A Document (Re)turn

Roswitha Skare
Niels Windfeld Lund
Andreas Vårheim
(eds.)

A Document (Re)turn

Contributions from a Research Field in Transition

PETER LANG
Frankfurt am Main · Berlin · Bern · Bruxelles · New York · Oxford · Wien

Bibliographic Information published by the Deutsche Nationalbibliothek
The Deutsche Nationalbibliothek lists this publication in the Deutsche Nationalbibliografie; detailed bibliographic data is available in the internet at <http://www.d-nb.de>.

ISBN-13: 978-3-631-56294-9

www.peterlang.de

Preface

This anthology on documentation theory and practices contains of many documents and many voices on documentation. This suits the occasion of the book well.

The book has two origins. One is the ten-year anniversary of Documentation Studies as an academic program at the University of Tromsø, Norway. Secondly, many of the articles are based on papers presented at the Document Academy Conference arranged annually since 2003 at the School of Information (until 2006, the School of Information Management and Systems, SIMS), University of California at Berkeley. We are convinced that with the advent of new media of communication, research from the vantage point of a generalized concept of the document becomes more and more relevant and indeed more fruitful.

We thank the contributing authors for their willingness to publish their work in this volume and for constructive dialogue regarding the manuscripts. Comments by participants at Document Academy Conference have been invaluable.

We are indebted to the Faculty of Humanities and the Department of Computer Science at the University of Tromsø, in addition to *Norsk tidsskrift for bibliotekforskning* (the Norwegian Journal for Library Research) for financial support given towards the publication of this edited volume. Our language adviser Margaret Hiley needs special thanks. Computer specialist Holger Hagan made the impossible possible in getting the fonts and the tables right.

Michael Buckland of the School of Information, UC Berkeley, one of the founding members of the Document Academy, has written the concluding chapter of the book outlining the enduring relevance of documentation research. We are especially grateful to him for theoretical and empirical advice, inspiration, as well as practical support.

Niels Windfeld Lund, Roswitha Skare, and Andreas Vårheim
December 2006

Contents

I The Concept of Document and Documentation

II Remediation

III Document Design and Aesthetics

IV Document Analysis

V Documentation in society

Epilogue

Niels Windfeld Lund

Building a Discipline, Creating a Profession: An Essay on the Childhood of "Dokvit"

In their book *Science and passion* (1985), Frans Gregersen and Simo Køppe define a scientific discipline by the following characteristics:
- a specific field of the world/reality
- a specific empirical and methodological tradition
- a specific conceptual framework
- a period of constitution
- a process of institutionalization
- a dimension of practice/societal relevance (32f).

Within this definition, I will study the first 10 years of existence, the "childhood", of "Dokvit", Documentation Studies, which was established in 1996 at the University of Tromsø in Norway. I will ask and try to answer the question of whether and to what extent it is possible to talk about Dokvit as a full scientific discipline according to the criteria mentioned by Gregersen and Køppe.

1 Documentation studies: a specific field of the world/reality?

If one sees the scientific disciplines as a coherent mapping of the world, dividing the world into disciplinary "countries", one could in principle expect that each discipline would cover a certain part of the world. But as everybody knows, neither in the "real" world with its nations, nor in the scientific world, are things that simple. Borders are changing, small countries as well as empires or superstates have been emerging and collapsing through history. The same is the case in regard to scientific disciplines, including attempts at inter-, multi- and transdisciplinarity.

One possibility is to see how scientific disciplines have emerged through history, just like nations, defining their territory and see how much power they can achieve in relation to other disciplines and in this way survive long enough to have a period of constitution and institutionalization and demonstrate a relevance for society, in other words to achieve legitimacy to become members of the United Disciplines of the world.

So if Documentation Studies is worth having a place in the United Disciplines, it should be able to define the territory, documentation. This approach implies not only answering the question of what is documentation, but also at a certain point to define the borders of documentation, to say what is *not* documentation.

Before the program at Tromsø started, a committee of librarians and faculty members from different disciplines formulated the general conceptual framework for the program, at this point without much knowledge of the documentation theorists such as Paul Otlet or Suzanne Briet. The choice of the name Documentation studies was not based on a paradigmatic critique of Library and Information Science, but on a much more pragmatic and general political interest in relation to the establishment of a National Library in Norway in 1989 and the closely related launching of a very broadly defined act of legal deposit in Norway, including documents of all kinds, including the new digital documents, but also broadcast television, radio and movies. Albeit unaware of the Otletian utopia of one large collection of all kinds of documents, the Norwegian act of legal deposit made the Otletian ideal explicit and challenged the Norwegian Library system in two fundamental ways, regarding open and free access and preservation. As long it is a matter of individual printed written documents, the library system is well suited for handling all kinds of documents in relation to open and free access. But when it comes to, for instance, recordings of broadcasted television, one may consider if the user should pay the producers and the actors for watching it like buying or renting a video. Next, in the case of preserving old film rolls as well as accessing and preserving the new digital documents, one has faced an immense challenge, due to the "intrinsic" nature of the documents.

This practical challenge created the perfect political justification and environment for the documentation program. At the same time, it did not only challenge the library system, but it also challenged the whole disciplinary system of the University. At the end Documentation Studies became a part of the Humanities in Tromsø, but locating it at the school of Social Sciences was also considered. In principle it could just as well be placed at the natural sciences. The question of whether Doc.Studies belongs to the natural sciences, the social sciences or the humanities is not that easy to answer. The paradoxical problem is that the answer could be positive in all three cases. When you are dealing with books in a library, you are dealing with the ideas expressed on the pages of the book, as well with a physical item to be shelved, as well as a socio-economic entity with a certain price. None of these dimensions of the books can be neglected since all three dimensions will be an issue some way or another in the library. In the case of digital documents the situation is more or less the same. In order to use a digital document, you have to have the right program and a running machine as well as access to the document. The latter may not be free, but may be managed by some media company requiring some kind of subscriptions. Finally you have to be able to understand it, for instance to understand a certain language. That means that you need traditions from all three scientific worlds in order to deal with these documents in the proper way.

One of the reasons for allocating the program of documentation to the humanities was that the overall theme for the program was how humans deal with documents. However, one may ask if humanities are dealing with what humans are doing in totality? If the program had been located in France or in other parts of a Latin/francophone world, this might have been the case, since the French notion of "Sciences humaines" covers sociology as well as medicine, psychology and studies of human expressions like linguistics and literary studies (Foucault 1966). In the anglophone world humanities is first and foremost the studies of human expressions like linguistics, literary studies, and art history. This is also the case in the Scandinavian countries including Norway.

The whole field of humanities in the anglophone sense is structured according to two main principles. One is the principle of medium, like the division between art history, literary studies, musicology and game studies as one of the newest disciplinary additions. The other principle is the geographical principle combined with the linguistic principle, dividing disciplines into English, Scandinavian, German studies, French/Romance languages, Slavic, Chinese/Asian studies and so on. Both main principles are very different in nature compared to the guiding principles of especially the social sciences but also the natural sciences. While the principles especially in social sciences and to a certain degree in natural sciences are dividing according to a certain perspective on a common object like sociology and psychology, dealing with two different dimensions of human life, or physics and chemistry, dealing with two properties of the natural world, the division in the humanities attempts to make a more concrete empirical division of separate objects either like a piece of literature, a piece of music or a painting or by a division between the English language and a Scandinavian language. The major problem facing Dokvit in this environment of the humanities is that it is more like sociology or physics, having a special perspective on human expressions, no matter if it is a painting, a book or a webpage. For Dokvit, a painting, a book or a website are all documents and they can all be analyzed as documents. There is no human expression that has unique privilege of being a document. It will always be a special kind of document, but not the only document! This implies an important difference between documentation studies and most of the disciplines in the humanities. The latter are generally interested in studying the unique qualities of their special kind of expression, for instance the uniqueness of novels, painted portraits or symphonies. The major reason for developing a special discipline for game studies, ludology, has been the uniqueness of games compared to literature or to visual art. In contrast to these disciplines, documentation studies is interested in comparing the different kinds of expressions, for instance comparing games and novels, to see the differences just as much as their common features. TIf you consider all expressions as different kinds of documents, you may study how they differ and how they are alike.

In addition to the comparative perspective, one may also add the important fact that many expressions nowadays are combinations of expressions like illustrations and text in printed publications as well as several media such as words, sound, still and moving images on webpages and so on. This is an increasing challenge for the classical disciplines, leading to a number of interdisciplinary attempts of studies of mixed media, like media studies and cultural studies. A crucial problem in these attempts is very often how to conceptualize the common object. Disciplines are mostly defined by their separate objects or methods and when an object goes across several disciplines, it becomes a dispute between the different disciplines whether one should use one or the other concept for the whole object. This can be illustrated by a recent discussion in the journal *Word and Image*. In volume 17 (no. 1 & 2), the theme is "Printing matters". In the introduction, the guest editors Graham Larkin and Lisa Pon emphasize how "the materiality of printed texts in early modern Europe is inseparable from that of images that were often produced by the same methods and the same people – often even on the same page" (Larkin and Pon 2001, 1). Later in the introduction they say: "While we have divided texts and images for reasons of conceptual clarity, we urge the reader to bear in mind the extent to which these stories are intertwined" (2). In a circular diagram, the two editors have tried to summarize their introduction. They have not distinguished between words and images regarding the history of both production and reception, but there is a division between descriptive bibliography/sociology of texts and connoisseurship/sociology of images. Why is this division necessary?

The idea of a sociology of texts in a broad sense derives from D.F. McKenzie. In his lectures on "Bibliography and the sociology of texts" he defines texts as including

> verbal, visual, oral, and numeric data, in the form of maps, prints, and music, of archives of recorded sound, of films, of videos, and any computer-stored information, everything in fact from epigraphy to the latest forms of discography (McKenzie 1999, 13).

Although Larkin and Pon appreciate the work of McKenzie and his focus on the history of production and reception of texts as recorded forms, they state the following argument for a separate sociology of images alongside a sociology of texts:

> As art historians, we are interested in proposing a similarly expanded

> role for connoisseurship; for present purposes we are calling this a sociology of images in order to reinforce the parallel with McKenzie's outlook" (Larkin and Pon 2001, 4).

When McKenzie argues in favor of a broad concept of text, "text" is constituted by the efforts of weaving a meaning together, no matter what kind of means you are using, in other words it becomes a matter of coherence. On the other side, when Larkin and Pon demand a conceptual distinction between visual and verbal means, it is due to the "inevitable" differences between images and words, becoming a matter of diversity and of recognizing the uniqueness of each medium. From this follow the traditional conflicts in the humanities between general disciplines like semiotics or cultural studies, covering all expressions of meaning, and separate disciplines for each kind of medium, words being dealt with by literary scholars and images taken care of by art historians. One may ask if it is the same kind of questions different disciplines are posing to their objects. What are the important questions for a document scholar in contrast to a literary scholar or an art historian?

Many students in documentation studies have been asking these questions through the years.

2 Documentation Studies: a specific empirical and methodological tradition

Following from the discussion whether Dokvit is a discipline within one, two or all of the three different scientific worlds, one may also ask if there is a special methodological tradition. If there is one, it is an attempt to develop a kind of complementary method drawing on all three scientific worlds. This development is closely related to development of the curriculum of Dokvit through the last decade, making guidelines for courses and projects in the programs.

Even if changes have been made, the main characteristics of the Dokvit tradition may be already seen in the introductory course in the first year 1996.

The very first students were asked to select a document and then approach it with the following questions:

1. who made it? (producer)
2. what kind of means are used? (media)
3. in which ways are these means being used? (traditions/modes)
4. what does the document actually document? ("content"/field/domain)

All four questions posed a huge challenge for the students. The first question about the producer became a challenge, for example when a childrens book was chosen and the question arose if the producer only was the author, or if the term also included the illustrator and, last but not least, the printer and publisher. It touches the whole paradigmatic traditions in literary and art studies, where the author and artist is in focus and the other human agents involved in the material and social process of production are excluded and considered as inferior to the analysis of the book as art or literature.

A similar problem arises when the second question about the means being used is addressed. In literary studies you might only consider, for instance, words used as metaphors or omissions which affect the reading, leaving it to readers to create the missing words. It becomes a bit more doubtful whether you should consider colors or the sizes of letters and the fonts being used as interesting for a literary analysis. This touches on another problem, the issue of the "content" of the document. Does the size of letters have any impact on the meaning or content of the book?

It was and still is a problem to truly define what means are. Means must be related to some kind of end or purpose. It requires that one goes into the very process of creating the document. This leads to the third question of how these means are being used.

If you have defined the means as letters, size of letters, colors, special words, illustrations, quality of paper, etc., then you may go further by looking at how letters are being used in combination with size, fonts and special words, in other words at how you construct a book. The same could be said about a painting, concerning how to use the brush, pigments and canvas in order to construct an artistic document. The major problem of studying the use of these means within the humanities is that the very practical use of the means is not the primary concern for the humanist, but rather to the contrary.

Erwin Panofsky wrote in 1938 about the object of Art History:

> In defining a work of art as a "man-made object demanding to be experienced aesthetically" we encounter for the first time a basic difference between the humanities and natural science. The scientist, dealing as he does with natural phenomena, can at once proceed to analyze them. The humanist, dealing as he does with human actions and creations, has to engage in a mental process of a synthetic and subjective character: he has mentally to re-enact the actions and to re-create the creations. It is, in fact, by this process that the real objects of the humanities come into being. For it is obvious that histori-

> ans of philosophy or sculpture are concerned with books and statues not in so far as these books and sculptures exist materially, but in so far as they have meaning. And it is equally obvious that this meaning can only be apprehended by re-producing, and thereby, quite literally, "realizing", the thoughts that are expressed in the books and the artistic conceptions that manifest themselves in the statues. (Panofsky 1955, 37-38.)

It is this attitude towards studying works of art which creates a serious problem for a document scholar working as a librarian or an art museum curator. The librarian as well as the curator cannot avoid dealing with the physical properties as well as with the thoughts embedded in the physical works in order to do their job properly. A teacher in high school as well as a university professor may be able to keep a distance to the physical realities of the works of art and keep an abstract relation to the world of art, but this also comes to an end when one moves into the digital world and takes a walk into a virtual library or museum. In that case, one has to handle physical means like a digital device in order to access the works of art.

Up till now it has been possible for many humanists to talk about content without mentioning or dealing with the physical properties or means, in other words to follow the path of Panofsky. The question now is whether this is also the case in a document analysis. The answer may at the first glance appear self-evident, but this is one of the most difficult questions, since it is a matter of defining what the document is about, in other words making an interpretation. This is what academics do in the other disciplines in the humanities, and one may leave it to them to do that job. But one may also claim that by doing this, one is defining and placing the material document in a specific cultural and social context, made possible by the producers and means being used in different ways as demonstrated by the three other preceding questions. Again one returns to the complexity of the production of the document. The problem is that content is not something inherent and essential within a physical document. The content of a novel or a short story is an interpretation according to a certain tradition for reading a novel or a short story. The whole hermeneutic tradition and most of literary studies are about searching for the best interpretation of a piece of art, whether it is a novel or a poem or a piece of music. The novel or poem is not different from other kinds of documents like photographs, music or paintings. A photograph may be considered a documentation of a famous person as well as one of your relatives, depending on who you are in relation to the person on the photograph. One may claim that words have more inherent content than photographs, but the only difference is that words are more general expressions and have been through a more general interpretation than is the case with more individual photographs. One may characterize the method used by a document scholar as a kind of deconstruction of the apparent or "obvious" content, followed by a more explicit placing of a document in a specific environment making it into a specific document.

This is also demonstrated in the two other projects of the first disciplinary semester. The second project was about doing fieldwork using the tradition of anthropological fieldwork, studying the production of documents in a specific field or organization or institution within a short period of time.

If one takes an art museum as an example, one may observe that a lot of different documents are made. The exhibitions can be considered as multimedia and complex documents, in which several works of art form parts of the total document. In addition to the exhibit itself you may have a catalogue, advertisements for the exhibits, postcards, and so on. Some of these documents may be considered worth studying in other disciplines, like the works of art exhibited, but the catalogue, the postcards and the letters between the curator and the artists, the sponsors, and the public authorities about the organization of the exhibits, will not be studied. This means that you not only have complexity regarding the exhibition itself, but also regarding the documents relating to the exhibit, more directly and indirectly. This also demonstrates the complexity of the sheer number of people involved in a production, and not just the few persons usually considered the main creators of the most important document, in this case the artists in the exhibit.

Finally, students in the first semester of the undergraduate program in documentation studies were asked to organize a database for some particular documents. This is not only a necessary qualification for being a librarian, but it is also trains people in organizing their own documents on a laptop and being able to annotate documents in order to retrieve them when they are needed. This leads again to the repeated question of the content of the document. The answer to this is quite simple: it very much depends on who you are and for what purpose you are using a document. In saying this, I am not claiming that the circumstances around the production of the document do not play any role in this. They are important, but it is mainly a kind of negotiation between the circumstances of the production and the actual current use of the document which forms the basis for an interpretation of what the content may be considered as. One example of this is the creation of a database of photographs in an interdisciplinary environment like the Norwegian Institute of Classical Studies in Rome, which serves students of Archeology as well as Art History. The very same photos of buildings may be interpreted in two distinctly different ways in relation to either Archeology or Art History. In the first case, it might be a matter of historical events or social organisation and in the latter case it might be a matter of style and special techniques of construction. Both interpretations are correct according to the different traditions within the two different disciplines. A third and different interpretation would be made if it were a database for educating photographers, where it might be important to focus on the angle and perspective of shooting the building. The most challenging task may be to make a database for a general library serving the general public. It is exactly in that situation, one may believe it is possible to make some kind of "general" description of the content. But it is only a matter of degree compared to the more specific databases. It is still a specific interpretation made within a specific culture, whether it is Norwegian or French or North American culture.

The result of this training should hopefully be that document students are aware of the complexity of documentation and that a document can never be completely isolated and considered to be essentially about one specific issue; instead, it must be viewed within a certain environment and how it has turned into a document analyzed.

This basic training in the first semester of undergraduate studies in Dokvit has been the elementary foundation for a larger student project on documentation. This project is undertaken in a selected field and approached from all three basic perspectives in Dokvit, embracing a physical dimension as well as social and cultural dimensions.

The students have so far been free to choose their specific field for the project. It has led to a large range of diversity of fields and themes, like "tombstones as documents", "horses as documents", "Picasso's *Guernica* as a document", "candles as documents", "concert as a document", "museum exhibition as a document", "management of an archive in a fishery factory", "comparative studies of the Bible in print and online", and many more. The very diversity of the projects demonstrates that the field of Dokvit may not be defined as a specific empirical field, but rather by taking a special perspective upon the world, viewing human life from a documentation perspective.

One may ask if it is at all possible to find any common issues in these projects which enable a common discussion among students and teachers. It seems to be possible, and three main themes have turned out to be crucial for the students and the beginning of development of a more specific field of research for Dokvit.

The first theme is the selection of materials, means or media of documentation. When you want to honor a dead relative, you ask for tombstone made of stone in order to keep it for many years instead of asking for a marker made out of wood; you would certainly not request one made of plastic or steel, even if these two materials may last just as long as stone. When you hold a concert, you also want the best instruments to play on in order to make the concert as good as possible. On the other hand, you may also use objects as instruments that are not usually used for music in order to make a new kind of music. In the latter case, it is a deliberate choice of material and means for the specific documentation process. No matter whether you are conscious of the consequences of the selected materials, the latter have always an impact on the resulting documents. When we ask the Dokvit students to consider what kind of materials have been used in the case they are studying, they also have an opportunity to follow up that question with a so-called contrafactual question: "what would have happened if one had used another kind of material". In one case study, two students studied a transformation of a printed book into a CD-Rom and realized that the possibilities inherent in the printed book and the CD-Rom were not the same. At the oral exam for this project, the students were asked about the possible consequences in the case of an opposite transformation, where a CD-Rom would be converted into a printed book. This unexpected question clarified not only the importance of materials used in different kinds of documentation, but also that the historical development of new kinds of documentation does not necessarily imply a simple increase of possibilities, but more a change of more or less dominant possibilities, the relations of power between different kinds of documentation. This is perhaps most clearly expressed by the French philosopher Jean-François Lyotard, who states that it is only digital data which really counts today.

> We can predict that anything in the constituted body of knowledge that is not translateable in this way will be abandoned and that the direction of new research will be dictated by the possibility of its eventual results being translatable into computer language. (Lyotard 1979, 4)

The second theme emerging in Dokvit studies is that of the human agent involved in the documentation process. If one takes the case of museum exhibition as a document, one may ask about the role of the architect in relation to the scientific curator in the case of archeological exhibitions. In the case of the reconstruction of an environment, one may make a compromise between a coherent presentation for the audience and the extent to which it is proved by the scientific observations. In the case of an art museum, one has the relationship between the artists and the curator to consider. In one exhibition in Oslo, a curator challenged the traditions of the art museum by bringing old works by some of the best-known artists like Munch together with very modern artists. This challenged not only the tradition of art museums, but also the hierachy of agents involved in art production. If one goes into the fields of music or film, one can also follow an ongoing struggle between different roles among the multiple agents involved in music (composer, musicians, conductor, manager, technicians) and film (director, artists, photographers, producer, playwriter, cutter).

Finally, the third theme dealt with can be formulated as traditions for documentation in different fields. Following from the two previous mentioned themes, throughout history strong traditions for how you document in different parts of society have developed. As mentioned by several document scholars, document types may be developed through a kind of negotiation of how to create a proper document (Briet, Brown and Duguid, Frohmann, Pedauque) inventing traditions for how to document in specific fields, like in arts, health care, religion, business, public administration and so forth. This offers the opportunity to go back in history and make historical studies of documentation tradition in various fields. At the same time it also creates the platform for a future-oriented experiment by asking if it is possible to change the tradition and to make an enquiry into the possible consequences of that change.

These themes lead all to one common approach, a comparative approach going beyond many traditional disciplinary borders that have become increasingly outdated due to the development of society as well as the development of new technology. But it was not only the borders that were not in accordance with new kinds of documentation; there was no updated conceptual framework to match the new forms of documentation, which were often a mix of formerly separate media made by new types of professional agents in new social settings. The creation fo such a framework was one of the main challenges for Dokvit and still is one of the most important tasks for development of a useful discipline for documentation studies.

3 Documentation Studies – a specific conceptual framework

One of the questions coming up repeatedly through the first 10 years is of course whether documentation studies really makes a substantial difference and is not just saying the same things in other words by using a new specific conceptual framework.

In order to do documentation studies and write articles and theses, one needs a distinct disciplinary language. One may ask why this is so urgent. Why cannot we just borrow concepts and theories from other disciplines? One reason could be that it might be difficult to see the difference from previous studies done within traditional disciplines, and then it could be argued why Dokvit studies could not be done in other departments. But the crucial thing here is that this conceptual framework is not supposed to provide a framework for a new kind of objects not dealt with in other disciplines. It is more a framework for making an analysis of the same empirical field, but from a different perspective and thus actually not focusing on the exact same objects. It is rather like in natural sciences, where you make a controlled experiment by defining the conditions for the experiment and the criteria for what you are studying, making the very character of the phenomena dependent on how you study them. This means that a book may be studied as literature as well as a specific form of documentation. This is one of the major differences compared to the other disciplines in the humanities which relate to specific empirical fields like literature or music.

Based on a general theory of documentation, a main conceptual framework has been formulated as consisting of three concepts on three different levels: documentation forms, documents and docemes (Lund 2004).

In order to create a coherent field for studies and research in documentation studies, it has been necessary to develop a general concept, *documentation form*, with a primary purpose to sort different kinds of documents in human life and society and thus to make some kind of classification of certain repetitive forms of documentation according to different fields and spheres as well as to different dimensions and features in relation to more inherent properties and qualities of certain kinds of documents. One may for instance consider books, journals and pamphlets with novels, short stories, poems and so on as having similar characteristics, all repetitively using letters in different ways to create texts, and thus belonging to a group of documents which may be characterized as literature, a relatively stable distinctive form of documentation different from film or theater which use bodily gestures and speech instead of letters. But you can also consider artistic documentation forms like literature or theater as distinct forms of documentation from political or administrative documentation forms like speeches, reports and forms.

One may wonder what the difference is between documentation form and the next analytical concept, the *document*? A book containing a novel is both a certain form of documentation as well as a certain document. When you primarily consider the book as a specific document and not as a form of documentation, you can make a more detailed analysis of the specific documents you are producing and see how they are made, using a more specific analytical model focusing on the producer, means and modes as described above. In this way it becomes possible to make more exact studies of different documents and still keep the analysis within a general and comparative framework of documentation studies.

Moving down to the specific analytical level of the single document, one faces a new problem regarding how to deal with the smaller parts of the document in a systematic way. In this regard, many students have turned either to semiotics or the more specific empirical disciplines as as sources of inspiration or models for detailed analysis.

The predominant conceptual framework of semiotics with its system of signs, the sign and, last but not least, the pair of signifier and signified, has been used by many students as an analytical tool on the microlevel of the document. One might consider a document not as a sign in itself, but more like a system of signs. But at the same time the use of the notion of signification creates a problem, because that way one more or less automatically moves towards a dependency on the theories of semiotics. This is typically shown in the discussions on the relationship between the so-called content and form/expression equal to the distinction between signified and signifier in the semiotic framework. If you in contrast this divide between an abstract "meaning" and physical "form" with talks about a meaningful formation whenever you express something or are impressed (that is, formed in a physically, socially and mentally distinctive way), you can go into that form and see how it is made up of a number of smaller distinctive parts.

This argument made it relevant to develop another analytical concept for the part of a document, resulting in the concept of the **doceme**. It is close to the concept of the document and relates to the same basic Latin verb and suffix as document, "docere" and "mentum". One may define a doceme as a part of a certain document. A certain doceme, like a photograph in a newspaper, may be a document in itself if it is made outside the newspaper. At the same time, the newspaper is not the same document if it does not have any photographs as illustrations. This leads again up to the first and general level of documentation forms, talking about newspapers as certain repetitive kinds of documentation. Some of them may have articles with illustrations, commercial ads and letters from the readers, but some may also have been formed without illustrations, or the opposite may be the case, with a lot of photos.

As a whole, you have a conceptual framework for documentation studies on the most general level as well as on the most specific level providing a kind of analytical scaffold for students and scholars in Dokvit, which creates something different from other studies of human life and society so far. One may ask whether this difference is just a matter of naming things differently or whether Dokvit has made a substantial difference in our knowledge about, for instance, how we express ourselves and communicate with each other. This may still, even after 10 years, be difficult to answer. It is a matter of constituting a corpus of knowledge labelled as documentation studies.

4 Documentation Studies – a period of constitution?

If one takes a look at either some of the projects made by students at Dokvit in Tromsø or at the issues dealt with in this book, it may be difficult to see a clear profile of questions and themes that contrasts to other disciplinary fields. Actually one might claim that there is nothing new in Dokvit and that everything it deals with has already been dealt with in many different disciplines including Library- and Information Sciences, Communication Studies, Media Studies, Cultural Studies and so forth. Nevertheless, if one claims any novelty for Dokvit, one will point to three major issues that also dominate this article.

The first main issue can be formulated in one question: "what is a good document?" This question goes into the practical craft dimension of making a concrete document using different kinds of physical means, but it goes equally into the social and cultural dimensions of documentation, regarding what is considered to be of high or low quality as well as efficient.

Next, Dokvit also cuts across a lot of different domains and related disciplines. It may be considered a kind of meta-discipline bringing a new kind of knowledge hidden inbetween the existing disciplines. In this way, it should not be considered as competing with, for instance, Art History or Literary Studies, but more as a supplement providing a comparative perspective to different kinds of expressions and media.

Finally, it also goes beyond the traditions of documentation studies related to libraries, archives and museums, from which it grew 10 years ago. It does not only focus on documents already made, but also on the very process of creation of documents by artists, doctors, bureaucrats, politicians and so on, considering the selection of the best means in the specific situations of documentation.

Two of the most important factors in this process of constitution of Dokvit knowledge are first of all to produce Dokvit-publications like this book, but it is just as important to educate Dokvit candidates, identifying themselves as Dokvit-scholars, ready to develop, sustain and implement this new kind of knowledge in society. For that reason it is important to have a certain degree of institutionalization of Dokvit.

5 Documentation Studies – a process of institutionalization

Dokvit or Documentation Studies became institutionalized in 1995 when it was officially agreed to establish a program of documentation studies at the University of Tromsø and to establish a number of faculty positions all devoted to documentation studies, but with different emphasis regarding the technical, social and cultural aspects of the field.

During the first decade of its existence in Tromso, Dokvit has grown to a full-scale program with B.A., M.A. and Ph.D. levels, and about 200 students have graduated on different levels and moved out into society as document scholars.

It has also started to develop an independent field of research on an international level within an international network called The Document Academy. So far, the Document Academy has organized a number of workshops and summer schools together with other document-oriented scholars and research communities. The most important of these is an annual conference for documentation studies, DOCAM (cf. www.thedocumentacademy.hum.uit.no), which has been held at UC Berkeley since 2003. DOCAM is a relatively small, but continually growing conference with an open agenda, exploring the possibilities of a document approach in research, business and the arts. Through these kind of activities, a kind of international document research community has emerged; one result of this is the fact that most of the contributors to this book are actually scholars regularly attending DOCAM or some of the other activities.

6 Documentation Studies – a dimension of practice/societal relevance

But at the very end, the criteria for whether a discipline of documentation studies will be sustainable in the future is a matter of whether it will be considered as relevant for society. One indication of relevance is the fact that candidates from the program get jobs not only as librarians, but also in many different kinds of fields with a documentation dimension, like in marketing, administration and health care, but also in the arts.

Almost in any corner of society, it becomes more and more important to document that you are doing what you are supposed to do, that you have not done anything wrong, and how good you are in doing what you are doing. Sometimes, documentation becomes more important than the very activity or person it is documenting!

7 References

Foucault, Michel, 1994 [1966]. *The order of things: An archaeology of the human sciences*. New York: Random House, Vintage.

Gregersen, Frans, and Simo Køppe, 1985. *Videnskab og lidenskab. Om humanioras videnskabsteori, videnssociologi, videnskabshistorie og samfundsmæssighed*. Copenhagen: Tiderne Skifter.

McKenzie, Donald Francis, 1999. *Bibliography and the Sociology of Texts*. London: The British Library.

Larkin, Graham, and Lisa Pon, 2001. Introduction: The Materiality of Printed Words and Images. *Word & Image* 17(1 & 2), 1-6.

Lund, Niels Windfeld, 2004. Documentation in a Complementary Perspective. In *Aware and responsible: Papers of the Nordic-International Colloquium on Social and Cultural Awareness and Responsibility in Library, Information and Documentation Studies (SCARLID)*, ed. W. B. Rayward. Lanham, Md.: Scarecrow Press, 93-102.

Lyotard, Jean-François, 1999 [1979]. *The Postmodern Condition: A Report on Knowledge*. Translation by Geoff Bennington and Brian Massumi. Foreword by Fredric Jameson. Manchester: Manchester University Press.

Panofsky, Erwin, 1993 [1955]. *Meaning of the Visual Arts*. London: Penguin Books.

Bernd Frohmann

Multiplicity, Materiality, and Autonomous Agency of Documentation

The growth of international interest in the "new" documentation, or "neo-documentation", can be traced to an impressive body of work now indispensable to the field, by Boyd Rayward, Michael Buckland, and Niels Windfeld Lund. Building upon Paul Otlet's and Suzanne Brier's pioneering ideas of the late nineteenth- to mid-twentieth century, these scholars have inaugurated new investigations of the relationships between documentary practices and a rich array of social, political, scientific, and cultural phenomena. The annual conferences of the Document Academy, which have been convened at the University of California, Berkeley since 2003, testify to the growing international interest in these relationships.

Documentation shifts interest from information to the document as a key concept for the disciplines of library science, information studies, and related fields. Recent years have seen a rise in studies of the social roles documents play, such as coordinating the work of institutions (e.g., see Brown and Duguid 2000; Star and Griesemer 1989), organizing epistemic communities (e.g., see Galison 1999), and manufacturing scientific knowledge (e.g., see Frohmann 2004a; 2004b; Latour 1987; Latour and Woolgar 1986; Poovey 1998; Shapin and Schaffer 1985). Studies such as these help expand the scope of research into the ways documents work across a wide range of institutions and practices. The document is seen as much more than an accidental vehicle for the communication of information, which in information studies is so often conceived as an abstract, immaterial, and mentalistic substance – Geoffrey Nunberg's "noble substance [...] indifferent to the transformation of its vehicles" (1996, 107), or Katherine Hayles's "disembodied information" (1999) – a conception that privileges research often transcending, if not simply by-passing, the social, political, scientific, and cultural worlds of documentation so important to Otlet and Briet.

In this paper, I single out three leading concepts of the informational model found questionable when attention turns to documents. The first is uniformity, which is one of the most salient properties of information, according to Nunberg's "phenomenology of information" (1996, 115–116). When conceived as abstract substance, information is the same stuff no matter what medium conveys it or what its content might be. Finding the appropriate philosophical elaboration of this uniform substance then becomes a prime directive of the theoretical imagination of information science. Documents, on the other hand, are multiple. They come in many forms, are made of many different kinds of material, and they have various institutional and cultural properties. Documentation counters information's uniformity with the document's multiplicity.

The second questionable concept is immateriality. Information is conceived as an abstract, mentalistic or "intentional substance" (Nunberg 1996, 110). This second property of information is connected to the first, because the nature of immaterial substance is uniform and unchanging. By contrast to information, texts, meanings, and semiotic entities such as signs and signifiers, documents are material, and their materiality has specific effects. Documents are things, often bearing marks or inscriptions, but, as Briet argued for her antelope in a zoo, unmarked things can also have documentary properties. The salience of the materiality of documents is the point of one of the reminders issued by John Seely Brown and Paul Duguid in their *The Social Life of Information* (2000) to corporate managers who would convert all of an institution's "information" or "knowledge" into electronic form. Brown and Duguid warn of the obliteration of important social relations dependent upon the physical properties of particular kinds of corporate documents. Just as information's uniformity underwrites its immateriality, documentation's multiplicity underwrites its materiality. The matter of documents takes many forms, not just in the variety of the physical properties of documents, but in the different kinds of mass or inertia exercised by them, which can be understood, analogously to the way matter is conceived in modern physics, as more than mere physicality. Documents gain mass or inertia by their institutional roles, which manifest both affordances and resistances. Documentation counters information's immateriality with the variety of the materialities of documents and their effects.

Finally, documentation questions assumptions of agency that follow from the mentalism of the informational model. In library and information science, these assumptions privilege research focusing on information practices that are seen as flowing from the consciousness of individual subjects (for discussions, see Frohmann 1990; 1992; and chapter two of Frohmann 2004a). Similar ideas may be found in related areas (e.g., see Mathiesen 2004). The privilege afforded to individual consciousness, and following from it, to human agency, is countered by documentation's recognition of autonomous and authorless documentation, along the lines of Michel Foucault's recognition of autonomous discourse. Information science's focus on conscious, human agency is connected to its concept of information as uniform, immaterial, mental substance. Just as the three concepts of the informational model found questionable by documentation are closely connected, so too are documentation's counter-concepts of multiplicity, materiality, and autonomous documentary agency. The following examples, taken from a time when the phenomenon of information had yet to present itself, are intended to illustrate these three concepts of documentation and the connections between them. The discussion is intended to show how the original documentation's sensitivity to the ways in which documents are woven into the fabric of our lives can be extended, but without appeal to the assumptions of the informational model.

In *Graffiti and the Writing Arts of Early Modern England* (2001), Juliet Fleming takes a very close and discerning look at the interplay of materiality and multiplicity in forms of writing quite different from those we encounter today. She argues that in early modern England there existed a mode of documentation whereby "inscriptional action" imbued matter with intelligence. In this pre-Cartesian world, where mind and spirit had not yet discarded their material form, but with modernism looming on the horizon, writing offered possibilities of experiencing imbrications of mind and matter quite foreign to the modern sensibility's allegiances to immaterial mental substance. In the writing practices Fleming surveys, mind encounters itself and intelligence is made manifest, not in the Cartesian mind's apprehension of its own clear and distinct ideas, but in the mystery of mind's relation to the sensible, material world. In early modern England, an inscription is not a record, a conduit, or a conveyance of immaterial substance – it does not communicate "information" as moderns understand it. It is an *event*: the manifestation of intelligence in matter.

Fleming is interested in how inscriptions function, not as mirrors of reality, but in ways more congenial to Deleuzian modes of analysis, which seek to know what inscriptions and documents *do*. She introduces us to documentary practices produced by "a way of understanding the relation of writing to the mind, and to the world outside it, that was not that of representation or reference" (164). Writing in a Deleuzian spirit (although her approach owes more to Jacques Derrida), she says her aim is to uncover "the logic whereby an object shaped by the art of man operates as a machine to 'occupy the brain and manage the will' of those who behold it" (121). The main features of this "machine", which we need to grasp in order to apprehend a mode of documentation now far distant from us, are its materiality and its agency. How can we think beyond "information" to the affective powers of the document's matter?

In Fleming's book, the multiplicity of documentation generates a profusion of examples, such as inscriptions on walls, rings, hair bracelets, clothing, emblems, tattoos, and pots. In each case, matter matters. George Puttenham's treatise of 1589 (*The Arte of English Poesie*), on the "ocular" beauty of visible poetry, is concerned with the "proportion" manifested in the material things of the sensible world. Intelligence in matter is exhibited by language in geometrical shapes, which manifests the "proportion" between apprehension and sensible things, and which is experienced as the appreciation of beauty, giving rise, in this case, to the pleasures of poetry. This early modern, English mode of documentation shows how the affective relations between mind and documentary matter operate as machinic assemblages, creating events of conformity and mutual accommodation of matter and intelligence, or as Puttenham put it (quoted in Fleming, 15), "this lovely conformitie, or proportion, or conveniencie betweene the sense and the sensible".

The "coat purchased by Charles VII of France in 1414, embroidered with 1,500 pearls, a third of which spelled out the words and musical notation of a song, 'Madam, I am the most joyous of men'", provides another example of how language "entered into relations with the material world" (10), and "where matter appears to bind thought" (13). It is one of several cases where we are "unable to distinguish between a poem, a jewel, an acoustical structure and a feat of embroidery" – another is "a miniature book in an ornamental binding designed to be worn at the waist" (10). Fleming's invitation to consider how matter is imbued by intelligence in a "historical moment when, as Marx put it, 'matter smiled at man with poetical sensuous brightness'" (13), can be taken up by reflecting on the difference between the beautifully embroidered verses of Charles VII's coat and one bearing simply non-textual, yet beautiful, embroidery. For the former, the material instantiation of inscriptions of language and musical notation are what matter. While even today we may readily admit to pleasures afforded by aesthetic qualities of visible language, we treat them as we would any pleasing non-linguistic design, because the inscription's "content", or "information", so we think, is radically separable from the material form to which we direct our aesthetic appreciation. But Fleming reveals a mode of documentation where the distinction we take for granted is not at all obvious, but even quite foreign. The mental and cognitive gestures of song are woven into Charles VII's "singing coat" in such a way that the power of its embroidered textual and musical inscriptions operates along lines of interplay of matter and intelligence.

The material properties of all writing, which underlie Derrida's concepts of *differance*, trace, and the deferral of meaning, are especially salient in the "posy", which is a kind of portable, poetic inscription designed for the eye, and whose point and purpose depends upon its singular instantiation in matter. Examples are short verses written on walls, on dishes meant to be taken home at the end of a banquet, "verses on fruit trenchers and in rings, and [...] mottoes, emblems, imprese, coats-of-arms and other heraldic or signature devices" (20). Posies were "[p]inned to trees and curtains, set upon conduits, and wrapped around gifts; or plaited into bracelets, embroidered on to clothes" (43). It is "the form that poetry takes in its fully material, visual mode, as it exists in its moment, at a particular site" (20). It cannot be properly understood as a conduit of information because, contrary to the products of our own documentary practices, it "has not achieved, and does not hope to achieve, the immaterial, abstracted status of the infinitely transmissible text" (20); it "cannot exist as text in the abstract" (43). The materiality of language was especially emphasized when the poetic epigram deliberately played upon matter's shape, as on posy rings inscribed with sayings like "Bent to content", or "A freend to the end". Fleming notes that to "draw attention to the line as a material mode of continuance and return [...] actively performs the thought it represents" (143). Posy rings are a mode of documentation in which inscriptions are not dead, inert, and lifeless matter awaiting human consciousness for life to be breathed into them, but intelligence actively at work in matter.

Emblems, or "devices", provide examples of how the materiality of documents achieves effects in civil life. Devices typically combine very brief sentences with pictorial support. They are designed to "create new objects of thought, giving 'marvell to the beholder' by producing effects of pleasure, hope or dread in the mind that apprehends them" (119). In general, they are "works of ingenuity, artificial things devised by art to distract or 'occupy' the mind by inviting it to supply the concepts to which they gesture; and they function to absorb the intellectual energies that they call into activity" (119). Among the most impressive examples in early modern England are family emblems, which engaged the minds and imaginations of those encountering them with the cognitive and affective gestures appropriate to their social status. These emblems were documents that worked like assemblages of mind and matter to maintain structures of social relations. As Fleming puts it, "to feel pleasure or dread in the presence of an object is to understand 'civill life' rightly as the product of humanly worked materials" (121).

Inscribed pots are another documentary form in which mind and matter are thoroughly intertwined. The potter's hands transmit mental gestures and affects – thoughts, imaginings, desires, feelings – that imbue matter with intelligence only in collaboration with the clay's accommodations and resistances. The finished pot emerges from the interplay of mind and matter, a characteristic amplified when, for example, inscriptions curve around the top of a mug, thus doubling the intertwining of the understanding and materiality. As Fleming puts it, such inscriptions demonstrate "the role of the materiality of space within the act of understanding" (158). Inscribed pots offer powerful examples of a mode of documentation in which "the impulses of the mind [...] take material form, and [...] material forms may consequently be understood as coagulated human thought" (152).

Fleming reveals a mode of documentation where intelligence and agency are not confined to the presumed immaterial mental substance of the human mind, but are active in the interactions of apprehension and the materiality of documents. The concepts of multiplicity and materiality help us understand a mode of documentation encompassing embroidery, posies, pots, emblems, wall writing, the shapes of visible language, and the many other cases found in her study. Her metaphor of a document as a machine that engages the mind connects these two concepts to that of autonomous agency.

The idea of documentary agency, and the study of what documents do rather than what they represent or mean, can be puzzling at first glance. Philosophies of action typically take intentionality, located in human consciousness, to be a necessary condition of agency. The allegiances to consciousness found in much of information studies also support the idea that it really can be only through human agency that whatever a document might be said to do actually gets done. But documentary agency can be motivated by at least three sources. First, we commonly attribute agency to documents. Books, fine art, films, and music move us greatly, or so we say. Much legal effort was expended in a famous Canadian multiple murder case to prohibit showing the perpetrators' video recordings of their brutal murders (the tapes were later destroyed), explicitly to spare the victims' families the pain of reliving their tragedy. In Chan-wook Park's film *Lady Vengeance*, similar video recordings are put to a different use, this time to rouse the victims' parents to exact their bloody revenge. Second, the performative actions of certain kinds of legal instruments, including those of adoption, citizenship, marriage and divorce, and those of incorporation, which bring legal individuals into existence, also provide examples of documentary agency. Third, much philosophical and theoretical work, especially from a post-structural stance, challenges the prejudice against attributing agency to non-humans. In his "posthumanist" analysis of scientific labour, Andrew Pickering (1995) sees it as a "dance of agency" wherein humans and the material things of the laboratory accommodate themselves to each other. Bruno Latour's long campaign against the separation of material, discursive, and social realms also features attributions of agency – even moral agency – to a variety of non-human "actants", including doors and automatic door-opening mechanisms. He observes that the effectiveness of both human and non-human agency depends upon alignments of many interlocking arrangements: "[a] scene, a text, an automatism can do a lot of things to their prescribed users [...] but most of the effect finally ascribed to them depends on lines of other set-ups being aligned" (Latour 1992, 240). And Ian Hacking, in a remark directly pertinent to documentary agency, says:

> Maybe I go further than Latour, for I might take inscriptions to be among the actants, right up there with fishers and molluscs, working and worked on, everywhere people go since the moment that our species came into being as *Homo depictor* (Hacking 1992, 36, note 1).

Latour's set-ups and alignments, and Pickering's "dance of agency", invoke Gilles Deleuze's and Félix Guattari's *agencements* (assemblages, or arrangements). At the beginning of their *Thousand Plateaus*, they write:

> We will never ask what a book means [...] we will not look for anything to understand in it. We will ask what it functions with, in connection with what other things it does or does not transmit intensities, in which other multiplicities its own are inserted and metamorphosed [...] A book itself is a little machine (1987, 4).

Their systematic rejection of representation and meaning, and their insistence on the affective powers of assemblages, are among the theoretical resources for neo-documentation's investigations of documentary agency, without appeal to mentalistic notions of information and its uses. These three motivations of the concept of documentary agency suggest three lines of research on whether and to what extent documentary agency is exercised: (1) how documents produce effects in individual lives; (2) how institutional practices confer performative powers on documents, and; (3) how theoretical resources such as those mentioned here extend the concept of agency to new areas of scholarship in documentation.

The concept of autonomous agency, together with the concepts of multiplicity and materiality, belongs to the theoretical resources that articulate what documents do without reduction to what individuals do with them. Individuals enter the picture only in the first of the three lines of research suggested above, and even then, the effects depend upon the document. Like Foucault's work on autonomous discourse, knowledge without a knower, and subjectivity without subjects, neo-documentation's use of the concept of autonomous agency recognizes significant documentary effects which cannot be traced to the consciousness of individual humans. In Fleming's work, the documentary agency exercised by her many examples of materialized inscriptions is non-authorial in nature. Wise sayings, epigrams, and received wisdom – written on walls, rings, pots, posts, skin, in hair bracelets, and embroidered on clothes – are no more the utterances of individual authorial subjects than are "a stitch in time saves nine" or "don't take any plugged nickels". But authorless discourse is not restricted to "sayings", as Foucault pointed out in his discussion of the "author function" in "The Discourse on Language". He says:

> All around us, there are sayings and texts whose meaning or effectiveness has nothing to do with any author to whom they might be attributed: mundane remarks, quickly forgotten; orders and contracts that are signed, but have no recognisable author; technical prescriptions anonymously transmitted (1972, 221).

He adds the statements of *disciplines* to this list, remarking that they belong to an "anonymous system [...] without there being any question of their meaning or their validity being derived from whoever happened to invent them" (222). In fact, *all* the statements Foucault considers in his archaeological and genealogical investigations are authorless. He argues that attributions of a document's "author" are explained by a historically contingent "author function", according to which a unifying principle – "the action of an *identity* whose form is that of *individuality* and the *I*" (222) – is imposed upon a particular group of statements. Documents and the statements inscribed in them long precede the advent of the author function. Their effects are products of autonomous agency.

Foucault's analysis in *Discipline and Punish* (1979) of the "power of writing" (189) exercised by documents in the apparatuses (*dispositifs*) responsible for "the constitution of the individual as a describable, analysable object" (190) has already been noted in documentation studies as a powerful example of autonomous documentary agency (see Frohmann 2004a, 148–151). To claim that documents have a central role to play in the constitution of individuality and the constitution of populations is to make a very large assertion. Yet Foucault shows how documents can be constitutive in this way: *constitutive*, not *communicative*. Essential to the apparatuses he studies was "a network of writing", "a whole mass of documents" and "a system of intense registration and of documentary accumulation" (Foucault 1979, 189). This specific exercise of documentary agency is, in Hacking's terms, a historical mode of "making up people" (Hacking 2002). Foucault shows how the statements he considers were repeated, not only in a literature, but in the many interlocking micro-practices of the legal, military, penal, and education systems. When a body of statements is embedded in a wide variety of such institutions and their specific practices, it escapes the voices and pens of its individual authors, and after a critical point, an identity, an individuality, or a population emerges autonomously. Documentation recognizes that the circulation of such statements does not occur in an ethereal medium. For Foucault, statements are material. Their circulation consists in the exchange, the handing over and the passing along of material things, according to embedded and authorized institutional routines. Through their inscription in documents, statements enter into assemblages of people, institutions, and practices. There is a direct route from Foucault's discourse analysis to documentation, because the analysis of specific historical instances of discourse and its effects opens upon investigations of assemblages or arrangements, in which the autonomous agency of documents is exercised through the mass or inertia of their institutionalized practices.

Foucault's analysis of the sixteenth-century *episteme* in the chapter "The Prose of the World" in *The Order of Things* (1994) offers a striking example of how materiality and autonomous agency together produce a powerful historical instance of a specific mode of documentation. In analyzing the importance of resemblance to Renaissance knowledge in terms of convenience (or contiguity), emulation, analogy, sympathy, and the signatures by which they are known, he sketches out a form of knowledge written in matter. Nature is stamped with writing, in the signatures by which resemblances are deciphered. We know, for example, that walnuts cure internal head ailments because the nut looks like the brain, and that "the eyes are stars because they spread light over our faces just as stars light up the darkness" (Foucault 1994, 28). The "face of the world", writes Foucault,

> is covered with blazons, with characters, with ciphers and obscure words [...] the space inhabited by immediate resemblances becomes like a vast open book; it bristles with written signs; every page is seen to be filled with strange figures [...] All that remains is to decipher them (27).

Language exists in the world as a material thing; it is forced "to reside in the world, among the plants, the herbs, the stones, and the animals [...] [i]t must [...] be studied itself as a thing in nature" (35). According to the grammar of Ramus, for example, "[w]ords group syllables together, and syllables letters, because there are virtues placed in individual letters that draw them towards each other or keep them apart, exactly as the marks found in nature also repel or attract one another" (35). The idea of language having meaning, and the semiology of signification, came later. In the sixteenth century, language has no signification; it is an infinite tapestry of resemblances between signs, but no relations exist between them and "signifieds".

One of the consequences of this *episteme* is that there is

> no difference between marks and words [...] The process is everywhere the same: that of the sign and its likeness, and this is why nature and the word can intertwine with one another to infinity, forming, for those who can read it, one vast single text (34).

Marks and words are equally material:

> language is not an arbitrary system; it has been set down in the world and forms a part of it, both because things themselves hide and manifest their own enigma like a language and because words offer themselves to men as things to be deciphered (35).

This is a mode of knowledge in which, as Fleming has also shown, words and things exist on the same, material plane. The writing woven into the fabric of the world comprises both signatures and language; written texts belong to the material world as much as natural marks, and are as much the objects of interpretation and decipherment. To a modern sensibility weaned on the distinction between observation and interpretation, and between what is apprehended through the senses and what is present to the mind in understanding a text, sixteenth-century knowledge appears to be a curious jumble of things linked by resemblance:

> an inextricable mixture of exact descriptions, reported quotations, fables without commentary, remarks dealing indifferently with an animal's anatomy, its use in heraldry, its habitat, its mythological values, or the uses to which it could be put in medicine or magic (39).

Foucault explains that "the reason for this was not that they preferred the authority of men to the precision of an unprejudiced eye, but that nature, in itself, is an unbroken tissue of words and signs, of accounts and characters, of discourse and forms" (39–40). Knowledge consisted in decipherment, not observation and demonstration as we know them. But since decipherment produced even more writing, knowledge became the "constant reiteration of commentary" (39). "Language", as Foucault remarks, "contains its own inner principle of proliferation" (40). When language is material, commentary upon written texts is no different than commentary upon animals, plants, the heavens and the earth – the "heritage of Antiquity, like nature itself, is a vast space requiring interpretation; in both cases there are signs to be discovered and then, little by little, made to speak" (33–34). The work of commentary is infinite and never complete because it is "directed entirely towards the enigmatic, murmuring element of the language being commented on" (41). It is not the speech expressing the modern *cogito*'s awareness of itself as thinking substance, but layers of written language superimposed upon nature and ancient texts, which can only reveal resemblances to the hidden and primal discourse it hopes to restore. Speech does not express thoughts arising in the mind; it is instead the always inadequate product of deciphering material, authorless writing. "One speaks", says Foucault, "upon the basis of a writing that is part of the fabric of the world" (41). Human speech is secondary, because the "interweaving of language and things, in a space common to both, presupposes an absolute privilege on the part of writing", and the "sounds made by voices provide no more than a transitory and precarious translation of it" (38).

The privilege afforded to writing in this sixteenth century *episteme* extends to documentation. Writing that generates more writing in the form of commentary is a machine for generating documents. But this mode of documentation is not rightly understood as a sixteenth century "information explosion." The documents it generates are not self-sufficient, signifying entities. They have no interiors, no *content* taking the form of "meaning" or "information". This documentary machine produces only more enigmatic matter, whose surfaces are caught in a web of resemblance. The power of this mode of authorless documentation drives an unceasing rewriting, seeking to duplicate an always hidden original text whose ultimate revelation – "the promised reward of commentary" (41) – would signal the collapse of the documentary machine by exercising a sovereignty over the entire *episteme*. Its force overflows the boundaries of documentary forms – whether book, manuscript, wall writing, or the many kinds of inscription investigated by Fleming – by writing the structure of resemblance into the fabric of the material world. In the sixteenth century, the affective powers of a wholly material and autonomous mode of documentation were visible everywhere, and drove the deciphering machine that generated the era's characteristic mode of knowledge.

The deeply thought work of Foucault and Fleming illustrates that powerful theoretical resources exist to continue and further the research inaugurated by neo-documentation. The concepts indicated in this paper supplement those already proposed (the others are institutions, social discipline, and history) as useful starting points for contemporary approaches to documentation (see Frohmann 2004b, 396–397). The work chosen for consideration in this paper is deliberate for another reason. Neither Fleming nor Foucault aim at grand theories. Instead, they put theoretical tools to work in their investigations of specific historical instances. Beyond suggesting that the concepts of multiplicity, materiality and autonomous agency are important theoretical tools for documentation, this paper is also intended to suggest that a similar method be considered for growth of the field at this early stage of its development. Because the interplay beween the multiplicity of documentation, its materiality, and its autonomous agency can be expected to take different forms in different historical periods and social circumstances, a useful approach would include those concepts among other relevant theoretical resources and put them to work in a variety of settings. Differences between specific cases test the value of theoretical resources in revealing the significance of particular modes of documentation. It is to be expected that concepts other than those proposed here will be central to other kinds of case. This attempt to show how the concepts of multiplicity, materiality, and autonomous agency illuminate documentary themes in the work of Foucault and Fleming extends an invitation to other researchers to expand the range of theoretical resources available to the field.

References

Brown, John Seely, and Paul Duguid, 2000. *The social life of information.* Boston: Harvard Business School Press.

Deleuze, Gilles, and Félix Guattari, 1987. *A thousand plateaus: Capitalism and schizophrenia.* Trans. and foreword by B. Massumi. Minneapolis: University of Minnesota Press.

Fleming, Juliet, 2001. *Graffiti and the writing arts of early modern England.* Philadelphia: University of Pennsylvania Press.

Foucault, Michel, 1972. *The archaeology of knowledge and the discourse on language*. Trans. A. M. S. Smith. New York: Harper & Row, Harper Colophon.

------. 1979. *Discipline and punish: The birth of the prison*. Trans. A. Sheridan. New York: Random House, Vintage.

------. 1994. *The order of things: An archaeology of the human sciences*. New York: Random House, Vintage.

Frohmann, Bernd, 1990. Rules of indexing: A critique of mentalism in information retrieval theory. *Journal of Documentation* 46(2), 81–101.

------. 1992. The power of images: A discourse analysis of the cognitive viewpoint. *Journal of Documentation* 48(4), December, 365–86.

------. 2004a. *Deflating information: From science studies to documentation*. Toronto; Buffalo; London: University of Toronto Press.

------. 2004b. Documentation redux: Prolegomenon to (another) philosophy of information. *Library Trends* 52(3), 387–407.

Galison, Peter, 1999. Trading zone: Coordinating action and belief. In *The science studies reader*, ed. M. Biagioli. New York; London: Routledge, 137–60.

Hacking, I. 1992. The self-vindication of the laboratory sciences. In *Science as practice and culture*, ed. A. Pickering. Chicago; London: University of Chicago Press, 29–64.

------. 2002. Making up people. In *Historical ontology*. Cambridge, Massachusetts; London: Harvard University Press, 99–114.

Hayles, N. Katherine, 1999. *How we became posthuman: Virtual bodies in cybernetics, literature, and informatics*. Chicago; London: University of Chicago Press.

Latour, Bruno, 1987. *Science in action: How to follow scientists and engineers through society*. Cambridge, Massachusetts: Harvard University Press.

------. 1992. Where are the missing masses? The sociology of a few mundane artifacts. In *Shaping technology/building society: Studies in sociotechnical change*, Wiebe E. Bijker and John Law. Cambridge, Massachusetts; London: MIT Press, 225–58.

Latour, Bruno, and Steve Woolgar, 1986. *Laboratory life: The construction of scientific facts*. 2d ed. Introd. by J. Salk. Princeton, New Jersey: Princeton University Press.

Mathiesen, Kay, 2004. What is information ethics? *Computers and Society Magazine* 32(8), June. Online: http://www.computersandsociety.org/sigcas_ofthefuture2/sigcas/subpage/sub_page.cfm?article=909&page_number_nb=1 (accessed 10 August 2005).

Nunberg, Geoffrey, 1996. Farewell to the information age. In *The future of the book*, ed. G. Nunberg. Berkeley: University of California Press, 103–38.

Pickering, Andrew, 1995. *The mangle of practice: Time, agency, and science*. Chicago; London: University of Chicago Press.

Poovey, Mary, 1998. *A history of the modern fact: Problems of knowledge in the sciences of wealth and society*. Chicago: University of Chicago Press.

Shapin, Steven, and Simon Schaffer, 1985. *Leviathan and the air-pump; Hobbes, Boyle, and the experimental life*. Princeton: Princeton University Press.

Star, Susan Leigh, and James Griesemer, 1989. Institutional ecology, 'translations', and boundary objects: Amateurs and professionals in Berkeley's Museum of Vertebrate Zoology, 1907–1939. *Social Studies of Science* 19, 387–420.

Johanna Drucker

Excerpts and Entanglements

1 Parts and holes

Otto Ege, early 20th-century philanthropist, famously, infamously, scattered the leaves of medieval manuscripts that these authentic treasures might provide pleasure and instruction to a broad and geographically distributed public.[1] The virtual aggregation of such dispersed rarities beckons on the current horizon as our new grail. Holy indeed the possibility of having one's page and sharing it too, with all the world, their grubby hands kept at the safe distance mediated through pixels, display resolutions, and the elaborate delivery system of the World Wide Web. But what is the document? Each leaf and page? The whole intact? Some original condition? The newly remade partial aggregate? Each, of course, and none.

As posed, the question about a document supposes a definition suitable for use in an instrumental, management mode. Subject to critical inquiry, the question dissolves and becomes more interesting.

We can enumerate an elaborate typology of kinds of documents – objects stretching the bibliographer's dream into a nightmare confrontation with items that stink, soak, and expand the protocol's physical and material decorum the way Isidore Isou's 1960 "book" *Chaos* (*Le Grand Désordre*) does when "shaken free" from its concealing envelope into a scatter of cigarette butts, detritus, ephemeral debris, and other trash meant to insult the reader's expectations. Literature? Letters? Try litter-a-ture and sign/sing a different tune, as Isou's experiment suggests.

Stretching the definition of a document along a material axis offers its own challenges to the structures of belief. But the conceptual axes that shoot through any point introduce another set of warps in our understanding.

---

1 Otto Ege was Dean of the Cleveland Institute of Art, Lecturer on the History of the Book at the School of Library Science, Western Reserve University, 1888-1951. This paper was originally drafted for presentation at the Document Academy meetings in Berkeley, at SIMS, August 13, 2003.

2 Identity and incompleteness

For instance, take this tenet of belief from the work of Jerome McGann: No document is self-identical (McGann 2002). The assertion suggests exponential possibilities. But does the concept of non-self-identicality comprise the field of inquiry we take to be a document? My argument is that our notion of a "document" has to be replaced by an idea of reading as an act of intervention and interpretation. But I hope to lead you there by a diverting route beginning with fragments and excerpts and leading through objects and artifacts to quantum poetics, 'patacritics, and radical constructivist approaches to cognition.

All documents are fragments. Let's begin with that premise. Even the most self-evidently complete document is an excerpt. All works are partial. Perversely, we could argue they are incomplete almost in inverse proportion to their appearance of completeness. Bibliographical studies taught us this. The great goal of recovery (of authorial intention or of the genealogy of a text through the traced history of its material manifestations) shows that authority and authenticity are surface features. They distract us from production processes and social histories. As McGann, and his contemporary, Donald McKenzie, demonstrated dramatically, texts are social productions, not the work of individuals. They are never fully present and never fully represent the complex processes of their production. Authors, we know from our French lessons in deconstruction, are themselves socially and historically created artifacts, the projected identity that arises from texts, implied and also inferred, rather than the author-itative source and origin of them.

Readers well-schooled in the last quarter century of theory will nod in agreement. Certainly, all language is found language. All texts are social documents. Authorship is a fiction. Identity is a mere feint behind which are the machinations and workings of a historically and culturally situated subjectivity. Ho hum. Yawn. But how do we get from these familiar precepts of deconstruction to fragments? Why post that image as a paradigm? The attempt to define a part of a document raises immediate questions about the "whole" we assume.

We like to think we know a fragment when we see it. The torn edges, ragged signs, announce the violent separation of the piece from its source. The excerpt, by contrast, sits with sound-bite perfection on the page, neatly, surgically extracted from its site of origin. The excerpt suggests a reductive modularity, capacity of discourse to be broken into consumable bits. David Moser, cited by poet-artist Ruth Laxson, says in her *Hundred Years of Lex-Flex*, "Quantum particles are the dreams stuff is made of" (Laxson 2003). Do I need to know more? Or even the full source? The citation. I have only the secondary source, Laxson, to cite – and the words of Moser appear in their brevity with a pretense of epigrammatic completion. All we need to know, to read that phrase, is bound up within it. Or so the excerpt says.

3 Trying excerpts

But how many texts are impervious to excerption? Trying to cut a crucial, telling phrase from the work of Paul Virilio's *Vision Machine* I found the task impossible. Deciding to test this (remembered from last year's teaching experience) perception, I opened Virilio at random, as per divination (rather than strictly scholarly) techniques. Lo and behold (you must admit, such language *is* appropriate under the circumstances), the section that came to hand was uncannily appropriate to our topic. So, here is a sample of this un-sample-able prose:

> Already at the beginning of the century, particularly in the United States, scraps of news film lying about the cutting room floor were no longer systematically swept up, "lost scenes" to be automatically incorporated into any old bit of junk that could be salvaged by the garbage collection, or, at best, the cosmetics industry. These began to be seen as "viewing matter", recyclable within the film industry itself (Virilio 1994, 50).

Something is missing. But the curious fact is that the more one goes on and extends the quote, the more the "missing" appears to extend:

> Once that happened, background reality re-surfaced, with blazing fires, storms, cataclysms, assassination attempts, crowd scenes [...] but above all, a mountain of material of military origin. These authentic documents, often judged at the time to be of no immediate interest, suddenly cropped up in the middle of feature films. Such subliminal sequences [...] (Virilio 1994, 50).

– I'll break off. Rather than helping close the elliptical loopholes in the text, the added bits just increase the sense of absent information in the ever-more porous framework of allusion and reference. The tissue-networked-fibrous (rhizomatic) nature of his prose doesn't permit excerption. That revelation led me to consider the distinction between excerpt and fragment, and hence, to the beginnings of thoughts for this paper.

4 Entanglements

Embedded and entangled, that, I thought, is the real condition of the fragment. And the excerpt? Let's just think about this. Fragments announce their dependence on their source. The language of Marjorie Levinson's study of *The Romantic Fragment Poem* is peppered with vocabulary conspicuously aware of this condition (Levinson 1986). She describes the fragment variously as "damaged", "incomplete", and "unresolved". The very condition of "irresolution" is a defining characteristic. Hers are Romantic fragments. and their particularity resides in their discursive claims to intentional fragmentary-ness (as well as the larger cultural context of celebration of incidental and accidental fragments). As Anne Janowitz has shown in her complementary study, *England's Ruins*, an ideological agenda was well served by this form, since the fragment, like its physical counterpart in the landscape, the ruin, provided an image against which presumptions of empire as whole and inevitable would be legitimated. The decay that engulfs the crumbling edifice suggests that the culture which is eroded is a part of nature and that Britain as an entity is an ancient as the geological formations to which such ruins appear to be about to return (Janowitz 1990).

Surely the fragment has a self-conscious character in the Romantic period, serving to provoke the melancholy strains of loss and nostalgia so utterly essential to the age. Fragments became the very image of the "damaged condition of Romantic poets" who followed Frederick Schlegel's edict that though the "works of the ancients have become fragments, the works of moderns are fragments at their inception" (Levinson 1986, 10). Schlegel wasn't speaking allegorically, but literally, about the production of poems deliberately embodying what another authority cited by Levinson – one Edward Bostetter – less than charmingly described as "extrinsically induced deformation of structural intention" (Levinson 1986, 11). Or, to put it another way, works that weren't finished even from the start. The implications of such an approach are more than decorative. We're not just talking about bits of statuary strewn about the garden to create a sense of an antique past whose decay is the foil to the fresh hopes of new youth or the impetus of empire. Though such descriptions are apt for the scene, they don't pull back the curtain on the rhetorical aim of the romantic fragment. This, in fact, struts on stage with the intention of disrupting claims of completeness, not just incidentally, by making works whose openings are left off (Wordsworth, began his poem "Nutting" on a "hemistitch" (a "half-line" an "open link") thus presumably leaving his meter hanging, its connecting wires sprouting like so many conspicuous chin bristles on the otherwise aesthetically well-formed work, that it might "provoke [...] an interpolative reception" (Levinson 1986, 61).

Of course, fragmentation has its own well-formed-ness and the art of creating bits of poesy that suggest they belong to a once whole work requires its own virtuosity. Just as the condensed language of a personals ad is meant to conjure, through the compressed iconography of its SWF, dancer's body, seeks mature companion for romantic interludes, walks in the rain, and candlelight dinners, an entire lived life indexed through this tiny inventory of handles. Yes, the Romantic fragment is an artful piece of text, deliberately showing what we now know to be the case of all work(s) that they are to be read, as Levinson puts it "against an ideal integrity and extensiveness" through acts in which the readers "mentally complete" the piece by generating missing parts.

As you do, here, following the zig-zag path of illogic in the stepping stone progress of this argument, characterized as it is by what (citing Levinson again this time citing Pierre Machery) can be termed an "determinate insufficiency" in which "incompleteness shapes the work" (Levinson 1986, 197). But my work, this task, my demonstration essays to exhibit not what Shelley referred to as "a lost and anticipated perfection" – that missing whole that gave the fragment birth – but rather, the persistent irritant of (Macherey again) "incompleteness in itself" as the "true reason for its composition" (Levinson 1986, 197).

Why?

5 Sacred associations

Because I'm intent on showing that that modern moment, quaintly antiquated as it may seem to be, marks the point of rupture with any objectivity for textual production or for our "getting hold" of the text or document as an object. Subjectivity, Rossetti's famous "inner standing point" for experience, again reiterated regularly by McGann, shifts the textual horizon from one whose coordinates are mapped against the constant sky to one which redraws endlessly from the point of view of the beholder. Linking our current work to the ruins in Romanticism, extending that fetishization of the fragment, we can find real use for this form and its ideas. The associational links between anything and anything are kept under constraint in many reading tasks. This is not surprising.

After all, many of the ways we have of reading and thus constituting a text are bred in approaches and attitudes towards scripture, whether we know this or not. Secular society, tending to believe in rational autonomy, forgets in us our inheritance of scholasticism as it morphed into scholarship. Sure we've changed. But what remains? Evelyn Tribble, writing of Robert Melanchton, a 1598 cleric advocating Protestant reform, notes that he declared a new mode of reading:

> "Now away with so many frigid, petty glosses, these harmonizings and disharmonies and other hindrances to the intelligence, and when

> we shall have redirected our minds to the source, we shall become suffused with the blessed nectar of divine wisdom" (Melanchton in Tribble 1993, 11).

Melanchton's argument was with Church doctrine, and the habit of creating extensive glosses in the surrounds of biblical text so that any individual reading was meant to be filtered through this consensual discussion of the learned, as Thomas More would argue, since the lay person might well get God's word wrong. The "central argument of reform-minded humanists", Tribble says, was to

> clear away the frigid petty glosses' of scholasticism, return to the source, and there experience the unmediated truth of scripture. The pure text reads itself–or rather, produces a moment of epiphany which erases the historical moment of reading (Tribble 1993, 11).

How unlike our current impulse, so pre-Socratic and Heraclitian, in which we imagine that we never dip twice in the same textual stream, that indeed the stream itself is reconfigured when we look away. As McGann is fond of saying, citing the inimitably unreadable George Spencer Brown's obscure opus *The Laws of Form*, "A equals A if and only if A does not equal A". We are all circumstance and situated-ness, subjective projection and inter-subjective mediation and exchange, seeing our texts engaged as instruments for communicative intercourse even as they offer their own "content" of genetically coded material.

6 Samples and sayings

And yet, the notion that "the pure text reads itself" is persistent in the garden variety of positivist approaches, to the poetic, the historical, and the logistical document. How much do we want the fabric of meaning to disintegrate searching in a desperate moment for a plumber's number in the Yellow Pages? How caught up in means when ends seem instrumentally urgent? Charles Bernstein, playing with these (all too often disappointed) expectations towards poetry, wrote in the poem "Thank You for Saying Thank You" in *Let's Just Say* (Bernstein 2003):

> Each line,
> word, & syllable
> have been chosen
> to convey only the
> intended meaning
> & nothing more.

I'll take up a series of examples here – bibles, the "burnt Boethius", a book by artist Gary Meres, one by the aforementioned Ruth Laxson, and the spectacular object of compulsive scholarly complexity, the Voynich manuscript – to see what each offers to my already radically dispersed image of the document:

Let's begin with bibles. Tribble makes a wonderful demonstration, in *Margins and Marginality* of the ways the physical appearance of the page participates in these assumptions about the authority of the text document. I'll reduce her subtle argument dreadfully, but she begins with the page of the *Glossa Ordinaria*, a "standard commentary on the Scriptures produced in the twelfth century". We see here the textual apparatus at work the mode Anthony Grafton characterizes in *The Footnote* as an "instruction for reading" – an exhortation towards a particular interpretation of the text (Grafton 1997).

Tribble contrasts these with later editions, in particular the *Great Bible* produced in English under license from Henry the VIII in 1539, has perversely done away with the gloss while leaving an indicator of the places in the text at which it might relevantly be inserted. These hanging hands, printer's marks, stand at the ready, like dead hypertext links, suspended and impotent. They mark an absent argument, suppressed through a combination of economic, logistical, and doctrinal reasons. "At those places where a hand appears [...] the reader is enjoined to make 'no private interpretation thereof'." The greatest fear of the English Church being that individuals might produce "private readings" in defiance – not of spiritual authority – but of the control asserted by the state over church matters for which they held authority. Tribble's excellent discussion details the correspondence of typographical appearance and attitudes towards authority – contrasting the polyglot complexity of the *Glossa Ordinaria* with the vertical hierarchy embodied in the *Great Bible*. Precluding access not only to the actual gloss but to its possibility, the Great Bible shows dramatically the extent to which the page has become the site of contested authority. The document is clearly fragmentary, and yet, can't be reconstituted through any of the acts of reading offered by the text left present.

Margins were once a space of dialogue, affirming or subverting the passages in the text. Paraphrasing Tribble, again, they offered manifest evidence of different glossing traditions – that of the exegete ("informed reader"), the insider ("privy to the secret meanings of the author"), the glozer ("obfuscating and distorting"), or other, rarer types – such as the anagrammatic reader decoding the possible structure of a text in esoteric ways (Tribble 1993, 75). Each of these modes of reading persists, however unmarked they become as the conventions of print gradually absorb the glossed text (so easily rendered with pen in hand, or added to in palimpsestic adumbration). But unmarked, they appear to disappear. The smooth page of the Gutenberg bible, printed in harmonious grey, even and even to this day a masterwork of printer's craft almost inconceivable under the technical circumstances, is the absolutely perfect image of the authoritative page, the scripture that seems to speak itself.

At a radical other extreme, texts whose material condition is fraught with damage, use, wear, tears, tatters, the weight of their history showing as frayed edge or even worse – water damaged or burnt. Kevin Kiernan's study of the "Burnt Boethius", tells a story of a text complicatedly transmitted through two very different artifacts. The first are charred fragments of a 10th century mss., in the British Library (Cotton MS Otho A.vi) the "only surviving copy of the Old English prose and verse translation of Boethius's Consolation of Philosophy by Alfred the Great (871-99)" severely damaged by fire in 1731, of which little remains legible (Kiernan 1998, 7-32.). And the second a transcription by Francis Junius, done in the 17th century, with interleaved and linked fragments of prose and poetry which match neither in length or details of their content. The figural opposite of the Great Bible, whose central text is present and all its commentaries missing, this text is absent in its original centrality but rendered by the tangential bits that describe that aporia through their many approaches to it (Kiernan 1998).

7 Dis-sociations

What is the document? And the text? They are never the same as each other. We read and the work is called forth, provoked. Junius's transcription may well have attempted to get at the actual content of the work, but as in the child's game of whisper down the lane each mediating act, we know, introduces its own encoded specificity. This need not fall into the realm of error, but the encoding matters, making of the text a new work. That's just the physical reality of transmission. Each embodiment is an interpretation. The creation of a "document" however, much as it depends upon the materiality of that textual substrate, is a more complicated matter yet.

Gary Meres' *Dead Man's Trail*, an artist's obsessive bookwork produced by Nexus Press in 2003, shows the principle of excerpted entanglement in one extreme (Meres 2003). The collaged pages bespeak their original sources by the memory invoked in their typography, but also, by the deliberate effort to communicate the processes of extraction and re-combinatoric art. Words, here, are shown to be all found, and the document created never out of whole cloth, even at that level of material production, but always as the product of circulating currency, language in the stream of human communicative exchange, captured and cut-up for re-use. The condition of all documents, to connect back into their source code and material history, only in Meres' case, as, more elegantly, in that of Ruth Laxson, the traces that betray that process beg for the Frankensteinian condition of text production to be seen as a metaphor of subjectivity. Language speaks us, the old deconstructionist theorists used to say, If Meres makes his gothic tale a pastiche fictional document, crafted from the hideous necrophilic remains of a vast corpus of pulp prose, an artifact of creepy dark-night adolescent angst and psycho-pathological textual cannibalism meant to create a frisson of grade B horror, then Laxson's borrowings are of another order altogether. Serious poetics struggle with the place of subject in history and historical subjectivity. Yes, language speaks us, she says, but we are human after all and the role of aesthetics is in the registration of that process in which critical decision-making can be marked. Her document, crafted out of bits and pieces, connects more directly to those lyrical poetics from which we started, ages ago, with Shelley and Coleridge and Wordsworth, marking their human condition as one of continual irresolution, of their poetics as a constant coming into being of a work.

But all these textual bits, with their artifactual richness, would still present only part of the argument in which the concept of the document is given its fuller exposition. Why?

Take the case of a fragment of an analytic work, that great mystery of unsolved manuscripts, The Voynich Mss. Still a puzzler, baffling scholars of all ilks and ages, the original work is in an encrypted code, indecipherable, if possibly legible through a complicated process that may or may not yield the secrets of what is, by all accounts, a strange alchemical treatise. The mss. is too complicated in its history for discussion here, and any Google search will lead you to the current state of compulsive scholarship, but I cite and show only one outstanding example interpretation to use as turning point and shift my discussion towards its final aspect. For here you see an image of a few words in the Voynich manuscript analyzed by the scholar William Newbold. Newbold became insanely obsessed. And his scribblings are his record of study of what he thought was micrographia, the code within the code of the illegible signs of an unreadable text. Breaking these glyphs down he saw the signs within, and rendered them discrete in order to recode them yet again. Newbold's approach, at the micro level of analysis, was a projected vision of hermeneutic possibility. The chimera of meaning, ever more elusive as Newbold proliferated his vocabulary of signs, became the endlessly conjured partner of his relentless pursuits. Meaning could not be mined, here, like ore, any more than it can in any first year literary studies class in which the document disappears and the students struggle to pour content out of the bucket of the page. But the embedded condition of meaning is here made starkly evident. The signs are rendered with a violent thrust of the nib into fibers and the eyes follow each hairline turn into an ever more detailed engagement.

8 Interpretation games

This is an apt place to turn my discussion towards the current consideration of "the document" at the intersection of new processes of interpretation. For these include the most pressing and real of logistical problems – those of electronic documents and digital surrogates, aggregates, virtual and simulacral. For if Newbold's capabilities for multiplying possibilities of meaning were in some sense limited by the optical tools available, then in the pixelated condition of digital storage, the lower limit would be minute indeed. The issue of scale is important, and all the more as the very processes of migrating traditional materials into electronic formats is always fraught with decisions about the constituent elements, the granularity of description. Text/document tensions were evident from the outset – as per Howard Besser's early discussions of the painful effects of ASCII entry on a work. Is it necessary to indicate pages within an electronic document? Or refer to it as a whole? If the format is PDF then are lexical units of any significance? If it is in ASCII then where are the margins? If the white space is rendered in facsimile then how accurate need a transcription be in making the arrangement of line breaks correspond to an author's original? Forget intention. I'm just talking description. But description IS interpretation. No "object" exists outside of cognitive construction. The simplest of problems raises a host of practical considerations and a wild bunch of theoretical questions, demonically batting the air around us as we try to resolve apparently simple issues like: What is the right unit for the "lexia" or lexical unit of a marked text? If we are, as we are, importing texts into e-space, then should they be chunked into elements that correspond to a paper-print-based original? Or to their electronic condition? And at what level of granularity? Paragraphs, words, sentences, characters? Every answer has its own objections.

We encountered these problems and many others, in our current project Ivanhoe. An electronic environment for critical studies, Ivanhoe is conceived in full recognition of all the theoretical dimensions I've alluded to thus far. But also, its dilemmas are only likely to resolved by following yet further along other pathways.

These are: quantum theory, 'patacritics, and cognitive theory of a radical variety. These three together shift the ground. An object in a quantum frame is created through an intervention, doesn't exist a priori. Patacritical modes of interpretation, grounded in Alfred Jarry's Pataphysics, the science of exceptions and imaginary solutions, alerts us to the particular rather than the general nature of all phenomena. And radical cognitive theory makes clear the dynamic relation between stimuli and the capacity to process information according to evolving models, or frames, of understanding–circumstances of co-dependent arising. Such an approach is systems-based, not empirical or positivist, and doesn't allow that documents pre-exist the capability of a beholder to conjure them or to be provoked into a relationship of meaning production in the proffered field of potentialities.

The design of the game of interpretation we named "Ivanhoe" was our field of inquiry for this research. In quick overview, our concerns in designing a game for *showing* the processes of textual interpretation were to make an electronic space that would force theoretical questions to the fore. These, very briefly stated, were: What is a document? How do we read? How could embedded/entangled interpretations be enabled? What are the elements of the interface design? What are the possibilities of using screen space to display the interpretive process, the subjective position of players in a game, the nature of a discourse field, and other issues in textual studies? The Patacritical demon, a concept that hovered on the edges of these discussions, embodied the notion of text as an intervention within a dynamic field of potentialities.

9 In-conclusion

The rhetoric of this paper is in part intended as a demonstration of an associational method, a para-pata-critical approach to the topic of what a document is, that scatters and relates parts to the whole through links of thought and readings, around the question that was supposed to be at the center: What is a document?

It is a particular, distinct, illusion, the image of an area created at the intersection of overlapping frames – of historical and social references, the projections of the reader, provocations of the text, constrained conditions, and potential responses – all within a poetical field. The term embedded, is not meant to suggest that a document is embedded in these many networks, like a nugget in earth, capable of extraction, but that it is constituted, the way a knot appears in a skein. The knotted entity is of and in the tangle that makes it. Excerpts *are* entanglements, its threads are material and cognitive, procedural and dynamic.

An artifact offers an illusion of stable ground on which to focus a projection that gives rise to an interpretation. A document is a set of contingently configured possibilities, a text is an encoded set of instructions for reading, an artifact is a material object that provokes and calls forth an interpretation. Interpretation intervenes in that quantum field.

I don't see a simple, positive material fact when I look at a document, I see fields of shifting relations momentarily stabilized in an artifact that exists in a continuum of temporal and spatial and quantum dimensions, only constituted through the framing acts of intervention.

10 References

Bernstein, Charles, 2003. *Let's Just Say.* Tucson: Chax Press.

Grafton, Anthony, 1997. *The Footnote. A curious history.* Cambridge: Harvard University Press.

Janowitz, Anne, 1990. *England's Ruins. Poetic Purpose and the National Landscape.* London: Basil Blackwell.

Kiernan, Kevin, 1998. King Alfred's Burnt Boethius. In *The Iconic Page in Manuscript, Print, and Digital Culture*, eds. G. Bornstein, and Th. Lynn Tinkle. Ann Arbor, MI: The University of Michigan Press, 7-32.

Laxson, Ruth, 2003. *A Hundred Years of Lex-Flex.* Atlanta: Nexus Press.

Levinson, Marjorie, 1986. *The Romantic Fragment Poem. A Critique of a Form.* Chapel Hill: UNC Press.

McGann, Jerome, 2002. Texts in N-Dimensions and Interpretation in a New Key. Online: http://www.humanities.mcmaster.ca/~texttech/pdf/vol12_2_02.pdf (accessed 31 July 2006).

Meres, Gary, 2003. *Dead Man's Trail.* Atlanta: Nexus Press.

Tribble, Evelyn B., 1993. *Margins and Marginality. The printed page in early modern England.* Charlottesville: University of Virginia Press.

Virilio, Paul, 1994. *The Vision Machine.* Bloomington: Indiana University Press.

Anders Ørom

The Concept of Information versus the Concept of Document

> "The resistance of texts to interpretation, and their power to engender many and conflicting readings, evaporates when they become information" (Peters 1988, 20).

> "Le livre a une longue histoire: chacun de ses elements, chacune de ses parties et de ses espèces est le produit d'un développement parfois très lent" (Otlet 1989, 363).

1 Introduction

The article discusses documentation science, its definition, object, and terminology in relation to the corresponding aspects of library and information science. The first part (2) treats the changes in the discourses of "Information" from the Late Middle Ages to the early 2000s. In general terms the article traces the changes from a discourse on the way the world is organized to a discourse on information understood either as a physical entity or as an (neutral) entity defined in relation to time (something new) and to accuracy. This main tendency from an understanding of "information" within an almost all-embracing context to an almost context-free concept is discussed contrastively in the light of recent developments in Library and Information Science (the physical paradigm, the cognitive schools, domain analysis and related views).

The second part (3) is a preliminary discussion of the actual use of the terms "information" and "document" in domain analysis.

The third part (4) is a tentative answer to the question: Why has the concept of "information" almost obtained a monopoly in the field of library, information and documentation science? The discussion (and analysis) includes prestigious, institutional and practical reasons (the status of front-line theories as general information theory and cognitive science, the technological and intellectual development of advanced information and information retrieval systems), the interdisciplinary use of the concept of "information", the idea of an information society and an information age, etc.

The fourth part (5) analyses relations and differences between the definitions and meanings of "information" and "document" in relation to epistemology, defining contexts, relation to the field of library, information and documentation, and furthermore in relation to core disciplines, and to what Niels W. Lund calls "line of convergence and line of divergence" (Lund 2001, 117[1]).

The last part (6) is a return to Paul Otlet's comprehensive *Traité de documentation* (1934). The *traité* is often considered to be the first systematic, modern work on the object of documentation (library and information science) and on the problems of organising information, in other words: the problems of knowledge organisation. The brief analysis of the *Traité* starts with a discussion of the recent reception of Otlet's contribution to library and information science. Next to this the three dimensions of "documentation" are expounded (a historical, a sociological and a systematic dimension), and Otlet's requirements for a documentation science ("une documentologie") are presented.

2 The concept of information: Historical changes and theoretical trends

In general, the term "information" is nowadays understood and used as an ahistorical concept. But the term has different meanings in specific societal and scientific contexts. This means that the word "information" is a polysemantic and problematic concept in the sense that it relates to very different contexts and is defined in different ways. The polysemantic aspect is a general characteristic of many widely used words (concepts) with a long history, but the word "information" is polysemantic to a very great extent because it is used in sciences and scholarly fields with very different epistemological foundations and in various discourses on society and politics. The word covers a broad range of meanings from the (functional) entities of perception processes to the designation of a radically new kind of society, "the information society".

Most scientific disciplines use the concept of information within the specific context of the individual science but there are some interdisciplinary semantic meanings within related theoretical and academic contexts. One of these meanings is that "information" is a physical object, another is that "information" is a "part" of meaning, a third is "information" defined as the cognitive content in an informa-

1 The Danish terms are *mangfold (divergence)* and *konvergens*.

tion act, in a fourth context "information" is understood as the *new* knowledge that an individual person acquires through reception and acquisition of the content of a message, in a fifth context the concept means an element of new knowledge added to our collective knowledge, and so on.

Peters (1988) has analysed the content of the concept historically. In the late Middle Ages "information" meant a discourse on the organisation of the world. In Renaissance science and religion the concept meant a discourse on the morphogenesis of the physical world (the origin and evolution of forms). In the empiricist philosophy of the Enlightenment the meaning shifted from objects in the world inform the senses, to the senses receive reports from the world.

In other words, the shift in meaning meant that the senses of the human being became the main focus. "Under the tutelage of empiricism, information gradually moved from structure to stuff, from form to substance, from intellectual order to sensory impulses" (Peters 1988, 13).

From the middle of the 19th century the context of the meaning changes from empiricism to bureaucracy. The new "bureaucratic" discourse objectifies "information" and alienates it from human perception.

In the 20th century the theory of information changes from a theory formed by the state bureaucracy and becomes a theory of signals, excluding the semantic dimension. The dominant post-war concept of information is dematerialised, and is defined in relation to time (something new) and accuracy. This conception is pushed to its (ironic) extreme by Theodore Roczak: "Information has taken on the quality of that impalpable, invisible, but plaudit-winning silk from which the emperor's ethereal gowns was supposed to be spun" (Roczak 1995, 3).

In the theory of signals, the object "information" has been naturalised and as a consequence of the naturalisation cleared of psychological factors in order to "establish a measure of information in terms of purely physical quantities" (Capurro and Hjørland 2003, 358). This naturalisation has been challenged and discussed heavily in the last decades during which "the tendency has been to re-humanise the concept of information; that is, to place it within a cultural context" (Capurro and Hjørland 2003, 360). This re-humanisation and the critique of reductionism are carried out both in the humanities and the social sciences. As an object, "information" is understood and conceived within a hermeneutic and historical framework. It means that "information" is understood as a concept dependent on both semantic and context. However, the general understanding of "information" and the dominant scientific concept are not – or scarcely – influenced by the re-humanisation and the critique of reductionism.

2.1 The concept of "information" in library and information science (LIS)

According to Hjørland (2000), the trend toward using the term information in institutions of librarianship and documentation is mainly related to: (1) an increasing interest in computer applications (or "information technology"), and (2) an indirect, theoretical influence of information theory (Shannon and Weaver) as well as of the paradigm of information processing in the cognitive sciences. These influences tend to reduce the study of documentary communication to the few aspects related to rationalistic computer science and cognitive science.

These new sciences have a nomothetic research ideal that has been "imported" to LIS. And in LIS there has been a tendency to define and "reduce" the object of the field in a way that makes it possible to formulate general laws. In order to come up to the standard of a nomothetic science, LIS has been "forced" to re-define and limit the complexity of its object (in the 1930s Paul Otlet made a great effort to cover all aspects of the object).

The nomothetic research ideal was first introduced and used in information retrieval, a research tradition that came into focus with the Cranfield experiments in the early 1950s. In these experiments the researchers operated with physical measures: basically counting relevant and non-relevant documents. The documents were handled *as though* they were physical objects one could count and calculate. This new kind of research, later called the physical paradigm, broke with a humanistic and sociological tradition in library science and documentation.

In contrast to the physical paradigm, the cognitive schools in information science beginning in the late 1970s operate with a rather high degree of complexity - but it is a complexity related to a limited field: information retrieval (IR). With the Cranfield experiments, IR had become the core discipline of LIS. The cognitive schools deal primarily with the interaction between the knowledge structures put down in an information (retrieval) system and the individual knowledge structures of the information seeker. In the cognitive schools, the scope has been broadened to include situational and to a certain degree social factors. In fact the development of the cognitive schools represents a growing understanding of the complexity of the object for LIS, but the limits of this understanding are set by the limits of the nomethetic research ideal.

In figure 1 some of the main characteristics of and differences between the physical paradigm and the cognitive schools are summarized.

The physical paradigm (The Cranfield paradigm)	The cognitive schools
Information (conceived as an entity) becomes the fundamental concept	*Cognitive structures* and *information* become the fundamental concepts together with the concept of *information needs*, (a concept that does not belong to cognitive theory.)
Characteristics: • A narrow focus (compared to documentation): Information retrieval • IR covers scientific information • IR becomes a rather well-defined scientific discipline – the core discipline in the new information science • Scientific knowledge is considered to be true knowledge • Scientific knowledge is considered to be universal and value neutral. It is not influenced by social and cognitive processes • (The historical dimension is excluded because it is a nomothetic theory)	Characteristics: • A broader spectrum of focal points (related to information retrieval) • In principle covers all kinds of information • Interaction in information retrieval is considered to be a complex phenomenon • Knowledge is relative in the sense that it is transformed by cognitive processes in the individual person • At the theoretical level the social dimension is excluded • Aims at an integrated theoretical framework • (The historical dimension is excluded because it is a nomothetic theory)

Figure 1: The physical paradigm versus the cognitive schools

In the 1990s, the physical paradigm and the cognitive schools were heavily discussed and criticized in the field of library and information science. The criticism was among other things directed towards the limitations of the nomothetic research ideal, the epistemological foundations of the dominant theories, and – as a consequence of these – the narrow understanding of the object of LIS. The approaches to library and information science prior to domain analysis and related views were also criticised for their exclusion of – or relatively simple conceptions of – the semantic (or semiotic) aspects of documents and documentation. This criticism and substantial reflections on the object of LIS resulted in alternative views on library and information science. These new views (with domain analysis probably as the one with most impact) aim at a non-reductionist approach to the study of information as an alternative to the earlier reductionist approaches.

Domain analysis and related views understand "information" in a hermeneutic perspective, a social and cultural perspective. Hjørland (2000, 38) expresses it this way: "[…] the object of LIS should be seen as cultural institutions (in particular science, scientific documents, (sub)languages, scientific communication and electronic databases understood as cultural institutions)." In the concluding statements of the same article, Hjørland continues along the same line of reflection: "[The] blocking in our field can to a large degree be avoided by changing the object of study from mental phenomena of ideas, facts and opinion, to social phenomena of communication, documents and memory institutions" (Hjørland 2000, 39).

In addition to this characteristic of the (re-defined) object, Capurro and Hjørland (2003) state that information professionals generally have a broad overview of information sources, and a knowledge of sociological patterns in knowledge production, of research paradigms, as well as of document types. Further the re-defined object "implies a sociological and epistemological approach to "the generation, collection, organization, interpretation, storage, retrieval, dissemination, transformation and use of information" (389).

This re-definition of the object of library and information science brings us in many ways back to the concept of "documentation" as it was coined in the 1930s.

3 "Information" or "document": a preliminary discussion

The redefinition of the object to a social phenomenon of communication, documents and memory institutions is according to Hjørland (2000) a strong argument for calling the field documentation science. Hjørland's argument for not changing the name is that "the terms LIS and IS are rather well established" and institutionalised. The way to solve the problem is to "make it clear that we are studying potentially informative objects" in library and information science (Hjørland 2000, 39). Potentially informative objects might include more than documents, but documents are the essential object of LIS (information with a broader scope could include other kinds of potentially informative objects). Concerning information retrieval theory, Capurro and Hjørland (2003, 383) write: "In our view, it is not too simple an idea to claim that information retrieval theory is in reality document retrieval theory and thus closely associated with library science."

From the point of view expressed in the quoted articles by Hjørland and Capurro, the crucial reason for *not* naming the field "documentation science" is that the terms "library and information science" and "information science" are institutionalised. It is of course to a certain degree a valid argument. But two problems would be better solved if the term "documentation science" became the institutionalised term instead of "library and information science". The first problem is that "document" is the central term that describes the object of the science. The other problem is the highly polysemantic concept of "information".

Capurro and Hjørland are very well aware of the problems related to the semantic aspect. They quote the British philosopher J.L. Austin:

> [A] word never – well, hardly ever – shakes off its etymology and its formation. In spite of changes in the extensions of and additions to its meanings, and indeed rather pervading and governing these, there will still persist the old idea [...] (2003, 350).

I would like to add that the same chain of reasoning is valid for the meanings of "information" after the Second World War. The word "information" cannot shake off the meanings developed in the context of information retrieval and library and information science. This "shaking off" has been tried many times with new definitions, revised delimitations, new criteria for a specific concept of "information" for library and information science. These changes, additions, limitations, and redefinitions of the meaning of "information" reflect more than the lack of a (mature) paradigm.

To use the term "documentation science", or "documentation studies", is not per se a solution. But it could contribute to a clarification because the term "document" is less blurred in general and is a more significant term for the object of library, information and documentation studies than the word "information" ("document" is of course a polysemantic concept as well). I am aware of Otlet's positivist position in his *Traité de documentation*, but his synthesis of "la documentation" is adequate for post-cognitive, sociological oriented positions in library and information science, as it is well known in Tromsø and elsewhere.

4 Why has the concept of "Information" almost obtained a monopoly in the field of library, information and documentation science?

I have touched slightly on this question earlier. On a general level, the answer is that "library and information science" is an institutionalised term. The use of this term and the nomothetic research carried out have contributed to the scientific prestige of the field. A substantial part of this research has been developed by the use of advanced technological and electronic information retrieval systems. Capurro and Hjørland write: "One reason for information scientists to prefer not to be linked to library science might be that important technological improvements were carried out not by people associated with librarianship, but by those affiliated with computer science. This preference is most probably the reason why they claimed to work with 'information, not documentation'" (2003, 283).

Scientific prestige is related to persuasion in the sense that the (library and) information science tries to convince (as all scientific and scholarly disciplines do) authorities, scientists, and institutions of its scientific "power" and value. This scientific "power" and value draw on the historical origin of the theories "imported" by (library and) information science.

With Shannon's information theory (1948), the term "information" had a great impact on the scientific as well as on the general prestige of the concept. This concept of information found in the (mathematical) information theory spread to biology (genetic information), physiology (the human brain as information processor), cognitive science and other sciences. (Library and) information science aimed at integration into the inter-disciplinary theories that drew on ground-breaking scientists, information theorists, computer scientist, and technicians. Nomothetic theories, the use mathematical equations, algorithms, and numerical abstractions were (and still are) considered to be of outstanding value.

Besides the aim of being a part of these prestigious and advanced front-line sciences, through the choice and institutionalisation of the label "(library and) information science" the discipline became associated with and (quite literally) "inscribed in" the information society with its global networks and advanced communication technologies. "Information" is – and was to a greater extent a decade or two ago – seen as the crucial element in a new economic era, and as the element that unites the interests of the states, the enterprises, and the scientific communities. It is often mentioned that the American Documentation Institute (founded in 1937) changed its name to the American Society for Information Science in 1968. The name given in the 1930s and the change in 1968 are illustrative for the transformations found not only in the field but also in the general development of the prestigious front-line sciences.

It is unsurprising that researchers in the field of library and information science as well as the numerous visitors in the field had a legitimate interest in entering the scientific frontline.

5 What is the relation between the concepts of "Information" and "Document" (Documentation)?

The document (re)turn started at a small scale in the late 1990s. The word "return" indicates that the researchers are going back to the roots of documentation science, or documentation studies in the early 20th century. In this return Paul Otlet is the central figure. Otlet constructed his terminology starting with the word "document" (defined as "signe et support"). From "document" he derived "documentation", which has two meanings: both the act of documenting, and the ensemble of document, the verb "documenter", the adjective "documentaire", the substantive "documentothèque" (documentation institute), "archives documentaries", "document types", "documentologie" and so on (Otlet 1989, 13).

A number of these terms are widely used in library and information science. A consequent and systematic use of the concept "document types" is found in Hjørland et al. (1997) where document types are described, categorised, and analysed from various angles among which are: an epistemological, a knowledge organisation, and a communicative point of view. The approach in this book is close to Otlet's approach in *Traité de documentation*. But the theory and typology of document types are treated as integrating parts of library and information science.

In his outline of a documentation science Niels W. Lund (2001) takes his terminological point of departure from the word "document", as did Paul Otlet (Lund's theoretical point of view (hermeneutics, semiotics) is – of course – different from Otlet's). Besides his theoretical reflections, Lund analyses some traditions for use of the word, because the concept of "document" is historically "loaded" with meanings that have to be taken into consideration in the definition of the term. In other words, "document" must be defined in relation to existing traditions for use. Lund traces four traditions that use "document" as a key concept. Thus in legal tradition, a document is understood as a "stabilising, societal symbol: the law". The document proves what is false and what is true.

In the historical tradition, the "document" traditionally points at the reconstruction of the past. But nowadays – according to Michel Foucault – the document no longer represents an inert material through which the historian tries to reconstitute what men have done or said, the events of which only the trace remains. History is now trying to define within the documentary material itself unities, totalities, series, and relations. According to the philological tradition, a document is first and foremost a material entity defined in opposition or complimentary to a work, or a text. The document is – in other words – the material manifestation of the text. The legal and some historical traditions accentuate the social character of the document as well its evidence of truth or false, right or wrong.

Another part of the historical tradition and the philological tradition emphasises the physical or material character of the document. Besides, we have the digital tradition that conceives of the document as a meaningful entity that does not depend on a physical support.

In the bibliographical field, Lund distinguishes between two traditions. The first tradition acknowledges a great variety of document forms and constitutes a general framework for talking about "documentation science", instead of bibliography. The second is connected to the dream of the universal book in which all the knowledge from the documents of the world is collected. This dream is based on the idea of *content* independent of form. The second tradition (or "paradigm") is guided by an interest in convergence and is considered to be the dominant in library and information science. The first tradition – the one that constitutes the framework of the re-defined documentation science – is guided by an interest in diversity.

The analysis of the historically "loaded" meanings of the term "document" constituted in different traditions leads to the conclusions that there is a "solidarity" between the form and content of a document and that (a) documentation science should follow the "line of diversity" in opposition to the dominant position in library and documentation science that follows the "line of convergence". These two "lines" have opposite epistemological foundations. The "line of convergence" follows a nomothetic research ideal and has "imported" its conceptual models from the sciences. The "line of diversity" has its foundation in the humanities, in hermeneutics, semiotics, and in Foucault's theories.

Lund analyses as well the etymology of the word "document". According to the *Oxford Latin Dictionary*, the verb "doceo" has five different meanings: to tell, to instruct, to demonstrate, to teach a person, and to produce a play. The suffix "–mentum" has two different meanings: that something is told, demonstrated etc., and the means used for this activity. When these means are used to tell or demonstrate something the result is a "document". Concerning the component "doceo", Lund emphasises that the meaning of "I tell or demonstrate", always implies an acting subject, i.e. a human agent in the documentation process. Lund continues his reflections from this starting point and proposes a model with four elements: human agent (author, creator), means, the method in which the means are used, and "document". The term "document" is thus defined in a human and communicational context. Accordingly, the term "documentation" covers both the process and the product. According to Lund "documentation" should be analysed at three levels: Documentation forms, documents, and "docems".

On the level of documentation forms, ways of documenting are studied:

- As they have been developed within a societal, scholarly or scientific field (for instance the health sector, art history, and biochemistry),
- In a historical period,
- Related to specific media, means and materials.

This brief sketch of Lund's *Outline* is meant to demonstrate two characteristics of documentation science. The first is the construction of the terminology based on the word "document", the second is the (theoretical) approach to the object: the "document" is viewed from a sociological (societal field), a historical, a media and a hermeneutic point of view. On a general level (leaving aside some aspects of a certain importance), the main difference between "domain analysis" and "documentation science" is the different degrees of coherence between theoretical point of view and terminology. "Domain analysis" (and to different extents related views) "inscribes" the document in a (library and) information science discourse, while "documentation science" returns to a development of the classical "documentation" with its object-coherent terminology.

Figure 2 is a synoptic comparison of "information" and "document" in a theoretical context. The figure does not include "domain analysis" and related views in the left column.

Information/ (library and) information science	*Document/ documentation*
A general, abstract theory of information → A nomothetic theory	A theory based on the historical development of document types and their social functions → An ideographic theory
Information understood in a non-specific context	*Document* understood in the context of the historical and social function of the production, distribution, and use of documents
The concept *Information* is not specifically related to the field of information, library and documentation science	The concept *Document* is – within a broader context – historically intimately related to organized collections of documents
Information retrieval is from the theoretical point of view the core discipline of library and information science	*Knowledge organisation* related to *document types* can be considered *a* core discipline in *documentation science, documentation studies*
The dominant theoretical conceptions in (library and) information science follow the "line of convergence"	Documentation theory is situated on the "line of divergence"

Figure 2: Information versus document in theoretical context

6 A return to Paul Otlet: *Traité de documentation*

Otlet has both been praised for his systematic work, his ambitions and his advanced ideas, and criticised for his epistemological foundation.

The Wikipedia article on Paul Otlet (2006) states:

> Paul Otlet devoted his professional life to the art of collecting, recording, organizing and disseminating knowledge. Although he lived decades before computers and networks emerged, what he discussed prefigured what ultimately became the World Wide Web. His vision of a great network of knowledge was centered on documents and included the notions of hyperlinks, search engines, remote access, and social networks. (Obviously these notions were described by different names.) Otlet not only imagined that all the world's knowledge should be interlinked and made available remotely to anyone (what he called an International Network for Universal Documentation) [...] (http://en.wikipedia.org/wiki/Paul_Otlet).

Traité de documentation: Le livre sur le livre was published in 1934, and according to Rayward "[t]he *Traité* is perhaps the first systematic, modern discussion of general problems of organising information" (Rayward 1994, 237).

On the one hand Otlet is viewed as a systematic and visionary author, and as the founding father of documentation. On the other hand he is viewed – and criticized – as an exponent of the positivist scientific view and epistemology that had great impact during his lifetime. Rayward's analysis of Otlet's *Traité* and of his essays on bibliography, decimal classification, documentation and related subjects leads to this conclusion:

> Otlet's thinking must be placed within a nineteenth century Kuhnian paradigm of positivist science, of the creation and dissemination of knowledge, that has long since been superseded. It can be argued that the solutions Otlet proposed for the problems of information storage and retrieval that were his almost obsessive concern failed because they reflected a naive view of the nature of knowledge and the dynamics of its growth. Otlet underestimated the complexity of the physical and social processes of scholarship and of the broader culture which supports these processes (Rayward 1994, 248).

Frohmann points out that "Otlet, like Bacon, subordinated the social arrangement in which information is implicated to epistemological principles" (Frohmann 2004, 34). In the case of Francis Bacon (1561-1626), the social arrangement was subordinated to an epistemology based on the human faculties (memory, imagination, and reason to which history, poesy and philosophy respectively corresponded). In the case of Otlet his (pre-analytical) positivism led him to – in Rayward's words – a reductionist and simplistic conception of knowledge. "After all, he seems to suggest, science produces in a quite straightforward way discrete, objective elements of knowledge. These give rise in an equally straightforward way to laws and generalizations" (Rayward 1994, 248). Otlet's conception of objective knowledge was the foundation for his vision of an encyclopaedic survey of all documented human knowledge. Otlet's ideas are at the "line of convergence".

I am not denying that Otlet's simplistic and positivist view of knowledge "permeates" the *Traité*, but this in itself does not mean that Otlet's principal work is irrelevant to the actual discussion of documentation studies. A kind of a "deconstructive" approach to the *Traité* points to different understandings of documentation implicit in the *Traité*. This is probably due to the fact that he was working on the book for a long time, and it is also due to the synthetic nature of the document type, the treatise, that condenses documents with different theoretical points of view: "Le traité est un ouvrage qui résume et condense, sous une forme concise et claire, nos connaissances les plus précises sur une science" (Otlet 1989, 129).

As a science, "la documentologie" covers a broad and rather heterogeneous object. The *Traité de documentation* has three important dimensions: historical, sociological and systematic. This means that Otlet viewed the object of "la bibliologie ou documentalogie" in a historical and social context as well as from a systematic point of view. The positivist epistemology finds its strongest expression in the parts on systematic and visions, while the historical treatment is marked by evolutionism, and the sociological parts deal with interrelations and interdependencies between documents and their societal and communicative contexts. The sociological parts are the least elaborated.

6.1 Reflections on *Traité de documentation*

This tri-partition in *Traité de documentation* of the object of documentation studies is a good starting point for some further reflections on the field. The book is a systematic treatise in the sense that it analyses all the elements of the object of "la documentologie" in a systematic way, proceeding from the general to the specific.

The document (or the book), the object, is at first given a general definition: "Un support d'une certaine matière et dimension [...] sur lequel sont portés des signes représentatifs de certaines données intellectuelles" (Otlet 1989, 43). This general definition has two noteworthy characteristics. The first is that it combines a physical support and meaning. The meanings of the documents constitute the materialized memory of mankind ("La mémoire materialisée de l'Humanité"). The second (and implicit) is that the concept includes document types ("des espéces de documents") that are not printed and bound, such as stamps, mile-stones, coins, labels, scientific documentary films, works of art, records, and musical scores.

The systematic analysis of the document is conceived by analogy with sciences as zoology. The analysis, or 'examen', of the document starts with the general and abstract concept and continues with the basic elements that constitute the document, the structure of the different parts of the document, and the document types ("les espéces ou familles d'ouvrages").

In his general presentation of the new, synthetic view on documentation Otlet uses biology as model. Biology has integrated a number of disciplines: physiology, zoology, botany and others in *a* general biological science. The objective of "la documentation" – the "documentation science" – is to develop "une science générale embrassant l'ensemble systématique, classé des données relatives à la production, la conservation, la circulation et l'utilisation des écrits et des document de toute espèce" (Otlet 1989,9).

Biology is characterized as a theoretic, explanatory, and evolutional science of all living beings. The documentation science aims at being a theoretic, comparative, genetic, and abstract science covering all books, all types and forms of documents, documentary institutions, production, conservation, circulation and use of all kinds of documents as well as including the historical and sociological context relevant to documentation. Like biology, documentation science is not a new science or discipline, but rather a synthetic science. It integrates disciplines like bibliometrics, bibliography, knowledge organisation ("l'organisation rationelle du livre et du document"), and document history, as well as many others .

Traité de documentation presents a synthetic and an analytic perspective on the object. This synthetic perspective integrates three dimensions of the study of the document: historical, sociological, and systematic. The objective of the organized documentation is to offer documented information on all kinds of facts and all knowledge. (It is relevant to notice that Otlet distinguishes between facts and knowledge.)

6.2 The historical dimension

According to Otlet, the historical development of the "document" is inscribed, or embedded in the history of civilizations. The history of the "document" is seen from a material and from an intellectual point of view. From the material point of view, the stages of development start with the invention of the writing and – at the time of the publication of *Traité de documentation* in 1934 – the development had reached the stage of the new substitutes for the book ("radio – phono – film").

From the intellectual point of view, the history of the book can be divided "en un nombre très divers de phases qui se confondent avec celles de l'histoire des sciences, des lettres, des arts, de l'éducation, de la vie économique, sociale et politique" (364). That the historical stages in the evolution of the book "follow" the history of the sciences and so on means that the history of the book has to be studied within a broad and differentiated context. Otlet makes several statements concerning the evolution of the book. In another context he writes that the evolution of book "reflects" what he considers to be the evolution of thought:

1. Primitive thought,
2. The literary expression of the moral, philological, and scientific thinking,
3. The established science(s), and
4. The new stage of the synthesized, documented, visualised, and mathematically based science (Otlet 1989, 39).

It is evident that the *Traité* belongs to the new stage according to Otlet.

The history of the books comprises also the history of the influence of the books, and in this sense it relates to the history of the ideas as well as to the history of human action. In the parts that treat the different document types, Otlet traces the history of individual document types, for instance the treatise. The history of the treatise is starts with Euclid and comprises treatises on political economy, history placed in their historical context. The book or the "document" is not studied for historical reasons only. "A detailed history of the book is an incomparable source of a real understanding of the book as it is today" (Otlet 1989, 38).

6.3 The sociological dimension

> Le livre naît dans la société; ce sont les circonstances de temps et de lieu de la Société qui donnent sa physiognomie propre. [...] Les circonstances sociales sont celles qui determinent les formes de la coopération intellectuelle ou materielle et les modalités commerciales ou outres selon lesquelles s'opère la diffusion des écrits dans le corps social (Otlet 1989, 29).

The book, the document, is a product of the society, and social conditions determine the forms of intellectual and material cooperation as well as determining the diffusion and dissemination of documents. Rayward writes: "The *Traité* begins with a long and exhausting general exposition about communication and information examined historically and from the point of view of various social and other sciences" (Rayward 1994, 238). Otlet deals with social networks, forms of intellectual cooperation, and the document is treated within a sociological framework that covers the intellectual and material/practical aspects of the "cycle" of the document: (intellectual and material) production, distribution and dissemination, criticism, scientific control and use.

The parts that analyse document types (Otlet 1989, 124-247) have a sociological aspect, although this is not the most important. This aspect is related to the social functions of document types. For instance some of the functions of the newspaper are to educate the masses, and to create or maintain movements in the public opinion. The documentary film has an educative function. The media and new books have impact respectively on the pattern of documented communication and their discipline. The television has (economic) consequences for the film and the book, and a new book can create a new discipline.

6.4 The systematic dimension

The Traité is first and foremost a systematic "summary" of documentation science. The historical and social dimensions are secondary. A systematic treatment was needed both in order to develop documentation science to the standard of other contemporary sciences, and in order to cope with problems within the field. One of the core problems that Otlet faced and handled was the continuously expanding universe of documents. Another was – what Francis Bacon also was aware of – the gaps in knowledge. A third was the lack of contextual relations among the documents. Concerning these problems Otlet writes:

> "(a) books present only some of the scientific data and so only a part of science (the incompleteness of books); (b) they present false as well as true knowledge (the errors of books); (c) they present the same thing more than once (repetitions); (d) they do not bring together information that is set out in several places, but divide it up and scatter it in innumerable volumes (fragmentation and dispersion); (e) they do not present the information set out according to its degree of importance (a mixture of the primary and secondary)" (Rayward 1994, 240. The quotation is Rayward's translation of: Otlet 1989, 373).

Systematic documentation and cooperation among libraries, archives, museums, offices of documentation, scientific societies, research institutes and so on were needed as well as standardized methods of handling documents and collection development.

An essential part of the *Traité* analyses and categorises document types. A brief presentation of this part can demonstrate Otlet's systematic procedure. Besides, the document types are central to the overall conception of documentation. He starts with a general definition of document types, and in this definition he draws on the former part where he has analysed the components of the document. After the definition (the documents form types that combine a part of the components in different ways) he distinguishes among bibliographic documents (printed books, journals, and so on), graphic documents (such as, for instance, literary and scientific manuscripts), and "substitutes" for the book. In the further classification of the documents, he addresses a number of dimensions such as the treated subject (philosophy, philology), the material form, the kind of reproduction, the documentary form, the intellectual form (encyclopedia, dissertation), the readers addressed (the general public, the specialist), and forms of addressing the reader (In Hjørland et al. 1997, there are corresponding dimensions of document categorisation).

Besides the printed document types and graphic documents (paintings, drawings and so on), the concept of "document" also includes documents that substitute for the book (art films, scientific documentaries are examples of document types among the multimedia documents). The general view is that all forms of documentation are complementary. The different document types are objects to different cycles of operations that take place in the various documentary institutions. These institutions have special functions in relation to the document. Among the operations is the rational organisation of documents (knowledge organisation) that is based on document types. The cycle of operations includes what recently often is defined as the object of information science: "Information science is concerned with the generation, collection, organization, interpretation, storage, retrieval, dissemination, transformation, and use of information" (Capurro and Hjørland 2003, 389).[2]

Though Otlet puts the main emphasis on the systematic dimension, all three dimensions must be considered as complementary, and documentation science ought to integrate the historical, the sociological and the systematic dimensions. Concerning the opposition between the "line of convergence" and the "line of divergence", the conclusion is that they are both expressed (in an implicit way) in the *Traité*. There is a tension between the two.

6.5 Science and documentation science according to Otlet's requirements, and a few concluding statements

Otlet treats the requirements for a science. In order to be a complete science, documentation science should meet eight requirements:

1. A general or specific object,
2. A specific point of view,
3. Generalizations, general facts, fundamental concepts, and laws,
4. Systematisation,

---

2 Capurro and Hjørland quote B.C. Griffith: *Key papers in information science.* New York: Knowledge Industry Publications (1980), 5.

5. Methods (research methods, logical procedures, argumentation procedures, classification, terminology, systems of measurement, etc.),
6. Organisation of labour (division of labour),
7. History,
8. Application of different studies and activities (Otlet 1989, 10).

The scientific ideal partially derived from biology and science in general is to a certain degree reflected in the requirements for documentation science: for instance in the use of terms such as "laws", "logical procedures", and "systems of measurement". Some of the requirements are general for science, social science, and the humanities, such as for instance the definition of "a general or specific object", "a specific point of view", "fundamental concepts", and (a kind of) "systematisation". History refers to the humanities, and division of labour to social science. These requirements point at documentation science as interdisciplinary, crossing the borders between the humanities, the social sciences, and the sciences. This is certainly not new in the discussion of the fundamentals of library and information science/documentation science. But in the light of the dominant nomothetic theories in library and information sciences as well as in the light of the views that criticise these dominant theories, Otlet's *Traité de documentation* is still a relevant book with interesting perspectives – in spite of the criticism its epistemological foundations has attracted.

The final question is: Which are the – possible and actual – theoretical advantages of a paradigm/view with the term "document" as a key concept? In other words: which are the arguments for a document return, for a documentation science in the year 2006?

Recent development in the field of library and information science (domain analysis and related views to different extents) criticises the dominant theories and research traditions in the field for reductionism, for a narrow understanding of the object, for the exclusion – or simplification – of the semiotic aspect of documents, and for the exclusion of social and cultural perspectives. This critique can be related to the conceptual history of information. The meaning and (consequently also the) context of the concept has narrowed down to a neutral, almost de-contextualised entity. Domain analysis and related views aim in the opposite direction, i.e. the direction of the contextually extended and complex concept of the "document". In other words the discourses on "document" have changed from more particular and restricted meanings to a multi-dimensional and integrated theoretical discourse. Document typology and knowledge organisation are well-developed (sub)disciplines in actual library and information science, and these (sub)disciplines have their basic foundation in Otlet's "documentation". The "document" is intimately related to organised collections of documents, and the "document" is understood in a historical, sociological, and systematic context by Paul Otlet, the founding father of "la documentation".

7 References

Capurro, Rafael and Birger Hjørland, 2003. The concept of information. *Annual Review of Information Science and Technology* 37, 343-411.

Frohmann, Bernd, 2004. *Deflating information: From science studies to documentation.* Toronto; Buffalo; London: University of Toronto Press.

Hjørland, Birger, 2000. Documents, memory institutions and information science. *Journal of documentation* 56(1), 27-41.

Hjørland, Birger, et al. 1997. *Faglitteraturens dokumenttyper i kommunikations- og videnskabsteoretisk belysning. Kategorier, medier, former, genrer, niveauer & kvaliteter.* Bind 1-2. Copenhagen: The Royal School of Library and Information Science. 6. foreløbige udgave.

Lund, Niels Windfeld, 2001. Omrids af en dokumentationsvidenskab: Anno 2003. *Norsk tidsskrift for bibliotekforskning* 16, 92-127.

Otlet, Paul, 1989. *Traité de documentation: Le livre sur le livre.* Liège: Centre de Lecture publique de la Communauté française de Belgique.

------. 1990. *International organisation and dissemination of knowledge: Selected essays of Paul Otlet.* Amsterdam: Elsevier.

------. 2006. Online: http://en.wikipedia.org/wiki/Paul_Otlet (accessed 12 August 2006).

Peters, John Durham, 1988. Information: Notes towards a critical theory. *Journal of communication inquiry* 12, 9-23.

Rayward, W. Boyd, 1994. Visions of Xanadu: Paul Otlet (1868-1944) and hypertext. *Journal of the American Society for Information Science*, 45, 235-250. Online: http://people.lis.uiuc.edu/~wrayward/otlet/xanadu.htm (accessed 12 July 2006).

Roczak, Theodore, 1994. *The cult of information: a neo-Luddite treatise on high tech, artificial intelligence, and the true art of thinking.* Berkeley, CAL.: University of California Press.

Schaanning, Espen, 1997. *Vitenskap som skapt viten: Foucault og historisk praksis.* Oslo: Spartacus.

Ørom, Anders, 2000. Information Science, historical changes and social aspects: a Nordic outlook. *Journal of documentation* 56(1), 12-26.

Gaute Barlindhaug

Analog Sound in the Age of Digital Tools: The Story of the Failure of Digital Technology

An important issue in the studies of new media has always been to explore and explain the relationship between technological evolution and cultural change. In this regard, digital technology has often been viewed as the single most important tool in the creation of many of today's new cultural expressions. In media relying heavily on computer technology, like blogs and MMORPGs the case is obvious, but digital technologies can also be linked to changes in more traditional medias like film, music and even literature. Many understand the emergence of these novel expressions as a result of new technology overcoming the limitations of earlier analog media. Following this argument, one would expect that producing innovative documents in a new millennium would be the result of a digital revolution that had rendered earlier analog tools absolute. Today's society has in general a positive attitude towards the introduction of digital technology, seeing it as an improvement on its analog predecessors. In this article I want to take a closer look at these assumptions by making a detailed investigation into the role of digital tools in the production of popular music, hoping to say something more specific about the relationship between technological innovation and cultural expressions.

From a certain point of view, it clearly looks like digital production tools are the dominating force in the western cultural expressions of today. The 80s and 90s produced a large range of digital hardware, culminating in a growing software and computer industry. Through the application of software, computers can be turned into powerful tools for the production of documents. Most literature describes the introduction and development of digital media as providing great freedom in manipulating information, both for consumers and producers. For most of us, "digital" equals "new and better". To a certain degree this is also true of musical production. Diverse software has been designed to make computers function as tools for both recording and producing sound. One important trend in this regard is the integration of a range of so-called software synthesizers into your music production. These are programs that function like real-life machines, but existing only in the software environment of the computer. A good example of this is "Reason", made by the Swedish company Propellerheads Software, a sound production tool with the graphic and functional appearance of a physical rack. Here the user can add units like drum machines, mixers and synthesizers, and on the backside of the rack you can connect the units together using colorful cables (fig1). Everything is very lifelike, but at the same time remains extremely virtual. "Reason" is exceptional in that it is a complete production environment, while most of the software synthesizers are made to function as a part of larger programs as plug-ins. These plug-ins are often simulating devices that also exist as hardware. At first this might seem like a prime example of the innovative development of digital media technology. But some aspects simply do not add up that easily. First of all: Why do we want software that functions like a real machine? After all, making word-processing software work exactly like a typewriter would not seem very novel. However, this is very much the case in music production. Secondly: With the plethora of software available, why are people willing to spend 1400 US$ on e-bay for a small battery-driven musical gadget from 1982, when you can get a software version for free? Academics have constructed a series of theories describing the impact of digital media, but how useful are these when trying to explain what is happening in a specialized field like music production?

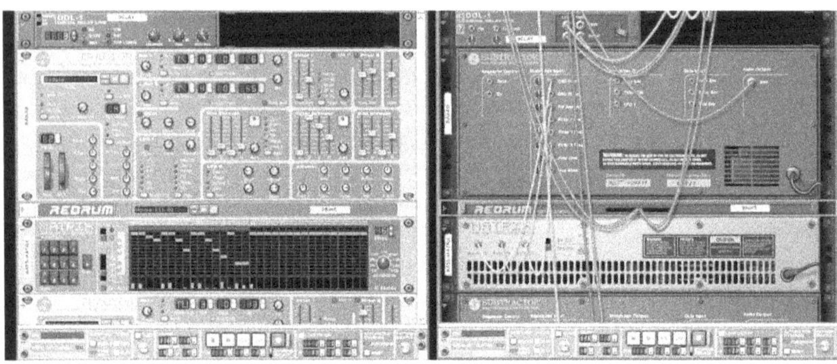

Figure 1

It has always been the case that older technological elements are taken up by digital media. In the 1970s and 1980s, analog elements were deliberately exploited as metaphors in the development of graphic user interphaces the idea was to use elements from traditional office work to construct a computer system that would be easy to understand for the workers not specialized in using computers. In the late 1990s, Bolter and Grusin published their theory of remediation, describing and explaining the relationship between digital media and its older counterparts. Inspired by McLuhan's claim that the contents of a media is another media, Bolter and Grusin focused on remediation as a process in which older technologies are absorbed into new digital media. In most of their examples the relationship between digital and analog media is one of competition, where the newer digital media tries to replace older technologies by appearing as an improvement. While a typewriter might be an important metaphor in understanding many word-processing software, the typewriter in its traditional form has been rendered obsolete by the software. Similarly, there doesn't seem to be any apparent reason to read a traditional newspaper when you can get the same information on the Internet. This remediation can also be seen as part of a "horseless carriage" phase of technologies, where we don't comprehend the novelty of inventions but instead relate them to more familiar media.

In music production, the relationship between new and old media is of a different kind. Software exists alongside its older analog counterparts, in a relationship much more complex than that of the metaphors and remediations we find in consumer media. These evolutionary contradictions in contemporary electronic music production are to a great extent a result of technology's role in musical aesthetics. This is an aesthetic dimension that makes it hard to use traditional academic theories to understand the relationship between music and the different technological media. To make a thorough investigation into the relationship between analog and digital tools, it is therefore important to view this relationship in relation to cultural expression.

By tracing the developments that created the premises for today's software synthesizers, I hope to achieve a wider understanding of the relationship between technological development and cultural expression, and in doing so reveal some shortcomings in established media theories. By way of example I will mostly focus on Propellerhead's "Reason" software, and try to explain its features in relation to cultural practice in musical production. The reason for focusing on electronic music is that it is a cultural form closely linked to the development of technology. Most of our understanding of digital innovations in our culture is derived from research into visual media, so by focusing on sound and music I hope to uncover some new relations. Furthermore, popular electronic music is from time to time used as an example to describe phenomena in contemporary technological culture. As I will show, sampling, a term from musical production, has also played a role in developing theories for other cultural fields, such as literature. In spite of this, the field of musical production has rarely been the subject of any thorough investigation outside the academic field of popular music studies.

Technology: tools or communicator

When trying to view electronic music in light of traditional media theories, it is crucial to point out that there is a tremendous difference in how academics and musicians perceive media technology. This difference also explains why media theories cannot explain what is going on in music production. Traditionally, academics think of media as something transmitting a message or functioning as the material basis for this message. There is a consensus that this material basis imposes constraints and influences what is communicated, and in that way affects the result. However, in connection with electronic music, the media is constituted by a longer production chain which goes far beyond the immediate material basis. Even if the material basis for the music is the same, what ultimately defines its aesthetics is what media was used in its prior production. In musical expression, technology plays a crucial role as a tool for production, and not only as a means for storage and distribution. It is also important to point out that much of the technology used in music production contains media that easily can be perceived both as storage and producer of content.

Because of musicians' focus on tools, the division between analog and digital technology is for the musician not about technical evolution, but rather a question of aesthetics. The evolution of cultural ideas and aesthetics are in these cases a result of the use of the technology, not only of its technological evolution. According to this, the material aspect of technology becomes an independent entity whose importance is not based solely upon its relative novelty. For fear of being seen as technological determinists, I think many academics have neglected these aspects of media technology. When put to closer scrutiny, the implementation of digital technology can therefore turn out to have quite a different effect than originally thought.

The importance of aesthetic property in media's material aspects is one of the reasons why the theory of remediation does not always comply to musical production. In media science this remediation is often explained in relation to the media's desire to achieve transparency, to effectively transmit a message. According to this view, the reproduction of older medial forms in digital media is motivated by the desire to render the digital media transparent. If we see media as a material vessel to store and transmit a message, the concept of transparency has a crucial role in the evaluation of media technology. Some forms of music might have similar concepts of transmitting something "authentic", like the sound of an acoustic guitar, and in these cases technology can often be seen as an obstruction in the communication of music. Gilbert and Pearson use the term "index of visibility" to describe this musical equivalent to transparency (Gilbert and Pearson 1999, 122). It is important to point out that Bolter and Grusin also talk of transparency in music, but they relate it to "liveness", the actual performance of music, and not anything to do with the tools used in the performance (1999, 42). The difference lies in the fact that Bolter and Grusin sees the live band as the source of music, whereas according to Gilbert and Pearson's "index of visibility", the band and its instruments could (in certain cases) be understood as an obstruction to perceiving the artistic ideas. This concept was very much a part of the 1960s folk music movement, where electric instruments were banned, but Gilbert and Pearson argue that in contemporary music this hierarchy has been broken down. Musicians do not look for transparency, but the rater looks for a media with a distinct mark, the actual mediation that can be incorporated into a new aesthetic expression.

Bolter and Grusin are also very much aware that media is not always used to achieve transparency, but is also used to create specific mediations (1999, 35). The problem is that their account of this is rather limited. In general they describe it as a fascination with media, without explaining what exactly is so fascinating about it. By example, they mainly focus on multiple remediations of different media into one media, like medieval altarpieces or in avant-garde and pop art collages.

The aesthetics of recording

The introduction and use of recording technology is a suitable starting point to illustrate how musicians understand technological media as a tool, and to explain the aesthetic difference between digital and analog technology. This is an example of a media that functions for both storage and production. In most media and documentation science the introduction of recording technologies is understood as enabling the fixation of sound in time, meaning you can record a segment of sound, share it with others and replay it at any time you want. This effect corresponds to that of the introduction of writing in relation to speech. When digital recording was introduced, the possibilities for authentic reproduction and effective distribution of sound were increased. Whereas analog recording had a destructive reproduction process, digital technology enabled the infinite cloning of sound.

However, if we turn to musicians and look at how they view recording technologies, the picture becomes a little different. Already in the late 1960s, multitrack recording studios were used to create music that was impossible to play live, in that way creating a work of art that did not exist prior to the recording process (Frith 2004, 115). A long range of artists, including musicians as diverse as Glenn Gold and Miles Davis, has used recording technologies to revolutionize the concept of music production. This is a concept that even Bolter and Grusin have noted (1999, 42). Brian Eno describes the introduction of multitrack recording as: "Now this is a significant step, I think; it's the first time it was acknowledged that the performance isn't the finished item, and that the work can be added in the control room or in the studio itself" (2004, 128). It is easy to understand how recording technology played an important part in the evolution of new types of instrumentations and arrangements, but my point is that through this creative process, not only was the performative role of the musician changed; the recording equipment used also defined what popular music was to sound like. By focusing on the recording as a creative tool, rather than just a container for a musical performance, the realisation emerges that different tools create different sonic experiences.

Because of the great technological difference between digital and analog recording, there is also a great difference in their sound characteristics. This plays an important part in the final artistic result. An analog signal is an electric wave that corresponds to a sound wave. When storing it on a magnetic tape you have to take into account the tape hiss, the background noise created by the magnetic particles on the tape. When you record to tape, you therefore have to record at a loud a level as possible to reduce the overall hiss. In this process you are likely to slightly overload the tape, meaning you record a bit louder than the tape can take. This results in a slight dynamic compression, making the sound more compact and generating a soft distortion, often characterized as a "warm" sound. With the introduction of digital technology, the possibilities for editing and combining recordings are greater than with analog tools. However it also introduced a different sound. When you record digitally, you have an analog-digital converter that samples the sound wave at a specific rate and bit depth. By reversing the process and recreating the waveform from the sampled points, the sound can be replayed (Mitchell and McCullough 1995, 60). If the sample rate and bit depth is sufficient, this sampling technique can digitally record and reproduce realistic sounds without any distortion and very little background noise. But these aspects, which are often described as the advantages of digital recording, have turned out to be a problem. During the sixties and seventies, the soft distorted, and compact sound of analog recording, had during the sixties and seventies defined how a recording should sound. Not only had recording technology enabled instrumentation and arrangement techniques that surpassed that of earlier live performance, it had also, as a by-product, defined popular music soundwise. When digital equipment was released in the early 80s, although it opened many new creative possibilities in regard to arrangements and instrumentation, its neutral and realistic sound did not have the sonic qualities associated with music production (Warner 2003, 21). It was easy to use but there was a reluctance towards it in the industry because of its lack of these sonic qualities. Even today most musicians and music producers, though they use digital recording, prefer the sound of analog recording technology and invariably employ strategies to achieve this sound quality.

The sound of yesterday today

The difference in sound between digital and analog technologies is not only evident in recording, but also in sound production tools like synthesizers. With analog recording technology, the aesthetics had become embedded in the culture through many years of use. But with analog synthesizers, the most profound aesthetic and cultural effect did not occur until after the digital technology had taken over the market. In this sense, the emergence of analog synth aesthetics is also the story of the conflict between commercial technological evolution and cultural practice. To understand the productional context of digital tools today, it is important to look into the events of this first technological counterrevolution.

This evolution of analog synth aesthetics is directly linked to the development of house and techno music in the late 1980s. In the summer of 1988 there was an explosion of electronically based dance music in rave and club culture. Much of this had its origin in Detroit, but it soon spread to the major cities of England and Germany (Rubin 2000, 111). Though much of this music formed part of a short-lived movement, it had a profound impact on the further development of all popular electronic music. The premise for the creation of this music was directly linked to technical innovations, but in a reactionary way. Academics writing on music technology in 1990 claimed that digital sound devices had taken over from their analog counterparts (Durant 1990, 181). In the formation of this new electronic music scene however, a series of discontinued analog machines produced by the Japanese "Roland Corporation" played a very important role. These were the drum machines TR-808 (1981) and TR-909 (1984), and the bass sequencer TB-303 (1981) (Berk 2000, 193). One reason for their discontinuance was that the early 1980s saw an emerging interest for drum machines featuring digital samples of real drums. For the average musician there was an obvious advantage of having a drum machine that actually sounded like drums, which was not the case with Roland's analog drum machines. In spite of this, Roland's president Ikutaro Kakehashin did not want to abandon the analog sound. In 1984 they released the TR-909, which he believed had the perfect blend of analog sounds and digitally sampled sounds (Vail 2000, 284). The cymbals and hi-hats were digital sounds, while the actual drums were still produced through analog circuits. The machine was not a success, and the year after it was replaced by the TR-707, featuring only sampled sounds. In conjunction with the release of the TR-808, Roland had also released the TB-303, a small portable device marketed as an electronic substitute for a bass player. As with Roland's drum machines, the TB-303 did not sound much like its real-life counterpart.

By the end of the 1980s, all these devices were considered outdated and were therefore cheap to buy on the secondhand market. For young and poor musicians these devices therefore became a starting point for making music, and instead of ending up sounding outdated, the use of this old equipment reinvented the sound of popular music. The deep "boom"-like bass drum sound of the TR-808 soon became a favorite with the emerging hip-hop acts (Cutler 2000, 111), whereas the more tight and punchy sound of the TR-909 defined much of house, techno and trance music. For bass-lines, the cheap TB-303 was a natural choice. By turning its resonance filter to the max, the machine would generate the extreme synth wail which came to define the style of Acid House.

The use of TR-909, TR-808 and TB-303 sparked an increasing interest in older synthesizers and drum machines. There was of course initially an economic reason for this renewed interest, since at that time the older analog equipment was cheap. However, this does not suffice to explain why the trend continued throughout the 1990s. In his book "Strange Sound", Timothy Taylor tries to explain the continuing trend by relating it to musicians' growing interest in earlier styles of popular music. However Tim Gane from the band "Stereolab", when interviewed by Taylor, claims that the only reason he uses old equipment is because he likes the sound of it, and does not link it to his interest for earlier popular music (Taylor 2001, 112). Another fact that speaks against Taylor's idea of retro romantics is that musicians in the 1990s used the old equipment in different ways than their manufacturers had intended. Music producer Trevor Horn recalls that, during the mid 1980s, he tried to think what a drummer could do while programming his drum machines.

> Nowadays people don't have a clue what a drummer can do, but they make the box go 'do do do da do baf', and it's fantastic, it's great ……… The way people get in to this sound these days is really quite unbelievable (Warne 2003, 146).

In addition to this, machines like TB-303, TR-808 and TR-909 were rarely used in popular music around the time they were in production. Thus there seems to be no definite link between a cultural nostalgia and the use of these vintage musical devices. This brings us back to the aesthetic dimension of technology, and again to the distinct difference in sound between analog and digital equipment. In the same way as the errors and inaccuracy of analog recording technologies were crucial in defining its sound, distortions and noisy sound in analog synthesizers is what makes them stand out from their later digital counterparts.

Amongst musicians, analog synthesizers and drum machines are, alongside other analog recording tools, described as having a "warmer" sound. Jim Scott, an engineer who worked at the Moog factory during the 1970s, has a personal theory about the sound of the analog synthesizer that can explain why it sounds "better" than its digital counterparts. As he explains, the internal sound processing of an analog synthesizer is done using the total frequency range of a sound, and even if you can't hear all these frequencies, they will affect the distortion of the sound (Pinch and Trocco 2002, 235). In digital processing of sound you can only work with a limited range of frequencies defined by the sampling frequency of the sample. Because of this, digital sound cannot be distorted in the same way as an analog, and therefore produces a "thinner" sound.

Why then, if digital equipment sounded so bad, did people start producing and using it? Besides producing a different sound, there were many productional and functional advantages of digital equipment. As mentioned earlier, digital recording enables a greater flexibility in editing. When it comes to sound productions, digital technology has made possible new ways of synthesizing sounds, such as the FM synthesis in the Yamaha DX7. Sadly, the manufacturers at one point made a turn in the development of digital synthesizers that was unpopular among many musicians. This happened when manufacturers started to focus on the possibilities of digital technologies in reproducing accurate sounds and copying real life instruments – in academic terms, trying to render the synthesizer transparent. While the traditional analog synthesizers had oscillators that produced square, sine and saw-toothed waveforms, the digital synths gradually exchanged these for sampled waveforms from actual instruments. In this way the synthesizer could hold a large sound repertoire of more authentic-sounding instruments. Among the first to use this technology was Korg, with the release of their M1 waveform synth in 1988 (Manning 2004, 301).

From the increasing interest in analog synthesizers in the late 1980s it can be concluded that it was precisely their failure to reproduce actual sound that made the analog synthesizers and drum machines aesthetically interesting. This analog equipment was especially used in the emerging dance music scene. In the beginning this was a result of economic concerns, but it eventually became the dominant aesthetics (Gilbert and Pearson1999, 124).

Functionality in analog technology

The reuse of analog synthesizers was not only motivated by their unique sound, but also by their functional advantages. The earlier analog synths usually had all their parameters accessible to the user in form of knobs and sliders. A good example of this is the design of the "minimoog", the first portable synthesizer to be produced. It was deliberately constructed with easy-to-turn knobs so that the musician easily could manipulate the sound while playing. According to Robert Moog, the inventor of the moog synthesizer, it was designed to be a musical instrument in all ways. It was not only an easy-to-play keyboard, but also a fast and intuitive instrument for sound production (Pinch and Trocco 2002, 224). With the introduction of more and more digital devices in the 1980s, these functions gradually became hidden behind a series of key combinations, resulting in a growing dissatisfaction amongst musicians. Today, manufacturers have learned from their mistakes and have reintroduced designated programming knobs.

Giving the user access to the programming parameters of a musical production tool gives the user only partial freedom. To achieve a greater freedom, the devices have to be turned "inside out", enabling the user also to configure internal structures of the machines, thus creating what is called a modular system. In the 1960s and early 1970s this was the standard design for synthesizers. The user can connect the components of the machine by using patch cords to arrange the path of both audio and controller signals. While the audio cords define the route of the sound through the system, the controller signals define how each module transforms the sound.

These modular systems of the late 60s and early 70s, were, and still are, extremely expensive and offered perhaps a bit too much freedom for the user. Still, the patch system lived on in hybrid synths like the Korg MS and PS series (produced 1977-1983). In these devices, some of the hardwired system can be overridden by a patch panel. The advantage with devices like these is that they can easily be used to manipulate sounds from external sources. By connecting them to other devices, the modules can be used as signal processors, transforming the sounds of other synthesizers and traditional instruments. In this way the modular system not only functions as a user interface, but it also doubles as communication standard between analog devices (fig. 2). These patch cord systems have a great flexibility in manipulating sounds, but are harder to use when it comes to sequencing melodies. When the synthesizer gradually became digital, the digital communication protocol MIDI (music instruments digital interface) was introduced to replace the analog patch cord system. The standard features of this system were mostly based on sending and receiving keystrokes from a keyboard, and not on distributing the actual audio signal. In this way the MIDI system was very good for notated music, but not as well-suited to manipulating sounds as the earlier analog system.

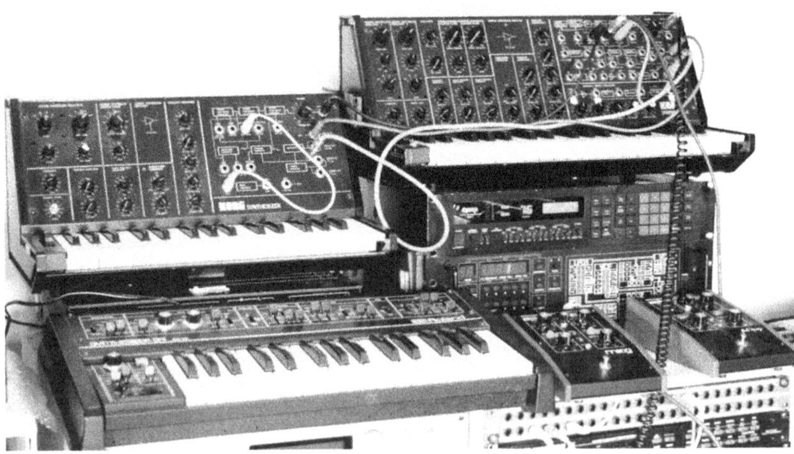

Figure 2

With the introduction of graphical music software, the functionality of modular systems has had a tremendous renaissance. In an academic context, this type of emulation or copying of functional aspects from older technology into newer media is usually understood as an attempt to draw on the user's familiarity with earlier technology. The use of the desktop metaphor is a prime example of this. This metaphor was established to give the user a familiar ground upon which to communicate with a computer in an office setting. In reference to musical production programs and equipment, the remediation of earlier devices must be understood in a much broader sense. In understanding for instance the Arturia virtual version of the Modular Moog system ("Moog Modular V soft synth"), familiarity cannot be the primary motive, simply because few of today's users have experience with modular Moogs. Thus, the motives for reproducing older user-functions in these cases are based on their creative abilities rather than as recognizable metaphors. The "Reason" software has several functions that are taken directly from the analog modular systems, which cannot be seen as merely functional metaphors either. An example of this is the "Matrix sequence", a module that sends out a cv-signal[1] varying in relation to user defined patterns (fig 1). By connecting a virtual cable to other devices in the program, all sorts of parameters can be controlled resulting in a rhythmic change in the sound structure. By reintroducing this vintage control system, unfamiliar to most young musicians today, "Reason" achieves a greater flexibility than what is found in more notation-based midi sequencers. Another software that is strongly based on the modular system is "Reactor", produced by Native instruments. Here you also use virtual cables for audio and controller signals to connect different components inside the program.

The use of digital tools in the 1990s

As I have shown, the development of commercial digital music tools in the 1980s did in some areas move away from what many musicians preferred. The digital devices lacked many of the sonic and functional aspects that electronic musicians looked for, and were therefore unable to make analog technology obsolete. However, the music technology in the 1990s was not purely an odyssey through vintage hardware. What many people associate with electronic music in the 90s is in fact the digital sampler. Although this can be seen as a contradiction to my claim of the importance of analog technology, I will argue that the sampler played an essential role in forming an aesthetics based around analog sound. The reason for this is rooted in how the sampler was used in the electronic music scene.

Originally an invention of the 70s, the drop in digital hardware prices made the sampler available to the general musician in the late 80s. Its design principle is the same as that of digital recording, taking samples of a waveform and storing them as digital information, hence its name. The invention of the modern sampler became fact when the digital information successfully was put in RAM memory cir-

---

1 Short for "control voltage signals" used to control parameters in a modular system.

cuits, easily retrievable by a keyboard controller. However the actual novelty of this design can be debated. The idea has much in common with the "Mellotron" of the 1960s, which stored actual analog sounds on different magnetic tapes attached to the keyboard.

When engineers started working on what eventually became the sampler, they wanted to create something similar to the M1 synthesizer, which could recreate the sound of traditional instruments. However, when the sampler became affordable for the general musician, its cultural impact was different. Nowadays people associate the word "sampling" with recording parts of music and reusing them, and not as a description of how analog/digital converters work. Taylor claims that using the sampler as an actual musical instrument is consistent with sampling and re-contextualizing parts of existing recordings, and not only with using it to reproduce traditional instruments (Taylor 2001, 152). In this way the case of the sampler fits in perfectly with a general discussion of digital reproduction. Andrew Goodwin's article "Sample and Hold" is one of the earliest examples of this. Here he discusses the sampler in view of Walter Benjamin's concept of "aura" (Goodwin 1990, 259). The understanding of the sampler as a recording device is also promoted by Chris Cutler in his article "plunderfonics". Here he views the sampler as a technical culmination of a "low" cultural tradition of using other people's recorded work as a basis for new artistic production. He claims that digital technology made sound piracy so easy that it made no sense not to engage in it. "Producing could be no more than critical consumption; an empirical activity of 'Pick 'n' Mix'" (Cutler 2000, 101).

A very peculiar aspect of the discussion around sampling was that it also crossed over into other cultural fields. In the late 1990s, there was a trend amongst some Norwegian authors to deliberately incorporate long quotes form other texts as an artistic strategy in their novels. To describe and explain this practice, many critics used the term "literary sampling". In 2001 Sussane Østby Sæther and Elin Fallen (2001) wrote an article, called "En Røff Guide til Sampling" ("A Rough Guide To Sampling"), which successfully demonstrates how sampling was perceived around the turn of the millennium. Their main point is that sampling is an aesthetic strategy based on a deliberate form of intertextuality, where the reader/viewer/listener recognizes the works as collage-like compositions based on well know elements. According to this view, sampling occurs when a specific element is deliberately moved from one context to another, and interpreted by the reader/viewer/listener in its new context. In this way they claim that the practice of sampling has much in common with the poststructural theories of Roland Barthes and Mikhail Bakhtin. It must be pointed out that their views are derived from a literary perspective, but they also claim that much of this is evident in musical and pictorial sampling.

Much of the academic understanding of "sampling" as an artistic concept is due to its appropriation by the existing discussion around intercontextualisation and digital reproduction. As Sæthre and Falles article shows, when combined with this existing discussion, sampling fits into a very neat theory. Another example of such a theory is Lev Manovich's account of artistic creation in new media as the selection and combination of preexisting elements, thus blurring the distinction between producer and consumer (Manovich 2001, 135). My question in regard to this is: how accurate are these theories in describing the effect of sampling technology on musical production? There is no denying that there are many examples where the sampler has been used to fuse parts of older existing recordings into new songs; the recontextualisation is an important aspect of the aesthetic experience. But if this is to describe all about the sampler, a sample must be something that always has a prior existence in different context to the sampler. In this view, the "sample" is something that is found (Sæther and Fallem 2001, 5). These thoughts promote the recording aspect of the sampler and its ability to reproduce something already existing. But as with the earlier described recording technology and sound devices, the use of tools for the production of music has a variety of effects. As Gert Lovink puts it: "The sample is not the expression of a fragmented world, it's the technological a priori of all information" (Lovink 2002, 259). This means that a "sample" can just as well be something new, and not existing prior to the sampling process. Even when basing a sample on an existing recording, the reuse of it does not have to result in a deliberate recontextualisation, but rather in the creation of a new cultural experience. An example of this can be seen in the use of the so called "Amen Break", a seven second drum rhythm sampled from a 1967 recording of "Amen Brothers" by the soul band "The Winstons". Although it is maybe the most frequently used sample, its origin is not generally known. According to Nate Harrison it has been used so much that it has become a part of our cultural subconsciousness, freed from any reference to an original context (Harrison 2004).

Harrison's account of the "amen brake" also shows how it was radically edited and rearranged and became an essential part of the aesthetics of drum and bass. In this use, the only thing remaining of the "amen brake" is the sound of the drums, not the rhythm. In this way we return to the important question of the aesthetics of sound, and especially vintage sound. From my point of view, the recording aspect of the sampler has not only been used to cut and paste from known songs, but also as a way to recreate the analog sound. When listening to music, most listeners will never recognize where a sample originates from; the only thing that gives it away as a sample is often its vintage sound. In this way the listener will not experience a recontextualistation of a specific musical piece, but rather a reuse of earlier sounds. This reproduction of analog sound, for instance vinyl sound, has been regarded as an act of romantic nostalgia (Norman 2004, 187). Holding this opinion, however, would mean missing out on all the creative innovations that have come out of experiments with earlier technology.

Digital reproduction of analog inaccuracy: a technological counterrevolution

When looking at how electronic musicians perceived the musical technology in the 1990s, we can perhaps sense a slight hint of technological determinism. By experimenting with older analog technology, the importance of the material technological aspects in forming a new expression became evident. The cultural use of technology had assigned aesthetic dimensions to audio tools, which carried great implications for the production of popular music. As a result of this material aesthetics, the creation of diverse musical expressions demanded a range of different technological devices. The problem that then occurred was that many of the discontinued synths and drum machines people wanted had become increasingly scarce and expensive. To get around this, people started searching for ways to regenerate the characteristics of different-sounding technology. Rather than merely seeing the sampler as a tool for deliberate melodical retextualizing, I believe it also played an important role in this regeneration of the older pre-digital sounds. Thus, sampling music from older recordings was not only motivated by a desire to recontextualize the melody, but also by a desire to recreate the sonic quality of the recording. This is particularly the case with drum samples, which can easily be reedited removing the resemblance to their original rhythmic use. If musicians sample acoustic drums, they generally prefer recordings from the 60s and 70s such as the "Amen Brake". These sounds were recorded with older analog equipment and have all the sonic quality of vintage technology. The sampler also turned out to be ideal for sampling sounds from old analog drum machines and synthesizers. In this way the sampler was not used to make accurate reproductions of acoustic sounds, but rather to reproduce the "inaccurate" sound of analog technology.

In the 1990s analog sound not only lived on through the use of samplers; manufacturers also saw this as an opportunity to start remanufacturing some of the earlier analog equipment. First out was a range of TB-303 reproductions, but it soon became evident that larger analog devices were too expensive to produce today. When the chief designer of Korg was asked whether he would start producing some of the old equipment, like the MS-20, he said it would be much more expensive to produce than the digital devices they now manufacture. This problem of economics was what eventually sparked the production of software synthesizers. Once again the legendary Roland TB-303 was among the first to be reproduced as software, under the sacral-sounding name of "Rebirth" (1996). These types of software are designed to simulate the circuits of the original device, recreating how its different components affect the sound. In this way the program can reproduce not just a single sound, but also the device's flexibility of sound synthesis.

At first glance, the software synthesizer might have much in common with the concept of remediation, but the key difference lies in the motivation behind its construction. The quest for transparency, which is so important for much of Bolter and Grusins understanding of remediation, is turned upside down by the software synthesizer. As I pointed out earlier, a musical tool that does not make a mark does not fit into the creative concept of electronic music production. As a consequence, the traditional concept of media transparency becomes comparatively uninteresting: digital transparency is only interesting when it is used to recreate the inaccuracy of analog tools. In this way the computer continues what the sampler started, namely the reproduction of the analog sound aesthetic that was lost with the introduction of the first digital tools. The software synthesizer is a result of a technological counterrevolution, fueled by a desire to revive pre-digital tools. Musicians do not look for transparent tools because the tools themselves have become an important part of the creative process.

Since academics in the field of media science mostly look at how we consume visual culture, they fail to recognize the rather strange relation between technological evolution and musical production. Because of this, they also miss some unique aspects of media technology and the production of cultural expressions. If we go back to the opening example of the computer functioning as a typewriter, a media scientist like Manovich would describe this as a misconception typical of the early age of digital media when the computer was perceived only as a tool. During the 1990s, he claims, this misconception was replaced with a growing awareness of the computer as a meta-machine for production, storage, distribution as well as media access (Manovich 2001, 69). This might be true in the realm of consumer electronics where it is popular to view digital media as blurring the role of the viewer/reader in relation to the producer. However, for musicians and probably many other specialist groups, the computer is most of all a tool for production. Being a meta-machine therefore involves an ability to function as diverse tools. In this specialized context, Manovich´s view that the computer has closed the gap between consumption and production becomes no more than a myth created outside the realm of artistic and cultural production. The true strength of the computer is that it sets the producer free, and gives him or her the choice too still use the typewriter if he wants.

What makes the computer interesting in the realm of music production is its ability to recreate the functional material aspects of earlier tools. The unique aspect of software synthesizers is that they do not just recreate the results of earlier tools, but also the tools themselves. Since music production in a sense is technologically deterministic, the computer as a meta-machine must also have to reproduce this technological materialism. Photo editing software strives in some instances to achieve the same materialistic aspects, though the use of plug-ins that try to copy the techniques of, for instance, crayon drawings. But the programs do not give you any actual crayons, they just add an effect that makes the picture appear as if it was produced with crayons. In the same way, today's metaphorical user interfaces do not have a functional materialistic resemblance to their real life counterparts, but are usually based on metaphorical resemblance. The files on a computer do not function like real life paper files, whereas the software synthesizer functions are as close to the original as possible. This makes the software synthesizer stand out from other acts of digital remediation. In this way, new media in the production of popular electronic music *is* analog media converted to digital representation, a statement Manovich claims to be more or less a popular myth (Manovich 2001, 49). In my view, the biggest achievement of digital technology is not the recontextualisation of text, but rather the provisions of tools. In order to recontextualise an earlier recording, no more than magnetic tape and scissors are needed, recontextualizing tools themselves on the other hand is a quality only attributed to digital technology.

However, the emergence of software synthesizers, even though its development seeks to revive analog technology, must not be seen as act of retro romantic. From the reproduction and recontextualisation of earlier tools, it is only a short way to start creating new tools. A good example of this is in fact Propellerhead's "Reason" software, which contains a series of vintage-like devices, but unlike "Rebirth", these devices have never existed in a physical form. All the synths, samplers and drum machines come with a distinct name and design; one can even read the serial number and production date on some of the virtual devices, dating them back to the early 1980s, even though they are all new inventions by the software designers. "Reason", therefore, presents itself as a simulation, but a simulation without an original. As argued above, since many people never have used the machines in real life, remediation of musical tools is not only about familiarity with older tools. People use the software versions of analog equipment because they want to achieve a specific sound and not because they already know how to use these tools. The motivation for software simulations is therefore driven by a more general cultural idea of analog technology, not merely by a wish to recreate specific historical tools. For the user the question is not whether or not "Reason's" tools have existed in real life, but rather that they correspond to the cultural idea of analog equipment superiority over digital technology. The counterrevolutional aspect of the software synthesizer is not about going back in time, but rather about the fact that the digital revolution as we know it has ended.

Convergence and divergence: the contradictions of digital technology

Some might claim that my argument about the software synthesizer as proof of the end of the digital revolution in fact proves the opposite. The computers' ability to reproduce analog equipment could easily be seen as the triumph of digital technologies. This view fits very well into the notion of media convergence, where all tools can be fused into the computer. But there are two problems in regard to this opinion.

The first problem with musical software is the lack of tactile aspects, a problem it shares with most other digital tools. As I have argued earlier, much of today's software, like "Reason", is trying to recreate not only the sound of analog technology, but also the functional aspects. The recreation of the latter is even more problematic than the recreating of analog sound itself. As I have pointed out above, analog equipment is renowned for its tactile controls, an aspect lacking in the traditional PC. Turning virtual knobs with a mouse simply does not feel the same as handling physical buttons. The digital tools are therefore lacking all of the performative aspects of early analog synthesizers. To solve this problem without spending a fortune on hardware, it is now possible to buy general purpose midi controllers that feature numerous slides and knobs. By attaching one to the computer through a USB port, it can be assigned to control the digital parameters of your software. An example of this can be seen in "M Audios" midi controllers, which combine piano-keys, knobs and faders. In addition to these general purpose controllers, there are also controllers made for particular software, such as the scaled-down Korg MS-20 that functions as a controller with the softsynth version. Because of this, it can be argued that even if the computer should manage to recreate the sound of analog technology, the computer as a physical device cannot be a substitute for the functionality of hardware. In this way, much music software is forcing the digital technology beyond its normal physical restrictions.

The second and most problematic issue with digital software is of course sound. As mentioned above, digitally created sounds are structured differently from analog sound. Even though a digital software version of a Korg MS-20 might sound like an analog synthesizer, the superior sound quality of the hardware version will by comparison make the software sound like something you really do not want to spend money on. As previously mentioned, Bolter and Grusin's concept of remediation implies that newer media reproduce older media as an act of supremacy over the older media form. Now, if we see the software synthesizer in relation to this, the remediation has much the opposite motivation when comparing digital and analog sound tools. The remediation of analog tools is in most cases accompanied by a growing consciousness of the lack of sonic qualities in traditional digital tools. There are of course many practical and economical advantages of digital technology, but there is always a sense that analog hardware can produce a "richer" sound. In a sense, digital musical tools have gone in the opposite direction than other digital media, and thus working against the "traditional" digital revolution. In opposition to the way all academic writing describes the evolution of digital technology, the more powerfully the computers have evolved, the more normal it has been to view digital musical tools in terms of a "horseless carriage", promoting what is lacking in digital media. In this way the software synthesizer re-actualizes the original analog equipment and digital tools are, in fact, eating themselves. When "Reason" makes a simulation of a series of imaginary analog devices, the program in reality helps to strengthen the notion that analog equipment is superior to digital. It is very much this notion that defines the need for this type of musical software. In addition, the way that "Reason" defines music production as a process involving a diversity of separate devices, works against the idea of the computer as the only production tool. In this way the convergence resulting from the production of software can be seen as fueling a technological divergence: namely, as upholding an interest for real analog hardware.

Conclusion

The conclusion of this article is that digital technology in music production does not have the novel status one might expect. Digital tools exist in a close relationship with their more vintage analog counterparts. The real novelty of software lies in its ability to respond to this relationship and revive instruments from the tar pits of technology, and to let people use them in new musical contexts. The strength of digital tools in the dawn of the 21st century lies not in their ability to copy and manipulate earlier texts, but rather to simulate and manipulate earlier tools, allowing the user to choose amongst all previous devices and even create new ones. Even though the software has many practical and economic advantages, it has to live up to the user's analog sound ideal. Furthermore, by following this quest for analog sound, digital technology helps to create an acknowledgement of analog aesthetics. This must not be seen as merely an act of nostalgia, but rather as a sense that the context of its use is what really makes a particular technology novel. The growth in popular electronic music is to a great extent a result of experimenting with cheap and outdated technology. Instead of always searching for new and better technology, electronic musicians have based their innovation on using whatever they could find and combining this into new cultural expressions. In musical production, the computer software is at the forefront of an ongoing technological divergence, where artistic expression is a result of both different technology and different usage. The success of the computer as meta-tool is not so much a result of the aesthetic qualities of digital technology, but rather a result of the cultural significance that vintage technology has achieved in opposition to the earlier digital production tools.

Though the development of musical tools differs a lot from how academics generally perceive technological evolution, one might, strangely enough, find a resemblance to this in how Marshal McLuhan described the fate of the horse after the introduction of the car. As McLuhan points out, the horse didn't disappear; it just changed its function from being a means of transportation to a means of leisure and entertainment (McLuhan 1964, 238). This might seem a strange comparison, however it illustrates the idea that new digital tools will not digest all earlier analog media. It also raises the awareness that novelty isn't all, and that older medias and technologies will live on and maybe even have a revival by being used in a new and different way. The introduction of new digital media has given us a choice; we don't use analog technology out of necessity, but because we want to. Our way of choosing is not necessarily linked to technical development, but rather to the cultural significance of material aspects and usage. It has too long been a tendency to make generalizations about the impact of digital media by focusing on the same empirical material, the consumption of visual culture only. By focusing on production of music, I hope to have brought some new empirical material forward and to have demonstrated alternative approaches in understanding the relationship between technical innovations and cultural expressions.

References

Berk, Michael, 2000. Analog Fetishes and Digital Futures. In *Modulation, A history of Electronic music: Throbbing Word and Sound*, ed. P. Shapiro; project director I. Lee. New York: Caipirinha Production, 187-201.

Bolter, Jay David, and Richard Grusin, 2000. *Remediation: Understanding new media*. Paperback ed. Cambridge, Massachusetts: MIT Press.

Campbell, Murray, Greated, Clive, and Arnold Meyers, 2004. *Musical Instruments, History, Technology & Performance of Instruments of Western Music*. Oxford: Oxford University Press.

Cutler, Chris, 2000. Plunderphonics. In *Music, Electronic Media and Culture*, ed. S. Emmerson. Aldershot: Ashgate, 87-114.

Durant, Alan, 1990. A New Day for Music? Digital technologies in contemporary music-making. In *Culture, technology and Creativity in the late Twentieth Century*, ed. P. Hayward. London: John Libbey, 175-196.

Eno, Brian, 2004. The Studio as Compositional Tool. In *Audio Culture, Reading in Modern Music*, ed. C. Cox and D. Warner. New York: Continuum International Publishing Group, 127-130.

Frith, Simon, 2004. Art vs Technolegy: the strange case of populare music. In *Popular Music, Critical Concepts in Media and Cultural Studies. Vol 2.*, ed. S. Frith. London: Routledge, 107-122.

Gilbert, Jeremy, and Ewan Pearson, 1999. *Discografies: Dance music, Culture and the Politics of Sound.* London: Routledge.

Goodwin, Andrew, 1990. Sample And Hold: Pop Music in the Digital Age of reproduction. In *On Record: Rock, Pop and the Written Word.* ed. S. Frith and A. Goodwin. London: Routledge, 258-274.

Harrison, Nate, 2004. *Can I get an amen?* Sound installation. Online: http://www.nkhstudio.com/ (accesed 11 June 2006).

Lovink, Geert, 2002. *Dark Fiber, Tracking Critical Internet Culture.* Cambridge, Massachusetts: MIT Press.

Manning, Peter, 2004. *Electronic and Computer Music.* Oxford: Oxford University Press.

Manovich, Lev, 2001. *The language of new media.* Cambridge, Massachusetts: MIT Press.

McLuhan, Marshall, 1964. *Understanding Media*. London: Routledge.

Mitchell, William J., and Malcolm McCullough, 1995. *Digital design media.* New York: Van Nostrand Reinhold.

Norman, Katharine, 2004. *Sounding Art: Eight Literary Excursions Through Electronic Music.* Aldershot: Ashgate.

Pinch, Trevor, and Frank Trocco, 2002. *Analog Days, The Invention and Impact of the Moog Synthesizer.* Cambridge, Massachusetts: Harvard University Press.

Rubin, Mike, 2000. Days of Future Past. In *Modulation, A history of Electronic music: Throbbing Word and Sound*, ed. P. Shapiro; project director I. Lee. New York: Caipirinha Production, 108-127.

Taylor, Timothy D., 2001. *Strange Sounds, Music Technology and Culture.* London: Routledge.

Warner, Timothy, 2003. *Pop Music- Technology and Creativety. Trevor Horn and the Digital Revolution.* Aldershot: Ashgate.

Sæther, Sussane Østby, and Elin Fallen, 2001. En Røff Guide Til Sampling. In *Utflukt: tidsskrift for kultur, kunst og samfunnsspørsmål.* 2001(1), 3-9.

Vail, Mark, 2000. *Vintage Synthesizers: Pioneering Designers, Groundbreaking Instruments, Collecting Tips, Mutants of Technology.* San Francisco: Miller Freeman Books.

Bernt I. Olsen, Niels W. Lund, Johan G. Bellika, Eirik Årsand, Per Hasvold, Gunnar Ellingsen, Alexander Horsch, and Gunnar Hartvigsen

Documents in Medicine: from Paper Documents to Quality-Healthcare?

1 Introduction

The US, as well as most Western nations, is experiencing a transformation from paper-based health documents to digital documents. In this study, we will explore how and why these changes are happening and aim at analyzing what the transformation from paper to electronic documents in healthcare might bring. We are also concerned about how this transformation affects our understanding of the notion of "documents", and in particular "medical documents".

The current replacement of paper-based information sources in health care has several causes. The development of new treatment methods and technological innovations as well as national health policy initiatives are some of them. These generate enormous amounts of information. For instance, the database Medline[1] grows by about 30.000 new publications each year, requiring specialized systems to organize all this information. Large hospitals also face this challenge. For instance, Haux (1998) argues that University Hospital of Heidelberg, with its 1700 beds, creates about 400,000 new medical records per year. These records contain 6.3 million pages and require 1.7 km of storage. Physicians create over 250,000 reports and 20,000 procedure reports each year. The service departments create around a million medical results.

These problems underscore that the traditional paper documents are insufficient in the modern healthcare system. Thus, future electronic documents will have to be dynamic and flexible, fully capable of supporting intensified documentation processes.

---

1 Medline is a bibliographical database with references to journal papers in medicine, nursing and odontology.

In this study, we will present some of the situations in which medical documents are produced. In particular, we will elaborate on how digital documents make a difference compared to paper based documents. To get a feel for what these documents are and will be in healthcare and how they actually come about, we will proceed along the following questions and lines:

- What is a document in healthcare?
- What makes medical information and medical information systems special?
- We will look at some specific cases/genres of documents:
    - Medical images
    - Collaborately created documents
    - The role of disease surveillance
    - Medical sensors

2 What is a medical document?

Interestingly, the terms "medical document" and also "clinical document" are frequently mentioned within the medical literature, but searching for some explanation on what actually lies behind the terms yields little information or discussion on what is meant by them. "Clinical" means direct medical treatment of patients, as in what is observed by a doctor: does the patient have a temperature, is he/she pale, does he/she have a fast pulse, etc. A clinical document would therefore describe clinical findings about the patient. "Medical" is, by the *Oxford English Dictionary's* definition: "of, relating to, or designating the science or practice of medicine in general, or its practitioners". From these two definitions one can argue that clinical documents are documents created during care, while medical documents are knowledge-containing documents used to implement care. It would seem that the "medical community" is not engaged in the discussion of what is meant by identifying something as a document, although the term is frequently used. Furthermore it seems that the meaning behind the words "document" and the process of "documentation" seems every bit as much blurred and ambiguous as it is in contexts other than medicine. The word "document", in its medical context, does not appear problematic in any particular way and apparently there exists a very good consensus about the meaning of it. In order to get an impression of what is considered as a document in healthcare let us first take a look at how the term is used. Please note that the following examples are quite randomly selected from the medical (informatics) literature.

The American Society for Testing and Materials' (ASTM) committee E31.25 was established "to develop standard electronic document representation of paper-based healthcare documents and forms", using XML for the purpose. In this context it is interesting to see their mention of "documents", exemplified in the following citation:

> In order to develop an electronic medical record, an electronic representation of the paper documents must be determined. However, standard description of the types of paper documents in medical records does not exist. A set of the types of documents in the medical record needs to be derived so that electronic representations of the documents can be developed (Sokolowski and Dudeck 1999, 148).

"Documentation", which generally concerns the process of creating a document, is in medicine very much associated with evidence of medical care (or healthcare), or the "legally" influenced report on how care was provided in a specific case (one patient) and is often collocated with the word "malpractice". The following is a quote from an article in the *Journal of Family Practice Management* authored by Teichman:

> Excellence in medical documentation reflects and creates excellence in medical care. At its best, the medical record forms a clear and complete plan that legibly communicates pertinent information, credits competent care and forms a tight defense against allegations of malpractice by aligning patient and provider expectations (2000, 1).

Teichman further states that physicians typically document patient care with a goal of effectively communicating with themselves. This is especially true for primary care like family practices. In other situations of patient care such as hospital settings, home care and nursing homes, this might also be the case, at least for example with patients with chronic illnesses, but within secondary and tertiary care, the documentation contains more communication between healthcare professionals. We will here make clear the distinction between the notion of document and the notion of documentation. In the case of the notion of document, it means the discrete limited number of data appropriate for a certain case, for example a consultation at the GP's office, which is the main focus. In the case of documentation, it is the recording of the whole process, each step in a treatment/care of a patient which is the focus.

We note the use of the term "record" in the previous quotes. In the medical setting "record" and "document" is related, "record" is typically used in the "Patient Record", the "Medical Record" or "Health Record". In other words, it would seem that the collection of documents concerning one patient's care or health is typically regarded as a record within healthcare. In his book on information retrieval (IR) within healthcare, Hersh points out in his definition of an IR-system that:

> An IR system consists of content, computer hardware to store and access that content, and computer software to process user input in order to retrieve it. Collections of content go by a variety of terms, including database, collection, or – in modern Web parlance – site. In conventional database terminology, the items in a database are called records. In IR, however, records are also called documents, and an IR database may be called a document database (2003, 4).

This is an interesting remark, even though we are not specifically interested in IR in this context, as it brings some clarification to the relationship between "record" and "document" especially since the author of the book is talking about IR within healthcare. Records are, in database terminology, defined as related data values or items physically stored together. In a relational database the equivalent might be a row (a tuple) in a table. This is interesting because it says that a document is a (small) set of related data and values, that create some meaning when grouped together. When a medical or health record is a collection of "documents" we could interpret this as "record" being the broader term, while "document" is the more narrow and specialized unit of information. This is how we could interpret the meaning behind the two terms in a medical setting.

Following this trail of thought, the medical documents are seen as parts of medical records and are "instantiated" either in an ad hoc manner, i.e. like narrative text, or according to some predefined structure, a template or the like. As for what goes into clinical documentation, quotes from the guidelines for *Good Medical Practice* (2006) by the General Medical Council provides a fair understanding:

> In providing care you must:
> [...] keep clear, accurate and legible records, reporting the relevant clinical findings, the decisions made, the information given to patients, and any drugs prescribed or other investigation or treatment (8);
> [...] Sharing information with other healthcare professionals is important for safe and effective patient care (25).

This quote points to two of the key elements of medical documentation: to record and document findings and actions and to inform colleagues or others who are involved in the shared care of the patient. From this we can also distinguish between the types of documents that store a documentation of objective observations (such as measured temperature, weight, height, etc.) and more subjective data, such as possible diagnosis and assessments of the medical condition of the patient, and the types of documents that are used for sharing care (such as referral notes and laboratory reports).

An important aspect of medical documentation is that it is created, maintained, and protected by the medical professional, but contains information about the patient. The patient has wide rights regarding insight into what is contained in the medical documentation, but cannot change or influence what is in the documentation directly. Because of the sensitive nature of medical information, a great responsibility lies on those who are responsible for the integrity and accessibility of the medical information. Access to medical documents is controlled by legislation that specifies who can access these documents and under what conditions. Such legislation usually also places a responsibility on the healthcare professional to not abuse the information and to maintain the privacy of the patient.

The use of medical documentation is not limited to the diagnosis and treatment of individual patients, but also plays an important role in monitoring practice (both in auditing one's own practice and reaching consensus on the best practice) and assessing population-wide trends (such as the outbreak of an epidemic, see section 4).

Health Level 7, an American non-profit organization, has in its Clinical Document Architecture (CDA) made an effort to standardize electronic clinical documents for exchange between systems and organizations using an XML structure. Having the "document" as part of the label, it is difficult to have a discussion about medical or "clinical" documents (or documentation) without taking a closer look at it. The CDA specifies the structure and semantics of a clinical document. A CDA is defined as follows:

> A CDA document is a defined and complete information object that can include text, images, sounds, and other multimedia content. It can be transferred within a Message, and can exist independently, outside the transferring message (Dolin et al. 2006, 1).

The CDA is mainly developed for interoperability purposes, making institutions able to exchange documents such as discharge summaries or progress notes. The CDA is "richly expressive" and contains text, images, sounds or any other multimedia content and is thus descriptive in terms of what we can expect from future health information systems. The CDA's mission is both to make information structured and interoperable and to make it interpretable by machines, so that they can be acted upon – by machines (like issuing alarms, reminders, etc), hence the adoption of XML for this purpose. The CDA is, like all standards from HL7, based on a framework called Reference Information Model, RIM. As the name suggests, this is a model of the grammar for the HL7 "language", i.e. it gives the basic building blocks of the language and the permitted relationships between them. The CDA is now being adopted quite widely within research as well as within clinical information systems and is a promising alternative when documents are being digitalized within healthcare.

The most interesting characteristic of medical information is the complexity inherent in such information. Since the 1970s, the field of Medical Informatics has had the creation of a worldwide exchangeable and interoperable medical- or health record system as a research goal, but it still remains distant. The issue of complexity, it is argued, is the main cause of the lack of such an electronic health record. The complexity of patient information is due to the fact that medicine in general mirrors the most complex organism that we know of, namely the human body. Furthermore, systems handling this information must meet requirements from a social and societal point of view (such as legal requirements etc.). Beale, in his comment in the IMIA Yearbook of 2005, uses the eight levels of complexity in living systems proposed by Miller (1995) to describe the task of making a information system, or an EHR, to support the task of giving health care, arguing that the complexity of life is relevant for clinical information systems at all eight levels – ranging from the micro-system level of the cell to the macro-perspective of the "super-societal" (global) level. Beale here argues strongly that the health information system differs from other systems in that the "complexity of life" it examines exists at all eight levels, and cannot easily be simplified by abstractions, but that the human patient needs to be captured in his/her entirety; any small detail might be important for care-giving and treatment purposes. This stands in contrast to other information systems that HISs are commonly compared to, like banking systems or ticketing/air travel reservation systems. In these systems, it is only a fraction of human activity that needs be modeled for a successful system. In addition to the complexity of the human body and the social and societal issues, the continually evolving medical knowledge base (e.g. Medline) creates further complexity, describing both the results of centuries of medical scientific achievement – an already overwhelming base of input to clinical decision making - along with an accelerating rate of new knowledge, crucial for success in research-intensive areas like oncology. Beale lists some interesting requirements for the health record:

- information and efficient user interface reflecting multiple levels of hierarchical biological and social organization;
- mobile patients;
- longevity of information (e.g. 100 years);
- multi-lingual;
- data shared and authored by multiple users simultaneously;
- integrated with knowledge bases such as terminology and clinical guidelines;
- wide geographical availability of a given record to multiple caregivers and applications;

- consent-based, potentially fine-grained privacy rules on information use (with exceptions for emergency access);
- multiple sources of constant change to requirements including medical technology, clinical procedures and guidelines, genomic/proteomic medicine;
- reliable medico-legal support for all users (Beale 2005, 302).

In addition to these requirements, one might also add the already mentioned potential size of the record, as some of the compounds might require terabytes of storage. However, as Beale points out, in all of the above requirements there might be at least one application or system more exigent than the EHR. The problem is that medical information needs encompasses multiple areas of ICT at once. As health care is provided, the assisting information systems need to perform at several of Miller's eight levels of complexity all at the same time, for different users with different needs. An example of the difficulty caused by this is the problems faced in the design of user interfaces for medical applications. Electronic information systems, in contrast to older (paper-based) systems have the potential to inform caregivers in almost any situation of nearly every aspect of the medical decision process. The risk of overloading the user with information, putting too much into one interface, is imminent and tempting for system designers. The problem at this point is: how does one know what is relevant at any point in time? How does the GP know what is relevant when referring patients to secondary care? Only the specialist, the recipient of the information, would know what to extract. Many applications fail at this point to attract users in clinical settings as the requirements for both user-friendliness and the felt usefulness of the application are extremely high. Health care workers are generally people with very little time to waste with systems that fail to inform them efficiently and are the first to stop using them (or refrain from starting to use them). Having the definition of HL7's CDA freshly in memory, the description of a "complete information object [...] that can exist independently from a transferring message" perhaps preceded by the word "minimum" might seem compelling in this context. The first apparent task is of course to build systems to make all the information available, the next to find appropriate methods of selecting the information most relevant to any particular situation.

3 Images in medicine

As we have now taken a look at the general "nature" of medical documents, we will move on to take a closer look at some specific concepts and cases within modern healthcare and the potential within technology and the digitization of medical documents, and the issues that they raise.

In medicine, images play a central role in the concept of a document. Their counterparts in everyday life are photos, illustrations, sketches, drawings and other examples from art or mass-media. However, images in medicine have very distinct properties, as they most often serve a very specific use in treatment, research or within medical education.

In medicine, an image, or a series of images, a 3D volume, a video, or any other visually perceivable entity, together with a minimum set of meta-data, is considered to be a medical document. That is: anything from a photo or a video to a 3D-model together with describing "data" is considered to be a document. The minimum set of meta-data depends on the context in which the document is used (or in other words: the purpose for which the document is created). In the context of patient care, the minimum set of meta-data comprises all information that is mandatory to fulfill the requirements of health service provision. For this purpose, especially information about the patient, the acquisition device, and the producer of the images is included. A special case are teleconsultations, where images or videos are captured and stored for documentation of the consultation. The project ENDOTEL led by Munich University of Technology (Horsch et al. 2003) has used the CDA document standard for this purpose.

In the context of medical education, the minimum set of meta-data comprises information needed to make the images a learning unit. This includes information such as author of the learning unit, and case data (e.g. age and sex of the patient, medical problem, therapy regimes).

Within the context of medical research, the minimum set of meta-data consists of information required by the trial protocol. Patient-identifying information is in this context either anonymized or pseudonymized. A special case are reference datasets for the validation of computer-based image analysis tools, such as computer-aided diagnosis tools: here, an image or imaging study together with meta-data needed for assessment of quality features (e.g. accuracy, reproducibility, robustness) can be considered a document (Horsch et al. 2005).[2]

Some examples may help to understand this definition. DICOM (Digital Imaging and Communications in Medicine) (DICOM, 2006) studies are documents in the context of patient care. A DICOM file representing a DICOM study on a computer includes a large header part containing detailed information about the patient, the health service provider that has performed the study, the imaging device, and the image acquisition parameters. ODITEB (Open Distributed Textbook, an eLearning application for tumor diagnosis with x-ray, CT, MRI, and endoscopy)

---

2 The bare pixel data of a digital image is not a document in medicine, due to the fact that it lacks necessary information that makes it a self-contained information unit.

cases are documents in the context of medical education (Horsch et al. 2000). Such an eLearning case comprises imaging studies together with non-identifying (anonymous) information about the patient and the case such as anamnesis, or an expert guided tour through the case. Mammo-iCAD (a current research project on computer-aided diagnosis for breast cancer detection of Definiens Inc., Munich, in collaboration with University of Erlangen and Munich University of Technology) cases are documents in the context of medical research. Such a case contains the breast images (mammograms) and a subset of patient data from the standard documentation used in mammography. In all these examples there are core meta-data which are essential for a document, including author(s), creation and modification date and time, and the property of being a self-contained information unit.

Documents for education and research are usually derived from documents which have been created in a patient care setting. For instance, in order to create an ODITEB eLearning case, DICOM studies are anonymized and non-identifying information from the patient record is taken and worked upon, providing a learning case for medical students.

In practice, medical images occur as parts of documents. So, looking at practice-relevant information units in medicine, one can always perceive the bare image without any meta-data as a part of a medical document. From this perspective, a DICOM image is a document with a structure defined by the DICOM standard, which contains an image or a series of images as a part of the document. Printed documents such as reports from a hospital to the primary care physician often contain images for illustration purposes (not for diagnosis). Information systems for pathology, microbiology, ophthalmology, etc. store visible light images and meta-data in a database, e.g. in an EPR system or a clinical trial system.

4 Multiple authored documents in healthcare

The medical domain is collaboration intensive by nature; many different participants are required in the act of caring for a patient. In hospitals, different kinds of clinicians bring their specialty area forth in the effort to give care to the patient, while in other settings such as home care and nursing homes several people share responsibilities in caring for multiple people. Within primary care, the most typical encounter in public health care (which accounts for about 90% of patient cases) cooperation also plays an important role. Documentation is a way of ensuring that someone else can easily take over care for the patient (i.e. secondary care, or another GP). Other than in the case of family practice kind of primary care, documents are rarely created in a medical context for only one person to see or use, and hence documents are both means for cooperation and artifacts that encourage cooperation, as we shall see. The role of cooperation within healthcare is strengthened by a current and worldwide emphasis on "patient-centric care" and "quality of care". Concepts as teamwork, the sharing of care for patients between clinicians, are regarded as crucial success factors in achieving increased quality of care and an improved health for the patient (Dichter 2003; IOM 2001, i.e. 27; Olender 2005). Shared care refers to clinicians who jointly treat the same patient, while continuity of care is the 'complete care' provided during all transitions, such as home to hospital, between institutions, and so on.

"Computer supported cooperative work" (CSCW) is a field of research that aims to understand the nature and characteristics of cooperative work so as to build adequate systems to support and enhance this cooperation. The nature of a collaborative activity is generally classified along the dimensions of time and space, that is – synchronous versus non-synchronous and same place (i.e. the people are in the same room) versus geographically distributed collaboration.

	Same time (synchronously)	**Different time (asynchronously)**
Same Place	*A meeting*	*A hospital ward*
Different Place	*Telephone call*	*Referred patient*

Table 1

All four modes of cooperation (see Table 1) are present when health care is provided in all kinds of medical issues and are traditionally supported in different ways. Documentation in a case of cooperative activity could be either conclusions made by the team or a report of a meeting. Cooperative activities spanning time and space have traditionally been mostly 'supported' by paper, either as paper journals (or parts of them) or forms and schemata, either transported between the cooperating parties or stored in a common place. We acknowledge that paper has a lot of qualities that make it well suited to support cooperative activities, as for instance medical records are small enough to be held in the hand while the doctor communicates with the patient, a nurse, or a specialist on the phone. The paper can readily be moved both within and between institutions, and has inherent (physical) limitations regarding unwanted distribution of sensitive data. Paper can easily be annotated for the next viewer or for later use. All of these qualities and many more are easily forgotten when documents are 'reproduced' or replaced by an electronic counterpart. But paper has also severe limitations when supporting collaborating parties or persons.

The introduction of information systems into healthcare has profound implications for the potential support and enhancement/augmentation of cooperation for the abovementioned quality of care issue and making the health of the patient at the centre of attention. The transition from paper to electronic documentation makes long-distance exchange of information and communication manageable. Information technology can provide for tele-consultations, bringing expertise and specialists to work in areas where it was nearly impossible before. Secondly, in the future, we expect to have health record systems that allow for both cooperative documentation of the care given to patients, allowing for authoring and editing by all types of clinicians and healthcare workers, suiting their need, from wherever they find themselves caring for a patient. Cooperation via IT-infrastructure brings forth new possibilities and requirements for documentation of care. Systems will allow for constructive and easy co-authoring of documents while at the same time also allowing for communication and coordination of activities.

Electronic documents are especially useful in terms of availability. Electronic versions of documents can easily be distributed to several locations at the same time. People can share both information, thoughts and ideas and work on the same document at just about any given time (only limited by the availability of the people themselves). The ease of distribution/availability of documents means that more people can be included into the care regime, which means there are better grounds for interdisciplinary cooperation, which in turn can lead to better care. Even the patients themselves can be encouraged, through availability of data about themselves and their health condition, to actively contribute and cooperate with healthcare personnel. This can be done through web interfaces containing parts of the patient record that the patient can access from home. Examples of such contributions are sensory equipment at the patient's home, or sensors to be worn by the patient, as discussed in chapter 6.

Research within CSCW has thrown light on several aspects of cooperative activities that have profound implications for systems that are built for health care purposes. Agreeing that cooperation and collaboration are important for the quality of given health care and the effectiveness of health systems means agreeing that all of these aspects must be taken into account in designing systems for the healthcare domain. Documents have a special role when it comes to cooperative settings in caring for patients. They can, for example, be seen as "collaboration mechanisms", helping in both coordinating and structuring work. Both paper and electronic documents can act as such mechanisms; thus for example in the co-located situation there are documents that are collaboration mechanisms, such as when physicians discuss an MRI image, lab reports, or any other such document. There are similarities between the co-located and the distributed collaboration modes that relate to the role and importance of collaborating mechanisms. In health care, documents (including forms, records, images, sounds, medical data, etc.) play an important role in collaboration as healthcare services are bound by legal requirements to document all actions and assessments related to the diagnosis and treatment of a patient. Digital documents have opened up new ways of collaboration and organization of work flow. They further enable completely new ways of performing care audits, both by allowing for more and better quality of documentation, and in allowing mechanisms for developing and controlling routines and protocols. The availability of electronic documents, along with communications tools, make them ideal for informing the cooperating people of each others' actions, creating 'awareness' within the cooperating party. Information technology and – systems can provide for quite outstanding support for cooperation in healthcare, but care must be taken when designing systems in order to use this potential to the highest possible degree. We are only starting to see systems designed with such issues in mind, and little empirical data exists on their use. The scientific body of knowledge on the subject of information systems supporting cooperation is perhaps still not matured to the level that the potential for 'augmented cooperation' can be fulfilled. There is still a lot to be learned about systems for collaboration and the documents that are to come from them.

5 Medical Documents for Population; 'aggregate' documents

At the other end of the scale from the patient-specific collaborately authored documents are population-specific issues. Today, disease surveillance is an important part of most countries' protection against epidemics and their global counterparts, pandemics. Most countries therefore have legislation that permits extraction of data from medical information systems for disease surveillance purposes. Disease surveillance today is dependent on specific 'documentation practices' and will likely remain dependent on a very wide range of information sources in the future.

An early example of the role of a document, and the documentation process, is the Broad street map, made by John Snow, a physician in the Soho area in London during the reign of Queen Victoria. From 1831 and onwards, London suffered from recurring cholera outbreaks that caused many deaths. Snow became interested in the cause and transmission of the cholera disease and used a map of the Soho area in London to plot the location of deaths caused by cholera. He used this map to show that there was a correlation between the water supply and deaths caused by the cholera disease. In his publication, "On the mode of transmission of cholera" (Snow 1965) from 1855, he argued that cholera was transmitted through contaminated water, against the more commonly held belief that cholera was transmitted through miasmata (i.e., bad air) (Frerichs 2001; Buechner et al. 2004). By looking at the map, everyone could see that the cases were scattered around the location of the Broad street pump. Snow managed to stop an outbreak, giving undisputable evidence for his theory, by convincing the authorities to remove the pump handle from the Broad street pump. John Snow is today regarded as a pioneer in epidemiology and is by some called "the father of modern epidemiology".

Today both we and the diseases that we are the carriers of travel faster and further than ever before. The SARS outbreak in 2003 showed how quickly a local outbreak of an unknown disease in Hong Kong spread to a lot of countries. The systems that are able to discover disease outbreaks have therefore become more important than before. Our ability to discover disease outbreaks is today limited by our access to digitally documented evidence of confirmed cases or digitally recorded documentation of actions that are caused by people affected by a disease.

Traditionally, it has been the medical laboratories that have been the data providers for the disease surveillance systems. The medical laboratories provide evidence for the presence of a disease from the samples that are provided by physicians. By counting the number of confirmed cases of a predefined set of diseases, typically in centralized institutions, we achieve some preparedness against the threat from contagious diseases. The record of previous cases provides data about the normal distribution of cases in the population. If the number of confirmed cases of a disease suddenly increases, we can discover the situation and potentially initiate a public health response to stop the outbreak.

A new threat which the disease surveillance system must face is bioterrorism. Bioterrorist actions may cause a large number of people to become ill simultaneously by spreading a disease agent through air, water or food. The fear of bioterrorist attacks has initiated research in syndromic surveillance systems (Henning 2004). The term "syndromic" refers to the set of early symptoms that characterize a disease. The goal of syndromic surveillance systems is to discover disease outbreaks as early as possible, hopefully early enough to initiate public health actions that can limit the effects of such actions. New data sources as school and work absenteeism, over the counter sales in pharmacies, and many other sources, have therefore become important. The most important source is the electronic patient record systems used by the health personnel that meet the patient. However, the text for documenting the chief complaints presented by the patient may cause problems related to misspellings, local slang and lack of a common terminology. If the routines for documenting a case are followed, and the documentation is performed immediately, this is a good data source for surveillance systems. However, the lacking utilization of electronic tools for documentation is limiting our ability to discover bioterrorist actions or naturally occurring disease outbreaks. To have an impact, syndromic surveillance systems may need to discover bioterrorist actions within the incubation period of the disease (Kaufmann et al. 1997, i.e. 88). A future source for syndromic and disease surveillance systems is therefore data provided by humans that volunteer data from sensors for disease surveillance purpose. A very relevant group are the diabetics that regularly measure their blood glucose level (Årsand et al. 2005). We will have a look at diabetes disease in relation to how sensory output is a part of medical documents later in the text.

Laboratory-based disease surveillance has limitations. It may take a long time to confirm the presence of a disease, we may not test for the correct disease in the laboratory, and it may take a long time before the data becomes available for the electronic disease surveillance systems, if the disease is unknown, how can we count occurrences of the disease electronically that lacks a classification? If the disease is new and unknown, as in the SARS case, we may not have a test that we can perform. We may therefore need to collect data about the symptoms of the patients, recorded by health personnel, and the category of tests that are performed to provide early indications of disease outbreaks. In the case of an unknown disease, we may lack a clear definition of the symptoms that we can use for screening, and the definition of the disease may change, based on updated knowledge which invalidates earlier definitions of the disease. Management of disease definition information is therefore also a challenge in being prepared for every possible outbreak of a communicable disease.

Another development that threatens our disease surveillance systems is the increasing availability and use of disease specific polymer chain reaction (PCR) tests by general practitioners. Unless the results of these tests are collected, our disease surveillance systems may become undermined from lack of case data. In the future we therefore need to develop disease surveillance systems that also collect case data from primary care physician's electronic health record systems.

Disease surveillance is a subject that requires thorough and accurate documentation, both in health care and, in the future, from other places. All sources of information are important in such a context, including other documents and documentation practices which, unlike today, are not specifically or explicitly made for the purpose of detecting epidemic outbreaks. They are differently sized 'streams' or 'rivers' of documents that altogether will contribute to the creation of powerful documents that detect epidemics or pandemics, hopefully early enough for us to take action. They will be powerful documents in that, like the map created by Dr. Snow, they will initiate actions against outbreaks or reducing the spread of diseases. However, finding signs of epidemic outbreaks is in many cases not trivial. It involves, in this context, searching through potentially large and distributed data-sets or documents. This approach is often labeled "data mining" within computer science. We will next briefly discuss this technique, which is regarded as very important in the future of health care.

As we have already discussed, patient databases and knowledge bases are growing rapidly within medicine and healthcare. With paper based information systems, this means growing mountains of paper documents that require a lot of storage space (patient records) and books and journals printed, delivered, indexed and filed for the use of medical decision making. With digital systems, it means growing patient databases and growing knowledge bases stored either in local systems where the data/knowledge is produced, or in centralized settings on servers. The transformation to digital documents offers some possibilities that are not available using paper documents. With paper, the information stored is not easily available, as documents have to be tediously collected in order to be available for evaluation in medical decision making. Furthermore, the information has to be processed by humans in order to be useful. The affordances of electronic documentation in regards of availability of the information and the potential for machine processing is given by the technique known as data mining. In essence, it means browsing through large amounts of data, looking for relevant (new) information and knowledge. This means that one can have agents or processes running that look for i.e. specific patters (one technique) either on a specific case (patient) level or in larger groups of people.

The increasing complexity of the medical field calls for tools that can keep up with this development. Having patient records available online enables automatic search routines and pattern matching. For example, the content of a person's record can regularly be used as a search filter in order to locate relevant medical information in medical databases and/or on the Internet.

For difficult cases where we have symptom descriptions, but not have been able to form a diagnosis, automatic pattern matching against other patients can help in the identification of the correct diagnosis. More general algorithms can be used to find similarities in medical data. This will be similarities between patient's records, between patient's records and medical databases, etc. Based on such a data mining system we can uncover relevant relationships in medical data, both expected and unexpected. For a document, this means that it will live its own life. The extension of the document occurs automatically.

The digitalization of documentation processes within healthcare has profound implications for the amount of available data in the future. Another factor that will contribute to this volume of information is the growing number of (digitalized) medical sensors. These range from hospital equipment that delivers data directly to patient records to equipment worn by the patient or body-sensors. It is likely that we will see this data present in future health records, along with patient contributions in various forms. We will now have a look at a specific and very relevant disease that illustrates this: the case of diabetes.

6 Sensory input - automatic documentation

Many chronic diseases need to be closely followed up in order to achieve better health prognoses, and medical sensors constitute good tools for this. Wireless communication technologies have exhibited huge progress the last years, with growth of facilities such as Bluetooth, ZigBee, WiFi, UMTS, and others. An increasing number of medical sensors support at least one of these communication standards, among them blood-pressure measuring systems, asthma peak aspiratory flow monitors and blood glucose measurement systems. Likewise, technological development has lead to miniaturized electronics that enable medical sensors either to be worn on the body with minimal inconvenience, or even to be implanted in the body. Based on one of the most common chronic diseases, diabetes, we will here briefly discuss both the state of the art and future perspectives of this technological progress, related to the change in medical documents and medical documentation.

The number of cases of diabetes worldwide in the year 2000 among adults (+20 years of age) was estimated to be 171 million (Wild et al. 2004). Most of the instances of the disease are defined as Type 2 diabetes (~92 %), where an unhealthy lifestyle is the main contributor to the imbalance in the essential insulin production and/or utilization system. Type 1 diabetes contributes to nearly all the remaining instances, where the cause is unknown and the individual's insulin production has stopped. For both types of the disease, the blood glucose level increases to unhealthy levels due to the defect in the insulin system. Thus, frequent use of blood glucose sensors is essential for this patient group as an aid in achieving healthy values and reducing chances of complications such as progressive development of retinopathy with potential blindness, nephropathy that may lead to renal failure and/or neuropathy with risk of foot ulcers, amputations, sexual dysfunction and substantial increased risk of cardiovascular diseases. For Norway alone, such complications are calculated to cost the country 3.5-4 billions NOK per year (Norges Diabetesforbund 2000). In addition to the artificial supply of insulin, physical activity and proper nutrition are actions, and thus parameters, that both patients and care givers need to relate to for achieving healthy blood glucose values. So are parameters such as weight, cholesterol level, micro-albumin, blood pressure, and so on.

People with diabetes are in regular contact with health care personnel like general practitioners (GPs), hospital nurses, diabetes specialists, foot therapists and eye specialists. Usually, these contacts result in the sampling of one or more of the parameters mentioned above. This data is stored in one or more electronic health record (EHR) systems. In Norway, a lot of data is still stored in unsynchronized systems. Data entered into EHR systems is stored in an underlying database, and the different medical documents are created real-time based on predefined report templates. Today, all the documents are both designed and generated by professional health care actors, i.e. none by the patients themselves.

Even though many of the blood glucose meters store the last measurements and have export possibilities to a PC, few of the hospitals or GPs have procedures for capturing these data in their EHR. Instead, the patients are asked to remember their last measurements at their annual, bi-annual or quarterly visits. Thus, the most important parameter for avoiding diabetes complications is still not utilized in medical documents, neither for use by health care personnel nor for the patients or relatives. The same is true for the two other most important parameters for people with diabetes; nutrition and physical activity data. The latter two are hardly ever captured at any health institutions. Prescriptions of medicines and measurement equipment are still not generated or transferred automatically to pharmacies, but issued as a paper document from the doctor to the patient (often handwritten).

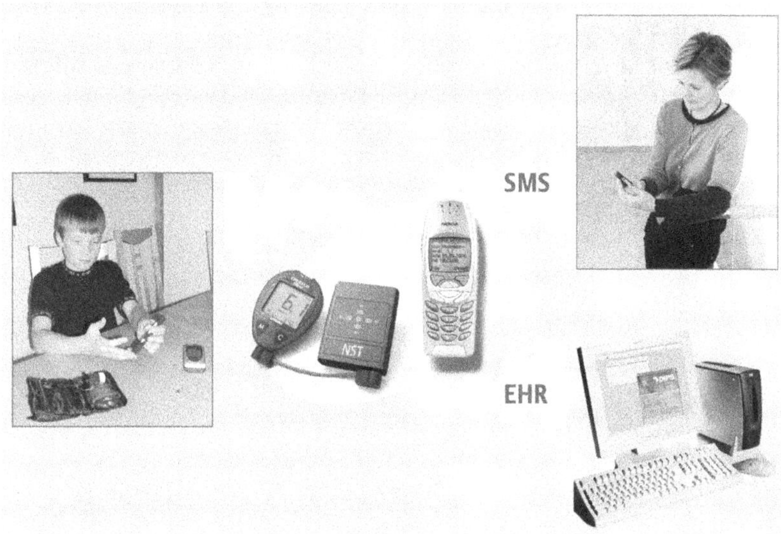

Figure 1: Automatic blood glucose data transfer to EHR and as an SMS to relatives. (Photo: Jarl-Stian Olsen/Hilde Pettersen NST)

A likely future scenario is that all important patient-sampled sensor data is stored, arranged, displayed and used by both the patient and the health care personnel to achieve an optimal health management. Prescriptions are automatically generated based on the actual use and effect of the medicine and measurement equipment, and transferred electronically to both pharmacies and patients. One of the projects at the Norwegian centre for telemedicine (NST) has designed and tested a concept that exemplifies part of this scenario for the blood glucose parameter. The prototype combines the short-range communication standard Bluetooth and GSM for long-range communication, in automatically transferring the medical sensor data both directly to an EHR system (Årsand et al. 2004) and to a relative's mobile phone (Gammon et al. 2005), see Figure 1.

If sensor data such as blood glucose were part of the EHR database, it provides an opportunity to generate novel medical documents to aid the patients, both in the treatment of illnesses and in prevention of getting them. Using data analysis prior to automatic document generation gives both the patients and the health care personnel answers to questions like: "At which time of the day are the parameters at a less healthy level?", "Which weekday(s) does the patient need to focus most on achieving healthy values?", "How many percent of the values are within the healthy range?", "How well regulated is this person compared to the average within her/his profile?", and so on. NST is also working with capturing and integrating nutrition and physical activity data (Eirik Årsand and Gunnar Hartvigsen, 2005) to provide a better clinical overview for this patient group. The idea is that the concept of direct capture of patient data into medical documents will shortly manifest itself in more patient groups, and even be used as a preventive measure among people at risk for developing certain diseases. Such an extensive use of patient-generated data needs subsequent routines for document generation, distribution and follow-ups.

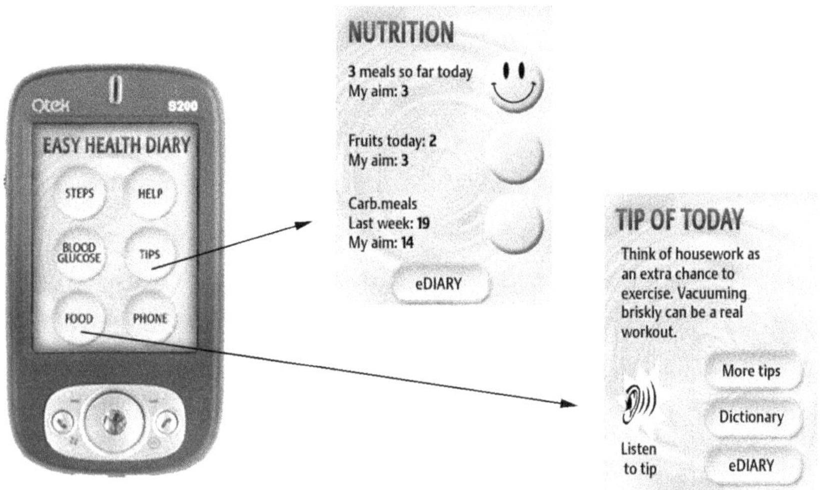

Figure 2: Example on Digital patient diary for people with diabetes; main menu and two example functions (Design: Årsand/Varmedal/Olsen, NST).

Future medical documents will, instead of mainly being either paper-based or electronic documents on hospital data terminals, to a large degree be constituted of electronically displayed information on the patients' stationary terminals (PCs, TVs) and mobile terminals (mobile phones, PDAs). The growth of digital patient diaries like the one displayed in Figure 2 is part of this scenario. So is the introduction of automatic computer-generated handling and feedback on the patient-sampled data.

7 Closing remarks

The notion of a "document" has profound relevance within healthcare. It is used for just about anything, from an X-ray image, a discharge report or a lab report to a prescription. Multimedia content is in some cases regarded a document. Aggregated and processed data is in the case of an epidemic a powerful document that can affect entire populations. The spectrum of objects called documents is, in other words, very wide. As we have touched upon in this essay, complexity plays an important role when speaking about documents in healthcare, both at the molecular level and the societal level, which documents within healthcare are operating on at all levels. Regarding documents as "complete information objects", as HL7's CDA does, provides us with a useful insight into the very crux of 'documentation' in this context. As the field of medicine and healthcare in general is highly complex, involving many people in the process of care-giving for patients, or also research and education, it is quite a challenge to produce such complete information objects at any given time. As documents are to be useful for such a broad range of people and uses with severe requirements for availability, security, informability and nearly every other aspect that could test the boundaries of information and communication technology, it is no wonder that standardization processes – trying to deal with the very issue of complexity – is having such a hard time making general models of the systems that deal with giving care to human beings.

There is a contradiction between the need for generalizing to build information systems and the specialization, where every patient, every human being has a need for a personalized treatment and follow-up, both in terms of medical treatment and social/cultural preferences. The tools available so far are classification and standardization, structuring and modeling information systems. Some issues are solved by such an approach, and others arise from it. Medical work, especially critical care, is exceptional by nature and collaboration-intensive. The most valuable resource in providing quality care is well-informed and competent medical staff. The paper-regime dominating healthcare from its infancy until now is rapidly being replaced by its electronic counterpart. Digital documents offer new opportunities, as information can be shared easily and be a part of electronic communication services on the Internet.

8 References

Beale, Thomas, 2005. The Health Record – why is it so hard? In *IMIA Yearbook of Medical Informatics 2005*, eds. R. Haux and C. Kulikowski. Stuttgart: Schattauer GmbH. Verlag für Medizin und Naturwissenschaften.

Buechner, Jay S., Constantine, Herbert, and Annie Gjelsvik, 2004. John Snow and the Broad Street pump: 150 years of epidemiology. *Medicine and Health Rhode Island* 87, 314-315.

Dichter, Jeffrey R., 2003. Teamwork and hospital medicine: A vision for the future. *Critical Care Nurse* 23, 8-11.

DICOM, 2006. Digital Imaging and Communications in Medicine (DICOM). Rosslyn, Virginia, USA, National Electrical Manufacturers Association (NEMA).

Dolin, Robert H., Alschuler, Liora, Boyer, Sandy, Beebe, Calvin, Behlen, Fred M., Biron, Paul V., and Amnon Shabo, 2006. HL7 Clinical Document Architecture, Release 2. *J Am Med Inform Assoc* 13, 30-39.

Frerichs, Ralph R., 2001. History, maps and the internet: UCLA's John Snow site. *SoC BULLETIN* 34(2), 3-7.

Gammon, Deedes, Årsand, Eirik, Walseth, Ole Anders, Andersson, Niklas, Jenssen, Martin, and Ted Taylor, 2005. Parent-Child Interaction Using a Mobile and Wireless System for Blood Glucose Monitoring. *Journal of Medical Internet Research* 7(5):e57.

Haux, Reinhold, 1998. Health and medical informatics education: perspectives for the next decade. *Int J Med Inform* 50, 7-19.

Henning, Kelly J., 2004. What is syndromic surveillance? *MMWR Morb Mortal Wkly Rep* 53 Suppl, 5-11.

Hersh, William R., 2003. *Information Retrieval: A Health and Biomedical Perspective*. New York: Springer-Verlag, Inc.

Horsch, Alexander, Balbach, Thomas, Melnitzki, Susanne, and Jürgen Knauth, 2000. Learning Tumor Diagnostics and Medical Image Processing via the WWW – the Case-based Radiological Textbook ODITEB.

Horsch, Alexander, Blank, Ricarda, and Doris Eigenmann, 2005. The EFMI reference image database initiative: concept, state and related work.

Horsch, Alexander, Itälä, Timo, Mikola, Tuire, Leonhardt, Petra, Tobman, Matvei, Nätscher, Catharina, and Helmut Sußmann, 2003. CDA-based Integration of a Teleconsultation Service into a Regional Electronic Patient Record System. *Medical Informatics Europe MIE.*

IOM (2001) Crossing the quality chasm: a new health system for the 21st century. Washington, DC, Institute of Medicine (US) Committee on Quality of Health Care in America. National Academy Press.

Good Medical Practice, 2006. Online: http://www.gmc-uk.org/guidance/good_medical_practice/GMC_GMP_V41.pdf (accessed 29 November 2006).

Kaufmann, Arnold F., Meltzer, Martin I., and George P. Schmid, 1997. The economic impact of a bioterrorist attack: are prevention and postattack intervention programs justifiable? *Emerg Infect Dis* 3, 83-94.

Miller, James G., 1995. *Living Systems.* Niwot; Colorado: University Press of Colorado.

Norges diabetesforbund, 2000. Noen fakta om diabetes – Program og handlingsplan 2001-2003. Oslo.

Olender, Lynda M.A.R.N., 2005. Hospitalists: A Chief Nursing Officer's Perspective. *Journal of Nursing Administration* 35, 497-501.

Snow, John, 1965. On the mode of communication of cholera. *Snow on Cholera* (Reprint). 2 ed. New York, New York: Hafner Publishing Co.

Sokolowski, Rachel, and Joachim Dudeck, 1999. XML and its impact on content and structure in electronic health care documents. *AMIA Symposium.* Washington DC.

Teichman, Peter G., 2000. Documentation tips for reducing malpractice risk. *Family practice management* 7, 29-33.

Wild, Sarah, Roglic, Gojka, Green, Anders, Sicree, Richard, and Hilary King, 2004. Global Prevalence of Diabetes – Estimates for the year 2000 and projections for 2030. *Diabetes Care* 27, 1047-1053.

Årsand, Eirik, and Gunnar Hartvigsen, 2005. A Wearable eHealth System for People with Type 2 Diabetes. In *Scandinavian Conference on Health Informatics SHI 2005,* eds. O. Hejlesen and C. Nøhr. Aalborg, Denmark: Virtual Centre for Health Informatics, Aalborg University.

Årsand, Eirik, Walseth, Ole Anders, Andersson, Niklas, Fernando, R., Granberg, Ove, Bellika, Johan Gustav, and Gunnar Hartvigsen, 2005. Using blood glucose data as an indicator for epidemic disease outbreaks. *Stud Health Technol Inform* 116, 217-22.

Årsand, Eirik, Walseth, Ole Anders, and Eva Skipenes, 2004. Blood glucose data into Electronic Health Care Records for diabetes management. In *HelsIT 2004*, ed. Ø. Nytrø. Trondheim, Norway: Norwegian Research Centre for Electronic Patient Records (NSEP).

Helena Francke

Negotiating Cognitive Authority: The Case of Scholarly Electronic Journals

The system of scholarly publishing provides a way to make public the results of research as well as theories explaining these results.[1] This serves two important functions in the scholarly community: the research results are spread to those who have an interest in or may be affected by the research; and the publication by a respected body functions as a guarantee that the results have some merit, that they are reliable (cf. Garvey 1979, 69). Furthermore, publication is an important path for scholars to qualify themselves for career moves. Over the past thirty years, the Internet has emerged as a medium that is regarded by many as revolutionising the possibilities for quick dissemination of recorded scholarly work to researchers all over the globe. But this development, with its rapid publishing and dissemination, has also led to the voicing of numerous concerns about the credibility of electronic journals and of electronic documents in general. Whereas the advantages of improved access are generally recognised, many within the academic world remain hesitant to trust electronic journals – hesitant, to use Patrick Wilson's term, in their readiness to accept them as cognitive authorities. To provide parallel publishing in print and electronic form is a way to meet this concern for credibility while also providing for ease of access. At the same time, numerous scholarly journals that only exist in electronic form ("e-only") have started up in recent years, some of them based on so-called Open Access models. Do the e-only journals face a prosperous future or are they only a passing phase? Can new media transform scholarly practices?[2] At the core of the future success of e-only journals lies their ability to convince people to regard them as authoritative institutions.[3] How we design material documents and how we make use of media-specific properties are likely to be influential factors in this endeavour (cf. Wathen and Burkell 2002). In the present article, I have focused on how these factors are

1 I will use "scholarly" to refer to academic, commercial, and independent research work from all disciplines, including science and technology.

2 This last question paraphrases the opening question in Simon Buckingham Shum and Tamara Sumner's 2001 article introducing their thoughts on developing the scholarly e-only journal *JIME* (*Journal of Interactive Media in Education*).

3 For an early example where this conclusion was drawn, see Turoff and Hiltz (1982); also Schauder (1994, 76-77).

used in e-only scholarly journals to negotiate cognitive authority. I will begin by discussing the benefits of extending Wilson's theory of cognitive authority to take document properties into account more specifically, before looking more closely at what such an understanding of cognitive authority might have to offer in an analysis of two journals: *assemblage* and *JIME*. Two strategies for becoming regarded as a cognitive authority for two different communities of practice will emerge.

Patrick Wilson describes a cognitive authority as having "influence on one's thoughts that one would consciously recognize as proper" (Wilson 1983, 15). The fact that scholars believe and trust cognitive authorities means that we are likely to act in ways which indicate that we accept their judgement, for instance by quoting a scholar's statements with appreciation or by allowing these statements to form a basis on which we design a research project.[4] In everyday life as well as in professional life, people find cognitive authorities, agents whose judgement and knowledge they trust, among people close to them as well as among strangers and institutions they regard as reliable and competent. One such type of institution within the research world is the scholarly journal (Wilson 1983, 168). To publish in respected journals is likely to increase the possibility that an article is read and is one way for scholars to achieve reputation among their peers. Wilson proposes that scholars seek reputation "not (or not exclusively) [...] for its own sake but for the recognition of cognitive authority that will be based on it" (1983, 43).[5] In order for their work to be recognised, their ideas to be spread, and their careers to be successful, it is of importance to scholars, particularly those who have not yet acquired reputation, to seek ways in which they can become cognitive authorities to a large number of people. One way of achieving this is to publish in journals which are in themselves viewed as cognitive authorities.

Wilson points out that a cognitive authority is always an authority to somebody else; she cannot appoint herself to be a cognitive authority (Wilson 1983, 13). However, there are methods that somebody or something (for instance a scholarly journal) can employ in order to market itself so that it will influence a person or group of people in their decision about its credibility. These methods may not always be consciously employed, or may be so institutionalised that they are barely reflected upon. In order for newly established journals to attract new and

---

4 Wilson moves between treating cognitive authority as something one is thought to be (the subjective complement of a sentence) or as a quality one is thought to have (the object). It has been difficult to avoid introducing the same ambivalence into this article.

5 Wilson acknowledges that there is no direct relation between reputation and cognitive authority, but the two are often linked to each other for reasons of convenience: "Reputation is not proof of wisdom, knowledge, or competence, but we take it as a reasonable basis for preferring to listen to one person rather than another" (1983, 23).

upcoming authors as well as authors who already have a reputation, they need to market themselves to readers and potential authors as cognitive authorities. In doing so they may try to draw on acknowledged cognitive authorities within the field by means of tying people who are themselves regarded as cognitive authorities to the journal in the positions of editors, editorial board members, or peer reviewers. The journal can also build on the trustworthiness of established organisations such as reputable publishers, learned or professional societies, or well-known indexing/bibliographical services. After a few years, the journal can make use of different types of quantitative measures which indicate that many people consider the journal's articles useful, such as journal impact factors, rejection rates, and visitor or downloading statistics. To a large extent this is a circular process. Journals draw on the cognitive authority of individual scholars in order to gain a good reputation in the scholarly community. In time, they may themselves come to be regarded as cognitive authorities. To publish in these journals will then give credibility and respect to new scholars, who in turn support other or these same journals by publishing in them, being members of their editorial boards or doing peer review assignments for them. It will not be possible for a journal to only rest on previous merits; rather, it will need to keep seeking out the cognitive authorities among future generations of scholars.

Wilson (1983, 166ff.) mentions three aspects that influence people's evaluation of texts (rather than people) as cognitive authorities. One aspect of importance for journal articles was mentioned above, namely the cognitive authority that we attribute to the people involved in creating a text or of people who recommend it to us. Another aspect is that of the text's publication history, including the institutional authority of the publishing house and whether the text has been used in different situations where its credibility has been taken into account, such as for instance an appreciative reference by another scholar, or awards or good reviews that a journal or individual article has received. Wilson's third aspect is the intrinsic plausibility that we find in the text, based on our own values and prior understanding of what the text is about. In connection to this, I will suggest an addition to Wilson's three aspects of criteria that we use in order to determine the cognitive authority of, in particular, texts. This fourth aspect has to do with the design and media-specific properties of material documents. These document properties, by which I mean the elements of the material form of the document, such as layout and the use of media characteristics and technology, correlate to our expectations and frames of reference, much in the same way as the text's intrinsic plausibility.[6]

---

6 That document properties are used by scholars when evaluating a website's cognitive authority is supported by the findings in Rieh (2002).

A document study of scholarly electronic journals

In the present article, documents are viewed as material artifacts through which we access texts. The design and medium of the document will influence not only the ways in which we may gain access to its text – if we can browse through it or find particular occurrences of terms through indexes or search facilities – but also to some degree how we interpret the text. Part of the text's meaning is intimately interwoven with the physical form of its inscription, such as the italicisation of a word or the positioning of an illustration on a book page. N. Katherine Hayles has emphasised that "*the physical form of the literary artifact always affects what the words (and other semiotic components) mean*" (2002, 25; italics in the original; cf. also Kress 1998, 67). I would argue that this is the case in all document types, even though usually attention is not drawn to it in such a conscious manner as it is in some artistic works. Although it is easy to assume that a "serious" document type such as the scholarly journal, unlike, for instance, an advertising brochure, is only about "content", this would indicate that it is possible to separate "content" from presentation, and thus access "pure information".[7] Rather, the document properties of scholarly publications determine how and when we can access them, how we can use and reuse them, and, indeed, how we understand them and what trust we place in them. We often only need a single glance to distinguish a print newspaper from a weekly, and both from a scholarly journal, without even browsing the titles or headlines. We do this based on such material factors as paper quality, size and thickness, and page layout, on the assumption that the products will follow the patterns that experience has taught us to pick up on. Many will notice that a similar familiarity with web genres and web-based document types has developed in the most recent years, after a certain initial uncertainty both among website designers and website readers as to what the conventions would turn out to be.

In designing websites for scholarly journals the question of what these conventions are and how they should be treated in the new medium naturally arise. Particularly interesting in this context are the journals that do not have a print counterpart or predecessor but are "born digital", the "e-only" journals.[8] The electronic medium of the web provides us with many opportunities. On the one hand, it can be used to mirror the print medium and to serve mainly as a distribution channel for documents that are intended to be printed out and read on paper. On the other hand, it provides opportunities for interaction, for multilinear read-

---

7 Cf. Bernd Frohmann's extended argument against this view in *Deflating Information* (2004).

8 In this article, "e-only" is mainly used to refer to journals which are born digital. In other circumstances, there are journals that started out as print journals or were published in parallel both as print and electronic, but which now only exist as electronic journals, and thus are e-only.

ing patterns, and for audio and video presentations that show similarities to for instance print, radio, and TV (Bolter and Grusin 2000, 44ff.; cf. also Meadows 1998, 202f.). My intention here is not to comment on those patterns that have emerged as accepted among e-only scholarly journals, or for that matter among scholarly journals in general on the web. Rather, I have taken a closer look at two specific examples of e-only scholarly journals in order to suggest which expressions such remediations (Bolter and Grusin 2000) of a document type can take and, in particular, how the document properties of the journals play a part in negotiating cognitive authority.

My investigation has taken the form of a "close reading" of the websites of the two journals. I have made a careful qualitative study of the documents' properties, with a focus on the choice and use of file formats and modes of representation,[9] page design, the existence of metadata, and the provision of methods for interaction.[10] The two journals differ in several respects, for instance with regard to their mission and audience, but they also show similarities. They both started up in 1996, which must be regarded as fairly early, and have from the beginning posted their articles on the web free of charge. They have limited institutional support, mainly from British university departments, and one of the journals has received research support for technological development (Buckingham Shum and Sumner 2001), but otherwise they rely on voluntary work. The journal *assemblage*[11] is published by graduate students in archaeology at Sheffield University. Archaeology is a discipline which has been suggested as particularly benefiting from electronic publishing, because there are possibilities of making data sets, large colour photographs, and excavation reports easily available and/or searchable in an electronic medium (Judith Winters in Campbell 2004, 148). *JIME*, the *Journal of Interactive Media in Education*,[12] is a multidisciplinary journal fo-

---

9 The term "medium" is a difficult one, used in many different contexts. I find it valuable to make a distinction between the modes by which a text (broadly speaking) is stored and presented, what Anna Gunder has termed "storage media" and "presentation media" (2001, 98ff.), and the semiotic forms of representation that Lev Manovich tentatively calls "media types" (2001, 19), but which I would prefer to term "modes of representation" in order to avoid confusion with "medium" (cf. Kress (1998) who speaks of modes of representation in this way, but seems to use medium for the same phenomenon). Examples of media would then be book, TV, computer, and CD-ROM, whereas examples of modes of representation are alphanumeric text, photo, animation, and film.

10 In the study, I mainly used the web browsers Mozilla Firefox 1.5 and Internet Explorer 6.0. I also had ample help from the Chrispederick.com Web Developer Extension for Firefox.

11 The *assemblage* website is available at http://www.assemblage.group.shef.ac.uk. My visits to the website took place in December 2005 and January 2006 and covered the first eight issues. Issue 9 was published in June 2006.

12 The *JIME* website is available at http://www-jime.open.ac.uk/. My visits to the website took place in July 2006 and covered the issues up to and including a preprint of the first article in 2006.

cusing on education and with a profile that stresses the innovative use of (interactive) new media. Articles are published as they are accepted, not gathered into issues, although in later years there have been quite a few special issues.[13] The audience of *JIME*, which the founding editors describe as "educational multimedia researchers" (Buckingham Shum and Sumner 2001), are generally computer literate and appreciative of the use that can be made of the medium to display examples of the toolkits and websites that are described in the articles.

In the following, I will report on the most striking ways in which document properties in the two journals work to create an effect which is likely to increase the possibility that researchers in each field will view them as cognitive authorities. The methods used by the journals draw on the cognitive authority of *persons*, on the cognitive authority of *institutions*, and invoke different forms of *remediation*. Examples of the first method are the use of a peer review system and references to awards and recognitions that have been given to the journal. What is the focus here is not the cognitive authority of the person as such, but rather how the medium is used and reconstructed to point to a person's cognitive authority. The cognitive authority of institutions influences the choice of standards, file formats, and web addresses used in the journals. Remediation is invoked in how the conventions and potentials of the print and electronic media are negotiated in a transition between the media, for instance regarding layout and the use of different modes of representation and of interactive features. It is important to note, however, that the methods are not clear-cut; the use of an open peer review system employs both the method of drawing on the cognitive authority of persons and of remediating the peer review system in the digital medium; and the correct use of standards is a reference to the cognitive authority of institutions, but the choice of file formats is also a remediation statement.

(Peer) reviewers as cognitive authorities

In most scholarly disciplines the peer review system, although a much debated phenomenon,[14] is held as a guarantor of high quality. A well-functioning peer review system is one of the factors that will convince scholars to look upon a scholarly journal as a cognitive authority. The peer review system is intended to serve

---

13 The editors of *JIME* have been diligent in reporting and reflecting on their ideas concerning the journal; for interesting background information see e.g. Buckingham Shum and Sumner (2001) and Sumner and Buckingham Shum (1998).

14 Cf. for instance Wilson, who views the peer review system as a way for academic disciplines to maintain a "professional monopoly" on their own work (1983, 51); Wennerås and Wold, who show evidence of "Nepotism and sexism in peer review" within medicine (1997); and Wager and Jefferson's review of "Shortcomings of peer review in biomedical journals" (2001).

two main purposes in the journal's work with the articles: firstly, it sets a quality threshold that the article must pass in order to be accepted for publication, ensuring that the claims in the article are credible and that the research has been rigorously conducted; secondly, the peer review comments propose improvements to the article, offering the author suggestions on how to make the article even better. The reviewer's role can thus be both that of judge and, in the most extreme cases, almost that of co-author.

For e-only journals the peer review system seems a vital practice to maintain in order to gain the trust of the scholarly community. Stevan Harnad has suggested that the web can in different ways be beneficial in facilitating a more open peer review system by publishing the review comments alongside the article itself (e.g. Harnad 1996).[15] Open peer review can be one way in which to counter critique that holds the system to be opaque and subjective. *JIME* has taken on this challenge, expressly to make "the review process visible [and] foster multidisciplinary debate" (Buckingham Shum and Sumner 2001), by making the peer review comments public and inviting anyone with suggestions to join in it. The system is incorporated into the article's architecture as a frame window next to the window with the article text. The window with the peer review comments contains, in the initial, private, stage, the reviewers' comments on the different sections of the article as well as the author's answers. These comments are then made public in the next stage, where the reviewers can continue commenting, and the public is invited to offer comments as well, either in direct response to the article or by taking part in discussions with the author and the reviewers. After this stage has been closed, the author rewrites the article with respect to the issues that have arisen in the comments, and the article is then published, still with the review comments available for public view and with the continued possibility for readers to comment.[16]

There are two further ways in which *JIME*'s attempts to make the peer review comments visible to the public contribute to increasing the potential of readers regarding the article (and the journal) as a cognitive authority. By encouraging both the appointed reviewers and other voluntary commentators to identify themselves,[17] the journal creates a situation where they may draw on the cognitive authority attributed to the commentators by the readers within the field of the arti-

15 Harnad has initiated such open peer review systems both in print in *The Behavioral and Brain Sciences (BBS)* (1978–) and in electronic form in *Psycoloquy* (1989–) (see e.g. Harnad 1992; 1996). Other examples of journals working with this type of peer review model are mentioned by Godlee (2002).

16 For a closer description of the review process, see Buckingham Shum and Sumner (2001).

17 See the "About JIME" page on the *JIME* website, /about.html (7 August 2006). For arguments in favour of this mode of conduct, see e.g. Godlee (2002).

cle. Some scholarly journals implement a system by which the reviewers of every article are identified by name, both to the author and to the readership. *JIME* takes this mode of procedure one step further by also publishing the comments of each individual reviewer. Furthermore, the journal presents each article as part of an ongoing discussion, where conflicting views and the conceptual understandings of different disciplines are allowed and even encouraged:

> JIME both legitimises and gives voice to dissenting views, alerting the reader that there may be a controversy behind the text, even though it has been accepted [...]. (Buckingham Shum and Sumner 2001)[18]

In his book on cognitive authority, Patrick Wilson spends some time considering the "knowledge industry", defined as "a group of people systematically trying to produce knowledge" (Wilson 1983, 39). Does the group of people who make up the institution of academia actually produce new knowledge, understood as generally agreed upon and closed answers to their questions, answers which the general public may put faith in? If so, Wilson concludes, the knowledge industry as a whole can be accepted as a cognitive authority. The "imaginary jury" that Wilson employs grants such institutional authority to the natural and formal sciences and, in a more restricted sense, to history (including the social sciences) and technology. Criticism, according to Wilson's jury, has no such institutional authority, although individual scholars can be viewed as cognitive authorities. Whereas Wilson is concerned with where the general public may assume cognitive authority, the members of the research community are likely to make their judgements differently, although not necessarily more discerningly. The quote above from the *JIME* editors indicates that the trust of scholars within the social and behavioural sciences may be gained by openly presenting multiple views and by highlighting rather than hiding controversy. Such a view agrees with a belief in scholarship which allows for a critical, social constructionist and plural view of truths about human behaviour, and is likely to also invite trust in the journal as a whole from this group of scholars.

At a later stage in the communication system of scholarly publishing comes another type of peer review, namely the published evaluative reviews of books or journal issues (cf. Fjordback Søndergaard et al. 2003), which, if we trust the reviewer, may be regarded as a recommendation to accept or refute the reviewed work as a cognitive authority (Wilson 1983, 168). Equivalents of appreciative reviews that occur quite frequently on the web are the awards that are presented to

---

18 Indeed, this is a practice which *JIME* also displays in other contexts. The invitation of comments on published texts or invited contributions is a guiding principle behind a couple of the special issues (2003, May 2004).

innovative or useful websites. Such awards are then often posted on the website in question as a mark of recognition and a sign to the readers that the website is worth their while. *assemblage* posts two such awards on their opening page. *JIME* publishes a short statement and the announcement of the special mention they received from an award-giving committee on a separate page, slightly hidden away on the website. Whereas not exactly the same as the praise often included in the blurb of a book or DVD in some countries, drawing attention to web awards is a way to associate the journal with something that is a common feature on websites and is likely to appeal to a specific kind of web-savvy audience.

Standards as cognitive authorities

The above example of peer review showed how *JIME* designs the journal website in order to incorporate the review comments and draw attention to its reviewers and authors, people who may serve as cognitive authorities to the readers. In a similar manner, organisations that are suitably acknowledged by the readers may provide a form of institutional authority. Regarding document properties, such institutional authorities can be found in the standards put forward by technological organisations such as the World Wide Web Consortium (W3C). That standards are followed is to a certain extent necessary, in order to allow for the construction of programs that will generate and display different digital formats properly. But when it comes to HTML, an absolute adherence to the standards is not required by most web browsers. Electronic journals make a choice as to which file formats, as well as to which versions of the formats, to use and how to follow the standards; these are choices that have consequences. For instance, the choice to publish the articles in PDF may indicate that the articles are mainly intended to be printed out and read in paper form, much as an offprint of a paper journal article. The electronic form is often viewed mainly as a distribution and storage channel.[19] To use some version of HTML is sometimes the result of a deliberate decision to apply hypertext links and other forms of distributed navigation in the articles. This is the case in both *assemblage* and *JIME*, and is most clearly developed in the latter journal. However, *JIME* does not limit the readers' options; the articles are also available in print-friendly versions in both HTML and PDF.

---

19 This is a view which may, but will not necessarily, change as we become more familiar with the electronic medium and solve some of the present difficulties. A clearly stated expression of this view from the very early years of web publishing comes from the editor of the e-journal *Surfaces*, Bill Readings (1994), who writes about the *Surface* articles: "The result looks exactly like an offprint from a learned journal, right down to the journal logo that ensures academic respectability. [...] The advantages of this procedure are manifold. Above all, the printed end-product [...] looks like a 'real' journal article." Cf. also Campbell (2004, e.g. 306); Schauder (1994, 91).

assemblage has gone through a number of different updates that are mirrored in the technique that has been used to publish it. HTML or, lately, XHTML has been used throughout as the basic technique, with additional image formats (mainly GIF and JPG) and the occasional multimedia file. In fact, the choice of HTML version in the issues seems to mirror the new developments in HTML (see Table 1).

Month-Year	**Issue – (X)HTML version used**	**(X)HTML version released**	**Month-Year**
		(HTML 2.0)	Nov 1995
Oct 1996	#1 <HTML>		
		(HTML 3.2)	Jan 1997
May 1997	#2 <HTML>		
Jan 1998	#3 <HTML>		
		HTML 4.0	April 1998
Oct 1998	#4 <HTML 4.0>		
		(HTML 4.01)	Dec 1999
		(XHTML 1.0)	Jan 2000
April 2000	#5 <HTML 4.0 Transitional>		
Aug 2001	#6 <HTML 4.0 Transitional>		
		XHTML 1.0 2nd ed.	Aug 2002
May 2003	#7 <XHTML 1.0>		
Dec 2004	#8 <XHTML 1.0>		

Table 1. Table showing how the (X)HTML versions used in *assemblage* follow the development of (X)HTML technology.[20]

The choice to switch to XHTML seems to have been delayed until the revised edition of the Specification came out in August 2002. This is also around the time when XHTML began to be more widespread on the web. In other words, it is apparent that the technical staff of *assemblage* have followed the development of (X)HTML closely. In issues 7 and 8, much of the presentation is governed by Cascading Style Sheets (CSS), a sensible consequence of the choice to use XHTML.

To a technologically aware reader, the conscious use of the latest available versions of HTML and of CSS in *assemblage* may be an indication that the journal's webmasters keep themselves informed of new developments in the HTML community. This is further emphasised by the inclusion on the "home" and "previous issues" pages and in issues 7 and 8 of an icon which states that the

20 The data on DTDs and stylesheets are based on an analysis of the "table of contents" pages and a sample research article page of each issue. The dates for when the HTML specifications were published have been taken from each individual specification, available via W3C (1995-2006).

pages have been validated against the W3C standards and found valid, which is one way of aligning the journal with the cognitive authority of W3C.

One of the concerns that is often expressed in relation to material on the web is how we can evaluate the credibility of the claims that are made. Guidelines intended to teach such evaluative skills often emphasise the importance of metadata. One source that is often pointed out as valuable when determining the publisher's authority is the URL, or web address.[21] Both *assemblage* and *JIME* have chosen to retain a URL which indicates their university affiliation (Sheffield University and the Open University respectively), rather than purchasing a web address that is based on the journal name. Both strategies could be viewed as emphasising legitimacy, either by pointing to a prestigious university's server or by establishing a trademark of its own. It is of course possible to use both strategies by allowing one address to redirect to the other.

Whose cognitive authority?

Unlike *JIME*, *assemblage* has changed a great deal over the years in regard to technology and design, as well as to the types of material that are included. The number of different types of contributions has been reduced over the years, causing the cancellation of such categories as "The *assemblage* fun page", "Words of Wisdom for Graduate Students", and the list of recommended websites. This is presumably because the editors have realised that journal publishing is time-consuming and therefore have tried to cut down on editorial material.[22] It could also be a result of new editors coming in; the turnover on editorial staff is understandably high, due both to the voluntary work it requires and to the restricted time during which people are graduate students. The result, however, is that the journal loses some of its playful student touch and takes on a look and feel that is closer to that of traditional print scholarly journals. This is further emphasised by the layout of *assemblage*, the eight issues of which display very different looks. Issue 1 is to a large degree a reflection of the time it was published in 1996. As a rather typical child of the early years of web publishing, it features different coloured backgrounds on different pages, an animated GIF accompanies the link to e-mail the editors, and the web pages make use of the full breadth of the browser window, with elements aligned left, right, and middle.[23] The first radical change of design for *assemblage* comes with issue 4 in October 1998. This issue

---

21 For instance in Barker (2005), Kirk (1996), and Smith (2005). Cf. also Rieh (2002, 155).

22 See the editorial in issue 6, available from: http://www.assemblage.group.shef.ac.uk/issue6/editorial.html (6 August 2006).

23 For an example of the design of a website from the same time, see for instance the HTML 3.2 Specification from early 1997, which has similar features (Raggett 1997).

makes good use of frames, an element introduced in the 4.0 Specification earlier that year. In subsequent issues, there is a move towards a stricter, tidier page with a naked black Arial font on white background and careful consideration of, for instance, line length and navigational features. The change seems in many ways to follow a prevailing development in web design in general and in this genre in particular, which could be seen as a consequence of the medium becoming more mature and finding its form. At the same time, this is a development which serves to make electronic scholarly journals more and more reminiscent of the typical print journal.

An e-journal's similarity to print journals was pointed out above as a factor that may be perceived as reassuring to some academics, and contributing to their readiness to consider the journal a cognitive authority. But academics looking for a print journal with easier and quicker distribution are not necessarily the only group that an e-only journal wants to reach. There is also a potential group of academics regarding the web as a medium with new and interesting potential, and who are quite open not only to increased distribution and access possibilities but also to new approaches to layout and to the inclusion of other modes of representation than alphanumeric text or still images. Since *assemblage* is primarily geared towards graduate students, the journal presumably finds the majority of its audience as well as its authors among younger scholars. Although this is not a guarantee that the audience is computer literate, it could be a contributing reason why the journal ventured in the early issues to attempt to create a sense of 'state-of-the art website'. By displaying good knowledge of how to handle the web medium and of the current web design trends, the journal can gain respect and trust from an audience which values and regularly makes use of web-based documents (cf. Wathen and Burkell 2002).

Both journals have also consciously attempted to include different modes of representation, *assemblage* through the section "State of the 'Arch'" in issues 3-5[24] and *JIME* by regularly encouraging its authors to contribute multimedia and/or interactive examples of the programs or toolkits presented in the articles. *JIME* also attempt to highlight such examples, both by pointing to them in connection with the article's abstract and by displaying a small icon in the table of contents next to the section in which the example is placed or described.[25] Indeed, one of the aims of the journal is stated as: "Through its innovative use of interactive Net-based media, to be an action research project which explores the changing face of journals, and more broadly, scholarly practice in the age of digital publishing and

---

24 For a short statement on the thoughts behind this section, see the introduction to it in issue 3, available from: http://www.assemblage.group.shef.ac.uk/3/3state.htm (7 August 2006).

25 See Buckingham Shum and Sumner (2001) and the "Quick user guide to JIME" page on the *JIME* website, /jime-help.html (7 August 2006).

communication."[26] *JIME* contains examples of interactive Shockwave flash and Java applets, as well as image, audio, and movie files. These take the form of excerpts of the projects presented in the articles as well as illustrations of experiments or of the underlying principle of an application. With an audience of educators and researchers who have an interest in interactive new media, such conscious inclusion of product examples is likely to correlate to the audiences' expectations and frames of reference in a way which makes them appreciate the services of the journal. Furthermore, the readers can "see for themselves" the products that are discussed in the articles, so that they can validate them directly. This will also provide a possibility for them to evaluate the trust they put in the journal's ability to select and include valuable articles.

A question of remediation

The two journals included in this study illustrate, in different ways, that at least two distinct strategies involving the journal's design and media-specific properties can be engaged in order to increase the journal's possibilities of being viewed as a cognitive authority by its audience: (1) the journal is made to resemble the print journal as much as possible; or (2) advantage is taken of the possibilities provided by the electronic medium through an emphasis on the use of multiple modes of representation as well as interactive functions. To discuss these two strategies in terms of remediation, a concept introduced by Jay David Bolter and Richard Grusin (2000), can help capture the nature of the relation between the e-only and the print scholarly journal.

Bolter and Grusin introduce the concept of remediation as a means by which to explain what they see as a competition for status among different media, where at the moment "Older electronic and print media are seeking to reaffirm their status within our culture as digital media challenge that status" (2000, 5). Depending on how the competition between different media is perceived, remediation will take different expressions. According to Bolter and Grusin, these expressions place themselves on "a spectrum of different ways in which digital media remediate their predecessors" (2000, 45). At one end of this spectrum we could place the first strategy where the reader is reassured that there is no difference between a journal in print and one that is online; it is merely a matter of difference in distribution method. In this way, the print medium is given prominence at the expense of the electronic medium, with an attempt to make the latter invisible. For instance, such respectful remediation takes the form of designing the e-only journal

26 Quote from the "About JIME" page on the *JIME* website, /about.html (7 August 2006).

so that the articles resemble those in a print journal, and in particular by providing PDF files intended to be printed and read on paper.

Moving further along the spectrum, a more radical strategy is chosen when the creator or user of a medium claims status for that medium on the grounds that it provides not only added value compared to other media, but in the best of cases offers a completely new and different experience. This is what happens when the editors of an e-only scholarly journal draw attention to the journal's use of modes of representation that are difficult or impossible to include in print, such as high-resolution and large size colour images, audio and video elements, or interactive media created with Java applets or Shockwave flash applications. A feature that is becoming increasingly taken for granted, but which is nevertheless revolutionary, is the provision of direct hyperlinks from references in the text to other documents on the web, something that (most of the time) facilitates and speeds up the process of following up on the article author's sources of inspiration.

Another example that points to added functionality in the new medium is the transparency and rapid interaction of a public peer review system. In the electronic medium the system can invoke a sense of direct communication between a large number of people, in a way which exceeds what a print journal publishing reviewers' comments alongside the article or "Letters to the editor" can achieve. In the design of *JIME*'s commenting system, there is also a clear emphasis on making the medium visible in the form of the different windows that appear on the computer screen and between which the reader navigates. This is one way in which the hypermediacy of the electronic medium is given prominence.

JIME demonstrates that an e-only journal can take different positions on the remediation spectrum in order to strengthen the journal's credibility and create an impression of professionalism. This is the case when *JIME* provides four different interfaces to their articles: two which make extensive use of frame and browser windows for advanced hyperlink navigation specifically adapted to be read on a screen, and two (in HTML and PDF) which are intended for printing. *assemblage*, on the other hand, seems to move from its earlier, more radical position that emphasises the differences between the media, to a form characterised by an attempt to make the electronic medium resemble print. However, the more recent issues of *assemblage* retain some of the features that particularly characterise the web medium, such as hyperlink navigation and a full-text search engine.

This article has identified two strategies for making use of the material document's design and media-specific properties in order to negotiate cognitive authority in e-only scholarly journals. The strategies employ different forms of remediation and are likely to be geared towards different user communities with the intention of gaining their trust. It is possible that both strategies can be employed simultaneously and thus appeal to both user communities, but this could also risk alienating users from both groups. The ambition in the article has been to illustrate that Patrick Wilson's theory of cognitive authority is useful in discussing the trust we place in electronic documents and to further develop the theory by introducing a fourth aspect that users take into account when determining whether or not to regard a text as a cognitive authority, namely its material properties. An objective has also been to show how empirical document studies can serve to highlight the role of document properties in the developing understanding of the social role that documents play in scholarly work. The influence of intellectual traditions on the system of scholarly communication has received a lot of attention lately. It is about time that we also recognise how this influence interacts with the materiality of the documents that play such a significant role in academic society.

References

Barker, Joe, 2005. *Evaluating web pages: Techniques to apply & questions to ask.* Berkeley, California: UC Berkeley Library. Online: http://www.lib.berkeley.edu/TeachingLib/Guides/Internet/Evaluate.html (accessed 6 August 2006).

Bolter, Jay David, and Richard Grusin, 2000. *Remediation: Understanding new media.* Paperback ed. Cambridge, Massachusetts: MIT Press.

Buckingham Shum, Simon, and Tamara Sumner, 2001. JIME: An interactive journal for interactive media. *First Monday* 6(2). Online: http://firstmonday.org/issues/issue6_2/Buckingham_shum/index.html (accessed 19 July 2006).

Campbell, Glen, 2004. *E-journal publishing in academic environments: A study of e-journal publishing projects and operations in academic departments and research libraries.* Ph.D. thesis, University of Strathclyde, Department of Computer and Information Sciences.

Fjordback Søndergaard, Trine, Andersen, Jack, and Birger Hjørland, 2003. Documents and the communication of scientific and scholarly information: revising and updating the UNISIST model. *Journal of Documentation* 59(3), 278-320.

Frohmann, Bernd, 2004. *Deflating information: From science studies to documentation.* Toronto; Buffalo; London: University of Toronto Press.

Garvey, William D., 1979. *Communication: The essence of science.* Oxford: Pergamon.

Godlee, Fiona, 2002. Making reviewers visible: Openness, accountability, and credit. *Journal of the American Medical Association* 287(21), 2762-2765.

Gunder, Anna, 2001. Forming the text, performing the work: Aspects of media, navigation, and linking. *Human IT* 5(2-3), 81-206. Online: http://www.hb.se/bhs/ith/23-01/ag.htm (accessed 3 August 2006).

Harnad, Stevan, 1992. Interactive publication: Extending the American Physical Society's discipline-specific model for electronic publishing. *Serials Review* 18(1/2), 58-61.

------. 1996. Implementing peer review on the Net: Scientific quality control in scholarly electronic journals. In *Scholarly publishing: The electronic frontier*, eds. G. B. Newby and R. P. Peek. Cambridge, Massachusetts: MIT Press, 103-118.

Hayles, N. Katherine, 2002. *Writing machines*. Cambridge, Massachusetts: MIT Press.

Kirk, Elizabeth E., 1996. *Evaluating information found on the Internet*. Baltimore, Maryland: Sheridan Libraries, Johns Hopkins University. Online: http://www.library.jhu.edu/researchhelp/general/evaluating/ (accessed 6 August 2006).

Kress, Gunther, 1998. Visual and verbal modes of representation in electronically mediated communication: The potentials of new forms of text. In *Page to screen: Taking literacy into the electronic era*, ed. I. Snyder. London; New York: Routledge, 53-79.

Manovich, Lev, 2001. *The language of new media*. Cambridge, Massachusetts: MIT Press.

Meadows, Arthur Jack, 1998. *Communicating research*. San Diego, California: Academic Press.

Raggett, Dave, 1997. *HTML 3.2 reference specification: W3C recommendation 14-Jan-1997*. W3C (World Wide Web Consortium). Online: http://www.w3.org-/TR/REC-html32 (accessed 2 August 2006).

Readings, Bill, 1994. Caught in the Net: Notes from the electronic underground. *Surfaces* 4. Online: http://www.pum.umontreal.ca/revues/surfaces/vol4/readings.html (accessed 5 August 2006).

Rieh, Soo Young, 2002. Judgment of information quality and cognitive authority in the web. *Journal of the American Society for Information Science and Technology* 53(2), 145-161.

Schauder, Don, 1994. Electronic publishing of professional articles: Attitudes of academics and implications for the scholarly communication industry. *Journal of the American Society for Information Science* 45(2), 73-100.

Smith, Alastair, 2005. *Criteria for evaluation of Internet information resources.* Online: http://www.vuw.ac.nz/staff/alastair_smith/evaln/index.htm (accessed 6 August 2006).

Sumner, Tamara, and Simon Buckingham Shum, 1998. From document to discourse: Shifting conceptions of scholarly publishing. *Proceedings of the SIGCHI Conference on Human Factors in Computing Systems, 18-23 April 1998, Los Angeles, CA*. New York: ACM Press, 95-102. Online: http://doi.acm.org/10.1145/274644.274659 (accessed 1 August 2006).

Turoff, Murray, and Starr Roxanne Hiltz, 1982. The electronic journal: A progress report. *Journal of the American Society for Information Science* 33(4), 195-202.

W3C (World Wide Web Consortium), 1995-2006. *W3C HTML home page*. Online: http://www.w3.org/MarkUp/ (accessed 5 August 2006).

Wager, Elizabeth, and Tom Jefferson, 2001. Shortcomings of peer review in biomedical journals. *Learned Publishing* 14(4), 257-263.

Wathen, C. Nadine, and Jacquelyn Burkell, 2002. Believe it or not: Factors influencing credibility on the web. *Journal of the American Society for Information Science and Technology* 53(2), 134-144.

Wennerås, Christine, and Agnes Wold, 1997. Nepotism and sexism in peer review. *Nature* 387(6631, 22 May 1997), 341-343.

Wilson, Patrick, 1983. *Second-hand knowledge: An inquiry into cognitive authority*. Westport, Connecticut; London: Greenwood Press.

Roswitha Skare

Text und Paratext und deren Remedierung im Film: Jens Sparschuhs Heimatroman *Der Zimmerspringbrunnen* (1995)

Der 1955 in Karl-Marx-Stadt, dem heutigen Chemnitz, geborene Jens Sparschuh war vor 1989/90 nur wenigen Eingeweihten in Ost und West bekannt. Weder systemfreundlich noch dissident schrieb Sparschuh vor allem Hörspiele, Kinderbücher, gab die Aphorismen Friedrich Hebbels heraus und veröffentlichte 1987 im relativ liberalen Buchverlag *Der Morgen* seinen ersten Roman. 1996 erhielt Sparschuh den Förderpreis der Stadt Bremen für seinen 1995 erschienen Heimatroman *Der Zimmerspringbrunnen.* In der Kurzbegründung der Jury für die Preisverleihung heißt es: "Jens Sparschuh widersetzt sich dem fortwirkenden Ernstfall der Teilung mit menschenfreundlichem Humor und einer humoristischen Liebe für die Absurditäten des Lebens" (Rudolf-Alexander-Schröder-Stiftung 1996, 7).

Der Zimmerspringbrunnen wurde von der Kritik fast ausnahmslos als Satire auf die deutsche Einheit positiv aufgenommen,[1] und wurde mit rund 90.000 verkauften Exemplaren[2] schon bald zum Bestseller. Bereits im September 1996 wurde die Bühnenfassung von Oliver Reese auf der Studiebühne des Berliner Maxim Gorki Theaters uraufgeführt;[3] 2001 kam der gleichnamige Film Peter Timms in die deutschen Kinos, der jedoch mit nur ca 42.000 Besuchern kaum die Erwartungen seiner Produzenten erfüllt haben dürfte.[4]

---

1 Vgl. bspw. das Hamburger Abendblatt vom 2. Januar 1996: "Der erste Roman, der dem Thema Wiedervereinigung komische Seiten abgewinnt."

2 Die Auflage der gebundenen Ausgabe bei Kiepenheuer & Witsch lag bereits bei beachtlichen 28.000; die Taschenbuchausgabe der Verlagsgruppe Bertelsmann erschien im Juli 1997 und hatte im August 2000 60.000 Exemplare verkauft.

3 Am 11. Dezember 1998 hatte das Stück an den Städtischen Bühnen Münster Premiere, am Maxim Gorki Theater wurde am 22. Juni 2006 die 242. und letzte Vorstellung gespielt.

4 Sparschuhs *Zimmerspringbrunnen* wurde von der Kritik häufig in die Nähe von Thomas Brussigs Bestseller *Helden wie wir* (1995) gerückt, der ebenfalls verfilmt wurde und mit seinen ca 186.000 Besuchern jedoch deutlich unter den deutschsprachigen Publikumserfolgen dieser Jahre lag wie bspw. *Sonnenallee* mit 2.557.018 Besuchern und *Lola rennt* mit ebenfalls über 2.000.000 Besuchern. Sowohl die Herstellung des Films *Der Zimmerspringbrunnen* als auch die Herausgabe auf DVD wurden von der Filmförderungsanstalt ökonomisch unterstützt. Vgl. dazu www.ffa.de. Die Besucherzahlen sind den Filmhitlisten auf diesen Seiten entnommen.

Die Handlung des Romans ist einfach: Der ca. 50jährige Hinrich Lobek, seit drei Jahren abgewickelt und arbeitslos, verbringt die Tage in einer Ostberliner Neubauwohnung zusammen mit seinem Hund Freitag. Die meiste Zeit liegt Lobek völlig initiativlos auf dem Sofa, beobachtet seine Frau Julia oder zieht sich in seinen Hobbyraum zurück. Durch einen Zufall – Lobek liest sein Horoskop und findet auf der Nebenseite eine Stellenannonce – bekommt Lobek Arbeit als Vertreter: Er soll Zimmerspringbrunnen für die Firma PHANTA RHEIn im Osten der wiedervereinigten Republik verkaufen. Trotz dieses beruflichen Erfolgs wird Lobek immer schweigsamer, der berufliche Aufstieg führt zur persönlichen Niederlage. Nachdem ihm seine Frau verlassen hat, widmet sich Lobek voll und ganz seiner neuen Arbeit und stellt in der gesamten Wohnung Zimmerspringbrunnen zur Inspiration seiner Verkaufsstrategien auf. Als sein Hund Freitag einen Zimmerspringbrunnen zum Durchbrennen bringt, bastelt Lobek ein neues Modell, das mit den Umrissen der DDR und dem Berliner Fernsehturm im Osten zum Verkaufsschlager wird: aus dem westlichen Modell JONA wird das östliche Modell ATLANTIS. Am Ende des Romans, zu Weihnachten, macht sich Lobek zusammen mit Freitag auf die Suche nach Julia. So verbringt er die Feiertage zusammen mit Obdachlosen im Berliner Bahnhof Zoo, rafft sich aber am Neujahrsmorgen auf und verläßt den Bahnhof. Der offene Schluß verrät nichts über Lobeks weiteres Schicksal.

Bereits an dieser kurzen Inhaltsangabe wird deutlich, daß Sparschuhs Roman nicht den Vorstellung eines traditionellen Heimatromans entspricht, wie dies der Untertitel "Ein Heimatroman" anzudeuten scheint. Interessant ist in diesem Zusammenhang, daß diese Genreangabe lediglich in der gebundenen Ausgabe des Verlages Kiepenheuer & Witsch zu finden ist. Weder Literaturkritik noch -wissenschaft gehen näher darauf ein, daß dieser Untertitel in der Taschenbuchausgabe durch die Genrebezeichnung "Roman" erstattet wurde, da der Begriff "Heimatroman" auf dem Cover das Buch zu klein gemacht und möglicherweise den Leserkreis erheblich eingeschränkt hätte.[5] Daß dem Autor der Untertitel aber durchaus wichtig war und keineswegs zufällig gewählt wurde, wird an dem unbestimmten Artikel deutlich, der ihn von den üblichen Genrebezeichnungen unterscheidet. In einem Interview antwortet Sparschuh zudem auf die Frage, warum er sein Buch im Untertitel einen Heimatroman nenne:

> Schlicht und einfach, weil der Held seine alte Heimat verloren hat. Ihm ist der Boden unter den Füßen weggezogen worden. Er macht sich auf die Suche nach einer neuen Identität, nach einer neuen Heimat. Wir leben in einer modernen Medienwelt, die durch die Globalisierung eine gewisse Zeit- und Ortlosigkeit hat. In dieser Welt ist

---

5 So Anja Neiß von der Verlagsgruppe Bertelsmann in einer elektronischen Post vom 4. Oktober 2000.

> das Heimatgefühl aber sehr wichtig. Der Mensch ist von seinen Instinkten her immer noch ein Tier. Es braucht sein Revier, in dem es sich zu Hause fühlt. Diese zeit- und ortlose Internetwelt kann einem doch Angst machen, oder? (Interview)

Im folgenden soll der Paratext und dessen Remedierung im Film bzw. DVD im Vordergrund stehen. Gezeigt werden soll unter anderem, daß der Untertitel "Ein Heimatroman" durchaus im Zusammenhang mit der erzählten Geschichte steht und damit Bedeutung für die Rezeption des Textes hat.

In seiner Studie *Paratexts. Thresholds of interpretation* (in Französisch bereits 1987 unter dem Titel *Seuils*) zeigt Gérard Genette mit Hilfe zahlreicher Beispiele, welche Rolle Titel, Untertitel, Vorworte, Umschlagtexte, aber auch der Bekanntheitsgrad des Autors, sein Alter und Geschlecht, sowie Preise, Ehrendoktorwürden u.ä. für eine Interpretation haben. Genette teilt den Paratext in den Peritext, der – wie Schutzumschlag, Titel, Gattungsangabe, Vor- und Nachwort oder auch verschiedene Motti – relativ fest mit dem Buch verbunden ist, und in den Epitext, der Mitteilungen über das Buch enthält, die in der Regel an einem anderen Ort plaziert sind wie Interviews, Briefwechsel oder Tagebücher. Genette geht dabei auch auf nicht-textliche Elemente wie Format und Umschlaggestaltung ein:

> Most often, then, the paratext is itself a text: if it is still not *the* text, it is already *some* text. But we must at least bear in mind the paratextual value that may be vested in other types of manifestation: these may be iconic (illustrations), material (for axample, everything that originates in the sometimes very significant typographical choices that go into the making of a book), or purely factual. By *factual* I mean the paratext that consists not of an explicit message (verbal or other) but of a fact whose existence alone, if known to the public, provides some commentary on the text and influences how the text is received (Genette 1997, 7).

Obwohl sich Genette in seinen Ausführungen zum Paratext auf das Buchmedium konzentriert, soll sein Begriff hier auch auf Film- und DVD-Medium verwendet werden. Dies ist relativ unproblematisch, da der Umschlag einer DVD in Größe und Format bereits an das Buchmedium erinnert und ähnlich wie ein Buchumschlag als Schwelle funktioniert, die in den Text bzw. Film führt; der Vor- und Abspann eines Filmes können mit den ersten und letzten Sätzen oder Abschnitten eines Romans verglichen werden. Durch die Verwendung von Genettes Begriffen soll außerdem gezeigt werden, daß neben dem literarischen Text auch der Paratext von der Remedierung beeinflußt wird.

Gebundene Ausgabe und Taschenbuch

Der Zimmerspringbrunnen ist ein relativ kurzer Roman; sowohl die gebundene Ausgabe von 1995 (11,9 x 19,5) als auch die Taschenbuchausgabe von 1997 (11,8 x 18,7 cm) unterscheiden sich wenig in Format und Umfang (160 bzw. 159 Seiten). Die deutlichsten Unterschiede zwischen den beiden Ausgabe liegen offensichtlich in der Umschlaggestaltung, zumal "modern publishing tends to neutralize these choices [typesetting and choice of paper, R.S.] by a perhaps irreversible tendency toward standardization" (Genette 1997, 34).

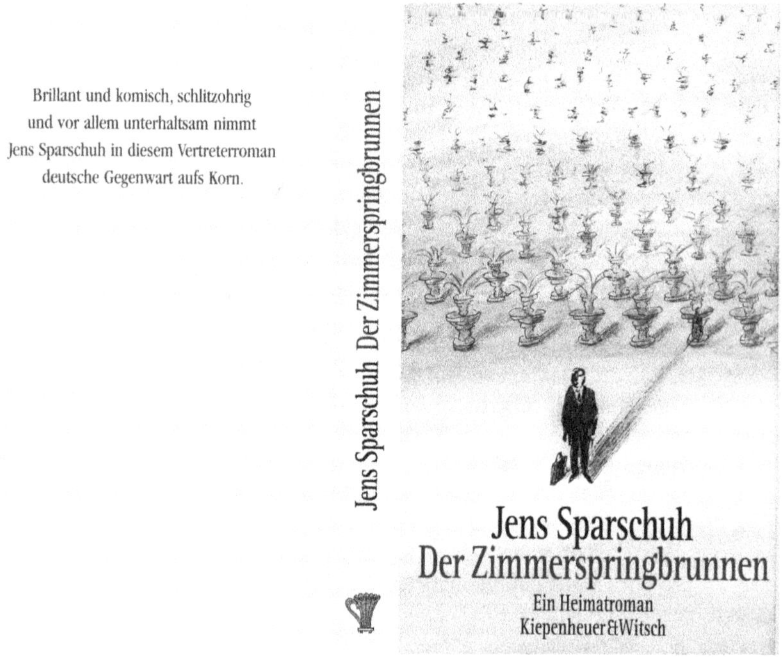

Der Schutzumschlag[6] der gebundenen Ausgabe ist hauptsächlich in blauen Nuancen gestaltet, wobei die Blaufarbe auch im Titel, im kurzen Text auf der Rückseite des Umschlages und nicht zuletzt im Leineneinband wiederkehrt. Die Aufmerksamkeit des Betrachters fällt zuerst auf die männliche Person in Anzug und Schlips, bevor sie durch dessen Schatten in den oberen Teil der Seite und mehrere Reihen von Springbrunnen gezogen wird. Die graphischen Elemente stehen dadurch im Verhältnis zum Titel und geben einen ersten Eindruck, die durchaus die Rezeption des Textes steuern können:

6 Der Schutzumschlag ist mit freundlicher Genehmigung des Verlags Kiepenheuer & Witsch abgebildet.

> The most obvious function of the jacket is to attract attention, using means even more dramatic than those a cover can or should be permitted: a garish illustration, a reminder of a film or television adaption, or simply a graphic presentation more flattering or more personalized than the cover standards of a series allow (Genette 1997, 28).

Der Name des Autors und der Titel des Buches haben die gleiche Größe, wobei der Titel durch die Wahl einer anderen Farbe hervorgehoben wird. Die Größe des Untertitels und des Verlagsnamens ist deutlich kleiner, jedoch ohne Probleme für den Betrachter zu erkennen. Die Aussage auf der Rückseite des Umschlages – ohne Quellenangabe – mag vom Verlag stammen und gibt einem potenziellen Käufer bzw. Leser weitere Hinweise zum Inhalt und Genre des Buches: "Brillant und komisch, schlitzohrig und vor allem unterhaltsam nimmt Jens Sparschuh in diesem Vertreterroman deutsche Gegenwart aufs Korn." Eine ähnliche Charakteristik findet sich im Klappentext, auch hier wird nach einer kurzen Inhaltsangabe mit den komischen Seiten des Textes geworben:

> Mit diesem burlesken Vertreterroman ist Jens Sparschuh das Kunststück gelungen, alle komischen und tragischen Aspekte der Ost-West-Spaltung aufzugreifen und ohne Larmoyanz durchzuspielen. Ein rasanter Gegenwartsroman und zugleich eine gekonnte Satire über den Erfolg.

Da Sparschuh 1995 für viele Leser noch relativ unbekannt war, kann man davon ausgehen, daß in diesem Fall weniger der Name des Autors als diese Beschreibung den Käufer bzw. Leser anzuziehen vermochten. Der Untertitel "Ein Heimatroman" setzt jedoch den Roman in eine Traditionslinie, die nicht unbedingt mit Komik, Ironie und Satire in Verbindung gebracht werden kann.

Der dominierende Raum im Heimatroman – ich stütze mich hier und im folgenden auf Karlheinz Rossbachers Typologie – ist das Dorf bzw. der Einzelhof in ländlich-agrarischen Gegenden, das Sozialmodell Dorf wird deutlich vom Sozialmodell Stadt unterschieden; es beherbergt andere Menschen als das der Stadt. Das Dorf wird traditionell als "Hort der Sicherheit" dargestellt; die Stadt als Ursprung des Feindlichen und Fremden ihm gegenübgergestellt. Der geographische Ort in Sparschuhs Roman ist die Großstadt Berlin. Allerdings ist Berlin bei Sparschuh lediglich in Form von kleinen, begrenzten Räumen, nämlich Wohnungen anwesend. Die Neubauwohnung Lobeks ist ein enger, abgeschlossener Raum, in dem alle Konflikte vor sich gehen. Die Wohnung liegt scheinbar im Nichts, weder andere Häuser noch Nachbarn existieren für Lobek. Während in Lobeks alter Wohnung am Rande des Prenzlauer Berges die Bewohner des Hauses durch ihre Geräusche anwesend waren, scheint Lobek hier völlig allein zu sein. So wird Lobeks Wohnung wie das Dorf im Heimatroman zum Zufluchtsort und topographischen Modell. Die Wohnung kann mit Rossbacher als "die große Welt in nuce" (Rossbacher 1975, 139) oder auch "Totalmodell in Abgeschlossenheit" mit einem "Charakter als Festung" (140) verstanden werden.

Der traditionelle Heimatroman ist Rossbacher zufolge ein Roman statischer Verhältnisse, weist aber trotzdem einen Reichtum an Handlung auf, um der realen Welt und den langen Zeitspannen gerecht zu werden. Im *Zimmerspringbrunnen* beschränken sich alle Handlungen Lobeks zunächst auf den Haushalt, wenn er nicht tatenlos auf dem Sofa liegt. Auch die Tatsache, daß er wieder eine Arbeit bekommt, verändert wenig an Lobek und an dessen Verhalten seiner Frau Julia gegenüber. Noch gegen Ende des Romans, als Julia ihn schon längere Zeit verlassen hatte, kann er sich nicht entschließen, ihr gegenüber aktiv zu werden.

Der mächtigste Motor von Handlung im traditionellen Heimatroman ist die Natur und daraus entstehende Schicksalsschläge, aber auch der Einbruch von Städtischem, von Kommerz oder einer Outgroup können für Aufregung und Handlung sorgen. Im *Zimmerspringbrunnen* löst Lobeks Abwicklung einen Schicksalsschlag aus, der zunächst einige Aktivität bei Lobek erzeugt. Nach mehreren erfolglosen Telefonbewerbungen gibt er jedoch auf und widmet sich dem Nichtstun. Veränderung und damit Bewegung in das Leben Lobeks bringt eine höhere Macht, das Wochenhoroskop und eine Annonce der Firma mit dem sprechenden Namen PANTA RHEIn, der den zweieinhalbtausend Jahre alten Satz des Heraklit mit dem Regionalgedanken verbindet. Eine Firma für Zimmerspringbrunnen in die Nähe philosophischer Überlegungen zu rücken, unterstreicht die Lächerlichkeit von Lobeks neuem Beruf, kann aber auch als Hintergrund für die Romanhandlung insgesamt verstanden werden: Alles fließt; alles ist einem konstanten Wandel unterzogen; nichts bleibt wie es war.

Im Gegensatz zum traditionellen Heimatroman begegnet uns mit Hinrich Lobek kein auktorialer Erzähler mit Überblick, sondern im Gegenteil ein Ich-Erzähler mit sehr begrenztem Blick, der die letzten drei Jahre in seiner Neubauwohnung in Ostberlin verbracht hat. Lobek hat scheinbar keinerlei Familie oder Bekannte und Freunde, jeder soziale Umgang fehlt, nachdem ihn seine Frau Julia verlassen hat. Obwohl Lobek sich an fühere DDR-Zeiten erinnert, z.B. die alte Wohnung, die Zeit seines Fernstudiums oder seine Tätigkeit für die KWV, die als Rückblenden eingeschoben werden, sind die Zeitverhältnisse im Erzählverlauf begrenzt und gehen keinesfalls zu einem Ur-Anfang zurück oder versuchen die Lebenstotalität Lobeks darzustellen. Die erzählte Zeit des Romans erstreckt sich vom Frühjahr/Sommer bis zu Silvester und Neujahrsmorgen, umfaßt also weniger als ein Jahr im Leben Lobeks und kann durchaus im Zusammenhang mit dem Gang der Natur gesehen werden. Lobeks Tiefpunkt ist zu Jahresende erreicht, am Neujahrsmorgen – ein ganzes Jahr mit neuen Möglichkeiten, liegt vor ihm – verläßt er das Pennermilieu.

Während die Gestaltung des Schutzumschlages der gebundenen Ausgabe sowohl in der Farb- als auch in der Motivwahl in Verbindung mit dem Inhalt des Romans steht, ist dieser Zusammenhang für die Taschenbuchausgabe[7] weniger deutlich:

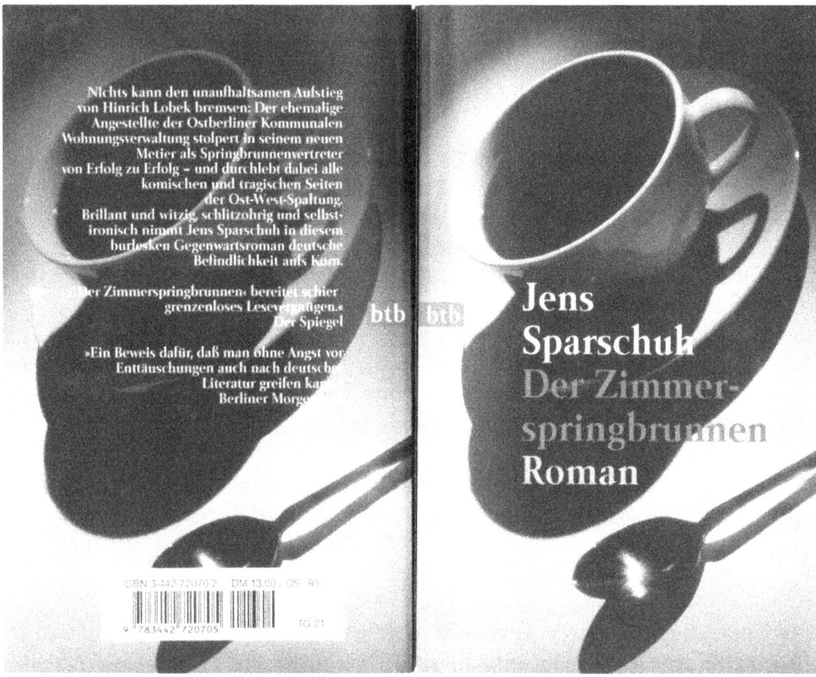

Die grüne Farbe des Umschlages scheint im Kontrast zum roten Titel und Logo des Verlages gewählt zu sein; Kaffeetasse und Löffel sind eher nichtssagend. Name des Autors, Romantitel und Untertitel sind gleich groß; der Titel wird jedoch durch seine Farbe hervorgehoben. Auf der Rückseite des Umschlages findet sich eine kurze Inhaltsangabe mit Begriffen wie "brillant und witzig, schlitzohrig und selbstironisch" neben Zitaten aus Rezensionen im *Spiegel* und in der *Berliner Morgenpost*, die den Roman mit positiven Bewertungen dem potentiellen Käufer und Leser empfehlen. Die Präsentation von Roman und Autor ist im Taschenbuch auf der linken Seite vom Haupttitelblatt zu finden, wobei der Klappentext der gebundenen Ausgabe etwas verändert und ergänzt wurde. So wird im Taschenbuch

7 Der Umschlag ist mit freundlicher Genehmigung der Verlagsgruppe Bertelsmann abgebildet.

sowohl der Bremer Förderpreis für Literatur von 1996 als auch die geplante Verfilmung[8] des Romans erwähnt. Zusammen mit dem gewählten Format wird dadurch auf den Erfolg des Romanes verwiesen:

> For undoubtedly the pocket edition will long be synonymous with canonization. On that account alone, pocket format is a formidable (although ambiguous – indeed, because ambiguous) paratextual message (Genette 1997, 21f.).

Für die Taschenbuchausgabe von Bertelsmann gilt zudem, was Genette zur Formatwahl sagt:

> The contrast between "trade edition" and "pocket edition" is, as we know, based on technical and commercial features, the most important of which is certainly not size [...] The contrast between trade and pocket, as a matter of fact, has much more to do with the old distinction between books bound in a stiff material and books bound in a flexible material (19f.).

Wie die meisten Taschenbücher ist auch die Taschenbuchausgabe des *Zimmerspringbrunnens* Bestandteil einer Serie: "btb. Aus Freude am Lesen", die sich mit folgenden Worten ihrem Publikum präsentiert:

> Bei btb erscheinen seit Mai 1996 liebevoll ausgewählte und hochwertig ausgestattete Bücher für leidenschaftliche Leser und Bücherfreunde. Die Autoren und ihre Titel stehen für ein individuelles Programm für individuelle Leser (http://www.randomhou se.de/btb/).

Die Umschlaggestaltung mag deshalb eher vom Serienprofil als vom Inhalt des einzelnen Buches abhängig sein, zumal der geringere Preis eines Taschenbuches nahezu automatisch zu einer weniger aufwendigen Umschalggestaltung beitragen mag. Die Beschreibung des Romans auf der Rückseite des Umschlages und die Zitate aus positiven Rezensionen kompensieren für einen Umschlag, der dem Leser kaum Anhaltspunkte zum Inhalt gibt. Geht man davon aus, daß der eher ungewöhnliche Untertitel "Ein Heimatroman" vom Leser registriert wird, kann man weiter annehmen, daß dessen Weglassung und Erstattung durch die eher übliche Genreangabe "Roman" beim Leser des Taschenbuches zu anderen Erwartungen an den Inhalt führt als beim Leser der gebundenen Ausgabe. Allerdings kann man auch damit rechnen, daß viele Käufer des Taschenbuches durch Rezen-

8 Der Begriff der Verfilmung wird hier wertneutral und synonym mit dem Begriff der filmischen Adaption verwendet. Zu Begriff und Begriffsgeschichte vgl. Bleisteiner 2001, 11ff.

sionen der Erstausgabe bereits eine Vorstellung vom Roman haben und damit weniger von peritextuellen Signalen abhängig sind.

Gemeinsam mit dem Verlagslogo, einem Löwen mit Flügeln, verspricht der Verlag seinen Lesern Qualität, wie dies Genette für Serien beschreibt:

> Today, therefore, "pocket size" is basically no longer a format but a vast set or nebula of series – for "pocket" still means "series" – from the most popular to the most "distinguished", indeed, the most pretentious; and the series emblem, much more than size, conveys two basic meanings. One is purely economic [...]. The other is indeed "cultural" [...]: the assurance of a selection based on *revivals*, that is, reissues (21).

Verfilmung

Obwohl die DVD in ihrer Umschlaggestaltung[9] an den Umschlag der gebundenen Ausgabe von Kiepenheuer & Witsch anknüpft und so Roman und Film deutlich miteinander ins Verhältnis bringt, fehlt auch hier jeglicher Hinweis auf den ursprünglichen Untertitel des Romans.

Wie auf dem Buchumschlag wird die Aufmerksamkeit des Betrachters zuerst auf die männliche Person auf der unteren Hälfte der Seite gelenkt und dann durch dessen Schatten in die obere Richtung. Allerdings ist der Titel durch die rote Farbe auffallender als auf dem Buchumschlag; gemeinsam mit den Vornamen der Schauspieler, die ebenfalls durch ihre rote Farbe hervorgehoben werden, wird so ein Rahmen um das Bild gelegt. Dies trägt auch dazu bei, daß der Name des Autors eine weniger zentrale Rolle einnimmt. Dagegen werden die Schauspieler und nicht zuletzt der Regisseur hervorgehoben. Der Name der Regisseurs wird zudem in Verbindung mit einem früheren Film gebracht: "Die neue Komödie von Peter Timm 'GO TRABI GO'".[10] Über dem Filmtitel und neben dem Blickfang des Umschlages wird zudem ein Satz aus dem Film zitiert: "Wenn alles zieht an einem Tau, erreichen wir das Weltniveau!" Indem dieser Satz im Film im sächsischen Dialekt vorgetragen wird – im Roman fehlt dieser Satz – wird eine Verbindung zur DDR-Vergangenheit und deren politische Schlagwörter hergestellt.

---

9 Vgl. http://www.filmposter-archiv.de/ (20.7.06). Im Falle des *Zimmerspringbrunnens* entspricht das Filmplakat dem ersten DVD-Umschlag.

10 *Go, Trabi, go* erschien 1990 und konstituierte "das neue Image des eigentlich doch ganz symphatischen 'Ossi', der mehr Glück als Verstand hat und immer irgendwie durchkommt" (Ivanović 2000, 227).

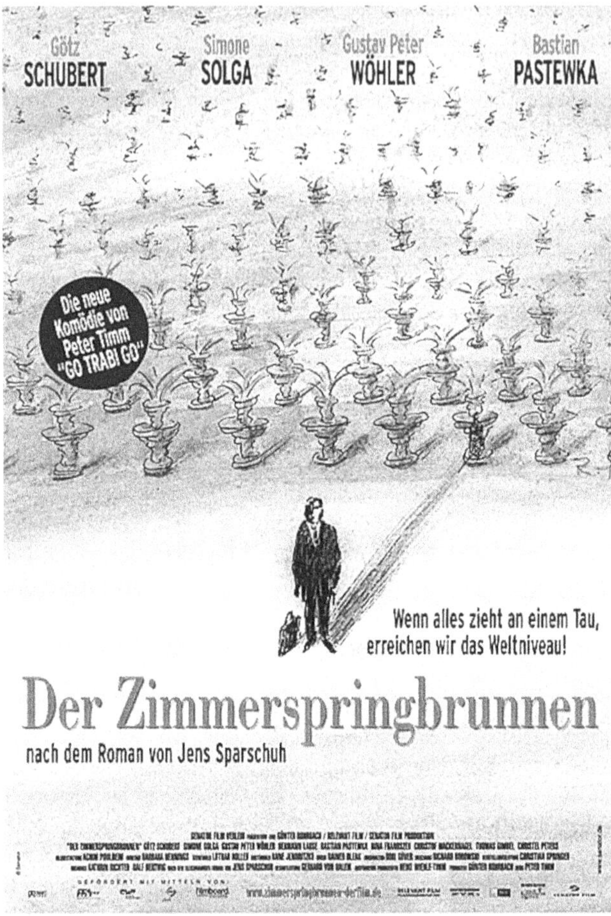

Wie in Büchern, kann sich jedoch auch der Paratext einer DVD verändern.[11] So weist eine spätere Ausgabe der DVD nicht mehr auf die Romanvorlage und deren Autor hin, sondern wählt Filmbilder für den Umschlag.[12] Die Bilder bekannter Schauspieler wie Götz Schubert und Bastian Pastewka können, ähnlich wie die Hervorhebung des Regisseurs, zum Sehen des Films anregen. Offensichtlich setzt man in dieser DVD-Ausgabe mehr auf die Kraft der Bilder, denn der Name des Regisseurs findet sich nur noch in kleiner Schrift am unteren Ende der Seite.

---

11 Vgl. Genette 1997, 6: "[...] a paratextual element may appear at any time, it may also disappear, definitively or not, by authorial decision or outside intervention or by virtue of the e-roding effect of time."

12 http://www.amazon.de/exec/obidos/ASIN/B0000798XF/preisroboterd-21/ref=nosim (26.9.06).

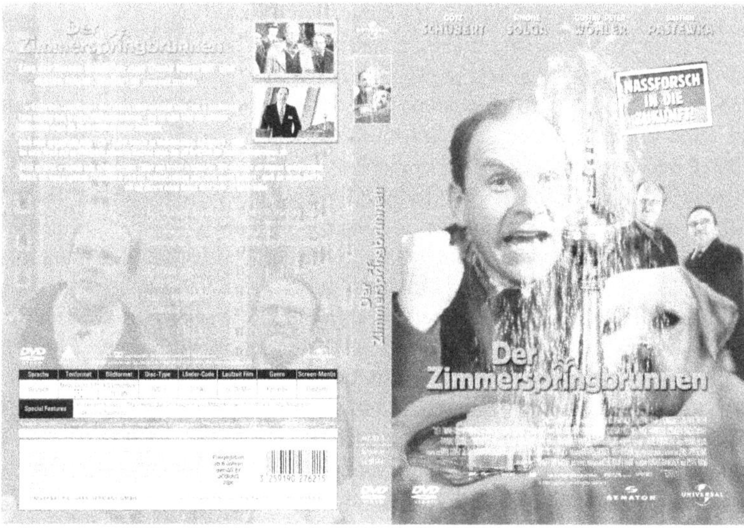

Wie auch in der Taschenbuchausgabe finden sich auf der Rückseite ein kurzes Handlungsreferat und Ausschnitte aus positiven Filmrezensionen, die vor allem die Komik des Films hervorheben. Dies korrespondiert mit der Genreangabe "Komödie" auf der Rückseite des DVD-Umschlages. Sowohl Titel als auch die Namen der Schauspieler heben sich in dieser Ausgabe durch ihre orange Farbe vom vorwiegend blauen Hintergrund ab. Lobek und dessen Hund dominieren gemeinsam mit dem Zimmerspringbrunnen Modell ATLANTIS den Umschlag in einer Szene, in der sich Lobek begeistert und engagiert zeigt. Die Farben der DDR werden in der DDR-Fahne im oberen Teil des Umschlages wiederholt; jedoch durch die Aufschrift des Slogans "Nassforsch in die Zukunft" fast verdeckt. Boldinger und Strüver – Chef und Kollege Lobeks in der Firma PHANTA RHEIn – betrachten Lobek wohlwollend aus dem Hintergrund.

Obwohl dieser Umschlag sich stark vom ersten DVD-Umschlag unterscheidet, entspricht hier der Paratext durchaus dem Inhalt, da die Verfilmung weniger die Tragik von Lobeks Leben als vielmehr die Komik seines Erfolgs in den Vordergrund rückt. Für die Verfilmung des *Zimmerspringbrunnens* gilt, was Bolter und Grusin für die zahlreichen literarische Adaptionen Hollywoods der 1990er Jahre beschreiben: "The content has been borrowed, but the medium has not been appropriated or quoted" (Bolter und Grusin 2000, 44).

Obwohl die Verfilmung der Romanvorlage gegenüber relativ treu bleibt, zwingt das Filmmedium und nicht zuletzt der Wunsch seiner Produzenten nach einer Komödie, zu inhaltlichen Vereinfachungen. So ist beispielsweise Lobeks Entschluß, sich als Vertreter zu bewerben im Film keineswegs schicksalhaft begründet, sondern geschieht auf Aufforderung des Arbeitsamtes. Das Verhältnis zwischen Lobek und Julia ist zwar auch im Film problematisch, aber keineswegs so aussichtslos wie im Roman. Dies liegt nicht zuletzt daran, daß Lobek im Film eher ein durchschnittlicher Arbeitsloser ist als der Sonderling des Romans, der stillschweigend seine Beobachtungen der Umwelt in einem Protokollbuch festhält; der Ich-Erzähler des Romans mit seiner begrenzten Perspektive ist im Film durch eine personale Erzählsituation ersetzt. Indem der Zuschauer die Handlung hauptsächlich 'von außen' sieht, entsteht ein größeres Gleichgewicht zwischen den Personen; der innere Monolog des Romans ist durch die Dialoge der Personen im Film ersetzt. So begegnet Lobek, im Film deutlich jünger und keineswegs in einer existentiellen Krise wie im Roman, seinem Filmpublikum sympathischer als der ehe tragische Romanheld, der weder mit der Welt noch mit seiner Ehe zurecht kommt. Für das Filmpublikum wird es deshalb einfacher, sich mit Lobek und dessen Geschichte zu identifizieren und in den Film einzuleben.[13] Zwar wird auch im Film Lobek von Julia verlassen, aber es besteht kein Zweifel, daß beide einander lieben. Der Film schließt mit einem deutlichen Happy End ab: Julia und Lobek finden zurück zueinander; nicht nur Lobek, sondern auch Julia ist nun arbeitslos, ihr Einkommen jedoch ist durch den weiteren Verkauf des Modells ATLANTIS gesichert. Durch die Filmmusik[14] – teilweise komponiert von Rainer Oleak und teilweise alte Pop Titel aus der ehemaligen DDR wie beispielsweise "Am Fenster" von *City*, "Als ich fortging" von *Karussel* und "Über sieben Brücken mußt du gehn" ursprünglich von *Karat* – bekommt der Film zwar mitunter einen nostalgischen Unterton, ist aber weit von der deutsch-deutschen Robinsonade entfernt, die im Roman durch die zahlreichen Anspielungen geschaffen wird.

Während Lobeks Hund im Film Henry heißt, trägt er im Roman den gutbürgerlichen Namen Hasso vom Rabenhorst, wird jedoch von Lobek in Freitag umgetauft (Sparschuh 1995, 20). Da sich die Handlung im Roman über einen längeren Zeitraum erstreckt, erfahren wir auch, daß sich Lobek immer mehr auf die vier Wände seiner Wohnung zurückzieht, in der er sich wie Robinson oder "der letzte Mohikaner" (39) fühlt, der gegen den Rest der Welt für sein Überleben kämpfen muß. All diese Anspielungen verweisen auf Daniel Defoes *Robinson Crusoe* und auf James Fenimore Coopers *Der letzte Mohikaner* – zwei Romane, die in spannender Form das Aufeinandertreffen zwischen Zivilisation und Natur themati-

---

13 Dieses Einleben in die Handlung wird von Bolter und Grusin als "immediacy" oder auch "transparent immediacy" bezeichnet. Literatur aber auch Film sind Beispiele dafür, daß Leser oder auch Seher das Medium – Buch bzw. Film – vergessen und sich in die Handlung einleben, obwohl sie wissen, daß es sich nur um eine Fiktion handlet.

14 Der Soundtrack zum Film erschien im November 2001 auf CD. Der Umschlag der CD nimmt das Umschlagmotiv der gebundenen Ausgabe von 1995 ebenfalls auf und stellt so einen deutlichen Zusammenhang zwischen Roman, Film und CD her. Umschlag und Titelübersicht finden sich unter http://www.amazon.de (19.7.06).

sieren und die zum Erfahrungshintergrund der meisten Leser in Ost und West gehören, da sie als Kinder und Jugendliche entweder die Romanbearbeitungen gelesen oder die Romanverfilmungen gesehen haben dürften. Die Anspielung auf die beiden Romane kann als eine Form des kulturellen Wissens gelesen werden, die einen Text nicht wirklich ins Spiel bringt, sondern nur die Erinnerung an ihn. Die Assoziationen, die sich für den Leser an Robinson und Lederstrumpf knüpfen, sind zentral; im Film jedoch fehlen diese.

Im Roman sind Sparschuhs Anspielungen so überdeutlich, daß es kaum zu einem falschen Verständnis kommen kann. Lobek fühlt sich immer wieder wie Robinson auf einer einsamen Insel, den Hund Freitag befreit er zwar nicht aus den Händen von Kannibalen, wohl aber aus den Umarmungen seiner Frau und am Ende geht er sogar daran, Freitag zu zivilisieren:

> "[...] – Das Leben, Mensch, das Leben ist unendlich viel mehr als Fressen, Gassi und Glotze! Man kann nicht so wie du bloß in den Tag hineinleben. Das Leben muß doch einen Sinn haben, einen Sinn, verstehst du! ... Jeder Mensch ... überhaupt: jede Kreatur ... man muß doch an etwas glauben in der Welt, verdammt noch mal!" (131f.)

Im Film begegnet uns Lobek dagegen weniger stereotyp, wie auch die anderen Personen weniger als im Roman mit den Requisiten der gängigen Stereotype von Ost- und Westdeutschen ausgestattet sind. Für Strüver ist im Roman der Osten "Neuland", in dem er alles für möglich hält; in den Augen Strüvers wird Lobek zum "Eingeborene[n]" (89).

> Im Umfeld des Briefkastenprojekts galt Strüvers Hauptinteresse den Sitten und Gebräuchen der Ostdeutschen. Er zeigte sich sehr daran interessiert, alles mit diesem Thema in Zusammenhang stehende in Erfahrung zu bringen. Er war froh, daß er die Ostdeutschen nun aus eigener Anschauung kennenlernte. "Der Ostdeutsche an und für sich ...", so begannen seine diesbezüglichen Betrachtungen (99).

Diese Sicht auf den Osten mag an anthropologische Untersuchungen fremder Völker erinnern, aktiviert aber auch die These von der Kolonisation des Ostens durch den Westen; die Romane Defoes und Coopers gelten gemeinhin als Klassiker der Kolonialliteratur. Erträglich werden diese Typisierungen lediglich durch die Tatsache, daß der Westdeutsche Lobek gerade in Form des Vertreters begegnet, wohl einer der denkbar lächerlichsten Gestalten, der sich noch von einem Arbeitslosen davon jagen läßt bzw. vom Wohlwollen der Besuchten abhängig ist. Die Ingroup-Outgroup-Personenkonstellation des traditionellen Heimatromans, in der "Hausierer, manchmal als Wander- oder Trödeljude" (Rossbacher 1975, 184) ihren Platz in der Outgroup haben, ist hier ins Gegenteil verkehrt: gerade der Vertreter wird im *Zimmerspringbrunnen* zum Helden, der sich allerdings nach wie vor wie ein Fremder den Wohnungen der Einheimischen nähert und nur mit viel Geschick in diese eingelassen wird.

Leitmotivisch strukturiert der Zimmerspringbrunnen sowohl Roman als auch Film. Verkaufen soll Lobek das Modell JONA, "ein etwa fingergroßer Walfisch (Typ U-Boot, metallic-Blau)", den Strüver als "Ereignisspringbrunnen, 'the new generation'" (Sparschuh 1995, 34) auf dem Vertreterseminar präsentiert. Der Prophet Jona, zwar vom Wal gefressen, aber gleichzeitig beschützt in dessen Inneren kann als Allusion auf die DDR und deren Einwohner gelesen werden, die zwar nicht im Bauch eines Wales, wohl aber innerhalb ihrer Grenzen gefangen waren, was sie jedoch nicht vor dem Untergang retten konnte. Ninive wurde durch die Warnung Jonas und durch die dadurch ausgelöste versagende Lebensweise seiner Bewohner gerettet; die DDR aber ging trotz aller Warnungen und Entsagungen seiner Einwohner ähnlich Atlantis unter. Indem Lobek das Modell JONA in das Modell ATLANTIS umbaut, läßt Lobek die DDR in der lächerlichen Form eines Zimmerspringbrunnens wiederauferstehen und erzielt damit ungeahnte Verkaufserfolge im Osten Berlins. ATLANTIS entwickelt sich zu einem "Kultgegenstand" (105), der sich vor allem in Kreisen eines "halblegalen 'DDR-Heimatvertriebenen-Verbandes', der erstaunlich gut und straff organisiert war" (106) gut verkaufen läßt. Lobek selbst ist von dieser Entwicklung überrascht und registriert sie eher unbeteiligt, obwohl auch ihn manchmals so etwas wie ein "Phantomschmerz" überkam, wenn er an früher dachte (105).

"Ostalgie" wird hier als ein Bedürfnis dargestellt, das Kinder noch nicht verstehen und auch nicht alle Erwachsenen teilen, das Lobek aber zum beruflichen Erfolg verhilft und ihm sogar die Stelle des Betriebsleiters Ost in Aussicht stellt. Ironischerweise ist es Lobek – ein abgewickelter Ostdeutscher, dessen Handlungen von Zufälligkeiten bestimmt sind – und kein skrupelloser Westdeutscher, der das Verlustgefühl der Ostdeutschen in klingende Münze verwandelt. Während im Roman offen bleibt, ob die Entdeckung von Lobeks Geschäftsgeheimnis Konsequenzen für seine Karriere haben wird, bringt sie ihm im Film eine Beförderung zum Verkaufsleiter Ost ein, die er jedoch an Strüver weitergibt.

Sowohl beim Buch- als auch beim DVD-Medium kann eine ähnliche Entwicklung beobachtet werden, was die Veränderung paratextlicher Elemente wie Umschlaggestaltung betrifft: Die spätere Ausgabe hat offenbar andere Voraussetzungen, nicht zuletzt materieller Art, auf die man zurückgreifen kann. Durch die gebundene bzw. die erste DVD-Ausgabe ist bereits ein Umfeld mit Rezensionen und Artikeln etabliert, die spätere Ausgaben beim Empfänger als bekannt voraussetzen können und so einen Rahmen für die nachfolgenden Ausgaben abgeben.

Das DVD-Medium macht zudem weitere paratextliche Elemente zugänglich:

> In film, although Genette does not mention it, "paratextuality" might evoke all those materials close to the text such as posters, trailers, reviews, interviews with the director, and so forth. The new media, in fact, have fostered an explosion of paratextual materials (Stam 2005, 28).

So findet man auf der DVD unter "Extras" unter anderen den Trailer zum Film, der wie Filmplakat[15] und DVD-Umschlag die Richtung angibt, in der die Produzenten ihren Film verstanden wissen wollen. Durch den Trailer erfahren wir, daß der *Zimmerspringbrunnen* von einem handelt, "der auszog, die Welt zu verändern und seine Heimat wiederfand"; eine deutsche Erfolgsgeschichte über Freundschaft, Liebe und alte Zeiten. Indem die Verfilmung diese Aspekte in ihrer Komik hervorhebt und die eher nachdenklich stimmenden Szenen des Romans, die Lobek in seiner Tragik zeigen, ausläßt, ist die Wegglassung des Untertitels durchaus logisch. Offensichtlich ging es darum einen unterhaltsamen und konsensfähigen Film zu schaffen. Der fehlende Untertitel der DVD wiederholt sich im Abspann, in dem wir erfahren, daß der Film "nach dem gleichnamigen Roman von Jens Sparschuh" entstanden ist, und ist damit durchaus stimmig, nicht zuletzt wenn man den humoristischen Ton des Films und dessen Happy End berücksichtigt. Während Lobeks weiteres Schicksal im Roman eher in negativer Richtung angedeutet wird, endet der Film nicht nur mit der Wiedervereinigung zwischen Lobek und Julia, sondern auch mit der Aussicht auf ein neues Springbrunnenmodell, das Lobek den Namen "Blühende Landschaften" geben will.

Da Aufzeichnungen von Theatervorstellungen selten der Öffentlichkeit zugänglich gemacht werden und deshalb von der Anwesenheit an einem bestimmten Ort und zu einer bestimmten Zeit abhängig sind, soll hier nur abschließend erwähnt werden, daß sich das Theaterstück, im Gegensatz zur Verfilmung, deutlich auf den Untertitel bezieht. Die Theaterfassung für einen Mann und einen Hund – der jedoch auf der Bühne nie sichtbar wird – überführt den Untertitel des Romans doppeldeutig auf das Theaterstück: "Ein Stück Heimat" spielt nicht nur auf das Genre Heimatliteratur an, sondern auch, daß hier mit Lobek und dessen Geschichte dem Zuschauer buchstäblich ein Stück Heimat präsentiert wird.

---

15 Vgl. http://www.filmposter-archiv.de/ (20.7.06).

Bibliographie

Bolter, Jay David und Richard Grusin, 2000. *Remediation: Understanding New Media*. Paperback ed. Cambridge, MA: MIT Press.

Bleisteiner, Angela, 2001. *Literatur im Medienwechsel. Eine Studie zur filmischen Adaption von Dramen Harold Pinters*. Heidelberg 2000: Universitätsverlag C. Winter (Anglistische Forschungen 292).

Genette, Gérard, 1997. *Paratexts: Thresholds of Interpretation*. Translated by Jane E. Lewin. Foreword by Richard Macksey. Cambridge: Cambridge University Press (Literature, Culture, Theory 20).

Interview mit Jens Sparschuh, 2006. Online:
http://www.djfl.de/entertainment/stars/j/jens_sparschuh_i_01.html (19. Juli 2006).

Ivanović, Christine, 2000. Wende im Film? Vorläufiger Rückblick auf ein Jahrzehnt deutscher Einheit im Film. In *Mentalitätswandel in der deutschen Literatur zur Einheit (1990-2000)*, Hg. von Volker Wehdeking. Berlin: Erich Schmidt Verlag (Philologische Studien und Quellen 165), 225-235.

Rossbacher, Karlheinz, 1975. *Heimatkunstbewegung und Heimatroman. Zu einer Literatursoziologie der Jahrhundertwende*. Stuttgart: Ernst Klett Verlag.

Sparschuh, Jens, 1995. *Der Zimmerspringbrunnen*. Ein Heimatroman. Köln: Kiepenheuer & Witsch.

------. 1997. *Der Zimmerspringbrunnen*. München: Verlagsgruppe Bertelsmann (btb 1300).

Stam, Robert, 2005. The Theory and Practice of Adaptation. In *Literature and Film. A Guide to the Theory and Practice of Film Adaptation*, Hg. von Robert Stam und Alessandra Raengo. Oxford: Blackwell Publishing, 1-52.

Verleihung des Bremer Literaturpreises 1996. Elfriede Jelinek. Jens Sparschuh. Laudationes und Reden. Hg. von der Rudolf-Alexander-Schröder-Stiftung. Bremen 1996.

Filmographie

Der Zimmerspringbrunnen

Land: Deutschland
Jahr: 2001
Produzent: Relevant Film, Senator Film Produktion
Video- und DVD-Anbieter: Universal
Länge: 94 Minuten
Erstaufführung: 29.11.2001/9.1.2003 Video & DVD
Produzent: Günter Rohrbach
Regie: Peter Timm
Drehbuch: Kathrin Richter, Ralf Hertwig
Kamera: Achim Poulheim
Musik: Rainer Oleak
Schnitt: Barbara Hennings

Simon Niedenthal

Documents of Light: Three Case Studies and a Preliminary Model for Organizing Light Knowledge

1 Documentation studies and the study of light

The area of Documentation studies offers a useful framework for the consideration of transdisciplinary subjects that do not respond fully to critical theories currently prevailing in the humanities and social sciences. This paper will apply a documentation approach to the study of light by examining case studies drawn from theatre, architecture and computer science. According to Documentation studies' extended definition of what constitutes a document, a theatre lighting plan, a computer algorithm, or even a light installation or fireworks show could be considered a document.[1] One consequence of the breadth of this definition is that it allows us to seek common organizing themes in a range of lighting practices. Scholars, scientists and lighting practitioners create, employ and perform documents that encode illumination knowledge, which can be understood as the manifestation, simulation or manipulation of light to a particular end. Taking a cue from computer lighting algorithms, which attempt to construct a symbolic description of the propagation of light in space, we can suggest a means of classifying documents of light in the broader sense, in a way that places the human body and sensorium in a central position.

The transdisciplinary study of light serves as a quintessential test of our commitment to question existing disciplinary boundaries, and to form new disciplines that better serve human needs. Indeed, light is in many ways an ideal subject for our times. Light remains a puzzling scientific limit case to in so many ways: it represents the ultimate in speed, though researchers have recently succeeded in stopping it by sending it through clouds of supercooled particles. Its nature as both wave and particle make light the quintessence of modern uncertainty. As a design substance it could be claimed that light will be the construction material of the 21st century.[2] Illumination has long been acknowledged as the basis for our

---

1 Thanks to Niels Windfeld Lund for his encouragement and support during my trips to Tromsø.

2 Perhaps the most poignant example of recent light architecture was the memorial to the World Trade Center and its victims in the fall of 2001.

perception of form and space, but there is a renewed awareness of its importance in the world of digital design. Through laser technology, the control of fiber optics and the phosphors of new digital media, light will bear the imprint of communication, record and expression. Light and its effects are richly evocative – light can be studied and manipulated as sense phenomenon, as mood regulator, electromagnetic radiation, or as the binding element of filmic media and architecture. Light is simultaneously physical and metaphysical. As a multifaceted phenomenon, light offers a perfect locus for developing new interdisciplinary discourses that attempt to bridge the gap between art and science that has drawn so much attention over the last 40 years (Snow 1993).

But the study of light has been awaiting new critical tools. Light as a transdisciplinary subject responds incompletely to two common interpretative models within the humanities and social sciences: semiotics and media theory. Although at least one writer has productively explored "codes" of illumination, it can be argued that the linguistically-derived study of signs offers a constrained, even counter-intuitive starting point for a deeper exploration of how a physical phenomenon such as light can "subconsciously matter" (Boone 1997, 86).[3] The limitations of semiotics as a means of interpreting sense experience has in fact recently spurred critical efforts aimed at decoupling our understanding of the senses and sense phenomena from linguistics, and insisting upon exploring the way in which the body creates its own meanings (Howes 2005). This approach acknowledges the contributions of McLuhan, whose media theory places the human body and sensorium in a central position.

Any consideration of light from a purely media theory perspective, however, quickly founders upon the fact that light can be either naturally occurring or artificially produced, and thus does not really qualify as a "medium" (one could, perhaps, substitute the older, more painterly definition of medium as a "binding substance"). McLuhan's simplest usage can serve as a test: a medium can be defined as a human process or artifact that functions as an extension of the senses (Ma-

---

3 Boone aims "to demonstrate how lighting-as-sign is functioning at the three basic levels of semiotic signification" (85). Part of the power of light, to my way of thinking, is that it does not "communicate" in the traditional manner of sign systems, and so we might need to expand our approach to the subject beyond semiotics to truly understand the way in which light can "subconsciously matter" (Boone quotes theatre lighting designer Tharon Musser on page 86). But Boone's handling of theatre lighting documents is particularly sensitive: "Three resources primarily inform my speculations on Rosenthal's use of light in West Side Story: production photographs, the focusing charts for the 1959 national tour of the show [...] and stage directions as they appear in the 1958 acting edition of the script. In order to speculate on the contributions made by Rosenthal's lighting design, I use both indirect evidence found in the focusing charts, color charts, and stage directions as well as the more direct evidence provided by production photographs" (84).

cLuhan 1998).[4] Moreover, the strength of media theory is in exploring the ways in which meanings arise within, and are inflected by conversations between media (Bolter and Grusin 1999).[5] The difficulty here of course is that light is manifested both within and outside of our experiences of media. We encounter illumination in representations, simulations and real space. The relationship between the domains is crucial. Let us presume a situation in which one views a movie of a dark alley, then leaves the theatre and walks down a dark alley. Are the two experiences analogous?[6] If so, then media theory cannot provide an exclusive vocabulary for our response to light. Some portion of our experience of light can survive abstraction to the film screen (to a 2nd plane), scaling (to a portion of our visual field) and dislocation in time and space. A transdisciplinary light studies can begin to provide terms of reference to help us understand this relationship.

So in order to move forward, it is clear that the study of light requires an expanded critical toolbox. One could begin by drawing from other obvious sources in the social sciences, including perceptual psychology, as well as natural sciences. But if one is to avoid fragmented and confusing arguments, it is also important to identify a framework of scholarly practice that can provide a kind of intellectual superstructure. Documentation studies, as outlined by Niels Windfeld Lund, can supply this sort of scaffolding: "Documentation Studies is defined as a new discipline dealing with forms of documentation by studying the production as well as reproduction of documents of all kinds" (Lund 1999, 45). One of the sources of Documentation studies' appeal is that it grows out of library and information sciences (LIS), and so is a capacious practice. As such, the discipline offers the "possibility to transcend the borders of film, literature, paintings, and other media, which are normally dealt with in a number of specific scientific disciplines for each kind of documentation" (45). Another benefit of Documentation studies'

---

4 McLuhan cites the electric light as a limit case early in *Understanding Media*: "The electric light is pure information. It is a medium without a message, as it were. [...] Whether the light is being used for brain surgery or night baseball is a matter of indifference. It could be argued that these activities are actually the 'content' of the electric light, since they could not exist without the electric light. This fact merely underlines the point that 'the medium is the message' because it is the medium that shapes and controls the scale and form of human association and action" (8-9).

5 This is the argument of Bolter and Grusin (1999): "No medium today, and certainly no single media event, seems to do its cultural work in isolation from other media, any more then it works in isolation from other social and economic forces. What is new about new media comes from the particular ways in which they refashion older media and the ways in which older media refashion themselves to answer the challenges of new media" (15).

6 The anecdotal evidence from cinematographers would suggest yes. In his memoirs, famed cinematographer Henri Alekan, who created the images for Cocteau's *Beauty and the Beast*, ascribes his education as a cinematographer to observation of light in nature, as well as to examinations of paintings (see Alekan's great book on cinematography, *Des lumières et des ombres*).

roots in LIS is that it inherits some of the taxonomic rigor of the parent practice. This is especially useful when dealing with the subject of light. A survey of writings on light uncovers a tendency towards flowery and poetic excesses, perhaps an unavoidable overcompensation that results when attention is directed towards a phenomenon whose omniscience and subtlety of effect leave it frequently ignored.[7] Indeed, the sketching of sense phenomenon taxonomies is one of the key tasks in the post-semiotic effort to recognize and reclaim our sense experience. Finally, documentation studies offers a vocabulary for moving beyond the prevailing reception theories, and allows us to redirect attention to the processes of making and using artifacts (Lund 1999).[8]

As a means of testing the usefulness of the documentation studies approach in the exploration of the processes of the documenting light scholar and lighting practitioner, I propose examining case studies drawn from three diverse and challenging domains: Shakespearean theatre scholarship, night architectural illumination, and computer lighting algorithm construction.

2 Lighting the Shakespearean stage

Imagine the plight of the Elizabethan theatre scholar: almost all of her conclusions regarding illumination in Shakespearean performance must be drawn from the indirect evidence of court expense accounts, second-hand reports from travelers' journals, and a few graphic sources. It is only in the past few years that theatre reconstructions (such as the new Globe) have enabled scholars to do photometric readings in environments that are themselves the result of speculation documentary evidence in the form of physical infrastructure and written material. Faced with these constraints, the theatre historian has had to become a masterful interpreter and manipulator of documents. In *Lighting the Shakespearean Stage*, R. B. Graves argues that the illumination qualities in outdoor and indoor theatres were not as different as previously thought, and that, unlike the highly directional lighting to which we are accustomed in the contemporary theatre, "early English lighting emanated from all around the actor, surrounding him with soft, indirect light. [...] The actors moved in the same light all Londoners moved in everyday" (Graves 1999, 232). The organization of each of Graves' chapters follows a similar pattern: an argument is constructed that ultimately allows the visualization of

7 Just try running a Google search on the terms "light studies"; the overwhelming majority of sites returned have a strong "New Age" flavor!

8 "Doc.Studies is primarily focusing on the producer or sender of the message and secondly on the use or reproduction of the documents" (Lund 1999, 45).

an illumination environment. This from the conclusion to his chapter on illumination of the outdoor playhouses:

> The general picture of the amphitheatres that emerges is one of a well-shaded stage with neither artificial light for general illumination nor the extreme contrasts of light and dark due to direct sunlight. As an actor came forward toward the foot of the stage, the light would increase slightly because the cover overhead intercepted less light (123).

Besides the rigor of his arguments, Graves' work is compelling because it allows us to more fully imagine the conditions of Elizabethan performance.

Although one can certainly savor the line of Graves' arguments, it is important to list the types of documents that he marshals to defend his thesis, and note the manner in which he employs each type. Graves' reasoning tends to move from what is known about an illumination environment to what can be deduced or must be argued, then back to more direct photometric evidence and interpretation. In his chapter on "Daylight in the Indoor Playhouses", for example, he begins by interrogating the written evidence concerning performance times, as this information allows the author to determine exterior light levels, given time of day and presumed atmospheric conditions. He then looks at court expense accounts to determine patterns of candle purchase, which allow for arguments on artificial light levels.[9] The next step is to examine existing examples of halls whose dimensions are similar to those of indoor playhouses, noting the placement of windows and predominating light qualities, as well as taking photometric readings of the light levels. Graphic sources are employed to several ends: architectural cross sections demonstrate spatial relationships and suggest illumination directions from windows, and an engraving from a book frontispiece shows the sort of relationship between window light and artificial sources that may have existed. Graves' concludes that though light levels were lower in indoor than outdoor playing spaces, the difference was well within the range of human visual adaptation:

---

9 Graves 1999, 129: "As it happens, the best estimate of candlelight employed indoors comes from a proposed article of agreement between housekeepers and hireling actors at Salisbury Court in 1639. In the agreement, the housekeepers agreed to pay half the cost of the lights, 'both waxe and Tallow, which halfe all winter is near 5 s a day'. As will be discussed in the next chapter, it is from such a figure that we can make a more-or-less intelligent guess about the number of candles used at Salisbury Court in the winter. Depending on their size and the proportions of expensive wax candles to cheaper tallow ones, the total number works out to about two to four dozen candles for each performance – a goodly number, to be sure, but in actual brightness not even equal to the power of one sixty-watt bulb." One convenient fact about studying candles as a light source is that their output corresponds to a common unit of measurement – the footcandle.

> In consequence, we must not think of the adult private theatres as dim, at least not in the early afternoon. On the contrary, we may imagine them as satisfactorily lit even by our own standards and entirely adequate by medieval and early modern standards (157).

We may draw several broad conclusions about Graves' use of light documents:

1. **Written evidence** is often (though not always) used to support arguments about light levels, the quantity of light present in the environment.
2. **Graphic evidence** is often employed for spatial understanding, and to answer questions such as: where were lights positioned with reference to the stage? Where were windows located? Where would shadows fall? Given that light intensity diminishes as it moves from its source, how much light could be expected to reach the acting area? What was the predominating light direction?
3. **Photometric evidence** is used to determine absolute illumination levels, and interpreted in conjunction with what we know about human visual response to light.

By nimbly manipulating these types of light documents, Graves is able to conjure a vivid imagining of the qualities of light under which Shakespeare's work was first performed.

3 Writing light

But scholars aren't the only ones who must master documents of light. Lighting practitioners who rely upon documents to communicate their designs to clients must, by necessity, be quite knowledgeable about what documents can, and cannot communicate about light. The conditions of night illumination offer a particular challenge to the documenting lighting practitioner, as nocturnal contrast ratios are often beyond the capacity of most filmic materials, and photographic results do not correspond well with the eye's visual range and capacity to adapt. Lighting designer Louis Clair has produced a number of large-scale light installations for urban spaces in Europe, Asia and Canada. In "*Écrire la lumière*", Clair wrestles with the limitations of different kinds of light documents, and proposes a technique of describing light "ambiances" (Clair 2000, 110)[10] as a means of constituting a communicable "light writing" (128) that can eventually aspire to the precision of musical notation Clair's development of the concept of illumination ambi-

10 I take responsibility for all translations from the article.

ances grows out of his dissatisfaction with the current media of light representation: "The lighting designer [...] creates images to present his project, but the images themselves remain subject to interpretation. They are unable to fully simulate contrasts of color or the perception of light in real space" (111). Though digital media offer the semblance of greater fidelity, 3d graphics fall short for similar reasons.

> Digital images remain, in spite of this precision, approximations, for, like other techniques, they can communicate neither the effects of vision in real space, nor the capacity of the eye to perceive gradations of light much greater than analog or digital media can reproduce (111).

Clair seeks to expand the realm of light documentation by moving away from imaging media towards literary description and the development of a taxonomy of light effects. His survey of light documents begins with the standard documentation that accompanies a project proposal. The light plan is "an inventory of elements to illuminate and several recommendations regarding the urban context in which they are found" (114). Far more important to the designer's intent, however, is the development of the appropriate ambiances. Clair derives the term ambiances from cinematography, but his use of the term is strongly influenced by literature: "The client couches his expectations in literary terms describing the feelings inspired by the light environment. The lighting designer must translate these terms into the values and vocabulary of light in order to create ambiances" (114). Clair outlines eight types of ambiances: festive, convivial, majestic, discreet, romantic, theatrical, poetic and functional. Each term is associated with specific social models and light qualities – "Festive ambiances are those which preserve the illumination qualities of festivals, fairs, etc. They are characterized by the presence of numerous sources of multicolored light in the space, quite brilliant, even aggressive" (116). The "values and vocabulary" of light through which the ambiances are conveyed include:

We may draw several broad conclusions about Clair's use of light documents:

1. **Characteristics of light:** quantity of light: flux in lux; quality of light: color rendering index (IRC); color of light: color temperature in degrees Kelvin; colored lights: expressed in usual terms, or in spectral curves (or in terms of color filters)
2. **Lighting direction:** elevation: high, low, frontal; plan: face, profile, reversal of daylight
3. **Shadows:** density, edge quality of shadows; existing shadows or those imposed by sources

4. **Contrasts:** hardness, positive or negative contrasts; contrasts of color temperature or filtration
5. **Illumination** in the visual field: qualities of the illuminated areas; composition of illuminated areas
6. **Character** of light sources: quality of the sources; disposition of the sources
7. **Animation** of light and shadows: used infrequently in permanent installations

Clair thus attempts to impose a higher-level taxonomic order upon the shared, often parametric vocabulary of the lighting designer. If his effort falls short, it is because his 8 ambiances – though perhaps useful – certainly cannot be considered an exhaustive list of the illumination environments one might want to create, and the mapping between higher-level ambiances and basic light parameters is not always made explicit.

4 The Phong algorithm

Night illumination and digital lighting algorithms share an important condition: it is always night in the computer. All computed illumination simulations must take into account everything we know about light and instantiate that knowledge in a way that imposes various economies upon the highly complex behavior that we observe in real space.[11] Lighting algorithms, then, demonstrate a kind of abstract, meta-level, though incomplete organization of light knowledge. The Phong shading algorithm can serve as an example. In 1975, Bui Phong at the University of Utah proposed a shading technique which proposed to advance the quality of computer generated images of three-dimensional scenes: "Human visual perception and the fundamental laws of optics are considered in the development of a shading law that provides better quality and increased realism in generated images" (Phong 1975, 311).

Here is a shading algorithm based on Phong's work (Manchester University notes on computer rendering):

$$I = k_d I_a + \frac{I_p}{d + d_0}\left[k_d(\mathbf{N} \bullet \mathbf{L}) + k_s(\mathbf{R} \bullet \mathbf{V})^n\right]$$

11 Producing a computer-generated rendering begins with the process of defining a geometric model expressed within Cartesian space. The visual characteristics of every surface must be determined and the position of lights specified. The renderer then employs lighting and shading algorithms to produce a 2d image of the computer generated environment.

The algorithm exhibits several key elements:

1. Vectors (N, R, L, and V), which represent **spatial information** about position of the viewer (V), the reflected ray (R), position of a light source (L), as well as the orientation of the surface at the point being shaded (N).
2. Exponential and fractional terms, the remnants of the inverse square law, which introduces falloff to the solution, the diminishing of **intensity of light** as it moves away from its source.
3. Material constants (ka, kd, ks) that represent the **characteristics of the surface** being shaded.

What sets Phong's function apart from previous solutions (including Gouraud) is the more accurate rendering of the specular highlights that appear on glossy surfaces:

> The first step in accounting for the specular properties of objects and the position of the observer is to determine the normal to the surface at each point to be shaded [...] it is only with this knowledge that information about the direction of reflected rays can be acquired, and only with this information can we model the specular properties of objects" (Phong 1975, 116).

Phong tested his algorithm by comparing computer renderings with photos of glossy spheres to demonstrate the presence of specular highlights.

As a system of organizing light knowledge, the algorithm draws upon three main historical threads. The observation that light bounces off a shiny surface at the same angle as it approaches was noted in a text on mirrors ascribed to Euclid, the Catoptrics, which had practical applications for those wishing to start fires (Park 1997, 59). The vectors (R), (L) and (N) instantiate this knowledge in the algorithm. The second historical document present in the algorithm – the inverse square law – is drawn from Newton's body of work, and applies to forces in addition to light (such as gravity) that emanate from a point source. The final historical echo is Johann Lambert's cosine law, which describes how the bright a diffuse (matte) surface appears depending on its orientation to a light source, first published in the Photometria from 1760.[12] The dot products, surface constants and vectors represent Lambert's insight in the algorithm. But of course it was Phong's elegant solution that brings the knowledge together in a form that allows a subset of light's behavior and effects to be efficiently demonstrated in computer renderings.

---

12 www.seds.org/~spider/spider/Misc/lambert.html (accessed 9 June 2006).

5 A Preliminary model for organizing light knowledge

The shading algorithm's character as a kind of meta-document gives us clues as to how to begin organizing light knowledge. However, for the algorithm to be truly useful we must expand our model beyond Phong's more limited intention. In insisting on a richer conception of the receiver of light than Phong's simple view vector, we can hope to accommodate more capacious understanding of light's significance and meaning to people. As we have seen in our examples of thought on light from theatre history, night illumination and computer graphics, light documents can be organized by imagining the human body in illuminated space. More particularly, we can examine light documents with respect to the way in which they encode the following kinds of knowledge about light:

a. Knowledge of the body and embodied mind
b. Spatialized knowledge of light
c. Knowledge of light sources
d. Knowledge of surfaces

Knowledge of the body and embodied mind obviously incorporates everything we know about perception and psychology, the visual and non-visual effects of light, our ways of thinking about light and its associations. Spatialized knowledge of light behavior informs our understanding of how light reverberates through a space, and, as we have seen in our survey of writings on light, can be extracted from graphic materials or encoded in algorithms – as Phong did – through the language of vectors. Knowledge of light sources encompasses everything we can observe and conceive about the sources themselves, often expressed through measurements such as color temperature and photometric readings, but also able to accommodate our poetic and artistic understanding. Finally, our knowledge of surfaces, so important to our evolutionary development and survival (Gibson 1987), accommodates both our tacit knowledge of things and all the ways we have developed to describe, represent and make surfaces. Obviously, many types of documents encode more than one type of light knowledge, so the model is something less than a rigorous taxonomy, but at least it can begin to help organize discussions about light between those who care about it.

6 Conclusion

Anyone proposing to reorganize existing knowledge structures has the burden of demonstrating the potential benefits of the task. I would argue that cutting a fresh cross-section through existing knowledge structures will have the benefit of bringing lighting practitioners and lighting documents into conversation with one another in a way that does not privilege existing disciplinary practices. A quick survey of current lighting design and research shows a range of recording practices. Cinematography and film lighting still exhibit a guild-like organization in which light knowledge is often tacit and passed from masters (or directors of photography) to apprentices (grips, gaffers, camera operators, etc). There is in effect no such thing as "cinematography research". Much of the lighting knowledge of great cinematographers inheres only in their film work, and accessing that knowledge is a very different task from, say, reading the sort of documents that emerge from the current scientific research on light. It is the aim of a study of light documents to facilitate the transfer of light knowledge from one group to another. The potential benefit of this transfer would be the application of light knowledge to new domains of illumination practice, with the goal of enriching our experience of light in our daily lives. It is through this sort of exchange that light can fulfill its potential as the construction material of the 21st century.

7 References

Bolter, Jay David, and Richard Grusin, 1999. *Remediation: Understanding New Media.* Cambridge, MA: MIT Press.

Boone, Mary, 1997. Jean Rosenthal's Light: Making Visible the Magician. *Theatre Topics* 7:1(1997), 77-92.

Clair, Louis, 2000. Ecrire la lumiere: De l'analyse du contexte au projet d'eclairage. *L'Architecture d'Aujourdhui* (Nov.-Dec. 2000), 110-128.

Gibson, James, 1987. *The Ecological Approach to Visual Perception.* New Jersey: Erlbaum Associates.

Graves, R.B., 1999. *Lighting the Shakespearean Stage.* Carbondale, IL: Southern Illinois Press.

Howes, David ed., 2005. *Empire of the Senses: The Sensual Culture Reader.* Oxford: Berg Press.

Lund, Niels Windfeld, 1999. Documentation Studies is close to LIS, but not quite the same! On the scientific and educational approaches in the Tromso curriculum for Librarianship. In *New Fields for Research in the 21st Century. Proceedings of the 3rd British-Nordic Conference on Library and Information Studies, 12-14 April, 1999, Borås, Sweden*, eds. M. Klasson, B. Loughridge, and S. Lööf. Borås: The Swedish School of Library and Information Studies, University College of Borås, 43-48.

------. 2004. Documentation in a Complementary Perspective. In *Aware and responsible: Papers of the Nordic-International Colloquium on Social and Cultural Awareness and Responsibility in Library, Information and Documentation Studies (SCARLID)*, ed. W. B. Rayward. Lanham, Md.: Scarecrow Press, 93-102.

McLuhan, Marshall, 1998. *Understanding Media.* Cambridge, MA: MIT Press.

University of Manchester notes on Computer Rendering, 2006. Online: http://www.sve.man.ac.uk/mvc/ (accessed 30 November 2006).

Park, David, 1997. *The Fire within the Eye*. Princeton, NJ: Princeton University Press.

Phong, Bui, 1975. Illumination for Computer Generated Pictures. *Communications of the ACM*, June 1975, 311-317.

Snow, Charles Percy, 1993. *The Two Cultures*. Cambridge: Cambridge University Press.

Maribeth Back, Daniel Billsus, Laurent Denoue, and David Hilbert

Designing and Using Complex Document Sharing Spaces: A Research Vision of Next-Generation Conference Rooms

1 Introduction

In the latter half of the twentieth century two visionary scientists wrote seminal papers that would drive the work of thousands of researchers. In "As We May Think" Vannevar Bush proposed a "memory extender" or "Memex" that has famously informed such inventions as hypertext, the Internet, and the World Wide Web (Bush 1945). Nearly fifty years later, Mark Weiser's vision of an everyday environment permeated with hundreds of small, wireless, interconnected computers created the field of ubiquitous computing (Weiser 1991, 1993). Weiser extended Bush's idea to include distributed hardware, and described how intricately networked systems impact not only on information design but also upon the design of physical spaces and objects. These two streams of work – Weiser's ubiquitous computing/pervasive information model of physical and mobile spaces, and Vannevar Bush's vision of artificial memory enhancement and information management – meet and intertwine in the design of smart environments for the workplace.

In particular, the conference room (or classroom, in the case of educational workplaces) is a nexus of information sharing, via documents or in real-life exchanges. Capturing and re-using the live content of meetings remains an open research issue. At the same time, next-generation conference rooms are often designed to anticipate new rich media presentation and ideation systems. Throughout the past couple of decades, many researchers have attempted to reinvent the conference room, aiming at shared online or visual/virtual spaces, smart tables or walls, mobile device integration, rich media support and teleconferencing systems of varying complexity. Current high-end room systems often emphasize high functionality, offering a multiplicity of thin, bright display screens (both large and small), along with interactive whiteboards, robotic/automatic cameras, and smart remote conferencing systems. (Liao et al. 2003; Liu et al. 2004; MacIntyre et al. 2001). Smart spaces and interactive furniture design projects have shown systems embedded in tables, podiums, walls, chairs and even floors and lighting. (Ishii and Ullmer 1997; Johanson, Fox, and Winograd 2002). Researchers at labs such as the MIT Media Lab and the Aware Home project at Georgia Tech (among others) have built smart networked objects, including interactive furniture, for home, personal and business environments (Omojola et al. 2000; Kidd 1999).

Added into the mix one can find a variety of meeting capture and metadata management systems, some automatic and some not, focused on capturing different aspects of meetings in different media: to the Web, to one's PDA or phone, or to a company database (Denoue et al. 2005; Mukhopadhyay and Smith 1999). Data flow and document management systems can be personalized or keyed to members of a particular group (Hilbert et al. 2005).

Exploiting the capabilities of all these technologies at one time, however, is a daunting task. For example, faced with three or more display screens for presentations, all but a few expert-level presenters are likely to opt for simply replicating the same image on all of the screens. If live annotations are written onto the slides during the meeting, what then happens to those annotations? Who "owns" them – that is, where do the digital copies of those documents wind up? How should the meeting's content be captured, stored, and retrieved for later consultation? Who determines what content is vital, and what is simply noise – too much meaningless detail?

In this chapter, we look at one research lab's integrated approach to this work. FXPAL (a multimedia research lab in Palo Alto, California) has been working on new document types and methods for handling them for more than a decade. The research process involves designing, prototyping and testing systems in our lab, and sometimes in other places as well, such as local universities and research institutes. Researchers often begin by observing users and envisioning how technology might support peoples' activities; then they build and deploy working prototypes to observe these ideas in use. This has produced numerous insights regarding document sharing and meeting room systems, their effects on users, and the social contexts in which they are embedded. The work we present here is specifically focused on rethinking methods for retrieval, presentation/use, archiving, and re-purposing of different kinds of documents within a corporate setting.

2 Function Follows Form: Smart Furnishings for Next-Generation Rooms

The design challenge in smart meeting room environments is how to choose which capabilities are vital to particular tasks, at a particular time or for a particular room, or are well suited to a particular person, within a particular culture, and then how to deliver those capabilities anywhere, anytime, in a highly usable – and useful – package. People increasingly expect to find the adaptable ease of use that they get from their personal devices in all the technology they encounter; how can designers leverage that expectation? We have been exploring the intersection of physical design of display spaces with embedded-systems furnishings that function as controllers for these smart spaces.

Rich media is usually understood to mean a combination of static and dynamic images and text, including teleconferencing and multimedia documents available locally or remotely. As displays become larger and more ubiquitous, the uses and designs of rich media will also change. How can we comfortably control, for example, three parallel video streams, along with presentation slides and a live remote presenter? What kind of content maps well into such a rich environment? How do local participants interact with the information they see projected around them, and how do remote participants interact with the same information?

Research shows that engaging, media-rich meeting experiences can increase both knowledge transfer and knowledge retention (Mayer 2001). The incorporation of media-rich engagement strategies in meetings creates a need to provide meeting participants with appropriate tools for managing these media – and ways to capture and reuse the meeting's content. In this section we describe our two most recent systems for rich media control in meeting rooms: the Convertible Podium, and the USE smart environments system.

2.1 The Convertible Podium: An Experiment in Smart Furniture Design

The incorporation of media-rich engagement strategies in meetings creates a need to provide the presenter with appropriate tools for managing these media. The Convertible Podium is a central control station for rich media document manipulation, including multi-screen multimedia presentation, shared annotation, and digital multimedia support for teleconferencing (Back et al. 2006). Designed for intelligent meeting support and capture, it is an intuitive, easily operated waystation for directing digital information. It is a valuable tool that can allow presenters to easily create and integrate rich media experiences into their work. It is also an experiment in integrating physical design and form with rich media functionality.

The compact, lightweight, mobile design provides multiple functionalities by converting its form. It converts from an rich media presentation podium to other functions including document capture, avatar representation for a remote presenter, and an interactive whiteboard. An important design imperative is that all hardware and software device controls are integrated into the structure of the podium. Similar to multi-purpose furniture or "Roomware" (Streitz 1998) the Convertible Podium combines its affordances as a regular podium with the capabilities of other presentation devices while maintaining its primary form and usefulness as a podium.

The Podium provides a focal point for the attention of the meeting and directs information in as many directions as required – both locally and remotely, via internet or intranet. It allows one person to manage multiple documents and streams of information directed to or from the conference room, or to multiple displays within the room. The Podium also controls the room environment: lights, sound, and projector controls.

A major criterion in this podium design is a form factor that is both elegant and functional. We also wanted to create an article of smart furniture with physical dynamics – that changed its physical shape as well as digital content. In this "transformer" metaphor, current functionality is mapped to the physical state of the object: function follows form.

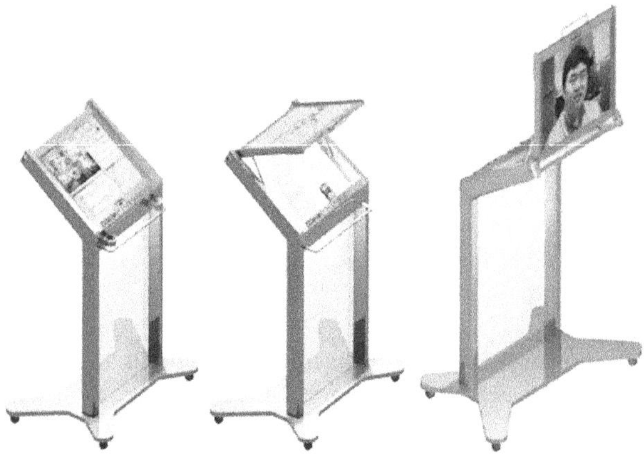

(A) (B) (C)

Figure 1. Design sketch: a convertible podium converting from a touch-screen podium (A), to a document-capturing device (B), to an upright mode that can be used for an avatar representation of a remote presenter, an interactive whiteboard, or an information board (C)

2.1.1 "But Where Do I Put My Laptop?"

Though the Podium is deliberately designed as a post-laptop device, it allows the use of many kinds of external and mobile devices including laptops, PDAs, cell phones, and portable USB/FireWire drives. Or, through the use of a smart-card RFID application called AnySpot (Hilbert and Trevor 2004) one's personal files can be securely uploaded from any networked computer on the LAN.

Mode 1: Presentation and performance. The Podium uses ePic, a rich media presentation application, as its primary presentation mode for showing slides, Web, video or other media [Liu et el. 2004]. Live annotation is available via touch screen (using finger or pen). Any image can be transferred to any screen with a flick of the finger across the touch screen; alternatively a sequence of slides and media can be pre-programmed to execute across any number of screens, in any order.

Mode 2: Capturing images and data. Digital images and real-time video demos are captured via onboard scanner and document camera. Images can be directed to room screens, to nearby or remote printers, or filed in a class-meeting media database.

Modes 3 and 4: Avatar/interactive whiteboard. Avatar/telepresence mode supports human-scale video avatars for teleconferencing. In an effort to enliven the static talking-head video image most people associate with online learning or videoconferencing, the Podium's avatar/telepresence mode features a life-sized, center-screen image of a remote presenter's face. The image appears on the Podium's LCD screen when it is fully upright, appearing there at approximately human head height, and can also appear on one of the room screens if desired. Remote presenters can control rich media multi-screen presentations from their remote locations, and interact with meeting participants via high-quality video and audio streaming. Networked interactive whiteboard and annotation systems with the Podium in upright mode enable local or long-distance group work such as planning, brainstorming and discussion. The drawing mode can also be accessed with the Podium's "hood" closed, so that a live presenter can draw on the touchscreen and show the drawing on room displays.

The Convertible Podium is an experimental system designed for one particular conference room (the Kumo conference room at FXPAL). As such, it is designed to match the meeting practices of one group of highly technical people, in a very specific space (a research space with a number of bleeding-edge technologies including multiple screens, automatic room controls, and an automatic meeting capture system and camera control system already installed). In contrast, our next system (USE) is designed for anyone to be able to "walk in and use" – including very busy, not necessarily technically oriented people such as high-level executives.

2.2 Usable Smart Environments: The USE Conference Room Project

Much of the smart conferencing work throughout the past two decades has focused on high functionality, usually systems that must be operated by technology experts (aka "wizards"). To date, nearly all "smart" rooms have these resident experts, who keep the room's systems functioning, and who often must be available on an everyday basis just to enable people to use the room. The systems in these rooms are designed for and assume the presence of these human "wizards"; they are seldom designed with users' activities in mind. In addition, people don't know what to expect in these rooms; as yet there is no technology standard for next-generation conference rooms.

The USE (Usable Smart Environments) project starts from a usability standpoint, with the aim of creating a "wizard-free" conference room: designed for ease of use, yet retaining next-generation functionality. Our first version of this system incorporates multi-display systems, local and remote document sharing and annotation, teleconferencing, and secure authentication (Back et al. 2006). The operational design is based in cross-cultural ethnographic studies on the way people actually use conference rooms; the first studies we did were on the meeting practices of an American CEO and a Japanese CEO.

In this project we focus on the fact that people enter conference rooms to create and maintain relations with each other, not to use the technology. This focus leads us to integrate the separate pieces of technology to support the natural activities of people meeting in the room, without giving them the added burden of making the technology work. The challenge here is to strike an effective balance between usability and new kinds of functionality (such as multiple displays, new interfaces, rich media systems, new uploading/access/security systems, robust mobile integration). The USE project has developed a flexible, extensible interface and architecture specifically designed to enhance ease of use in smart environment technologies. The architecture allows customization and personalization of smart environments for particular people and groups, types of work, and specific physical spaces.

USE rooms are designed as physical "smart spaces" designed to allow people to interact easily with highly functional meeting tools, including new kinds of document services. Particularly appropriate in the new smart conference room environment are "corporate memory" technologies, such as the personalization services and knowledge capture and retrieval systems FXPAL has been developing; these are described below.

3 Pervasive and Personalized Information Access: AnySpot and PIPs

In the early 1990s, Mark Weiser envisioned a world in which "each person is continually interacting with hundreds of nearby wirelessly interconnected computers" (Weiser 1993) which ultimately "weave themselves into the fabric of everyday life until they are indistinguishable from it" (Weiser 1991). A key component of this vision is pervasive information: being able to utilize any content or service, using devices that are always at hand, over networks that don't tie us down. While we have come a long way toward this ideal, seamlessly accessing and sharing documents while mobile remains challenging.

Our goal was to develop a novel pervasive document platform that would bring us closer to Mark Weiser's vision by simultaneously addressing the following pervasive information needs:

Weaving into the fabric of everyday life. We wanted to provide powerful pervasive information capabilities while minimizing impact on users and organizations. This meant we did not want to assume users would adopt new storage practices (e.g., web repositories), operating systems (e.g., distributed file systems), or special client technology (e.g., VPN client software or thin client devices).

Fast personalized access. We wanted to help people find their files quickly. In mobile scenarios where users are under time pressure and are using portable and embedded devices with limited user interfaces – such as mobile phones and office copiers – personalization can dramatically reduce the need for browsing and searching, greatly speeding access.

Portable and embedded interfaces. Supporting pervasive information access means realizing that users will not always have a laptop or desktop close at hand. This implies the need for a wide variety of interfaces for both portable devices (e.g., cell phones) and embedded devices (e.g., office copiers).

Thus, we developed AnySpot, a web service-based platform for seamlessly connecting people to their personal and shared documents wherever they go. AnySpot goes beyond existing systems by providing fast personalized access to documents stored in a variety of existing file systems, through a variety of portable and embedded interfaces.

3.1 Weaving into the Fabric of Everyday Life

In order to support people's existing work practices without requiring them to adopt new storage systems, operating systems, or client interfaces, we developed web service wrappers for existing file systems that provide a standard interface for important file access functions such as *GetFiles* and *GetHistory.* While in the office, users access their files as always. But once they leave the office, AnySpot extends secure access to users' files and history to other devices and networks.

3.2 Fast Personalized Access

In our previous work on personalizing shared document devices, we observed that mobile users were often in a hurry when accessing their files, and typically wanted to access the same files they had most recently accessed while in the office (Hilbert and Trevor 2004). Thus, AnySpot collects users' file histories to form a "personal information cloud" interface (Figure 2), that allows mobile user to quickly access their most recently accessed files. This dramatically reduces the need for searching and browsing.

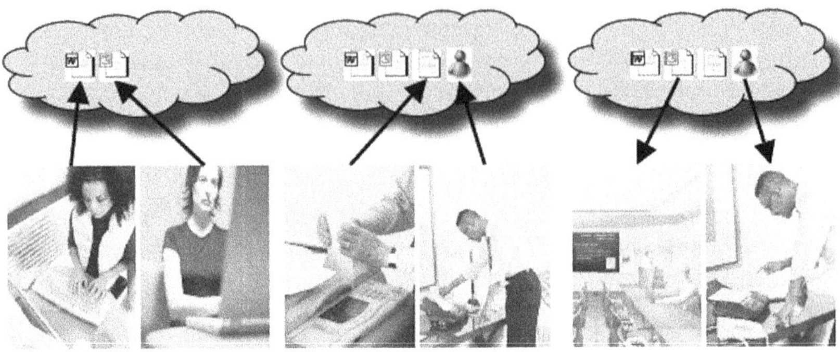

Figure 2. Personal information clouds are populated by data we touch throughout the day (left). They are also populated when we use non-traditional computing devices, such as copiers or fax machines (center). Our information clouds can then be used to personalize and augment the capabilities of existing shared devices, such as podium PCs and fax machines (right).

3.3 Portable and Embedded Interfaces

Because our web services architecture allowed us to separate the system logic from the user interface, we were able to develop a wide variety of specialized interfaces on top of our platform. For instance, the Personal Interaction Points (PIPs) system (Hilbert and Trevor 2004) now leverages AnySpot to allow users to walk up to any PIPs-enabled presentation device in an organization identify themselves using a smart card, and instantly present files directly from their "personal information cloud". We also integrated third-party document services to allow cell phone users to print (NetPrint) and fax (InterFax) their documents from their cell phones, extending our previous work on network-based services for extending cell phone capabilities (Schilit et al. 2002).

Our experience with anySpot suggests that web services can provide a compelling framework for personalization and for pervasive computing. They allow independently developed systems to be combined in non-anticipated ways. The ability to cleanly separate logic and interfaces allows novel clients to be built quickly to support portable and embedded applications. The ability to easily connect services allows devices with limited capabilities (like mobile phones) to leverage more powerful networked services for increased capabilities (like faxing and printing).

4 Creating and Using Corporate Memory: ProjectorBox and PalBar

In a landmark article, over a half century ago, Vannevar Bush envisioned a "Memory Extender" device he dubbed the "Memex" (Bush 1945). Bush's ideas anticipated and inspired numerous breakthroughs, including hypertext, the Internet, the World Wide Web, and Wikipedia. However, despite these triumphs, the memex has still not lived up to its potential in corporate settings. One reason is that corporate users often don't have sufficient time or incentives to contribute to a corporate memory or to explore others' contributions. We are investigating ways to automatically create and retrieve useful corporate memories without any added burden on anyone. In this section we discuss how ProjectorBox – a smart appliance for automatic presentation capture – and PAL Bar – a system for proactively retrieving contextually relevant corporate memories – have enabled us to integrate content from a variety of sources to create a cohesive multimedia corporate memory for our organization.

Corporate memory has been a hot topic in management and computer science since at least the early 1990s. Despite great interest in technologies to help organizations leverage past experience, expertise, and other collective resources, in practice, corporate memories often fall short of expectations. There are numerous challenges in developing effective corporate memories, including problems in asset capture, representation, retrieval, and reuse. For instance, most people will not do extra work to contribute to a corporate memory without proper incentives, particularly when the benefits accrue to someone else at some later time. Fortunately, many organizations already produce useful information that can be hosted on corporate intranets and tapped for corporate memory purposes. However, given the variety of available information and users in even a moderately sized organization, it becomes extremely difficult for employees to stay abreast of all the potentially useful information that may be helpful at any given time. This problem is exacerbated by the fact that sources of corporate information are often heterogeneous and distributed. Users must not only realize that there may be useful corporate information relevant to their current task, but they must know where to look, and possibly consult multiple sources.

Problems of resource discovery and information overload have plagued us for some time on the World Wide Web. With so many online resources available to us, how can we stay abreast of all the potentially useful information without spending all our time searching and filtering? In a corporate setting, these problems have palpable costs. When we are unaware of relevant information and human resources, the quality, efficiency, and satisfaction of our work suffers. When separate corporate units are unaware of one another's activities and expertise, they unnecessarily duplicate work.

The goal of FXPAL's research on Corporate Memory is to produce technology for more effective knowledge capture and utilization. We are investigating techniques that allow employees to contribute and access information seamlessly, i.e. without significant usage overhead. We believe that this can be accomplished by making both information capture and retrieval part of established work practices. For example, giving a presentation in a conference room, bookmarking a web page or sending email to a colleague are activities that result in corporate content that can be captured automatically. Similarly, activities such as accessing a web page or an email message can be interpreted as an implicit expression of an information need, which allows us to retrieve potentially relevant information proactively, i.e. without explicit user requests.

ProjectorBox, an autonomous presentation capture appliance, indexes virtually every presentation and meeting in our corporate conference room, allowing video segments to be retrieved based on content (Denoue et al. 2005). And PAL Bar, our proactive retrieval system, brings together content from these heterogeneous sources into a unified multimedia corporate memory (Billsus et al. 2005).

4.1 Seamless Presentation Capture: ProjectorBox

Presentations are ubiquitous. But presentation archives are rare due to the cost of purchasing, setting-up, and using current recording technology. As a result, useful information passes through projectors all the time and is lost.

Current approaches assume that presenters, facility operators, or audience members will adjust their practices to garner the benefits of automatic presentation capture. In our experience, even the most modest assumptions – e.g., that presenters will use specific software, upload their files, or start and stop recordings – are unrealistic. ProjectorBox is our attempt to create a presentation capture solution that users can simply "plug-in and forget".

ProjectorBox captures, indexes, and archives presentation slides and audio without any user input. It is an RGB-based appliance that intercepts video information as it is sent from presentation devices, such as a presenter's laptop, to display devices, such as a projector. This means it can capture content from any presentation device – including a non-preconfigured guest presenter's laptop – running any presentation software. It goes beyond existing approaches by automatically creating easily searchable and skimmable archives.

Despite their advantages, RGB-based solutions introduce considerable challenges. In order to automatically produce high-quality archives suitable for browsing, retrieval, and reuse, an RGB-based solution must infer high-level information from the video signal. For instance, the system must: (a) distinguish between presentation and non-presentation content, (b) detect boundaries between contiguous presentations to structure content for browsing and retrieval, and (c) extract text to support content-based retrieval. We now briefly discuss how we address these challenges.

4.1.1 Detection of Presentation Content

Our first challenge was to automatically separate presentation content from non-presentation content. For example, when recording a presentation, we would like to exclude images of the desktop and the presenter selecting the presentation file and starting the presentation software. We address this problem using an automated image classification approach. As a first approximation to identifying presentation content, we focused on identifying slides. We apply commercially available optical character recognition (OCR) to extract the text from images, and use the text bounding box heights as the main feature for classification. The intuition is that most presentation slides use larger fonts than typically appear on a computer desktop or in other applications. As a result, text bounding box heights are a useful cue for detecting slide images. The resulting classifier can reliably distinguish between presentation and non-presentation content (Hilbert et al. 2005).

4.1.2 Presentation Segmentation

Because ProjectorBox may run continuously in a room used by multiple people for multiple presentations, we also needed to automatically detect presentation boundaries to allow them to be browsed and retrieved as cohesive units. We adopted a time-based approach in which presentation boundaries are defined whenever the elapsed time between two successive slide images exceeds a user-definable threshold (e.g., 20 minutes). This approach emphasizes precision in segmentation over recall. That is, adjacent presentations may be erroneously grouped together, but a single presentation is rarely erroneously split into multiple presentations. We make it easy for users to manually adjust presentation boundaries.

4.1.3 Presentation Retrieval

Finally, users want to retrieve presentations based on content and access captured media non-linearly, as opposed to having to play through it sequentially (Abowd 2000, Chiu et al. 2000). We use optical character recognition (OCR) to extract text from slide images and create a full-text index so users can retrieve slides based on content. Our slide skimming and playback interfaces allow users to easily skim and skip around presentation content non-linearly.

4.1.4 User Interfaces

ProjectorBox's web interface supports two methods for quickly retrieving content. The main page (Figure 3) shows a list of dates and times in a calendar-like list, indicating when content has been captured. If the date and time of a specific presentation is known, this page provides a single-click solution to presentation retrieval.

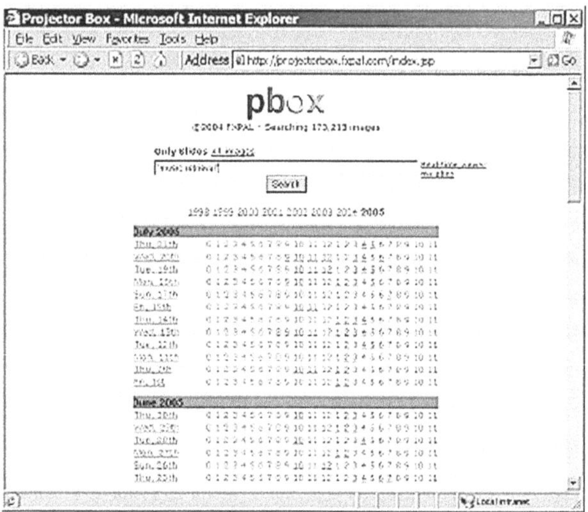

Figure 3. The main page.

The main page also provides full-text search of all captured presentations, allowing users to retrieve slides by content. The search results page (Figure 4) shows matching slides organized by date. Moving the mouse over a slide shows an enlarged version with the matching query terms automatically highlighted in yellow, and plays back the associated audio clip.

When the user clicks on a date or time or clicks on a slide in the search results, the day viewer page (Figure 5) shows thumbnail images of slides captured that day. Here, too, moving the mouse over a slide shows an enlarged version and plays the associated audio clip. This page makes it easy for users to skim around presentations to locate slides or segments of interest. Double-clicking on an image brings up a slide player for playing back content sequentially or skipping backward and forward through slides.

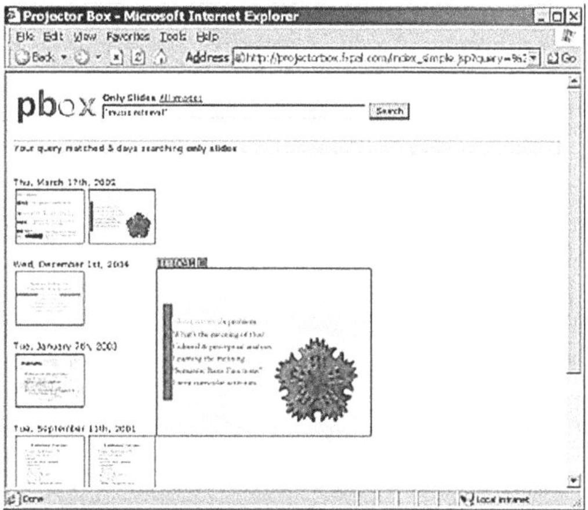

Figure 4. The search results page.

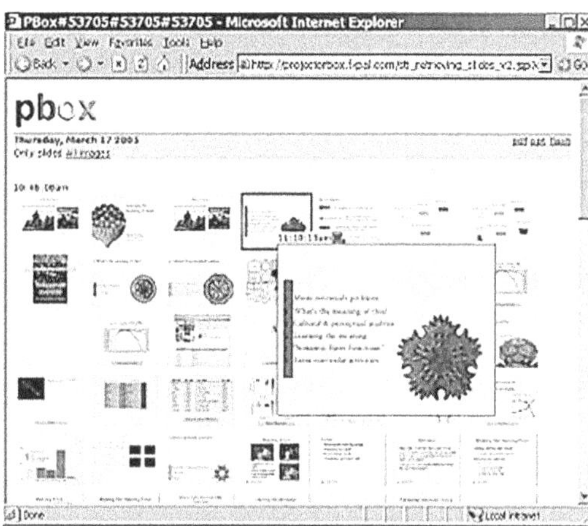

Figure 5. The day viewer page.

In a user study we found our results supported our initial vision and design decisions; ProjectorBox was both easy to use and useful (Hilbert et al. 2005). Automatic slide and audio capture helped users review missed presentations and stay informed about "what's going on" within the organization. Our users expressed a desire for more support to find personally relevant presentations they missed and to stay aware of what was going on in the organization. We have since begun investigating new services that leverage ProjectorBox's archive to bring relevant information to users' attention. These include awareness and proactive retrieval interfaces, as well as content-based browsing for information discovery. In the following section we discuss FXPAL's proactive retrieval system.

4.2 Seamless Content Discovery: PAL BAR

PAL Bar is a proactive contextual retrieval tool, specifically designed to support seamless access to relevant corporate content. In the following sections we briefly review the system's recommendation UIs, its architecture, and the recommendation algorithm. In addition, we show how the combination of seamless capture technology, such as ProjectorBox, and seamless discovery technology, such as PAL Bar, has enabled a fully integrated multi-media corporate memory system that supports capture and discovery of content without any added burden on anyone.

PAL Bar's main purpose is to proactively recommend content related to the user's "context", such as a currently displayed web page or email message. The concept of contextual proactive information retrieval is not new (Budzik et al. 2001; Rhodes 2000), but unlike other systems in this field, PAL Bar was specifically designed for corporate information access: as described in the algorithm outline below, PAL Bar's recommendation algorithm utilizes information about the organization. In addition, PAL Bar supports multiple alternative recommendation interfaces, allowing users to choose between more or less subtle ways of being notified about corporate resources.

4.2.1 Recommendation UIs

PAL Bar is a toolbar for web browsers and is currently available for MS Internet Explorer and Mozilla FireFox. Its initial design was quite simple, consisting of only four buttons and a search text field (Figure 6).

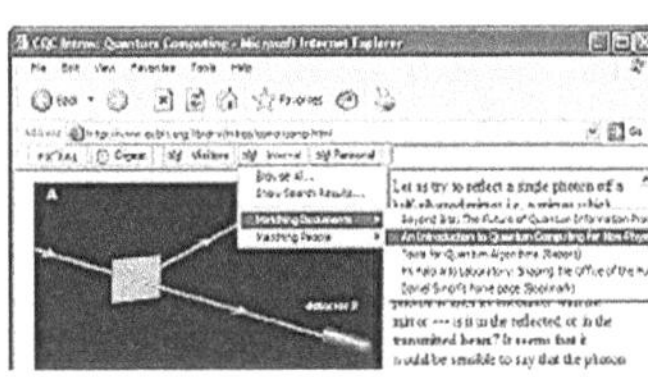

Figure 6: PAL Bar's Initial Recommendation Interface

The three right-most buttons acted as the system's first recommendation interface: these *recommendation buttons* are typically grayed out, but change color (from gray to red) when the system recommends resources related to the currently displayed web page. When the user clicks on a red button, the system shows a drop-down menu containing lists of recommended resources. Clearly, this interface was subtle and unobtrusive. However, its recommendations were almost universally ignored. Based on a small-scale user study conducted at FXPAL, we designed and implemented three additional user interfaces: *translucent recommendation windows*, a *SideBar* interface and an email-based *recommendation digest* that the system periodically sends to PAL Bar users.

4.2.2 Translucent Recommendation Windows

Our initial recommendation interface was so subtle that our users tended to forget that it was there. We decided to occasionally display recommendation notification windows in cases in which the system judged a recommendation to be of exceptionally high quality. Recommendation windows are small, partially transparent windows that fade in on the corner of the user's screen, similar in style to the translucent email notification windows in Outlook 2003. The windows display a link to the recommended document, the document type, and the generated query terms. Users can also resize the windows to taste to show a document preview consisting of snippets extracted from the document, with the query terms highlighted. For example, the web page displayed in 7 generated the recommendation window shown in 8. Recommendation windows automatically fade away after a short delay unless the mouse cursor is moved over them. There is, of course, a fine line between making our recommendations more noticeable and making them overly invasive or annoying. We addressed this by making our window design small and understated and making the relevance threshold for triggering a window quite high. A follow-up user study at FXPAL revealed that the recommendation windows led to a significant increase in accessed content, but several users stated that PAL Bar had become more distracting. In addition, the recommendation windows did not address the fact that users may be engaged in other tasks and may therefore not want to interact with the window or recommended content right away. The following two interfaces address this issue.

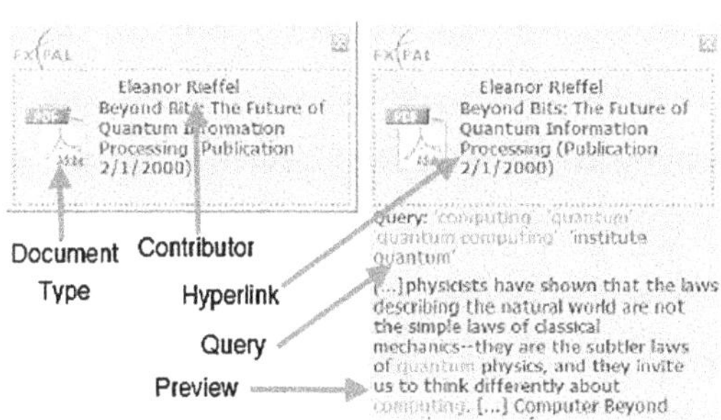

Figure 7: Translucent Recommendation Windows

4.2.3 Sidebar Recommendations

The Sidebar interface is similar, in principle, to the recommendation windows, i.e. particularly relevant recommendations are immediately brought to the user's attention. However, instead of rendering recommendations in a separate window that appears and disappears proactively, recommendations are added to a *Sidebar* interface that remains constantly visible on the right side of the screen. When the user clicks on a recommendation, the Sidebar opens a window similar to the one shown in Figure 7. In summary, this interface does not force users to interact with recommendations right away: recommendations do not fade away after a few seconds, i.e. users can access them whenever they have time to do so. Arguably, the interface is also less obtrusive than the recommendation windows, because the Sidebar only updates its content, but its size and appearance remains unchanged.

4.2.4 Recommendation Digest

The recommendation digest is different from all three interfaces described above: it does not proactively bring recommendations to the user's attention. Instead, the digest is a document that lists particularly relevant recommendations the user might have previously missed. By clicking the digest button (see Figure 6), users can request digests that contain a subset of the recommendations presented during the preceding hour, day, or week. Alternatively, users can request that digests be sent periodically via email. Most PAL Bar users currently receive an automatically generated digest document once a week.

To determine which recommendations to include in the digest, we use a recommendation aggregation approach designed to restrict digests to only the most relevant information. The intuition underlying this process is that items that were recommended multiple times to the same user over a specified period of time (potentially based on multiple different contexts) are more likely to be related to the user's information needs or interests than items that were recommended infrequently or only based on a small number of visited pages.

5 Seamless Media Capture and Discovery

PAL Bar, when integrated with seamless capture technology such as ProjectorBox, leads to a compelling end-to-end corporate memory solution that supports seamless media capture and discovery without any added burden on anyone. The scenario described here exemplifies the core idea that is driving our research on corporate memory and automated information dissemination: knowledge capture and reuse as byproducts of established everyday work practices.

UbiSight is an FXPAL system that automatically records videos of presentations or meetings, based on motion and audio tracking. Since *UbiSight* does not capture any textual content, retrieval of automatically recorded videos is challenging. However, *ProjectorBox* addresses this problem: since *ProjectorBox* stores the exact time of every recorded slide, the resulting index can be used to locate video segments that correspond to displayed slides. In short, ProjectorBox serves as a full-text slide *and* video index.

This means that in addition to textual documents, PAL Bar is now able to recommend automatically recorded meetings and presentations. For example, consider a scenario where a researcher at FXPAL visits a web page about "collaborative filtering". Based on the text of this page, PAL Bar proactively generates a query that retrieves a set of corporate documents related to this topic. Figure 8 shows how the Sidebar interface renders such a set of recommendations. The first recommendation in this set is a presentation that was automatically recorded by *UbiSight* and *ProjectorBox*. In the scenario shown in Figure 8, the user selected this presentation, causing the Sidebar to display a recommendation window that allows the user to browse and access individual slides.

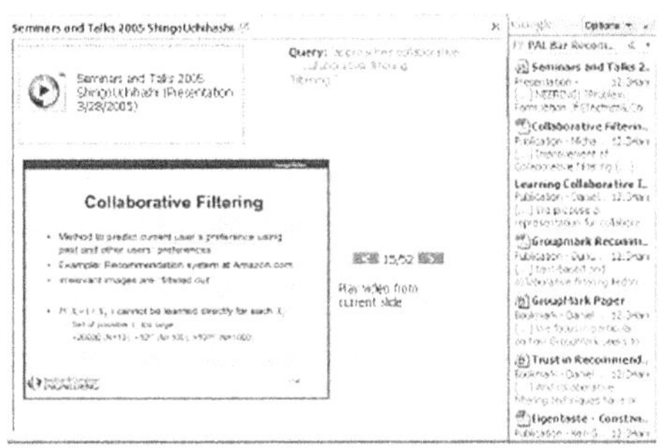

Figure 8: Sidebar and a Selected Recommendation

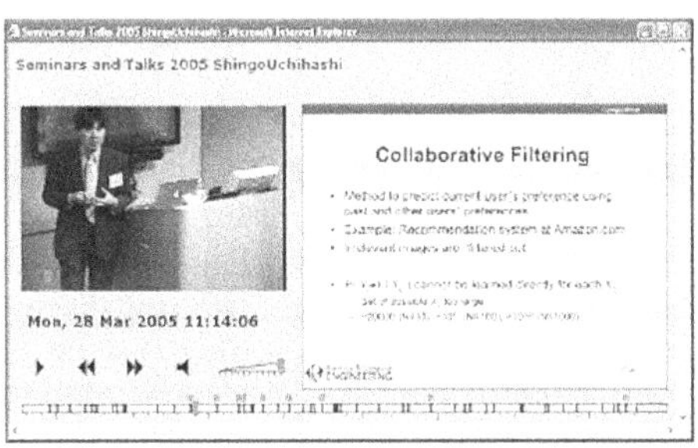

Figure 9: Corporate Memory Media Player

Since the system also has access to corresponding *UbiSight* video, the user can start FXPAL's video and slide player to play back the recommended presentation (starting at the currently displayed slide). Figure 9 shows FXPAL's corporate memory media player: video is played back on the left side of the window, while corresponding slides are shown on the right side. The timeline at the bottom of the window allows users to see slide transitions (vertical bars) and to navigate to any slide. Slides that match the user's original context, in this case a web page on "collaborative filtering" are considered particularly relevant and are marked with bold squares above the timeline.

In summary, the integration of *PAL Bar*, *ProjectorBox* and *UbiSight* enabled a powerful corporate memory system for completely seamless information capture and discovery. While a formal evaluation of the utility of the system integration will be the subject of future work, we feel that we are one step closer to realizing Vannevar Bush's Memex vision for organizations: we have built a fully automated "Corporate Memex".

6 Conclusion

We have presented a set of research technologies for creating, sharing and retrieving knowledge within a corporate setting. Ranging from the integration of physical design for rich media control to personalization of a pervasive computing environment and the automatic capture and retrieval of information, these systems have enabled us to integrate content from a variety of sources to create a cohesive multimedia corporate memory for our organization. The system integration and usage scenarios described in this paper exemplify the core ideas that are driving our research: a union of the visions of both Mark Weiser (ubiquitous computing) and Vannevar Bush (the Memex).

7 References

Abowd, Gregory D., 1999. Classroom 2000: An experiment with the instrumentation of a living educational environment. *IBM Systems Journal* 38, 508-530.

Back, Maribeth J., Surapong Lertsithichai, Patrick Chiu, Jonathan Foote, Don Kimber, John Boreckzy, Qiong Liu, Frank Zhao, and Tadashi Matsumoto, 2005. The Convertible Podium: A rich media teaching tool for next-generation classrooms. *Proceedings of ACM SIGGRAPH 2005*. ACM Press: Los Angeles, CA.

Back, Maribeth J., Gene Golovchinsky, John Boreczky, Pernilla Qvarfordt, Anthony Dunnigan, and Laurent Denoue, 2006. The USE Project: Designing Smart Spaces for Real People. Workshop position paper. *Proceedings of the Eighth International Conference on Ubiqutious Computing (UbiComp 2006)*. San Diego, CA.

Billsus, Daniel, David M. Hilbert, and Dan Maynes-Aminzade, 2005. Improving Proactive Information Systems. *Proceedings of the Tenth International Conference on Intelligent User Interfaces*. San Diego, CA, 159-166.

Budzik, Jay, Kristian Hammond, and Larry Birnbaum, 2005. Information Access in Context. *Knowledge-Based Systems* 14, 37-53.

Bush, Vannevar, 1945. As We May Think. *The Atlantic Monthly*. July 76(1), 101-108.

Chiu, Patrick, Ashutosh Kapuskar, Sarah Reitmeier, and Lynn Wilcox, 2000. Room with a Rear View: Meeting Capture in a Multimedia Conference Room. *IEEE MultiMedia Magazine* 7(4), 48-54.

Churchill, Elizabeth, Les Nelson, Laurent Denoue, Jonathan Helfman, and Paul Murphy, 2004. Sharing Multimedia Content with Interactive Displays: A Case Study. *Proceedings of the 2004 Conference on Designing Interactive Systems*. ACM Press, 7-16.

Cruz, Gil, and Ralph Hill, 1994. Capturing and playing multimedia events with STREAMS. *Proceedings of the Second ACM International Conference on Multimedia*. ACM Press, 193-200.

Denoue, Laurent, David M. Hilbert, John Adcock, Daniel Billsus, and Matthew Cooper, 2005. ProjectorBox: Seamless presentation capture for classrooms. *Proceedings of the World Conference on E-Learning in Corporate, Government, Healthcare, & Higher Education (E-Learn 2005)*. AACE Press, 1986-1991.

Hilbert, David M., and Jonathan Trevor, 2004. Personalizing Shared Ubiquitous Devices. *Interactions* 11(3), 34-43.

Hilbert, David M, Matthew Cooper, Laurent Denoue, John Adcock, and Daniel Billsus, 2005. Seamless presentation capture, indexing, and management. *Proceedings of the International Society for Optical Engineering (Optics East)*. 6015, 305-313.

Ishii, Hiroshi, and Brygg Ullmer, 1997. Tangible Bits: Towards seamless interfaces between people, bits and atoms. *Proceedings of the International Conference on Computer Human Interaction 97*. ACM Press, 234-241.

Johanson, Brad, Armando Fox, and Terry Winograd, 2002. The Interactive Workspaces Project: Experiences with ubiquitous computing rooms. *IEEE Pervasive Computing* 1(2), 67-75.

Kidd, Cory D., Robert Orr, Gregory D. Abowd, Christopher G. Atkeson, Irfan A. Essa, Blair MacIntyre, Elizabeth Mynatt, Thad E. Starner, and Wendy Newstetter, 1999. The Aware Home: A living laboratory for ubiquitous computing research. *Proceedings of CoBuild 99*. Springer-Verlag LNCS 1670, 191-198.

Liao, Chunyuan, Qiong Liu, Don Kimber, Patrick Chiu, Jonathan Foote, and Lynn Wilcox, 2003. Shared interactive video for teleconferencing. *Proceedings of the Eleventh ACM International Conference on Multimedia*. ACM Press, 546-554.

Liu, Qiong, Yong Rui, Anoop Gupta, and JJ Cadiz, 2001. Automating camera management for lecture room environments. *Proceedings of the International Conference on Computer Human Interaction 01*. ACM Press, 442-449.

Liu, Qiong, Frank Zhao, John Doherty, and Don Kimber, 2004. An EPIC enhanced meeting environment, *Proceedings of the Twelfth ACM International Conference on Multimedia (Video Demo)*. ACM Press, 940-941.

Liu, Qiong, Xiaojin Shi, Don Kimber, Frank Zhao, and Frank Raab, 2005. An Online Video Composition System. *IEEE International Conference on Multimedia & Expo*. Amsterdam, The Netherlands, July.

MacIntyre, Blair Elizabeth D. Mynatt, Stephen Voida, Klaus M. Hansen, Joe Tullio, and Gregory M. Corso, 2001. Support for multitasking and background awareness using interactive peripheral displays. *Proceedings of the International Symposium on User Interface Software and Technology 01*. ACM Press, 41-50.

Mayer, Richard E., 2001. *Multimedia Learning*. Cambridge University Press, Cambridge.

Mukhopadhyay, Sugata, and Brian Smith, 1999. Passive capture and structuring of lectures. *Proceedings of the seventh ACM International Conference on Multimedia (Part 1)*. ACM Press, 477-487.

Omojola, Olufemi, Post, E. Rehmi, Matthew D. Hancher, Yael Maguire, Ravikanth Pappu, Bernd Schoner, Peter R. Russo, Richard Fletcher, Neil Gershenfeld, 2000. An installation of interactive furniture. *IBM Systems Journal* 39(3-4), 861-879.

Rhodes, Bradley J., 2000. *Just-In-Time Information Retrieval*. Ph.D. Dissertation. Massachusetts Institute of Technology, Media Lab.

Stallman, Richard M., 1981. EMACS the extensible, customizable self-documenting display editor. *Proceedings of ACM SIGPLAN SIGOA Symposium on Text manipulation*. ACM Press, 147-156.

Streitz, Norbert A., Jörg Geissler, and Torsten Holmer, 1998. Roomware for Cooperative Buildings: Integrated design of architectural spaces and information spaces. *Proceedings of CoBuild 98*. Springer-Verlag LNCS 1370, 4-21.

Trevor, Jonathan, David M. Hilbert, Daniel Billsus, Jim Vaughan, and Quan T. Tran, 2004. Contextual contact retrieval. *Proceedings of the Ninth International Conference on Intelligent User Interfaces*. ACM Press, 337-339.

Weiser, Mark, 1991. The computer for the 21st century. *Scientific American* 265(3), 94-104.

Weiser, Mark, and John Seely Brown, 1993. Some computer science issues in ubiquitous computing. *Communications of the ACM* 36(7), 75-84.

Wood, Kenneth R., Tristan Richardson, Frazer Bennett, Andy Harter, and Andy Hopper, 1997. Global Teleporting with Java: Towards Ubiquitous Personal Computing. *IEEE Computer* 30(2), 53-59.

Carol E.B. Choksy

Contracts: Documents Creating Context[1]

In this study, I will examine written contracts in various settings, as an anthropologist might, to see how they function within a society. If current archaeology and historical interpretation are correct, we learned to write and then to read in order to create, execute, enforce, and dispute contracts. Lawyers will tell you that while the physical document is not the actual contract, the concept represented in it as an enforceable agreement is; but they are observing contracts from the perspective of the law, not from history or anthropology, i.e., how people actually use them.

The document itself plays an important role in "literate" cultures and either continues to exist or reappears even when religion and law do not support it. I will argue that contracts act within a specific context, but also that they represent a particular context. To put it another way, contracts not only refer, they also predicate. Contracts reach out into the environment and shape it, while being shaped. As an utterance, a contract is formulaic, like political oratory, prayers, or charms. This formulism is required to limit responses to it from the environment: from the parties, the scribe, the enforcing authorities, and society in general. I conclude that contracts specifically, and documents generally, assist us to create, define and maintain societies. Society is a documentary society.[2] One axiom of that conclusion is that "literacy" as we understand it, the ability for large segments of the population to read and write, is not necessary for a society to be considered "literate". In explanation, documentary society predates what we call literate society.

If Schmandt-Besserat (1992) is correct, the clay tokens and complex tokens found in many parts of the Ancient Near East represent our first contracts as well as our first attempts at writing. The tokens themselves were eventually encased in a clay

---

1 I would like to thank Debora Shaw of the School of Library and Information Science at Indiana University for her helpful comments.

2 As research has demonstrated, differentiating societies as literate and non-literate does not take into consideration the many forms of literacy. I am not certain calling a society a "documentary" society is much better, but it does serve to distinguish societies like our own that are completely dependent upon documents not attached to our bodies to define who and what we are from societies where documents would be the body, as in circumcision, attached to the body, as with clothing denoting role or social state, or created only occasionally for special purposes, like communicating with deities.

envelope.[3] Then the envelope was imprinted with the contents and signed. The clay envelope became the certification that what was inside was correct and accurate. Legal documents created to enforce the contracts developed along the same lines. The document was written and then put inside an envelope with various seals and notations attesting to the veracity of the document inside. We do not know if there were copies made of early documents or if the documents were registered with the authorities, as this evidence has not survived. The language and content of the contracts was formulaic. For example, Sumerian loan contracts always included commodity and amount, names of the contracting parties with the verb "šu ba-an-ti", and repayment clause (Skaist 1994, 22). Among the Sumerians, documents are called "dub" and the scribe "dub-sar". In Akkadian, documents are called "ṭuppum", whereas in Elamite they used the term "tup-pi". This entered Old Persian as "dipīm" where the scribe was called "dipīvar".

Parthian and Sāsānian 250 BCE to 642 CE contracts, sometimes called "dib", were most often written documents. These were written by a scribe called a "dibīr". After being written they were signed, sealed, witnessed, and registered with the appropriate authorities. Each party received a copy of the contract. To be legal, the document itself had to be dated, had to mention the names of all parties, the value of the goods involved, and a period of time for the contractual obligations to be valid, and it had to be witnessed (Choksy 1998, 194). These were also formulaic in language and required content. The corresponding Greek term for document at this time is "ταβέλλα".

In the Roman world from the time of Constantine's 323 CE constitution, written documents, or "tabulae" including contracts, became more important in the law. Contracts in particular were drawn up by scribes called "tabelliones", who, in some instances could testify to the authenticity of a document if the document had not already been filed in the courts. Justinian's constitution of 528 CE instructed the tabelliones to read the document aloud to the two parties to ensure it reflected what they wanted. Again, the language and content of the contracts is formulaic (Pryor 1981, 6-7).

In contrast, Romano-Visigothic law of the 9th century did not require written documents, but did require contracts be authenticated during the day and before witnesses using a required set of gestures (Pryor 1981, 9; DiMatteo 1998, 76). Later medieval European laws of the 13th century recognized a contract as having been consummated by a handshake and either the paying of "God's penny" to a charity or earnest money. There was no requirement that the deal be made in front of witnesses (Pryor 1981, 14). Some Europeans of the early Middle Ages were comfortable making contracts without writing them down. Even today, verbal

3 http://anthro.binghamton.edu/ Fistikli Web Site/ Images/Photo_Albums/ Shaped-Clay_Photo_Album/pages/ tokens_jpg.htm (accessed 5 December 2006).

contracts are still a recognized form of legal contract. The apparent basis for verbal contractual practices at that time stems from the Church canon law regarding truthfulness as the basis of contracts (Lesaffer 2000, 182), quoting Matthew 5:34-37,

> But I say to you, Do not swear at all, either by heaven, for it is the throne of God, or by the earth, for it is his footstool, or by Jerusalem, for it is the city of the great King. And do not swear by your head, for you cannot make one hair white or black. Let your word be 'Yes, Yes' or 'No, No;' anything more than this comes from the evil one.

Disputes were settled in ecclesiastical courts wherein perjury was considered a serious sin (Lesaffer 2000, 184). The glossators of the 13th to the 16th centuries tried to rationalize the difference between Roman law relying on written contracts and canon law relying on verbal contracts by trying to identify the point at which the contract is made, rather than the difference in their different linguistic statuses, i.e., verbal and written. Clearly, earthly power in the form of a contract did not agree with the Church's city of God. One of our current terms for documents recognized as being important is "record". This is an word whose roots mean "from the heart", which stems from the time in English law when humans were the only witnesses permitted in a court of law. This, of course, changed beginning in the 12th century when documents began being permitted in court (Clanchy 1993).

When Roman law was "rediscovered" in 12th century Europe, so too were written contracts. From this time on in continental Europe, the tabellio was called a "notarius" and the tabula was called a "notula". This shift from our Near Eastern heritage to our Indo-European heritage is curious in that the words for the person drawing up the contract and the contract itself both derive from the Greek "γιγνώσκω" meaning knowledge, learning, or judgment. Hence, a notarius is a person of knowledge, whereas the tabellio was just a scribe, a person who creates a "tab". The Roman world could take writing of contracts for granted because contracts had been written from time immemorial. The medieval European world did not take the writing of contracts for granted, giving them a higher status as reflected by the new name for the scribe and the the document. Pryor, in his *Business Contracts of Medieval Provence,* traces how the notarii of the 12th through the 14th centuries who were re-inventing the contract experimented with different linguistic formulations, eventually settling on the pre-existing language of Roman law (Pryor 1981, 22-27).

Medieval Muslim contracts at first had a mixed legal status. The Qur'ān sura 2:282 requires that contracts be written, "O believers, when you contract a debt one upon another for a stated term, write it down, and let a writer write it down between you justly". However, several schools of jurisprudence did not recognize written contracts as valid. Muslims paid no attention to the schools and continued creating written contracts. Medieval Muslim contracts were created, signed, witnessed, and sealed in the same way as Parthian and Sāsānian contracts were, with one exception. People stopped registering their documents with official government repositories. Instead, the documents were given to "a trustworthy person together with an unofficial covering letter which stipulated the relationship of the contracting parties to one another" (Choksy 1998, 197). Islamic schools of jurisprudence did finally catch up with the Qur'ān and accepted practice and eventually condoned and even supported written contracts.[4]

Elsewhere along the Silk Road, written contracts held a clear status as being the preferred method of creating enforceable obligations. The oldest Tibetan contracts are not found in Tibet, but further west along the Silk Road in East Turkestan and Hexi. Most of them were found in the Dunhuang Caves and are dated roughly in the 9th century. They also appear not to have been written by native speakers of Tibetan. They incorporate formulae from other languages found along the Silk Road, including Khotanese, Chinese and Uighur. These contracts are sealed in two different ways: there are stamp seals of the witnesses and "finger seals" (Chinese huazhi) of the parties. Finger seals are ticks made on the document at each joint of the person's finger (Takeuchi 1995, 1-10). These documents are as formulaic as from any other part of the world. As Takeuchi says in his *Old Tibetan Contracts*,

> Formulae played the most important role in the contracts, where the whole text must be written in accordance with the formula. Consequently, each contract consists of stereotyped and peculiar expressions, which are not always grammatically analyzable and can be understood only in consultation with the underlying formula (Takeuchi 1995, 4).

The tradition in China from the 7th to the 15th centuries was for the scribe to read the contract aloud before the parties signed it. Early in this time-span contracts among the people had no legal status, only ownership posted in the government register was officially recognized. Despite this, people did make contracts for land as if they owned it or wanted to purchase it (Hansen 1995, 10). As the centralized government weakened, especially during the Yuan Dynasty, 1277-1368, when the Mongols ruled, contracts became increasingly important to prove ownership. The contracts are as formulaic as anywhere else. Interestingly, the Dunhuang Cave that held the few Old Tibetan contracts also held about 250 contracts from this period in China. Some of these contracts were what we would call "chirographs". A chirograph has the same text on two different parts of the paper, but is torn or cut so that each party can have the same wording in the contract. To demonstrate

4 http://beinecke.library.yale.edu/papyrus/oneSET.asp?pid=1214 (accessed 5 December 2006).

that the two come from the same page, they can be fitted back together and the text compared. This was also very common in 12th to 14th century England. Witnesses in China were also liable for the debt of the borrower (Hansen 1995, 1-16).

Formulaic written contracts precede what we understand to be literacy (cf. Harris 1989). The preservation of this document type in so many different environments in the northeastern hemisphere is also a testament to their ubiquity and quantity. We observe the persistence of contracts where they are not recognized by juridicial schools in medieval Muslim countries. We see their gradual reinvention in Europe of the 12th century (Pryor 1981, 8-11).[5]

Contracts usually name the date, the parties, the offer, the obligation, and various other things like when the contract is consummated, periods of time involved, and settlement should there be a disagreement. The wording itself is very formulaic for many different reasons: because of custom, because the law requires it, because the lawyer's experience is good with a particular formulation. This formulism reminds one not so much of legal issues as of charms and prayers. "Knock on wood", and "good-bye" are only a few of the prayers and charms we say in our daily lives in the U.S.A. We claim that we say them without recourse to superstition or even a cognizance that a deity is being summoned as with "good-bye" (from "abide with God"), but like the formulaic written contract, we seem to need them to communicate with sureness.

What is the purpose of formulism? Recent linguistic work focusing on language production would make it a "tool for social interaction" but limits that interaction to manipulation, asserting separate identity, or asserting group identity, i.e., what one can effect upon the world (Wray and Perkins 2000, 13-14). The creation of a contract, as we have seen, involves at minimum four parties wishing to affect each other: the scribe, the enforcement environment whether official or unofficial, and at least two parties. One clue can be found in the work of political anthropology, specifically in the work of Maurice Bloch. In his study of Merina oratory he describes the limitations not only on the content, but on the method of speaking,

> First, the orator's words are almost entirely not his own, in the sense that he sees them as handed down from the ancestors. He will have learned all the proverbs, stories and speech forms and his main aim is to repeat them as closely as possible following the Malagasy custom. Not only is the orator strictly limited in what he can say, but freedom of intonation and loudness which he would have in ordinary conversation is almost totally non-existent. His choice of gesture and also of posture is fixed for him by the rules of oratory. Finally, the usual grammatical choices, which exist between different voices for example, has been diminished, as have his possible choices of voca-

5 Pryor says the use of written contracts did not entirely die out.

> bulary. Merina speech acts can be seen as a continuum from polite to impolite speaking and oratory is so 'polite' that the choice of what can be said and how it can be said has largely disappeared (Bloch 1975, 8).

Bloch points out that these highly formalized utterances are a form of social control, but a form that is very one-sided and coercive – the speaker being backed by society against the listener, hence fraught with power relationships (6). What if both sides agreed to an exchange without coercion or the need to demonstrate social hierarchy? Those two parties join together within the contract to exert social control over society and each other through formulaic language and content. The contract constrains possible responses from society as well as the parties to the contract and requires action from all. Having signed the document a party cannot repudiate the signature. Having written the document, the scribe must attest to its fair representation of the desires of the parties. Having received the document into its existence, society must now enforce the contract and does so, even when the law or the government do not. Options for response are significantly reduced. As Bloch notes, "In other words, as soon as you have accepted a form of speaking in an appropriate way you have begun to give up, at a bewilderingly rapid rate, the very potential for communication" (15). Communication density goes down as formalism goes up.

This formulism is by no means a holdover from a less rational and more superstitious time and place. Contracts do not represent the stereotypes we believe we find in the "other". Homi K. Bhabha in his "The Other Question: The Stereotype and Colonial Discourse" has demonstrated that colonial discourse is rife with this pretended empirical claim about "the other",

> Fixity, as the sign of cultural/historical/racial difference in the discourse of colonialism, is a paradoxical mode of representation: it connotes rigidity and an unchanging order as well as disorder, degeneracy and daemonic repetition (Bhabha 1983, 18).

Contracts, while fixed, are actually designed to leave unspecified many things that help us to negotiate on a situation-by-situation basis what we "mean" within the contract, i.e., the contract is a way of fixing but not fixing meaning to serve our purposes. When we colonize the past, we make the same mistake. Elizabeth A. Meyer's recent book, *Legitimacy and Law in the Roman World* (2004) makes an unfortunate mistake in claiming the use of contracts in Roman life was an extension of charms and prayers, thus demonstrating that the superstitious Romans gave the tabulae themselves a power the rational Greeks did not. The Romans had clearly degenerated from their honored ancestors.

Language	Word	Some of the Meanings
Sumerian (Archi 2003, 30)	dub-	tablet
	dub-sar	scribes
Akkadian (Veenhof 2003, 88)	ṭuppum	a term used for all kinds of written documents.
Elamite	tup-pi	tablet
Old Persian	dipīm	inscription or document written on stone clay, etc. rather than with ink
	dipīvar	person who perserves or keeps document; a scribe, secretary or clerk
Classical Greek	ταβέλλα	writing tablet or note
	γιγνώσκω	perceive, learn, come to know, judge [from Old Persian zainti-]
Middle Persian (Pahlavi)	dibīr	scribe or secretary
	dibīrestān	school
	dibīwar	secretary
Roman Latin	tabula	a board coated with wax and used for writing, writing-tablet; account books; a document, deed (of a legal, business, or similar nature); a record or records.
	tabulārius	an accountant, book-keeper, or similar
	tabulārium	a collection of inscribed tablets; a record-office or registry.
	tabella	wooden, usually wax-coated, tablets threaded together to form a notebook; a tablet or (pl.) tablets forming a document of any sort.
	tabelliō	one who draws up legal documents, notary.
	tabellārius	a letter-carrier, messenger, courier; a clerk or book-keeper
Medieval Latin	notārius	a short-hand writer, stenographer; a person drawing up documents of a legal, business or similar nature
	nota	A mark attached, imprinted, etc., in order to identify or distinguish; a brand or other mark (on animals, etc.) [from Greek γιγνώσκω]
	notula	a contractual obligation
New Persian (Farsi)	debir, dabir	scribe
	debiri, dabiri	writing, secretariate
French	tableau	mathematical table or picture

Why, from the time humanity could write, did it feel the need to have written contracts? Why do we write contracts when our jurists do not recognize them, as was the case in early medieval Islamic lands? Why do we keep writing them even when the government does not recognize them, as in 6th to 13th century China? Why do we write them when we do not know the language in which they are written, as with the Old Tibetan contracts of the 9th century? Why do we rediscover written contracts, as 12th century Europe did? As utterances, contracts are our proxies for our actions. Two parties could certainly meet and make an exchange of goods and services, but wherever we find writing, we find written contracts and the rediscovery of written contracts. The law may have different requirements for contracts as witnesses, but as we have noted in medieval European and Islamic lands, contracts persisted even when the law did not recognize them.

It should be pointed out again that the idea of contracts goes beyond the realm of economics. There are marriage contracts and adoption contracts. Thus, our current U.S. view of politics is that the Constitution is the citizens' contract with each other, to "ordain and establish a more perfect union". Many sects of the three major monotheistic religions view the believer as having a "covenant", a contract, with a deity.

Contracts are one of the more extreme forms of formulaic language and they are also one of the more common forms of social control. These are documents acting, documents being our continuous proxies to enact social relations. As our proxies, contracts do more than just memorialize our action, witness our action, and organize our action. Contracts enact. They reach out into our environment and call forth a specific response from the entire society, not just the two parties to the document (Meyer 2004). Documentary societies use contracts to assist us to create, define, and maintain society. I would argue that the primary function of documents in society is to create, define, and maintain society itself.

References

Archi, Alfonso, 2003. Archival Record-Keeping at Ebla 2400-2350 BC. In *Ancient Archives and Archival Traditions: Concepts of Record-keeping in the Ancient World,* ed. M. Brosius. Oxford: Oxford University Press, 17-36.

Bhabha, Homi K., 1983. The Other Question: The Stereotype and Colonial Discourse. *Screen* 24.6 (1983), 18-36.

Bloch, Maurice, 1975. Introduction. In *Political Language and Oratory in Traditional Society,* ed. M. Bloch. London: Academic Press, 1-28.

Choksy, Jamsheed K., 1998. Loan and Sales Contracts in Ancient and Early Medieval Iran. *Indo-Iranian Journal* 31 (1998), 191-218.

Clanchy, M.T., 1993. *From memory to written record: England 1066-1307*. 2nd ed. Oxford: Blackwell.

DiMatteo, Larry A., 1998. *Contract Theory: The Evolution of Contractual Intent*. East Lansing, MI: Michigan State University Press.

Hansen, Valerie, 1995. *Negotiating Daily Life in Traditional China: How Ordinary People Used Contracts, 600-1400*. Yale: Yale University Press.

Harris, William V., 1989. *Ancient Literacy*. Cambridge, MA: Harvard University Press.

Lesaffer, Randall, 2000. The Medieval Canon Law of Contract and Early Modern Treaty Law. *Journal of the History of International Law* 2 (2000), 178-198.

Meyer, Elizabeth A., 2004. *Legitimacy and Law in the Roman World: Tabulae in Roman Belief and Practice*. Cambridge: Cambridge University Press.

Pryor, John H., 1981. *Business Contracts of Medieval Provence: Selected Notulae from the Cartulary of Giraud Amalric of Marseille 1248*. Toronto: Pontifical Institute of Mediaeval Studies.

Schmandt-Besserat, Denise, 1992. *Before Writing: Volume I, From Counting to Cuneiform*. Austin: University of Texas Press.

Skaist, Aaron Jacob, 1994. *The old Babylonian loan contract: Its history and geography*. Ramat Gan, Israel: Bar-Ilan University Press.

The New Oxford Annotated Bible, 2001, 3rd ed., ed. Michael D. Coogan. Oxford: Oxford University Press.

Takeuchi, Tsuguhito, 1995. *Old Tibetan Contracts from Central Asia*. Tokyo: Daizo Shuppan.

Veenhof, Klaas R., 2003. Archives of Old Assyrian Traders. In *Ancient Archives and Archival Traditions: Concepts of Record-keeping in the Ancient World*, ed. M. Brosius. Oxford: Oxford University Press, 78-123.

Wray, Alison and Michael R. Perkins, 2000. The Functions of Formulaic Language: An Integrated Model. *Language and Communication* 20 (2000), 1-28.

Philippe Bootz, and Xavier Hautbois

Time Measures in Documents: The model of "Motifs Temporels Paramétrés"

1 Introduction

This article aims at presenting the model of "Motifs Temporels Paramétrés" (Parametrized Time Motifs) which can help to locate "Unités Sémiotiques Temporelles" (Semiotic Time Units) in artistic documents *in context of their reception.* Based on the aural reception of sound documents, this model is also pertinent when dealing with audiovisual and multimedia documents.

Led by François Delalande, musical semiology turned towards the issue of the reception of sound documents, taking for granted that a musical sign could not be treated in absolute terms; indeed, the relevance of an analysis can be authenticated only by referring to studied behaviour: "it is always a matter of establishing connections between elements in sound configurations and *human behaviours*, either productive or receptive" (Delalande 1991). That is why the semiotic analysis program that he proposes is focused on strategies of listening (typical-listening) which condition us to perceive sounds in a particular and precise way.[1] In collaboration with researchers and composers from the Laboratoire de Musique Informatique de Marseille (M.I.M.) (Laboratory of Computerized Music of Marseilles), he led a selection and a classification of extracts from musical works based on their aural reception and according to criteria of time significance. Nineteen "Unités Sémiotiques Temporelles" (UST) have been compiled in this classification (MIM 1996). "A UST is a category of equivalent musical snatches which have a precise time significance linked to their morphology, even out of their musical context" (Delalande in MIM 1996, 18-19).

The UST system devised by the MIM proved relevant in the analysis of documents extracted from entire musical works (MIM 2002). Moreover, the existence of UST as semiotic units linked to time-related mental representations has been given substance to by recent UST categorization experiments, based on musical extracts provided by the MIM. These spatial representations seem to fit with a

1 On this topic, see the example of Debussy which he developed in Delalande (1989).

spatial coding of time. The name of UST, often relating to specific movements,[2] is highly relevant in this regard.

The relevance of UST seems to extend far beyond the strict boundaries of sound documents. Using definitions and properties of the signified levels of these units as detailed by the MIM, we have noted in multimedia products (*La colonie* by Alexandre Gherban,[3] *Avec tact* by Antoine Schmitt[4]), in experimental movies (*Rhythm 21* and *Diagonal symphony* by Hans Richter,[5] *Etude n° 8* by Oskar Fischinger[6]), and in experiments with lights (*Opus 161* by Thomas Wilfred[7]), visual patterns that are strongly analogous to UST in music. If it is true that UST are really linked to time-related mental representations, that system could constitute a broadly "a-media" semiotic system, independent from any specific media, and could be applied to any kind of document.

Nevertheless, the description provided by the MIM is not sufficient to widen that system to include all media. Indeed, that description is essentially qualitative and uses metaphoric terms as well as a exclusively musical vocabulary. On the level of the signified, the use of metaphors raises no problem, but as regards the signifier level, they hardly provide an efficient description. On the other hand, the use of a musical vocabulary in the description of a signifier complicates the formal analogies between the world of sound and the world of the visual. That is why, in that field, analyses deriving from that description have remained purely qualitative.

Thus, it proved necessary to propose a more abstract and systematic description of these UST on the level of their signifier, a description which would no longer rely on musical variables any. We named this "Motif Temporel Paramétré" (Parametrized Time Motif). Of course, the components thus defined remain carried by sound variables, as they are carried by other variables in visuals.

This work on the signifier enabled us to proceed to sound syntheses of UST. Then we tackled the MTP analysis of a visual work on a quantitative level. The MTP system also happens to be easy to program and should help us elaborate simulations or facilitate the relationship between sound and image in multimedia.

2 Some examples of UST: *Qui tourne, Qui veut démarrer, Trajectoire inexorable...*
3 Published in *alire12*, cd-rom, Villeneuve d'Ascq, MOTS-VOIR, 2004.
4 Available on the author's website, http://www.gratin.org/as/avectact/index.html.
5 Centre Pompidou, Musée National d'Art Moderne.
6 Centre Pompidou, Musée National d'Art Moderne.
7 Luminous machine, Carol and Eugene Epstein's collection, Los Angeles, 1965-1966.

2 Methodology

We have focused on the sound-morphology of multiple sound extracts provided by the MIM, so that we could detect time-variation rules in them, not to describe them accurately, but in order to detect oppositions between UST signifiers. Our analysis is thus not a signal analysis, but a semiotic analysis based on a set of oppositions. It is based on the actual UST classification, even though it enabled us to characterize the types of examples provided by the MIM, which a purely qualitative approach could not have done.

As a result, these variables were named pertinent variables, and MTP determines their structure in time.

We have described this system in a graphical and analytical meta-language. The graphical language is well adapted to a standardized representation of the time variations of pertinent variables; the analytical language provides us with a clear description of the subdivision of the system into its constituent parts.[8]

We have adapted the analysis method based on the way the sound "sounds" and not on its signal analysis. This made the perception of pertinent variables easier, which can occur in a rather complex way in musical snatches. Further, the observation of wave files and sound graphics helped us measure the quality of some parameters. Eventually, simulations gave us the opportunity of improving our analysis.

3 Overview of the system

3.1 The system units

UST provide us with an iconic transcription of time shapes, that are often also characteristic of states of motion. Hence, they form a semiotic system with no corresponding cutout,[9] so that it is legitimate to focus only on the study of their signifier, knowing that only the association of a signifier with a signified constitutes a sign. That signifier level, that of MTP, forms an articulate system organized in distinctive units. Indeed, a UST cannot be split into smaller signifying units, whereas a MTP is organized on several levels. Before we describe precisely each level of articulation and each UST, let us establish an overview of the system units.

8 Let us consider the suggestive impact of formulae in chemistry.

9 The vocabulary we use is that of Klinkenberg (1996), "système sémiotique à decoupage non correspondant".

A "Motif Temporel Paramétré" describes the signifier of a UST by using time functions which represent the overall appearance of the time-pattern of the pertinent variables *v* on the length of the UST.

Two pertinent variables *v* are enough to describe the signifier of a sound UST. We named them F and I. These abstract variables are characteristics of the signifier but they are materialized by physical parameters of the sign stimulus. Thus, the variable F is materialized by the "melodic" aspect of the sound (frequencies evolving in time). The variable I is principally materialized by the intensity of the sound, but, in certain cases, it can also be by its brilliance, or in other words: the spectral richness of sound.

Each UST is systematically described with these two variables. Nevertheless, the pattern of only one of these variables suffices to perceive the UST in a great many cases. Consequently, we named it "main variable of the UST". When the UST does not possess such a variable, the two pertinent variables are of equal importance, for the perception is as influenced by the time-pattern of one as it is by the time-pattern of the other.

In a sound, distinct time-layers may be noticeable and pertinent for time semantics. In that case, a full set (F, I) shall be identified in each layer. These layers evolve simultaneously in the Motif and only their association affects the time-pattern that is identified on the semantic level of the UST. In a multilayer Motif, one layer at most is to have a main variable; it is called the main layer of the Motif.

UST are organized in phases. A phase is a part of the Motif which presents a strong opposition to the preceding and the following parts.[10] That opposition only concerns the main variable of the UST when the latter is characterized by it. It concerns the two pertinent variables simultaneously when both are of equal importance.

The temporal function of a pertinent variable shows one or several profiles following one another. A profile is a specific fragment of time which stands in opposition to those adjacent to it. It is based on a rule of association of elementary functions called profilemes. These profilemes help us build indiscriminately the profiles of the two variables F and I.

10 The precise definition of the phase is given in the following section.

3.2 Profilemes

3.2.1 Parameters

Profilemes are characterized by three parameters: their shape, which defines the look of the elementary function's time-pattern, their amplitude and a characteristic length, most often their actual length.

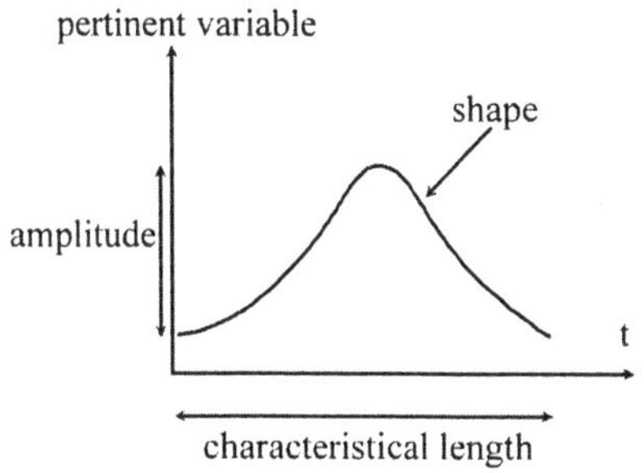

Figure 1: examples of parameters of a profileme

3.2.2 Parametrical specificities

a) Shape specificities

We have devised a list of thirteen profilemes. They are divided in six classes, each one described by a normalized schema and a formula:

- the constant shape. Three profilemes belong to that class:
  - the *plat* (flat shape), formula: Pl. It designates a little variation of the *v* variable of about an average value which does not vary significantly from the characteristic length.
  - The *constante stricte* (strict constant), formula: Cst. Unlike the *plat*, the *v* variable of this profileme remains strictly constant in time on the characteristic length. On the level of frequencies, it may represent a sustained, resonant, or repeated note.
  - The *constante nulle* (zero constant), formula: O. It is a *constante stricte* of no amplitude at all. It applies only to the I variable and helps us situate a rest in the music.
- the linear shape: its pertinent variable evolves monotonously in a linear way in time, and its steep incline gives the impression of speed. In our system, no profileme is opposed to another by the worth of that steepness, so that the value of the slope on the diagram is unimportant, provided that it is not zero. In the analyzed extracts, the variation direction (ascending or descending slope) is not pertinent on the signified level, so that this class has only one profileme: L.
- the curved shape: the pertinent variable evolves in a non-linear, monotonous way in time and its curved shape gives a feeling of acceleration. The value of that curve is not significant in the example, unless it is zero. Two

profilemes are to be distinguished depending on the direction of their variation. The ascending curve is classified as C+ and the descending one C-. In MTP for which the variation direction is not pertinent, these two classes are indiscriminately called C.

- the bell-shaped curve: in the profileme, the pertinent variable rises and then falls in time. Rectangular and triangular forms belong to this category (among other geometrical shapes). It is not the round shape of the bell which defines it, but the existence of an ascending front and a descending one on its characteristic length. There are two symmetrical profilemes and two dissymmetrical ones. The symmetrical ones are:
    - the *pulse*, called Π, in which the variable is zero if not placed on a short segment of time constituting the characteristic length of the profileme.
    - the *cloche symétrique* (symmetrical bell), classified as Cl, in which the ascending and descending parts develop along the whole characteristic length of the profileme.

The asymmetrical profilemes are asymmetrical because of the pertinent variation of their slope. They are distinguished by the steepness of their ascending line: respectively the *cloche dissymétrique à front raide* (dissymmetrical bell with a steep line), called Cl+ and the *cloche dissymétrique à front lent* (dissymmetrical bell with a gentle line), called Cl-. They spread along the whole characteristical length.

- the *peigne de Dirac* (Dirac comb), called pD: it is a periodically repeated peak. Unlike the others, it has no noticeable amplitude or shape. That shape only plays the role of an operator which enables us to draw periodical profiles. It is never directly observed.
- the *séquence ordonnée* (ordinate sequence), noted séq. It is a musical motion which possesses a proper temporality different from the preceding shapes. Its time structure is not defined here, and it constitutes a shape perceived as slowly structured in time.

The basic profilemes are made up of the 12 profilemes other than the *peigne de Dirac*.

- Schematic representation and formulae of the profilemes:

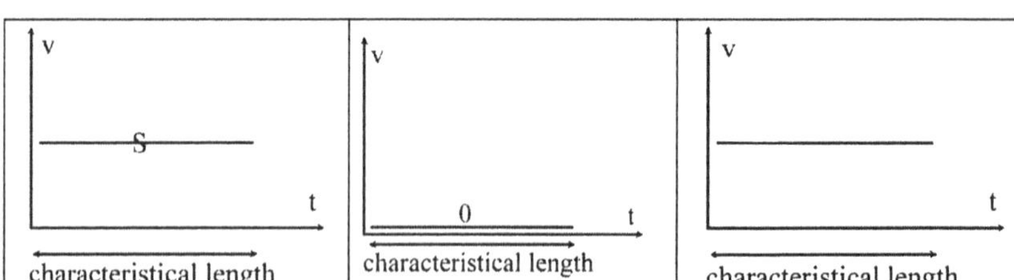

Cst	0	Pl

Figure 2: constant shapes

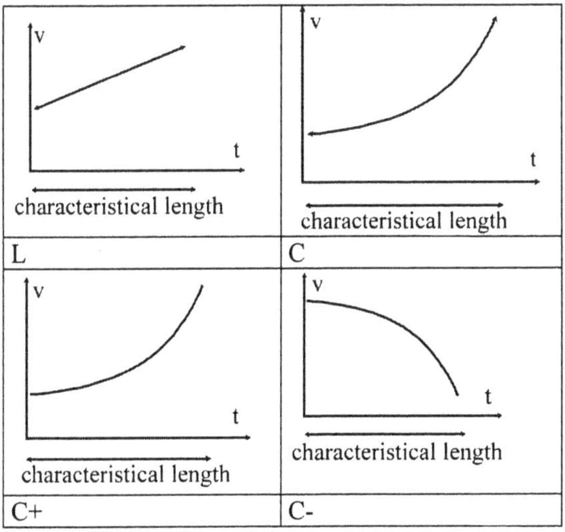

Figure 3: linear and curved shapes

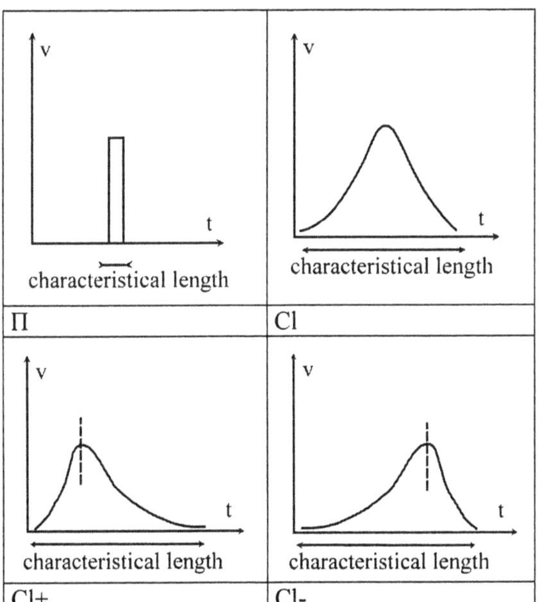

Figure 4: bell-shaped curves

The *peigne de Dirac* as well as the *séquence ordonnée* will not be directly represented by their real shape on normalized schemata, but by specific symbols.

The *peigne de Dirac* will be represented by a vertical dotted line topped by the T value of its period. In front of that line is placed the indication "Me" to point out that what is contained in that zone constitutes the elementary Motif which shall be repeated in the profile.

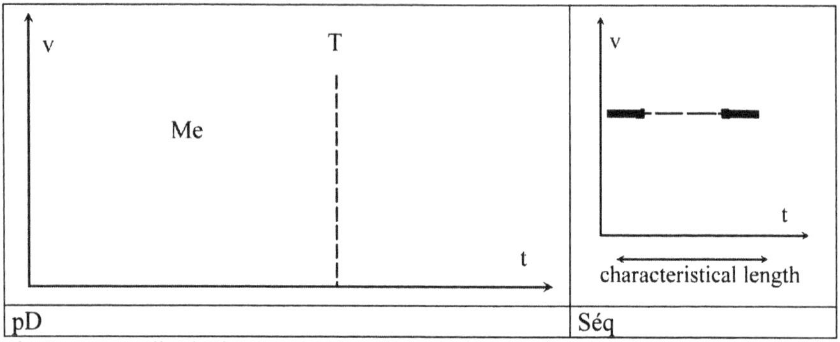

Figure 5: normalized schemata of the *peigne de Dirac* and of the *séquence ordonnée*

b) Length specificities

Because they are built from the 4 characteristic lengths T0, T1, T2, and T3, the characteristic length of a profileme can belong to 6 value fields noted by the symbols *T0, T1, T1=T2, T2, T3, T2 or T3*. The T0 field corresponds to the value that is necessary to perceive a profileme. As regards sound variables, that value is about 300 ms. The T1 field typically corresponds to a duration shorter than 1 second. T2 corresponds to a length of several seconds. This T2 field seems to correspond to the length during which the profileme can be treated in working memory. T3 corresponds to a duration longer than 10 seconds, which is too long for the correspondent characteristics of the profileme to be treated in working memory.

These fields correspond to categories. The frontier between two adjacent fields has no signification. Thus, depending on the sound context of the profileme, a length of 0.9 second will sometimes be identified as a *T1*, sometimes as a *T2*. In certain cases, the field of ambiguous values between T1 and T2 is identified as a field in opposition to the others. We called it *T1=T2*. The measures we took on fragments of sound gave lengths in that field a value of approximately 1.5 s. Thus, *T1* is opposed to *T2*, and *T1=T2* is opposed to both *T1* and *T2*.

The field *T2 or T3* indicates that the corresponding length may get a value comprised between a few seconds up to more than ten seconds, or even a few dozens of seconds.

3.3 Profiles

3.3.1 Assembly grammar of profilemes

A profile is ruled by one of the following operations that affect the basic profileme:

- identification: the profile is directly made up of the basic profileme.
- the convolution of a basic profileme by a *peigne de Dirac*: the convoluted profileme is reproduced periodically depending on the period of the *peigne de Dirac.*
- the multiplication of the basic profileme by a *pulse*: the profile is made up of a fragment of the basic profileme (that which corresponds to the value of a *pulse* not equal to zero), the rest of the profileme being thus reduced to a zero value.
- the convolution of a basic profileme by a *peigne de Dirac* followed by the multiplication of a curve (C+ or C-): the profileme is reproduced periodically and its mathematical envelope evolves in that reiteration according to the curve C+ or C-.

It is easy to gather these assembly rules under a formula. If we note P the profile and pf the basic profileme, * the convolution and X the multiplication, we shall note these 4 rules respectively:

P = pf ; P = pf * pD ; P = pf X Π ; P = (pf * pD) X C+ (or P = (pf * pD) X C-)

Two successive profiles can be opposed by the amplitude of their basic profilemes, one being of a weaker amplitude than the other one. These oppositions in amplitude are marked by an arrow on the schema of the profileme and by the notation {+/-} in the formulae. Note that the amplitude of the *constante stricte* is always that of the end of the preceding profile.

3.3.2 Specificities of periodical profiles

In a periodical profile, the basic profileme can present variations in shape or in amplitude during its reiteration. These variations are noted by the symbol ≠ in schemata or in formulae. Moreover, the period of reiteration can also vary from one elementary Motif to another one. In that case, it can increase strictly, reduce strictly or vary randomly in one direction or another. According to the rise or fall of the period, that variation is indicated by Pmin →Pmax or Pmax ← Pmin in schemata and formulae.

3.3.3 A stricter definition of the phase

When a Motif has a main variable, a phase is always constituted by a profile of that variable.[11] When a Motif has no main variable, a phase is made up of two si-

11 This latter being related to the profiles of the other variable which occurs at the same time.

multaneous profiles, one of each pertinent variable. A change in phase is effected only when these profiles differ *simultaneously* in every variable. The number of phases in the Motif is then equal to the number of profiles in the variable which possesses fewest of them. Practically, all multilayer Motifs have but one phase.

In the Motif, phases follow one another sequentially. In certain Motifs, one or several phases can recur. That repetition may be a redundance (some repetitions are then noted (n) on Motifs or formulae) or a periodical repetition (convolution of repeated phases with a *peigne de Dirac*).

3.4 Time Motifs

Certain Motifs are delimited in time, in other words: their length is significant. Others are not delimited in time, that is, their length is infinite on the signifier level, even if the length of their stimulus is obviously a finite one.

3.5 Normalized schematization and formulae

In schemata, the two pertinent variables use the same horizontal time axis: F is directed upwards and I is directed downwards. When the Motif has a main variable, it is noted on the corresponding axis. Profiles are separated by vertical dotted lines. The value of the characteristic length of the profileme is indicated under its shape. Phases are not noted. A thicker vertical dotted line indicates the end of the Motif. In the case of a Motif delimited in time, the field of its complete time-width is noted behind this line. The distance which separates the limit of the former profile from the limit of the Motif has no signification in this schema. Each layer is the object of a schema and layers are separated by the symbol +. When the Motif has a main layer, it is the first represented. When a profileme is multiplied by a curve, the envelope (the curve) is noted in dots.

In formulae, the Motif is delimited by square brackets. The profiles of pertinent variables are separated by a comma. The first variable indicated is I, the second one is F, according to the notation [I: formula of the profiles/F: formula of the profiles]. The field of the Motif's length is noted after the square brackets when it is delimited in time. Phases are noted by commas separating the two notations: I/F. The main variable, when it does exist, is noted by the letter p in front of I or F.

3.6 UST

With these representation conventions, UST constitute the following system:

UST	**Motif Temporel Paramétré** (Normalized schemata and formulae)	
Par vagues (Wavy)	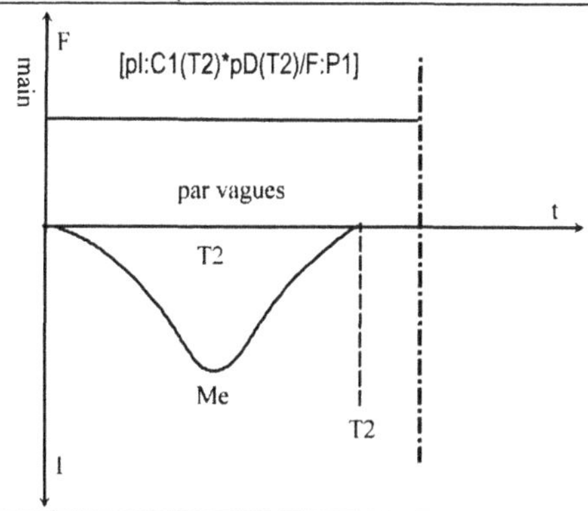	1
Obsessionnel (Obsessive)	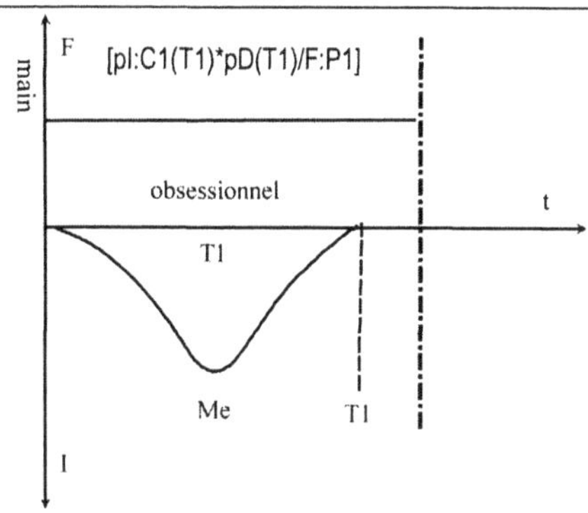	1
Qui tourne (turning)	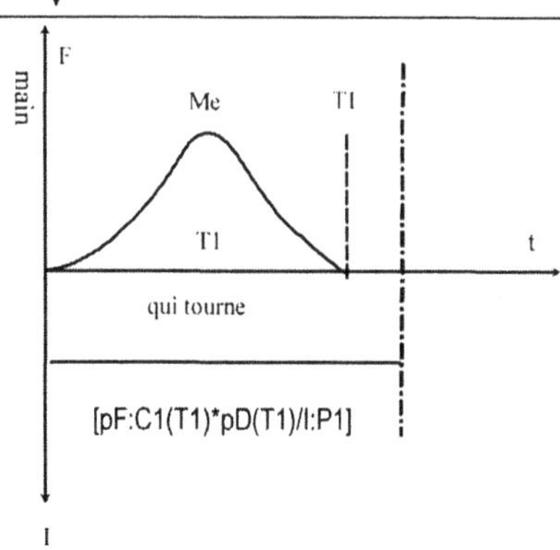	1

	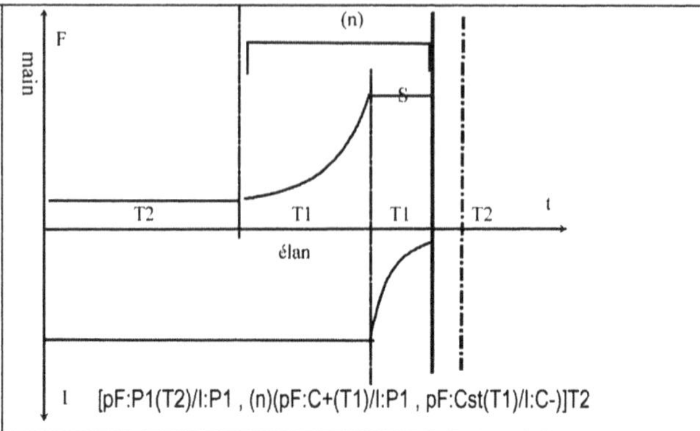main F (n) S T2 T1 T1 T2 t élan I [pF:P1(T2)/I:P1 , (n)(pF:C+(T1)/I:P1 , pF:Cst(T1)/I:C-)]T2	
Élan (Run-up)	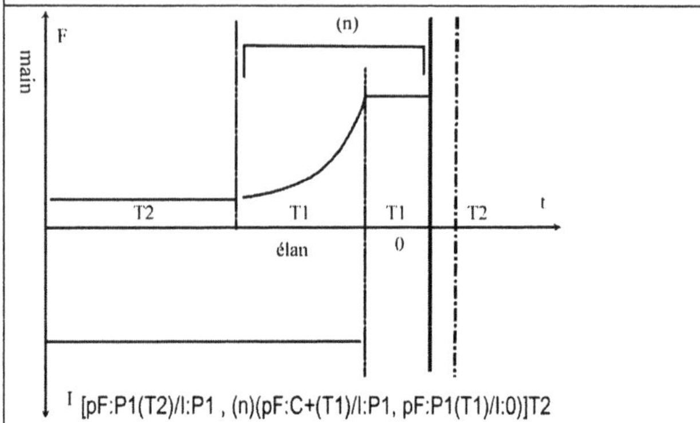main F (n) T2 T1 T1 T2 t élan 0 I [pF:P1(T2)/I:P1 , (n)(pF:C+(T1)/I:P1, pF:P1(T1)/I:0)]T2	3
	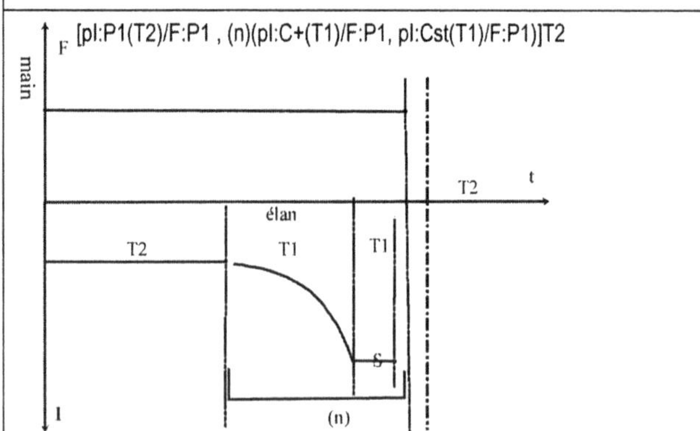[pI:P1(T2)/F:P1 , (n)(pI:C+(T1)/F:P1, pI:Cst(T1)/F:P1)]T2 F main T2 t élan T2 T1 T1 S I (n)	

<table>
<tr><td rowspan="1">Chute
(Fall)</td><td>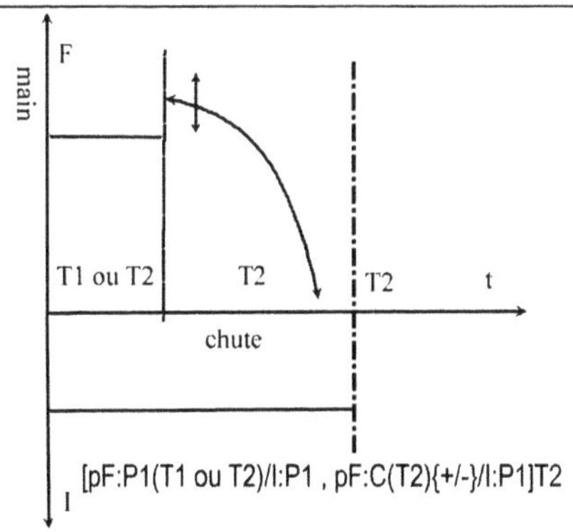
</td><td>2</td></tr>
<tr><td rowspan="2">Trajectoire inexorable (Inexorable trajectory)</td><td>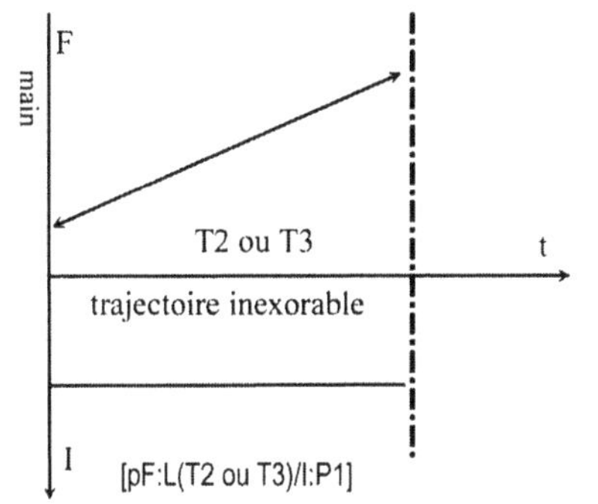
</td><td rowspan="2">1</td></tr>
<tr><td>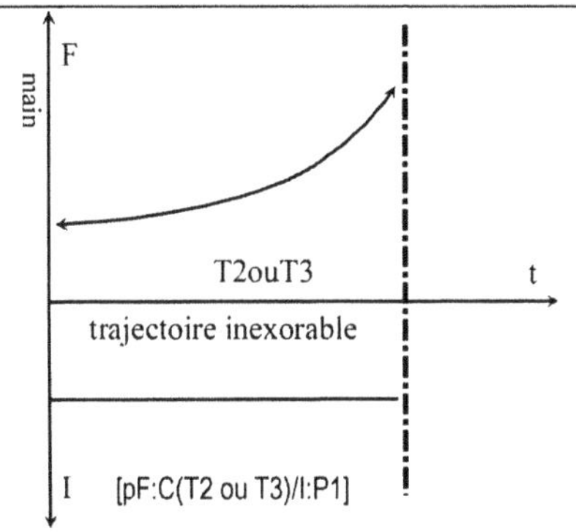
</td></tr>
</table>

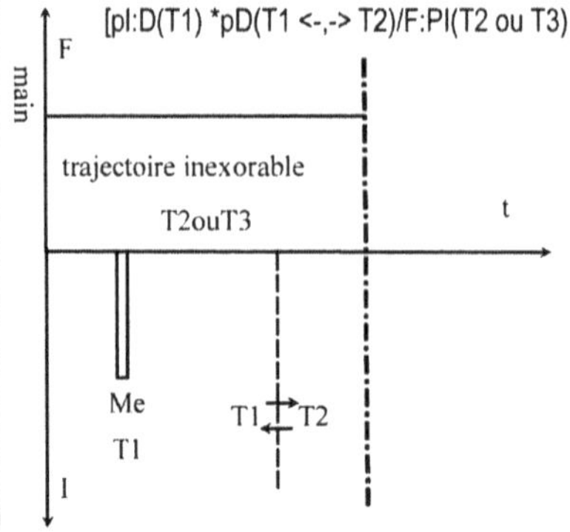
[pl:D(T1) *pD(T1 <-,-> T2)/F:PI(T2 ou T3)
F
main
trajectoire inexorable
T2ouT3
t
Me
T1
T1
T2
I

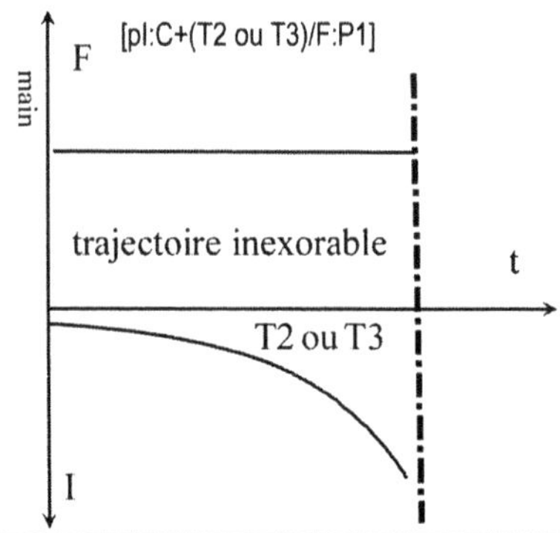
[pl:C+(T2 ou T3)/F:P1]
F
main
trajectoire inexorable
t
T2 ou T3
I

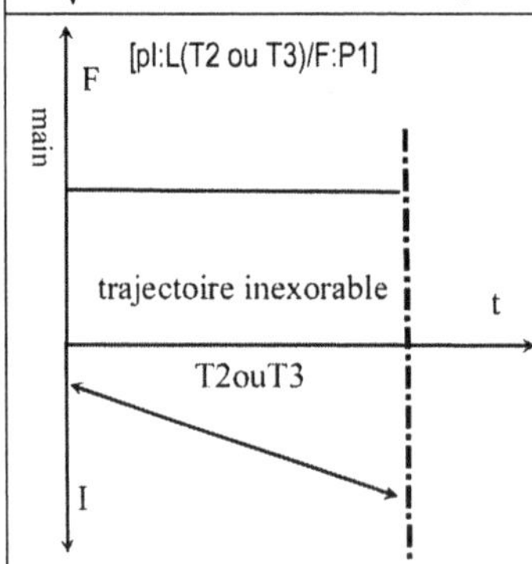
[pl:L(T2 ou T3)/F:P1]
F
main
trajectoire inexorable
t
T2ouT3
I

<table>
<tr>
<td rowspan="2">Sur l’erre
(on the ways)</td>
<td>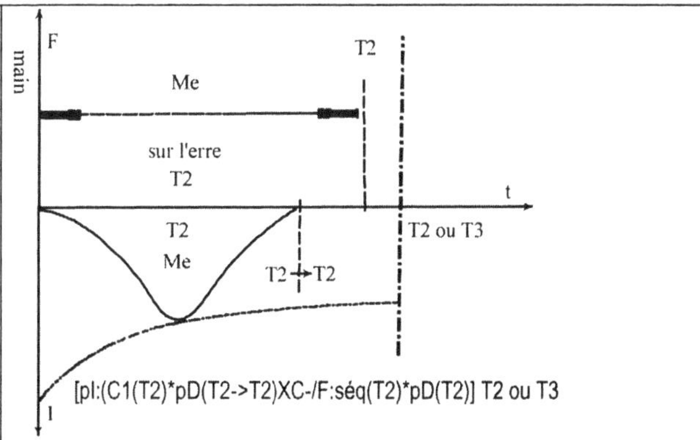
</td>
<td>1</td>
</tr>
<tr>
<td>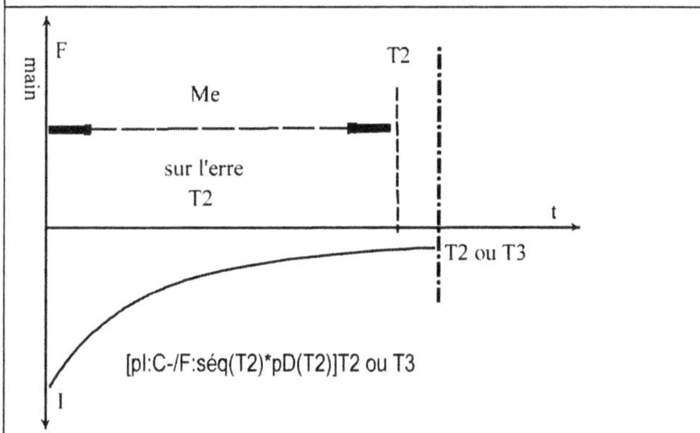
</td>
<td>1</td>
</tr>
<tr>
<td>Étirement
(Stretching)</td>
<td>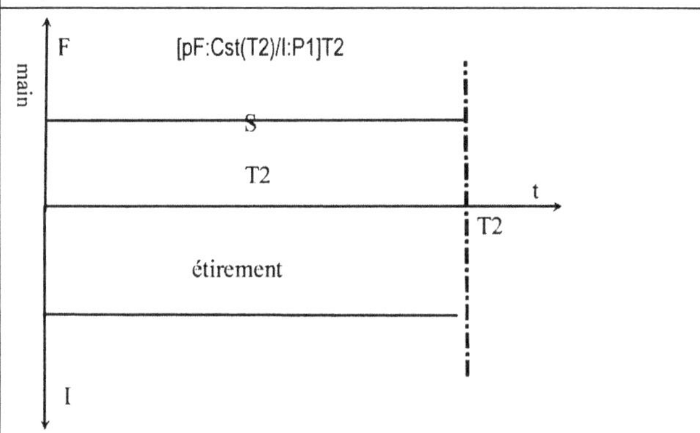
</td>
<td>1</td>
</tr>
</table>

Freinage (Braking)	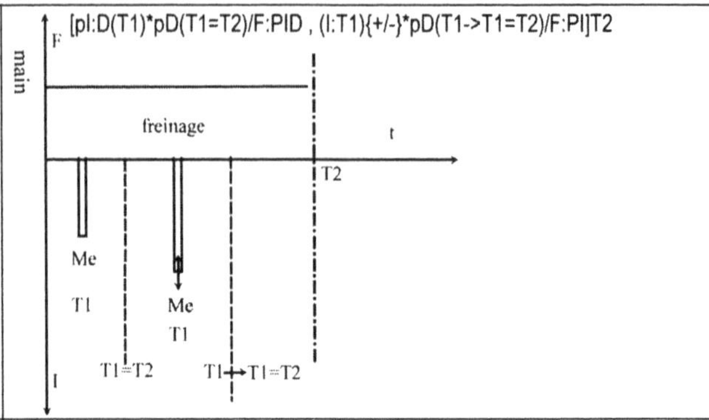	2
Contracté-étendu (Tense/ Stretched out)	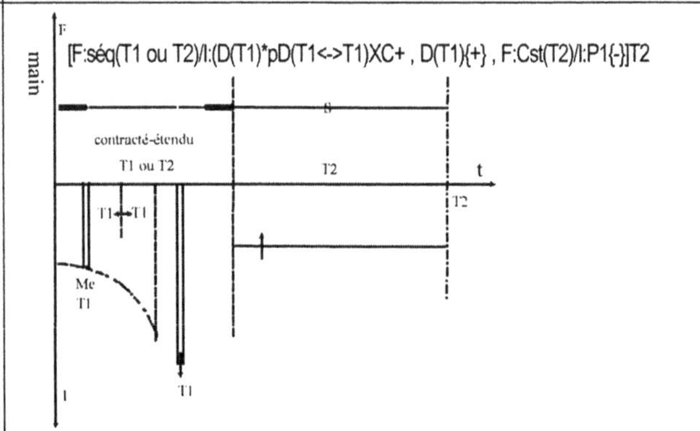 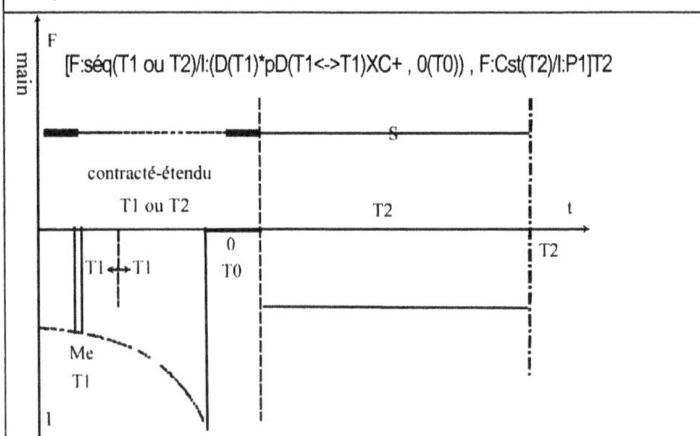	2

Suspension-interrogation (Suspension/ Question)	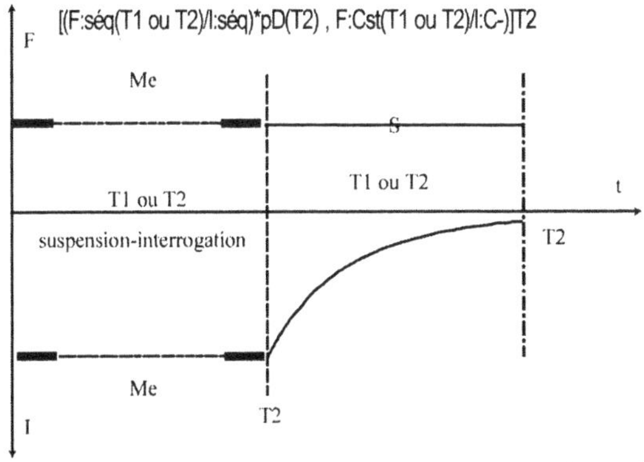	2
Qui veut démarrer (Which wants to get started)	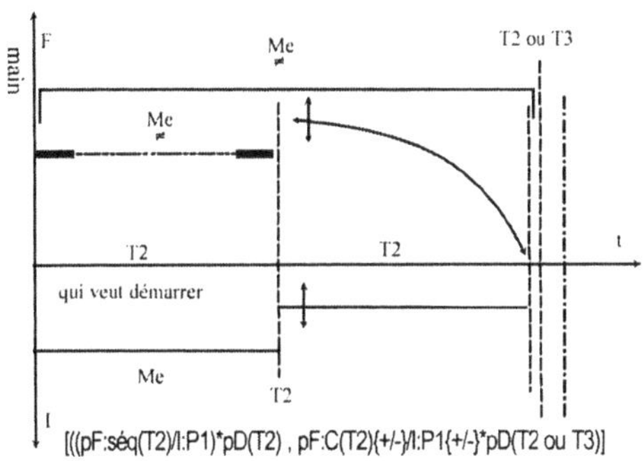	2
Sans direction par divergence d'informations (Directionless because of informational divergence)	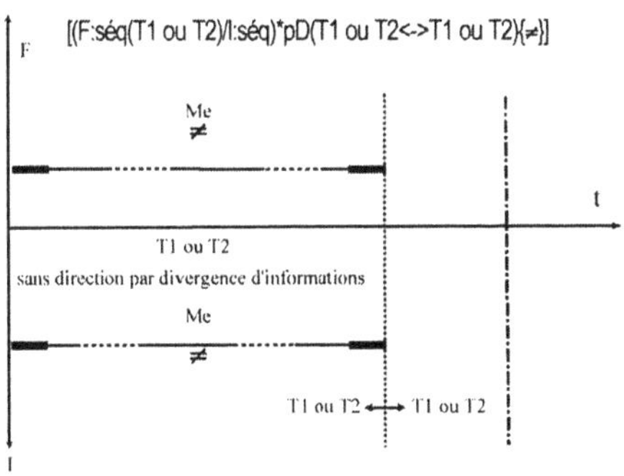	1

<table>
<tr><td>Sans direction par excès d'information (Directionless because of too many pieces of information)</td><td>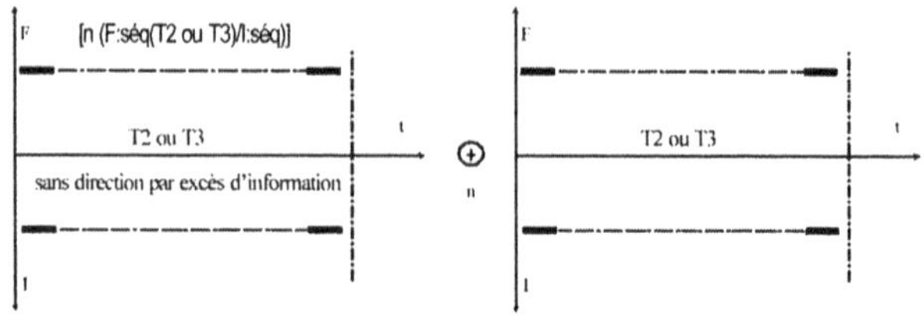
</td><td>1</td></tr>
<tr><td>Stationnaire (Stationary)</td><td>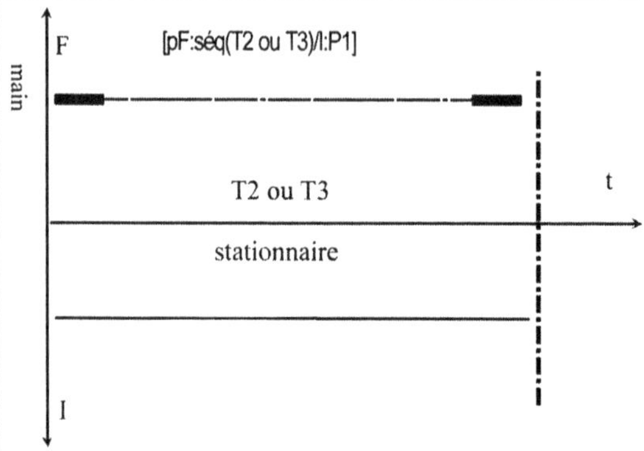
</td><td>1</td></tr>
<tr><td rowspan="2">En flottement (Floating)</td><td>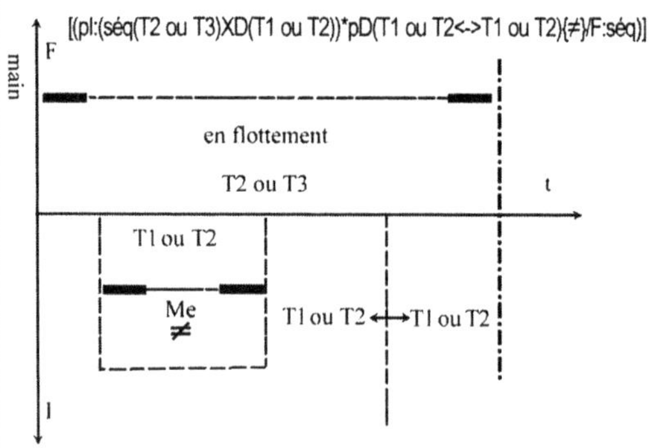
</td><td rowspan="2">1</td></tr>
<tr><td>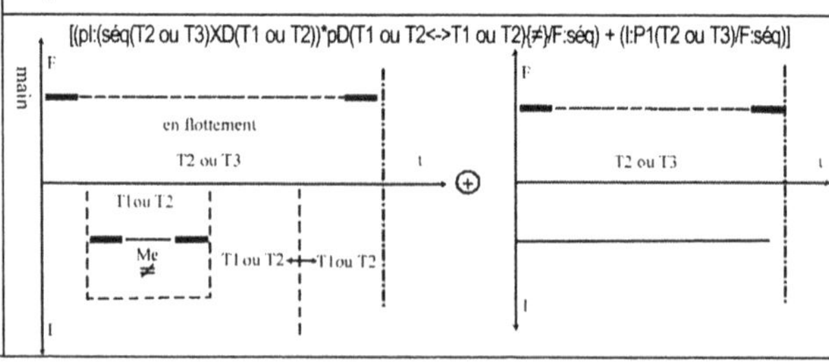
</td></tr>
</table>

<table>
<tr>
<td>En suspension (Suspended)</td>
<td>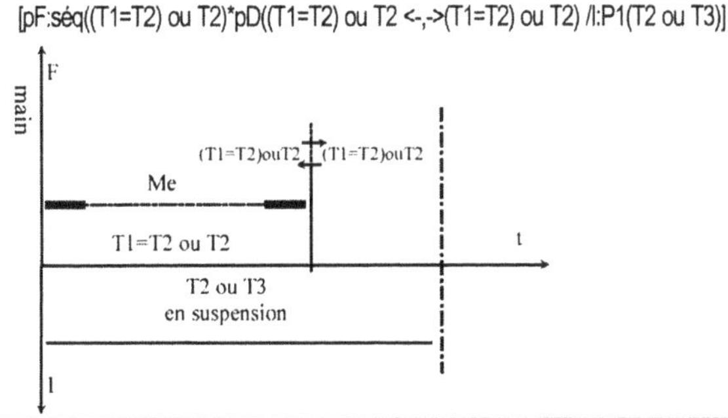
</td>
<td>1</td>
</tr>
<tr>
<td>Lourdeur (Heaviness)</td>
<td>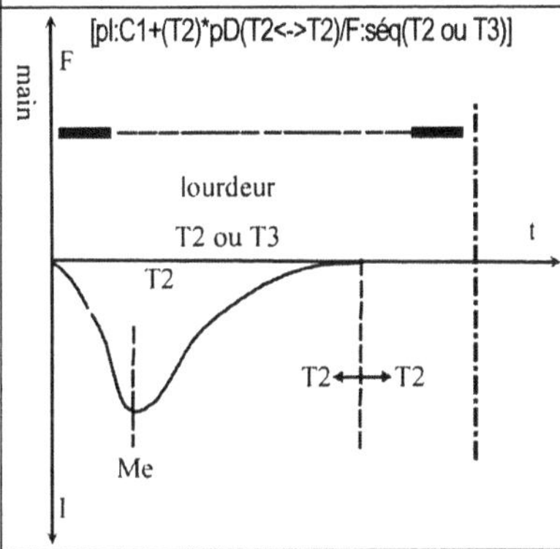
</td>
<td>1</td>
</tr>
<tr>
<td>Qui avance (Moving forward)</td>
<td>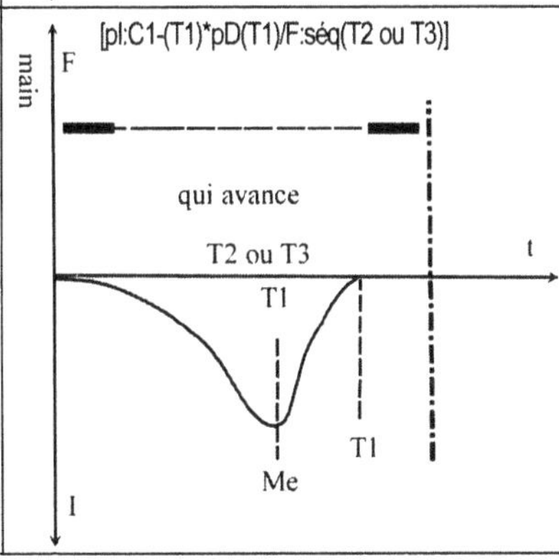
</td>
<td>1</td>
</tr>
</table>

4 MTP synthesis

The 21 MTP corresponding to the 19 UST were synthesized with the help of the OpenMusic V5.0 software, a graphic programming environment developed at the IRCAM and designed specially for computer-assisted composition.

We have worked directly from an initial sound-file to which we have applied intensity and frequency filters. All the simulations have been realized from a sound extract from the musical piece *La création du monde* composed by Bernard Parmegiani.[12] That extract presents a sound texture focused on comparatively stable frequencies. It hardly changes and only serves to fill the MTP with a sound texture. We could have proceeded from other sound-files, but the more noticeable characteristics a sound-file has (melodic trait, percussive rhythm, etc.), the less the UST produced by filtration are considered typical.

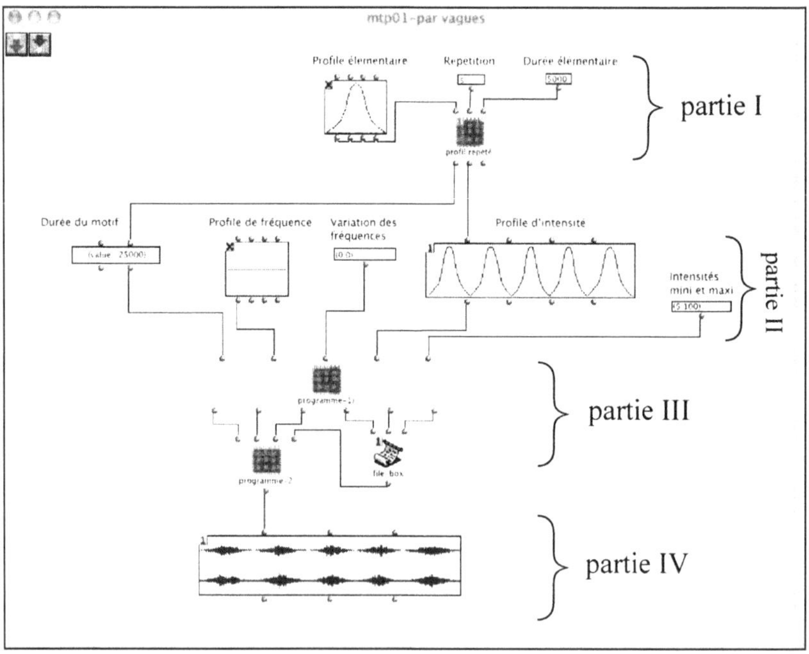

Figure 6: simulation of the UST *Par vagues*.

The simulation program has been devised to allow the easy realization of a vast corpus of sound-samples, by playing on the different parameters and on the choice of the initial sound-file. Here is the example of the simulation of the UST *Par*

12 *Lumière*, in *Métamorphose du vide*, 5'38 to 6'06.

vagues (Figure 6): The elementary profile corresponds to the profileme we used (here a bell-shaped one), and the adjacent boxes make its characteristics more prescise: characteristical length (500 ms) and many repetitions in the *peigne de Dirac*. The total length of the Motif is then calculated (2500 ms) and the program builds up a comprehensive intensity profile. The frequency profileme is then introduced (here a *plat*), as well as its variations, whose every boundary is given in relative values regarding the actual sound frequency. Program 1 calculates the filter we get, corresponding to the MTP. Program 2 applies it on the original file (file-box) and the wave-file of the simulation is saved on a disk and displayed on the terminal box.

Here are the simulations we got:

UST	Length of the MTP	Frequency profile (F)	F variations	Intensity profile (I)	I (min max)
Par vagues	25000	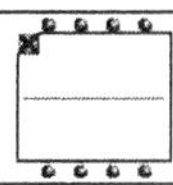	(0 0)	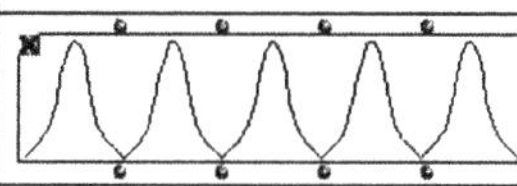	(5 100)
	In this simulation, we have used a bell-shaped, elementary intensity profile, length: 5s (T2), repeated five times. A variation in bell-shaped brilliance increases the pertinence of the UST.				
Obses-sionnel	9000	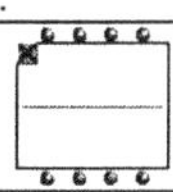	(0 0)	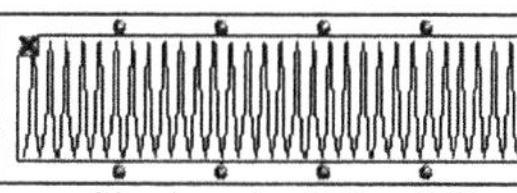	(5 100)
	The intensity profile has a bell-shaped elementary profile, length: 300ms(T1), which is repeated 30 times. The tighter the bell is, the more pertinent the simulation is.				
Qui tourne	18000	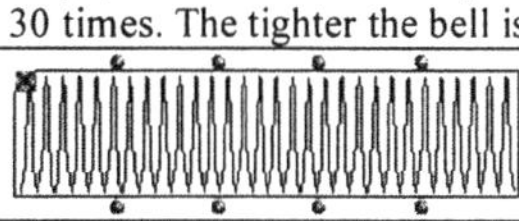	(0 500)	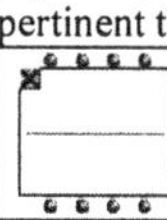	(100 100)
	Here, it is the frequency profile which is based on a bell-shaped elementary profile, length: 600ms (T1), repeated 30 times.				
Élan (in F)	3000	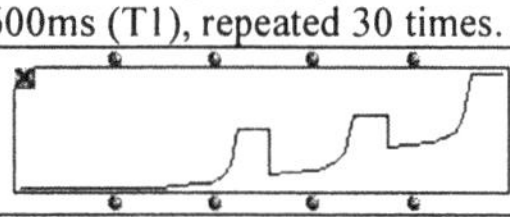	(0 2000)	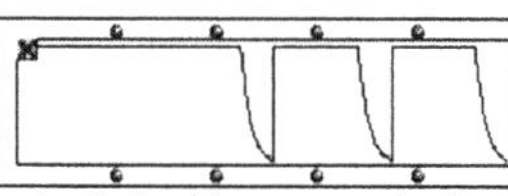	(0 100)
	In this simulation, we chose three successive *élans in F*. In this case, only the first *élan* needs a preparation. A reducing of the intensity is needed on each layer to draw a frontier between the *élans*.				
Élan (in I)	1500	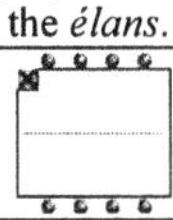	(200 200)	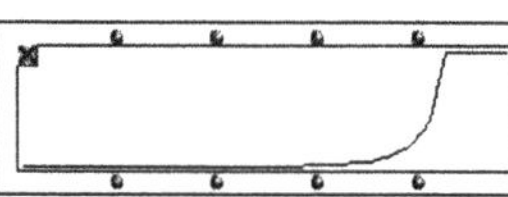	(10 100)
	Here, we have reproduced a simple *élan in I*. As in the case of an *élan in F*, the exponential profile has to be a short one.				
Chute	5000	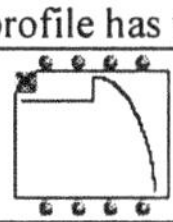	(0 2500)	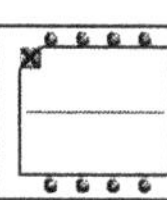	(100 100)
	We have added a slide in the frequency profile to insist on the triggering of the fall. The curved profileme is comparable to that of the *élan* (the *Chute* might be ascending), but of				

	a greater length (T2 instead of T1).				
Trajectoire inexorable (in F)	20000	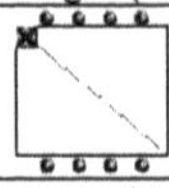	(-2400 2400)	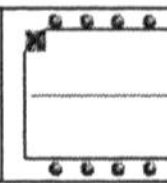	(100 100)
	Here we see a slowly decreasing linear function of the frequency. An ascending function is also suitable.				
Trajectoire inexorable (pulsed in I)	15000	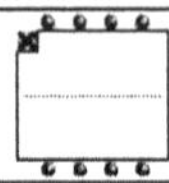	(0 0)	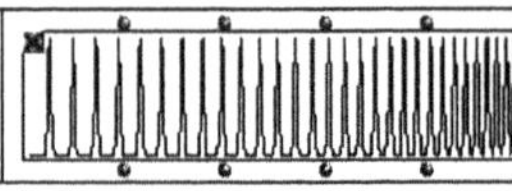	(0 100)
	Here is a *peigne* in intensity with an acceleration. A slowing-down of the *peigne* leads to the same UST.				
Trajectoire inexorable (in I)	20000	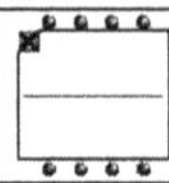	(0 0)	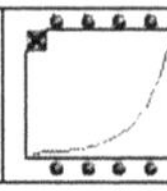	(10 100)
	In this example, we have used a slowly increasing curved function of the frequency. That simulation does not correspond to any example of the CD; but it was admitted as a *Trajectoire inexorable* by MIM members.				
Sur l'erre	10000	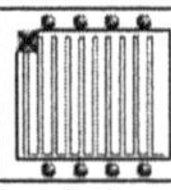	(0 600)	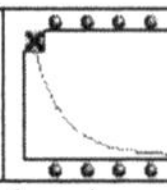	(0 100)
	In this simulation, there are two alternative notes, forming an interval of three semitones, while the global intensity exponentially decreases (10s).				
Étirement	8000	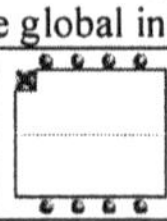	(200 200)	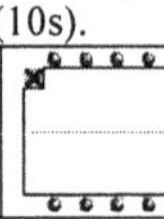	(100 100)
	Here, we have taken a short extract (0.1s) from the initial sound-file, deprived of any frequency variation.				
Freinage	2500	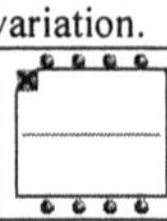	(600 600)	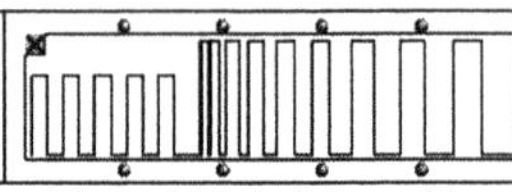	(0 100)
	This simulation is based on a regular *peigne* of intensities, which is followed by a decelerating *peigne*.				
Contracté étendu	15000	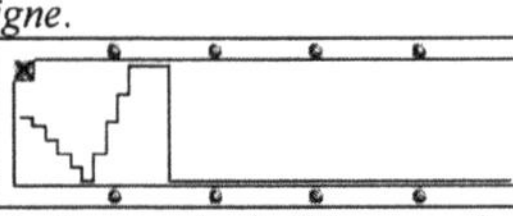	(0 600)	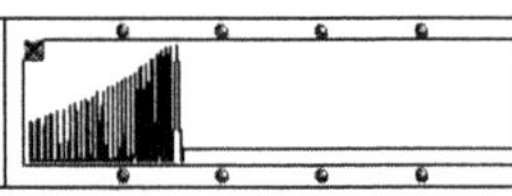	(0 100)
	As regards frequencies in this example, the time-function uses two profiles: one is random and by layers (4s) and the other one is constant (11s). On the intensity level, the time-function is formed by a sequence of three profiles: the first one is organized in accelerated peaks of increasing amplitude, the second one is a very short impulse and the last one is a *plat*.				
Suspension interrogation	10000	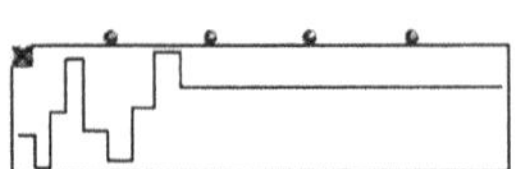	(0 600)	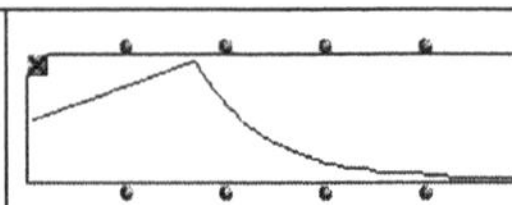	(0 100)
	In this simulation, frequencies evolve according to a sequence of four values repeated with variation (slowly moving with changes in height) during 3s, followed by a constant phase (7s). Intensities vary according to a first ascending and linear profile, then to a decreasing and curved second profile.				

Qui veut démarrer	10000	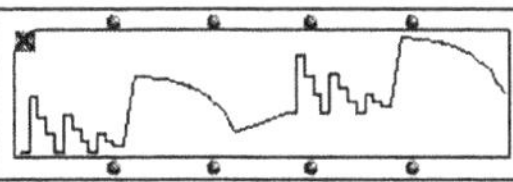	(-1200 1200)	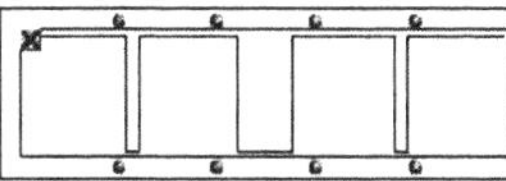	(0 100)
	Here, frequencies evolve according to an organized sequence, followed by a decreasing curved shape, the ensemble is repeated with variations in height. The intensities are constant here: frequencies are separated by some rests (0 intensity).				
Sans direction par divergence d'information	25000	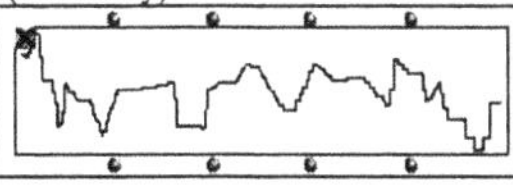	(-2400 2400)	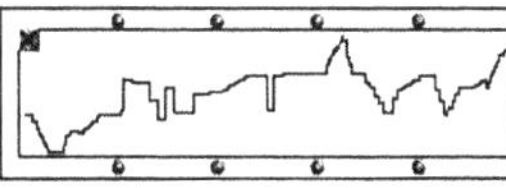	(10 100)
	In this example, frequency and intensity variations are sequences (motions) of random length and speed.				
Sans direction par excès d'information	15000	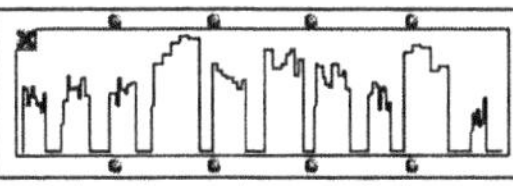	(-1000 0)	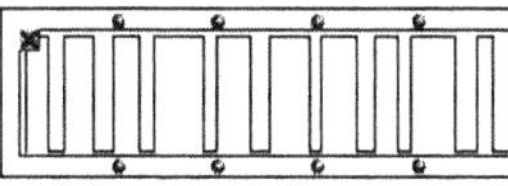	(10 100)
	This simulation is made up of the superimposition of four sound-files we got from four profiles of the type displayed. Each frequency profile is made up of constructed sequences of random length and speed. Intensity profiles are flat, they separate sequences from one another. Here, we have taken four tracks of frequency variation so as to constitute different layers of sound: (-1000 0), (500 1500), (2000 2500) and (3000 3500).				
Stationnaire (cyclique)	32000	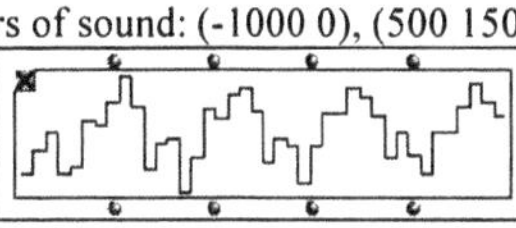	(0 600)	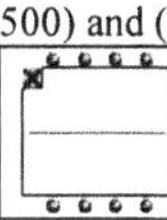	(100 100)
	Here, we use a cycle of frequencies slowly repeated four times (8s each) with variations.				
Stationnaire simple	20000	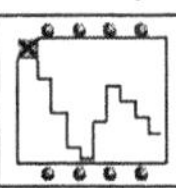	(-600 0)	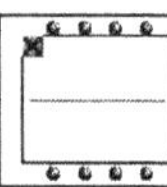	(100 100)
	To simulate this UST, we have taken four slowly marked out (20s) values, random in frequency.				
En flottement	20000	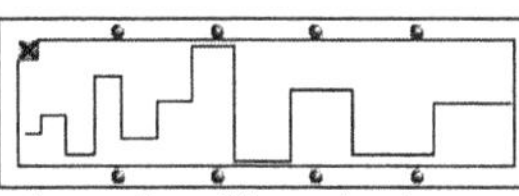	(0 2400)	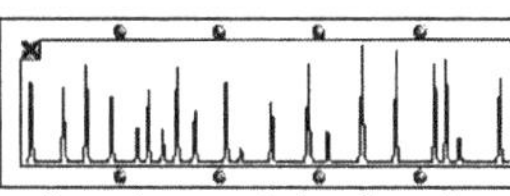	(0 100)
	Low density peaks of intensity (separated by rests often close to 1s), of random position and amplitude, provide a selection of snatches whose frequencies are, in themselves, random. In this simulation, the continuum is a rest.				
En suspension	15000	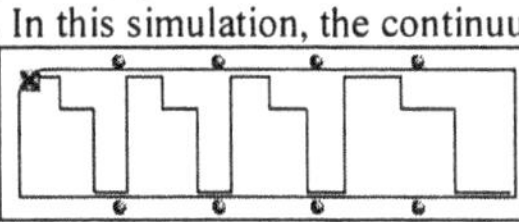	(600 1200)	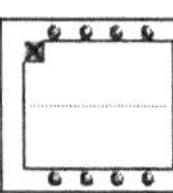	(50 50)
	In this simulation, we have used a cell of three frequency values, repeated four times slowly, while the intensity is constant.				
Lourdeur	20000	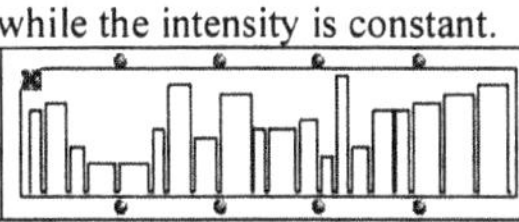	(0 1200)	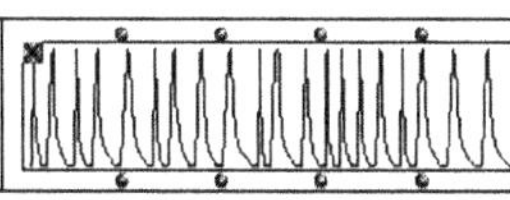	(0 100)
	The present UST is simulated thanks to large irregular bell-shaped profiles (of variable length about 1s) applied to the intensity, and combined with layers of random frequency.				
Qui avance	15000	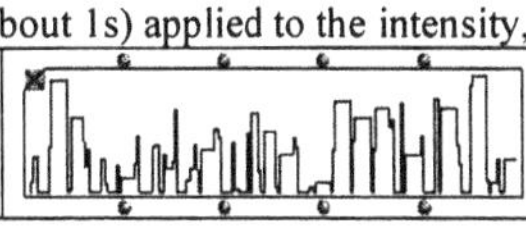	(0 2000)	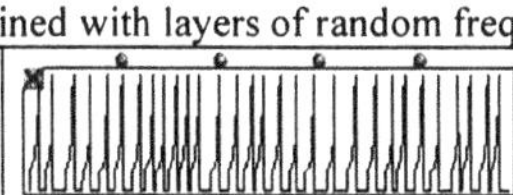	(0 100)

	Here, we have set up groups of three values random in frequency, separated by rests of variable length, with an intensity profile increasing on the three notes. The sound which is produced by that simulation is added to the transposed initial sound, so as to create a seemingly necessary continuum.

5 Application of this model to visuals

The first observation of the application of the MTP model occurred during Kari Beate Tandberg's presentation of a work during the Document Academy Summer School at the University of Tromsø in June 2005. She wanted to transcribe into music a picture representing a stretch of water on which raindrops were starting to fall. To make that transcription, she captured the time variation of the image luminosity integrated in the whole picture. Then, she got a relatively flat time-curve, randomly punctuated by short and irregular peaks. This curve is typical of MTP 17, which characterizes a UST *En flottement.* Consequently she used the curve to synchronize a sound generator which produced a continuous background noise on which sound events – functions of the peak level – were added. That sound was really *En flottement.* It should be clarified that Kari Beate Tandberg did not know about the theory of UST and that her approach was an artistic one, not a simulation. However, this example shows that the analysis in MTP can happen to be totally pertinent for the analysis and the synchronization of multimedia works.

We also made a quantitative analysis in MTP and UST of *Rhythm 21* by Hans Richter. This work was chosen because of the scarcity of time-related variables in it: the piece is composed of black and white rectangles on backgrounds of the opposite colour, whose surfaces and positions vary. We were able to cut that work in MTP precisely and totally, without any problem. We were able to find several UST, the main one being the *Trajectoire inexorable.* Only two pertinent variables are used in that work, F being here materialized by the size of the elements and I by their position. In visuals, these variables are not conveyed by any particular rectangle but they characterize a group pattern of the geometrical parameters (centre or edge elements): position and size.

An important phenomenon was noted during this analysis: MTP do not depend on the work but on the analyzed document in context of its reception. That distinction was already very clear in the analysis of sound documents: UST and MTP are not inscribed in the score, instead they crucially depend on the musical interpretation, so as to have the MIM composers struggling over the correct execution of the examples they themselves have composed. The importance of the context of reception is just as great as far as visuals are concerned. The analysis was made on a digitalized video file and depending on the screen that was used (analogical or flat), the UST and MTP varied in certain spots in the file.

6 Conclusion

Our model provides an operational basis on which to set up simulations, and also provides numerous quantitative criteria. It is open enough to be applied broadly, and it should be interesting to seek how other sound classifications, especially those established on great lengths, could be deconstructed into profiles and profilemes. The deconstruction system which we propose can be applied to them. Such a deconstruction should permit the determination of how UST are combined together in these classifications. Finally, our model succeeds in its main aim, which was to provide a description adaptable in computing. That model easily allows the taking into account of more than two variables and it can be applied to the field of visuals. Visuals being tabular and non-linear, it is probable that the simple transposition of Motifs into variables is not sufficient to describe the entire units which we are to encounter.

The analysis in MTP also shows that the reading of an audiovisual artistic document is largely dependent on the context of its reception and that it could not be applied to a theory based on the philology/hermeneutics interrelation; reading an artistic document consists in living its effective perception and not in intellectually reconstructing a hypothetical referent document.[13]

7 References

Daquet, Alice, 2004. *Étude de la pertinence psychologique des "Unités Sémiotiques Temporelles", mémoire de maîtrise de psychologie cognitive 2003-2004 sous la direction de Charles Tijus et Stephen Mc Adams.* University of Paris.

Delalande, François, 1989. La terrasse des audiences au clair de lune: essai d'analyse esthésique. La prise en compte des écoutes-types comme points de vue d'analyse. *Analyse musicale* 16, 75-84.

------. 1991. L'analyse musicale, discipline expérimentale? *Analyse musicale* 23, 11-20.

Klinkenberg, Jean-Marie, 1996. *Précis de sémiotique générale.* Liège: De Boeck & Larcier.

MIM, 1996. *Les Unités Sémiotiques Temporelles, éléments nouveaux d'analyse musicale.* Marseille: MIM.

13 Such a document may exist in a digitalized video file, but certain computerized works such as the adaptive poetical generators take into account the absence of that document in their conception.

------. 2002. *Les Unités Sémiotiques Temporelles, nouvelles clefs pour l'écoute, outil d'analyse musicale*. CD-ROM. Marseille: MIM.

Richard L. Anderson, Brian C. O'Connor, and Jodi L. Kearns

The Functional Ontology of Filmic Documents

1 Message and Meaning

More than a quarter century ago, film theorist Bertrand Augst asked, "Why can't we use a computer to measure and speak of filmic structure in the same way we can for verbal text?" (Augst 1981) We had then sophisticated means to extract key words from word-based texts and we had various forms of structural analysis at varying levels of granularity. Yet difficulties for film studies arise from the "literary metaphor." This is not to say that there is no discourse mechanism at work in films, only that attempts at one to one correspondence between the frame and the word or the shot and the sentence or similar impositions of the verbal form onto the image form have failed. Films are not word documents. Films do not have a rigidly defined grammatical structure. Images are not words. Shots are not sentences (Pryluck 1976), indeed "shot" is ill-defined (Bonitzer 1977).

Precisely because filmic messages are not word messages, they provide a means for probing the complementary relationship between message and meaning. We examine here a few phases of our probing of filmic documents, and the relationship between structure and meaning. We have taken the liberty of sketching the earlier phases and of presenting the most recent in somewhat more detail. Considerations of the early phases, among other issues of document use, led to the functional ontology construction as a foundation for this probing and for wider concerns within the arena of messages, meanings, and uses.

2 Functional Ontology Construction

Functional ontology construction (FOC) is a pragmatic approach to studying problems in information science concerning the relationship between documents and behavior (Anderson 2006). One of the underlying principles of the FOC approach is the notion of a binary model of the document. Function or meaning has an independent but complementary relationship with the structure of the document. This idea is consistent with Shannon and Weaver's information theory (1949), semiotic theory (Eco 1976), Wittgenstein's "language games" (Blair 1990), Skinner's (1957) theory of verbal behavior, and Dawkins' (1976) theory of memetics. Before proceeding further it is necessary to discuss the notion of functional ontology.

The functional ontological space provides a common ontological context for behaviors such as information seeking or browsing and the documents that would satisfy the user's needs. This concept is similar to the behavior analytic notion of behavioral environment. The functional ontology is the set of environmental stimuli and historical factors that have function for an individual at a particular point in time – those things that select behavior. This usage of the term ontology is closer to the philosophical usage (Flew 1986) than the technical use of the term in information science.

In information science, ontology describes a categorization system such as the Library of Congress system or a hierarchy of categories such as Yahoo's web directory. This use of the term is more akin to the notion of a foundational or upper ontology (Smith 2003); an ontology that contains "everything that is the case" as Wittgenstein (1922) pursued in the *Tractatus Logico-Philosophicus*. We suggest that this is the notion of ontology at the core of much Library and Information Science work. Wittgenstein's (1953) later work on language games suggests that the relative nature of language games makes the concept of a universal ontology untenable. This position marked Wittgenstein's break with the logical positivists. Bertrand Russell was highly critical of this position and suggested that Wittgenstein was "tired of serious thinking and invented a doctrine which would make such an activity unnecessary" (Russell 1985, 161).

If one accepts Buckland and Liu (1995) and Copeland's (1997) criticism of the state of thought in information science and their explanation of the problem as being the dominance of a positivistic philosophical orientation, then one requires the rejection of a positivistic ontology in favor of a functional ontology. Smith (2003) suggests that

> the project of building one single ontology, even one single top-level ontology, which would be at the same time non-trivial and also readily adopted by a broad population of different information systems communities, has largely been abandoned (115).

Ontology within the context of this work is simply that which exists within the environment of an individual. The functional ontology is comprised of those elements of the individual's environment that have behavioral function. Ontology as traditionally used in information science emerges as a consequence of the collective instances of individual behavior.

We conceptualize a document as a bundle of attributes or signals. The term signal is preferred for two reasons. First, the term signal has a dynamic connotation. The FOC approach has an underlying assumption that the relationship between users and documents is a system of selection, which requires the examination of change over time. Second, if one were to use the FOC strategy in a research or engineering setting, then a signal detection approach would be a likely tactical approach to the problem at hand. The signal detection approach is used in our examination of Bellour's "System of a Fragment" (Bellour 2000).

When an individual interacts with a document, the signals that make up the document become part of the individual's ontology and may acquire behavioral function for the individual. This notion will allow the application of the behavior analytic technique of functional analysis to the analysis of the relationships between the user and the document. FOC is a direct application of the behavior analytic technique of functional analysis. Skinner (1953) discusses the general approach taken here in *Science and Human Behavior.*

> The external variables of which behavior is a function provide for what may be called a causal or functional analysis. We undertake to predict and control the behavior of an individual organism. This is our "dependent variable" – the effect for which we are to find the cause. Our "independent variables" – the causes of behavior – are the external conditions of which behavior is a function. Relations between the two – the "cause-and-effect relationships" in behavior are the laws of a science. A synthesis of these laws expressed in quantitative terms yields a comprehensive picture of the organism as a behaving system (35).

The continuing evolution of our model and our analyses of documents are grounded in the approach Skinner describes.

3 Initial Model of Filmic Documents

Our initial approach and first publication in this arena were made in the mid-1980s with technology that has already slipped into antiquity – analog videodiscs and an Amiga 1000 desktop computer (O'Connor 1991). The first success of the approach was to reduce the enormous amount of time required to do film analysis by hand and eye. Early film analysis required sitting with a projector and watching and writing and timing quickly or using the equipment of a film editor and looking frame by frame at the filmic text. We had hard-wired the videodisc player to the computer; written programming that enabled control of the image – normal speed, forward, reverse, high speed, frame-by-frame; and written programming that allowed gathering and display of data right on top of the film image on the monitor.

More significantly, we recast our model of the document. Instead of seeking some algorithmic relation between the shot and the word or sentence, we thought back to the fundamental activity in key word extraction from a verbal text at the time – looking for blank spaces or punctuation marks. This was fundamentally a matter of looking for points of discontinuity in the signal stream. The basic idea was to go through a text character by character; if the character was a letter or number, hold on to it for some future activity; if the character was a blank space or punctuation mark, stop looking at the data stream and go perform an activity such as checking the collection of letters just accumulated against a stop list or dictionary.

We reasoned that we could simply look at some attribute of the film and so long as the signal remained within certain parameters, keep going; but when there was a "significant" change in the data stream, stop and perform some action. With this early system we were limited in what we could measure automatically. The result was a set of experiments that still required human engagement with the document and the technology; however, the speed and certain digital capabilities opened new avenues.

We looked at the filmic text as a three-dimensional signal set. There were 24 frames (US film standard; 25 European) or still photographs per second of standard running time. The individual frame was comprised of pixels addressable on X and Y axes; any set of two or more contiguous frames represented time across a Z axis. The frame was the constant addressable unit with addressable points within the frame. We also looked at the same system as the potentially changing set of values for any one or more pixel locations.

At the time, measurement of color values and edges was beyond the abilities of our system. However, we could measure the size of any segment of a frame and location of any pixel or set of pixels. Moving the cursor to a point on the image on the screen and clicking the mouse gave the X, Y coordinates of the point; clicking and holding the mouse down enabled the drawing of a rectangle of any size up to the size of the entire screen. Releasing the mouse caused the software to calculate the area of the rectangle, print the value to the screen, and store it for future calculations. Generating and storing the coordinates of the initial point in the rectangle enabled calculation of changes in location across frames, as well as changes in size across frames.

Using these simple capabilities we sought a means to calibrate our calculations to some aspect(s) of film structure and meaning. We found two films with nearly identical "topics" but two widely varying audience reactions. Both film segments presented approximately 50 women running marathons in urban settings. One, made by Olympic documentarian Bud Greenspan, produced adjectives such as "dynamic", "exciting", and "engaging"; while the other, a local Moscow coverage of the Goodwill Games, produced audience reactions of "dull", "boring", and "snoozer." We reasoned some aspect of the production – the message structure – must account for much of this difference in reactions and set about to measure structural differences.

We drew rectangles around the women in each frame – one rectangle around the group if more than one woman was in the frame; one around the most central of the women in the group; and one around the single woman if there was only one. We recognized that a rectangle is not the same as an outline of the two-dimensional form of each woman or group, but reasoned that rectangular framing had the strength of Western art traditions and would likely hold a stable relationship to the actual female shapes. We established a set of strict criteria for just where to start and stop the rectangle.

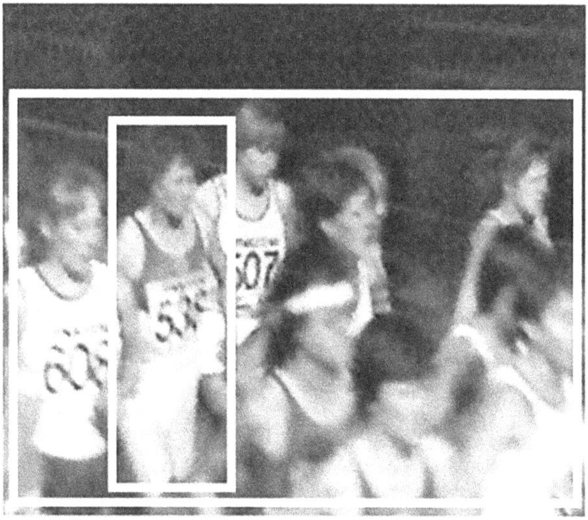

Figure 1. Adapted screen shot of rectangle concept.

From this rectangle data we could derive the percentage of the frame occupied by each woman or group and just where in the frame they were. Simply looking at the size and location of the rectangle in each successive frame enabled us to describe points of change and derive duration of screen presence. Applying these processes to our two marathon film segments we discovered that the exciting film left its subjects on the screen only one third the time that the snoozer did. The longest period without change in the first was 19.1 seconds, in the second 61.88 seconds. The mean on-screen time in the exciting piece was 4.99 seconds, in the dull work 14.98 seconds. When we looked at the differences in the areas of the rectangles we found nearly a 2:1 difference. The exciting piece averaged 55767 pixels per rectangle, while the dull one averaged 28394 pixels.

Both the screen time and the rectangle areas fit with standard film production practice and with work that had, at that time, recently been done by Watt and Krull on television viewing preferences (Watt 1979; Watt and Krull 1974). On the whole, the closer the subject is to the lens, the more engaging; and the more rapidly the image changes (up to a point) the more engaging. We also noted that the points where there were significant changes were points where we could extract a representative frame (e.g., first frame after the point of change) and have a set of key frames.

We accomplished a first order analysis of the document structures by using the native elements of the film and by referring directly to the film, not to some vague definition of "shot" or "Close Up". Of course, we had not yet reached an entirely software-based analysis and we were able to speak of relationships between frames and across sets of frames in only a very crude manner. We had stepped away from the literary metaphor and established the potential of a numeric representation to provide a robust and stable means of description and analysis.

4 Measuring Filmic Structure

Audience verbal reactions to the set of marathon videos and television form attribute measurements of James Watt led us directly into a study accomplished in 2000 (Watt 1979). Watt had calculated rates of structural change in television programs of the 1970s with precise articulations of Shannon's 1947 algorithm from the *Mathematical Theory of Communication* (Shannon 1949). While acknowledging that program content is not insignificant to the longevity of popularity in television programs such as *Sesame Street* and *Mr. Rogers' Neighborhood*, Watt's focus was on form, or structure, rather than content.

With interpretations of Shannon's formula to specific form attributes of videos, Watt measured complexity of structural attributes such as the number of sets and scene changes per episode, dialogue dependence, and character appearances. In congruence with Shannon's model, complexity of structural attributes of videos yielded results called *entropies*, where – in a Shannon sense – entropy expresses the average rate of structural complexity in a communicated message. Audience reactive descriptors to the 2 marathon films ("dynamic", "exciting", "engaging"; and while "dull", "boring", and "snoozer") are argued to represent reactions to structural complexity of the 2 films. Watt and Watt & Krull similarly recorded audience reactive descriptors ("exciting", "interesting", "surprising", and "boring") and correlated these reactions to specific moments in the television programming with structural complexity measurements representing moments of high or low entropy.

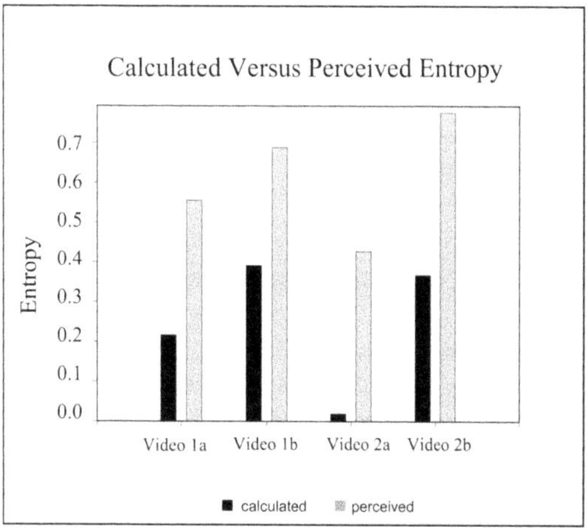

Figure 2. Relation of calculated entropy to children's perceived entropy.

In this phase of our work we used children's reactions o pairs of videos on the same topic, with one video produced expressly for children and one expressly for adults. Entropy measurements of seven form attributes of videos were calculated, and showed significantly greater structural change in the children's videos than in those for adults. Child viewers were shown one of these two sets of documents and then asked a series of comparative judgment questions that would be used to quantify their perceptions of structural complexity of each film. Comparative judgments simply quantified responses elicited from viewers who were asked to place small stickers on line graphs displaying polar reactions to certain questions.

The comparative judgment graphs were expected to elicit perceptions about the changes in the program information viewers may have felt after watching a video. These emotive descriptions – interesting, exciting, funny, boring, surprising – were the very adjectival representations of entropy. We asked the viewers, for example, *Did you find the program boring?* The viewer independently placed her stickers on the line graphs in response to six such questions and the specific locations of the stickers were translated into numerical representation on the same scale of the calculated measurements. Figure 2 shows similar trends between the mean calculated entropy measurements and the mean perceived entropy measurements. Clearly, corresponding results are not identical values, though one can see that the relationships between perceived entropy values show similarities to the relationships between the calculated entropy values. The relationships between the sets of videos suggest that a calculated entropy value could render a numeric representation for these and other videos for child audiences that reflects the opinions of the child viewers.

These data support our hypothesis that there would be a significant positive correlation between mechanically calculated entropy measurements for a set of videos and the perceived entropy measurements made by child viewers of the video sets. Thus they can be used as useful and predictive elements of representations of children's videos, akin to Augst's vision.

5 Measuring Distraction in PowerPoint Presentations

We have explored structural distraction in PowerPoint documents in an attempt make our general model more robust by stepping beyond video into a message that uses words, sounds, photographs, and videos. We reasoned that with formulae derived from Shannon's equation, we could offer a numerical representation of what makes the PPT presentations of some of our colleagues exciting and entertaining, while others' are boring and predictable.

Since, anecdotally, audiences use the same reactive descriptors to PPT presentations that were observed in the previous studies of film structure, it seemed reasonable to measure PPT structure by the same algorithm. Entropy measures of PPT form attributes were selected to specifically address elements of multimedia presentations that make them different from traditional presentations (overhead transparencies, mimeographed handouts, greyscale photocopies), such as sound effect occurrence, slide transition incidence, picture dependence, mixed fonts, and others.

Values for ten form attributes were calculated. Scattered among the results were extreme instances where entropy measured high – higher, in fact, than at any other point in the individual PPTs. *Entropic burst*, we called this instance of high entropy communication. The entropic burst is the moment at which cognitive structure strays from the anticipatory response (Hayes 1993); or that instant that all else is forgotten (Wilson 1999) and the viewer accepts that it is okay to react to the surprise. One recognizes the entropic burst when the presentation is momentarily structurally different than the standard or normal structure established by the author and presenter. Perhaps a sound effect is used to emphasize a major argument, or a slide transition effect occurs mid-presentation to introduce a new topic.

Since entropy is a measure of structure that ranges from near stasis 0 (zero) to near complete chaos as it approaches 1 (one), the effect of a message of any length greater than one bit takes place over time. One way of stating our observations would be to say that at or near zero, the structure of a film, or a PPT, or any message would exhibit little or no surprise; while at or near one, surprises would be so frequent as to become ordinary. One might say at the middle of the curve – a normal curve – there is sufficient familiarity for a change of structure to be surprising. At those moments where entropy is near the top of the curve, the message has the least structural distraction.

A secondary, simple equation – $DF = (|0.5 - H|) * 20$ – was derived as a measure of a document's structural distraction factor (DF). To illustrate, if entropy of color occurrence was 0.13063 (low: end of the curve), the distraction factor of color occurrence for this particular presentation was 7.38732 (high); if entropy of sound effects was 0.52626 (high: middle of the curve), the distraction factor of sound effects for this particular presentation was 0.52528 (low) on the familiar of "1 to 10" scale.

We present the concept of entropy measures of document structures and the corollary distraction factors as precise quantitative ways to speak about documents. This does not mean that there is one or some small set of "perfect" structures for a particular message, nor is there a formula to ensure distraction-free messages, especially since the meaning is also dependent on the viewer.

6 Fine Grain Calibration of Signal Structure to Meaning

While the marathon film study, the children's videos study, and the Power Point Presentation study demonstrated rigorous means for speaking of document structure and its relationship to meaning, we were working only at a macro level of both analysis and the definition of meaning. We could correlate precise structural attributes with "dynamic, exciting" and "boring, snoozer" or with "I would really like to see that again." Also, human observation and determination of some points of change were still required. As more sophisticated means for analysis of the signal set became available, we faced an intriguing problem: how might we relate structure to a finer granularity of meaning?

For an answer, we turned away from aggregated reactions of many people to the reactions of one person. Exceptional cases may very well be lost in the statistical aggregation and methodological formalism found in most studies in information science. These exceptional performances fall into the tails of the statistical distribution and would likely be explained away as variance or discarded all together. Gilbert (1978) suggests that the key to improving performances lies within the tails of the statistical distribution – the exceptional performances and the spectacular failures. The case study that follows is an examination of the behavior of an exceptional individual, film theorist, Raymond Bellour, of whose work Augst commented: "It remains exemplary in the rigor and precision of the analysis performed and, to date, it is still the best example of what a genuine structural analysis of a filmic text could attempt to do" (Augst 1980, 1).

7 Description of the Bodega Bay Sequence

Bellour's rigorous analysis of the Bodega Bay sequence of *The Birds*, "A System of a Fragment" (2000), provided a record of his engagement with the signal set of a portion of the Hitchcock film. The sequence is, on the face of it, rather simple. A young woman, Melanie Daniels, sets out in a small motorboat with a pair of lovebirds in a cage. She crosses Bodega Bay to leave the birds as a gift to catch the attention of a young man, Mitch Brenner. She enters the Brenner's house, leaves the birds, and returns to the boat. She returns across the bay. Mitch spots Melanie crossing the bay. Mitch drives around the bay to the pier where Melanie will be arriving. A sea gull strikes Melanie and cuts her head before she reaches the pier. Mitch helps Melanie out of the boat and they walk toward a shop to tend to the wound.

When Melanie is on the bay, Bellour points out, we are presented with a classic Hollywood structural attribute: alternation – we see Melanie looking, then that at which she looks, then Melanie again. This alternation continues until she arrives at the house. While she is in the house we simply observe her behavior, except for a brief look out the window at the barn. Bellour sees this scene in the house as a "hinge" in the design of the film. It disrupts the pattern of alternation, while it also takes Melanie off the water and brings her indoors.

As Melanie returns to the boat, we see what looks rather like the beginning of her trip – she is getting into the boat and heading off. However, Mitch sees her; then, she and Mitch acknowledge one another. Bellour refers to the scene in the house (the hinge) and the double act of seeing as the "two centers" of the Bodega Bay sequence.

As an integral component of his analytic method, Bellour includes photographic frames from the Bodega Bay sequence – key frames. Ordinarily, these are the first frame of each shot in the sequence. In our analysis, we operate at the level of the individual frame (29.97 frames per second in the system of digital video with which we worked). We refer to Bellour's shot numbers and to his two primary divisions: "A" for Melanie's trip across the bay, her time in the house, and her return to the boat; "B" for her return trip in the boat. According to Bellour's analysis and textual description of the Bodega Bay sequence, the following elements should be present in the physical document: key frames and key frame sets, alternation, and two centers – the "hinge" sequence and a second center.

The relationship between the physical structure of the Bodega Bay sequence of *The Birds* and Bellour's description of the structure of the sequence is the primary concern of the functional analysis. In other words, what physical attributes of the sequence prompted Bellour to make the statements he made about the film?

Catania (1998) defines "a tact as a verbal response occasioned by a discriminative stimulus". A discriminative stimulus is a stimulus that occasions a particular response and is correlated with reinforcement. In this particular case, the tacts or verbal responses of interest are the statements about the Bodega Bay sequence made by Bellour (2000) in *The Analysis of Film.* The discriminative stimuli are the physical dimensions of the film that prompted Bellour to make the statements he did. The reinforcement in this case is assumed on the grounds that *The Analysis of Film* is considered to be a seminal work in the film theory community and Bellour and others applied the same types of analysis to other films.

8 Structural Analysis of the Bodega Bay Sequence

Techniques for measuring physical attributes of video documents have existed for some time. Dalianas, Allen and England (1995) reviewed a number of automated techniques for the segmentation of video documents that included the analysis of raw image differences between frames, a number of histogram based techniques, and an edge detection based approach. However, in choosing a technique for structural analysis of a video document, the nature of the question one hopes to answer must be taken into account. Macro-level approaches such as those taken by O'Connor and by Kearns and O'Connor (2004) measure the structure of an entire film or message in Shannon's (Shannon and Weaver 1949) terms. Bellour described the Bodega Bay sequence in fairly microscopic detail. An approach such as those we described earlier would not be granular enough to match adequately Bellour's description of the sequence. It should be noted that Kearns's (2005) concept of "entropic bursts" might provide a finer grained Information Theoretic approach for the task at hand. The segmentation techniques reviewed by Dalianas, Allen, and England (1995) provide the level of detail necessary for the detection of key frames and framesets in Bellour's analysis, however the techniques would not be appropriate for detecting alternation or detecting the centers within the sequence as identified by Bellour.

The ultimate goal in analyzing the structure of the Bodega Bay sequence was to find the elements of the physical structure of the film that prompted Bellour to make the statements (tacts) he did about the film. To accomplish this task, it was necessary to look at the structure of the segment on at least two levels. First, Bellour breaks the sequence into "shots" or frame sets and selects key frames. This requires an examination of individual frames. Second, Bellour describes alternation between the frame sets, the unique character of the "hinge," the two centers, and the gull strike. These tacts are descriptions of the relationship between frame sets.

In standard digital images each and every color is composed of a certain amount of red (R), a certain amount of green (G), and a certain amount of blue (B) – with black being the absence of any R, G, or B and with white being maximum of each. In the frame images we captured there is a possibility of 256 shades of red, 256 shades of green, and 256 shades of blue, for a possible palette of over 16 million colors. Deriving a histogram of each of the RGB components or the aggregated values distributed across an X-axis of 255 points (the zero origin being the 256th) yields a fingerprint – a color distribution map – of each frame.

It would seem obvious that within the large number of frames in a film (~30/sec) there is likely to be a little bit of variation in color distribution from frame to frame; however, this variation will be small in sequential frames depicting the same objects with the same composition and lighting, and the variation will be larger as the objects change or the composition changes or the lighting changes. Perhaps one of the most appealing aspects of mapping color distribution is that it is an entirely software-based process. There is no necessity for human intervention to determine and mark what is to be considered the "subject" or how many pixels (percentage of frame area) make up some viewer-selected object.

9 Method

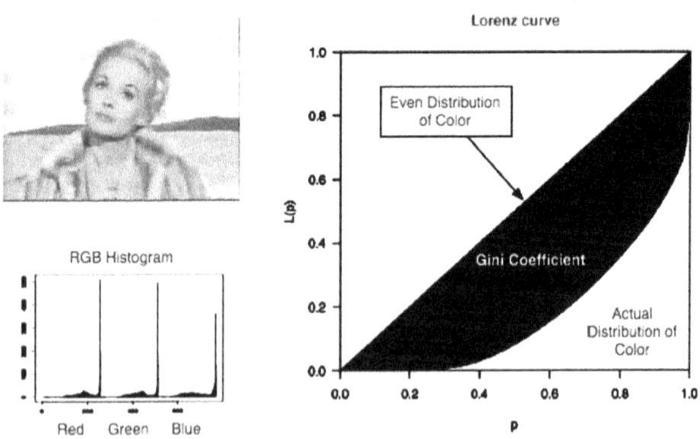

Figure 3. Gini coefficient as "finger print" of frame RGB data.

The Bodega Bay sequence from *The Birds* was extracted and converted to AVI format from the 1986 Video Disc version of *The Birds*. The resulting file was segmented into 12,803 JPG image files. RGB histograms were generated for each of the 12,803 frames using the Python Imaging Library. A Lorenz transformation was then performed on each histogram. The Gini coefficient was calculated to generate a scalar value representing the color distribution of each frame, as in Figure 3. Differences in Gini coefficients between successive frames were calculated as a measure of change across frames.

10 Detection of Key Frames and Frame Sets

Figure 4 shows the absolute value of the difference between the Gini value of a particular frame of the Bodega Bay sequence of *The Birds* and the previous frame. The mean difference between frames for all frames is 0.003826, which is represented on the graph by the (upper) horizontal line. The mean difference between Bellour's key frames was 0.075678. The difference values fall into a bimodal distribution. The difference values of key frames and the proceeding frame were an order of magnitude higher than the difference values between frames that were not identified as key frames.

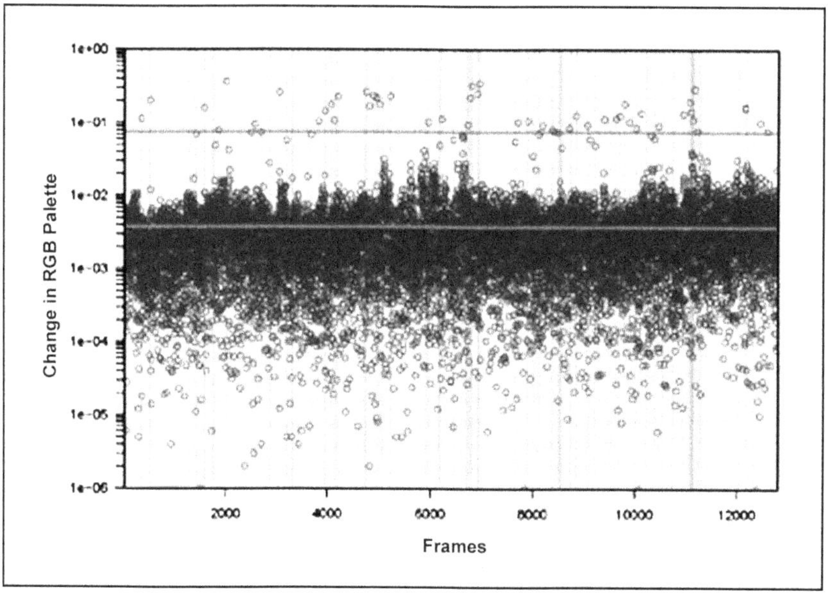

Figure 4. Order of magnitude difference distinguishes key frames

11 Analysis of Frame Sets

Figure 5 shows the Gini coefficients of each frame of the segment broken down by shot number, presenting the "flow" of the color distributions across the time of the film sequence together with some key elements of Bellour's tacts. Once Melanie is underway, we see in the graph of Bellour's shots 15 through 31, a distinct graphical presentation of "alternation" – Melanie, what she sees, Melanie, what she sees, and so on.

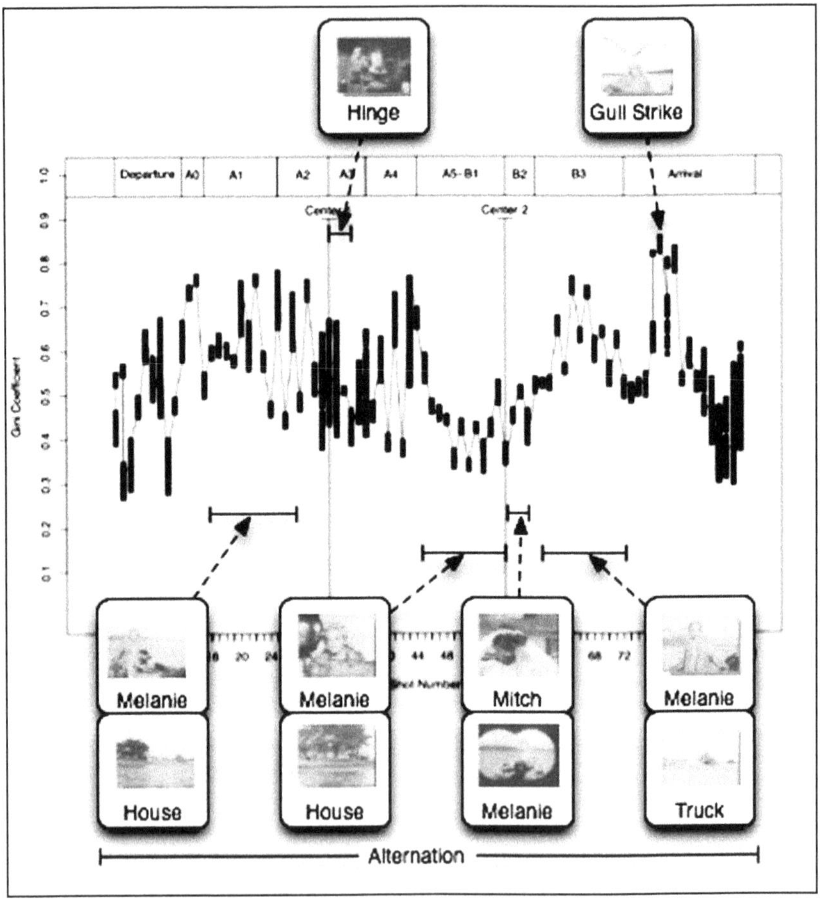

Figure 5. Map of Bellour's tacts onto shot RGB data.

The RGB graph does not necessarily indicate that there is alternation in the sense of Melanie/dock/Melanie/dock/Melanie; however, one would still be able to say that there is alternation of the RGB pallets, regardless of whether a human viewer would say that the same objects were in front of the lens. Such an RGB alternation might have its own discursive power.

Bellour's "hinge" sequence runs from frame number 5219 to frame number 6447 – Bellour's shot numbers 32 – 36 (A3). Bellour also refers to this sequence as the first of the "two centers." It would make some sense, then, that it would be in the vicinity of the center and the final frame number 6447 is very near the center of 12,803 frames. More significant is the distribution of the Gini values – they are clustered more closely to the .5 line and they display much less variation than we see in most of the rest of the graph. Given the different form of the distributions on either side of the "first center" it is not untenable to assert the graphic appearance of a hinge.

What is not so immediately evident graphically is the second center – that point in the sequence when Mitch sees Melanie – a second center in that it breaks up the rhyme of the trip out and the trip back for a second time. That is, Melanie has exited the house and heads back to the dock and the boat. It seems that after having been in the house – the first center – Melanie will simply head back; however, Mitch's discovery of Melanie and the eventual union of "hero and heroine for the first time in the ironic and ravishing complicity of an exchange" (Bellour 2000, 53) interrupt the simplicity of the return.

Bellour suggests that the second center "stands out less starkly;" however, it does stand out. Shot 43, whose large number of Gini values suggests both its length and the varying data set, is where Melanie moves along the dock and into the boat. Shots 44 and 45 begin the pattern of displacement along the Gini value that was typical in the earlier alternation. This alternation pattern develops strongly between 48 and 54 – alternating Gini values remain almost fixed in place along the Gini axis and they occupy a narrow band of the axis. At 55, the shot crosses the 0.5 boundary and the subsequent Gini values suggest alternation again, though of a more widely distributed sort. It is during this fragment that Melanie has watched Mitch, then, at 54 Mitch runs to the house and at 55 Melanie stands up and tries to start the motor. The second center displays a form of alternation, but this takes place in a manner that presents almost a mirror image of the alternation in the trip out – the alternation here "hanging below" the 0.5 line. As the second center closes, the alternation repeats the pattern of the trip out – all the Gini values arcing above the 0.5 line.

12 Discussion

The order of magnitude difference between the mean differences for key frames and non-key frames presents a numerical representation of the key frame tact. Thus we have a precise, numerical way of speaking of the key frames identified by Bellour, as well as an automated way of detecting those frames.

The clustering of Gini coefficients in the "on water" sequences with distinctly different and separated patterns presents a numerical representation of the alternation tact. Melanie's Brenner house sequence presents a distinctly different numerical and graphical representation, giving us the hinge tact. The numerical and graphical "bunching up" in the representation of Mitch's discovery of Melanie and their double seeing alternation presents us with the second center and a means for speaking precisely of the two-centers tact.

Bellour does not speak to any significant degree about the gull strike on Melanie, though the strike is often mentioned in other discussions of the Bodega Bay sequence. The entire strike is approximately one second of running time and may have been too microscopic for Bellour to address in his analysis. However, the numerical analysis and graphical presentation present a striking data set. Almost every frame presents a Gini value significantly different from its predecessor. This is a very high entropy portion of the sequence – several rapid changes in the data stream in less than a second of running time is a very different pattern from that of any other portion of the film. One might suggest that digital frame-by-frame precision might have enabled Bellour to speak of this brief fragment.

The close correlation between the frame-to-frame analysis and Bellour's writing suggests that the use of an expert analyst's response to *The Birds* indeed demonstrates the utility of the FOC approach to this problem. Perhaps one of the most significant consequences of the close correlation is the availability of a "vocabulary" for description and analysis. A fundamental problem with previous systems of analysis has been the reliance on words to describe visual, time-varying documents. Setting about describing, analyzing, and indexing word-based documents with words is simple, though not necessarily easy or trivial. One can extract words from a document; use some rule for selecting certain words; and then subject the document and the representative words to scrutiny. If the supposed representative words do not occur frequently or at all in the document, no synonyms occur, and no words of some higher or lower lever of specificity occur, then we can easily say the words are not significantly representative. Since there have been no one-to-one correspondence between words and images or parts of images; since there are no precise standardized terms for entropy values of production attributes of videos (that is, "fast-paced" and "beautifully lighted" are not precisely defined); and since words are not native elements of the image track, there is no reliable way of speaking precisely of attributes and changes of attributes across frames. Being able to represent these attributes and time-varying states of the attributes at the pixel, frame, frame set ("shot"), sequence, and document level with the same processes and terms should enable deeper and more fruitful analysis.

At the same time, the same techniques provide means for discovering structural elements. It would be too facile to suggest that we now have a robust mechanism for automated description of filmic structure; however, we do at least have a robust automated means for mapping the structure. One could run any film through a frame by frame comparison of RGB and be able to state that certain portions remain stable for some time, then change; and at some points, rapid changes take place – the points of change, the points of discontinuity in the data stream, represent points where something different is happening. One function of such points of continuity might be as indexing points – pull out, for example, the 40 frames at which there is the greatest frame-to-frame change and have a rough "index" of the film. Find the one, two, or three most frequent RGB fingerprints and use representative frames with those values to present the "look" of the film.

Perhaps even more intriguing, and a likely avenue of rewarding research, would be the use of RGB fingerprints in classification. Do all of Hitchcock's films, or at least those from a particular period, share the same fingerprint patterns? If De Palma is the heir to Hitchcock, do his films actually bear a numerical similarity to Hitchcock's films? Do music videos and early Russian documentaries (e.g. Vertov's *Man with the Movie Camera*), films with very different structures from the classic Hollywood films studied by Bellour, yield useful numerical descriptions?

Of course, most videos are made up of more than simply RGB data. Multiple sound tracks for voice, narration, sound effects, and music significantly increase the amount of data available for analysis; however, there is no reason that these time-varying data could not be described using a similar numerical and graphical technique.

As demonstrated here, the data available for analysis is not limited to the signals available in the physically present document. Bellour's analysis of *The Birds*, in essence, becomes another signal or memetic attribute of the document. Other critics who have commented on *The Birds* or viewer reactions to the piece could be analyzed in the same manner that was applied to Bellour's work. Every person who interacts with a document and commits some permanent behavioral product of that interaction contributes to the document's signal set for subsequent uses.

In some sense, this becomes a fundamental aspect of the setting for considering the relationship between the document/message structure and the semantic meaning. The additional signal, for example a review, can have a significant impact on whether a document is accessed and on how it is evaluated for fitness to a given information need. The document is not necessarily static with the same impact on any given user; rather, it is an evolutionary process. The concept of document as evolutionary process receives more discussion in Wilson (1968).

Bellour (2000) sought means to explore and represent video documents with the precision already applied to verbal documents at the micro and macro levels. He sought means to go beyond what Augst termed the "gratuitousness and arbitrariness of impressionistic criticism" (1980, 2). The FOC approach offers the opportunity to do so; to enable speaking directly of the native elements (e.g. the RGB components and their changes across time); and, to paraphrase Godard, to confront vague ideas with precise images.

13 References

Anderson, Richard, 2006. *Functional ontology construction: A pragmatic approach to addressing problems concerning the individual and the informing environment*. Ph.D. Dissertation. Denton, TX: University of North Texas.

Augst, Bertrand, 1980. Commentary on Raymond Bellour's "Analysis of a segment from The Birds". Course handout.

------. 1981. Personal communication over coffee, Berkeley, CA.

Bellour, Raymond, and Constance Penley, 2000. *The analysis of film*. Bloomington, IN: Indiana University Press.

Blair, David C., 1990. *Language and representation in information retrieval*. Amsterdam; New York, NY: Elsevier Science Publishers.

Bonitzer, Pascal, 1977. Here: The notion of the shot and the subject of cinema. Bertrand Augst translation for course handout translation of Voici. *Cahiers du Cinema* 273(February), 5-18.

Buckland, Michael K., and Ziming Liu, 1995. History of information science. *Annual Review of Information Science and Technology 30*, 385-416.

Catania, A. Charles, 1998. *Learning* (4th ed.). Upper Saddle River, N.J.: Prentice Hall.

Copeland, Jud. H., 1997. *Engineering Design as a Foundational Metaphor for Information Science: A Resistive Postmodern Alternative to the "Scientific Model"*. Ph.D. Dissertation. Emporia, KS: Emporia State University.

Dalianas, Apostolos, Allen, Robert B., and Paul England, 1995. Comparison of Automatic Video Segmentation Algorithms. *Proceedings of the SPIE Conference on Integration Issues in Large Commercial Media Delivery Systems*, 2-16.

Dawkins, Richard, 1976/1989. *The Selfish Gene*. Oxford, UK: Oxford Press.

Eco, Umberto, 1976. *A theory of semiotics* (Advances in semiotics). Bloomington: Indiana University Press.

Flew, Antony, 1984. *A Dictionary of philosophy.* New York: St. Martin's Press.

Gilbert, Thomas F., 1978. *Human competence: engineering worthy performance.* New York: McGraw-Hill.

Kearns, Jodi L., 2001. *A mechanism for richer representation of videos for children: Calibrating calculated entropy to perceived entropy.* Ph.D. Dissertation. Denton, TX: University of North Texas.

------. 2005. Clownpants in the classroom? Entropy, humor, and distraction in multimedia instructional materials. Paper presented at the Document Academy 2005, Berkeley, CA.

Kearns, Jodi L., and Brian C. O'Connor, 2004. Dancing with entropy: form attributes, children, and representation. *Journal of Documentation* 60(2), 144-63.

O'Connor, Brian C., 1991. Selecting Key Frames of Moving Image Documents: A Digital Environment for Analysis and Navigation. *Microcomputers for Information Management* 8(2), 119-133.

O'Connor, Brian C., Jud H. Copeland, and Jodi L. Kearns, 2003. *Hunting and gathering on the information savanna: Conversations on modeling human search abilities.* Lanham, Md.: Scarecrow Press.

Pryluck, Calvin, 1976. *Sources of meaning in motion pictures and television.* Manchester, NH: Arno Press.

Russell, Bertrand, 1985. *My philosophical development*. London: Unwin Hyman.

Shannon, Claude E., and Warren Weaver, 1949. *The mathematical theory of communication.* Urbana: University of Illinois Press.

Skinner, Burrhus F., 1957. *Verbal behavior.* New York: Appleton-Century-Crofts.

Smith, Barry, 2003. Ontology. In *The Blackwell Guide to the Philosophy of Computing and Information*, ed. L. Floridi. Malden, MA: Blackwell Publishing, 155-167.

Watt, James, 1979. Television form, content attributes, and viewer behavior. In *Progress in Communication Sciences 1*, eds. Melvin J. Voigt and G. J. Hanneman. Norwood, N.J.: ABLEX, 54-90.

Watt, James, and Robert Krull, 1974. An information theory measure for television programming. *Communication Research* 1(1), 44-68.

Wilson, Patrick, 1968. *Two kinds of power: an essay on bibliographical control.* Berkeley: University of California Press.

------. 1999. Personal communication at lunch, Berkeley, CA.

Wittgenstein, Ludwig, 1922. *Tractatus logico-philosophicus.* With an introduction by Bertrand Russell. New York: Harcourt, Brace & company, inc.; London, K. Paul, Trench, Trubner & co., ltd.

------. 1953. *Philosophical investigations.* Translated by G.E.M. Anscombe. Oxford: Basil Blackwell.

Vesa Suominen

A Structural Approach to the History of Documentary Contents: Documentation Studies for Librarianship

1 Introduction

In this article, my aim is to find and illustrate the proper scholarly basis for librarianship, basing my search and illustration on a specific idea of the library. As an introduction, I shall shortly discuss the possible disciplinary contexts where we in a way or another could conceive of the library.

Documentation studies is a disciplinary current which can be regarded as a part of a wider field that could be called library information and documentation studies (LID). I use the notion of LID studies as a comprehensive term for a 'family of disciplines' like information science, documentation studies, but also others appeared in history under names such as library and information science (LIS), bibliography, book studies/history, etc. This field is characterised by the absence of an established disciplinary map, and consequently we could also list as independent parts of LID disciplines or disciplinary currents that in other contexts are considered as parts of information science, such as information retrieval, information seeking, information management, or bibliometrics.

By documentation studies I here mean primarily a disciplinary current that sometimes has unofficially been called the 'neodocumentation movement'. The word documentation itself within LID classically comes from the Otletian idea (e.g. Otlet 1935) in the beginning of 20th century, and thereafter it has had a history connected to the ideas and practices of the so-called information services and leading to disciplinary level phenomena such as "informatics" (see e.g. Mikhailov and Giliarevskii 1971). So-called neodocumentation has its origins in the last decades of the 20th century, and it consists of the interest some scholars have had in the concept of document and documentation (e.g. Buckland 1997, Lund 1999 and 2004, and Frohmann 2004, especially 199 ff., to mention just a few). As institutional manifestations could be mentioned documentation studies at the University of Tromsoe and the series of Document Academy (DOCAM) meetings. I perhaps can count my own work as one of the various relatively independent roots of neodocumentation, too (see e.g. Suominen 1990 and 1997). My own interest has especially been to outline a scholarly basis for our understanding of the library and librarianship as an alternative to the one provided by (library and) information science, which is my theme in this paper, as well.

Information science, if compared with documentation studies, may be more established, but at the same time it perhaps is more restricted by assumptions that are not as fertile for understanding the basic aspects of library and librarianship. In information science, the issues of library and librarianship are considered as one field where the results of research could be applied, as a "R&D activity", to put it in words by Ingwersen (1992, 4). Consequently the library and librarianship are, without further reflection, subsumed to the (in themselves somewhat dubious) "scientific" notions of information science, such as "information seeking", "information need" etc. (cf. Järvelin and Vakkari, 1988[1]), with inherent tendencies towards methodological individualism, userism (see e.g. Suominen 2004) and flatly rationalist understanding of man's social and cultural existence. The result is that when trying to grasp, what a library is, we only can ask what we use a library for, and then we can only make a library intelligible as a tool for our immediate use. We would not ask what the function of a library is in a wider and more fundamental cultural and social reality and in the cultural and social dimensions of our own existence.

In my view, documentations studies – as quite a young disciplinary current, consequently having the merit of not being crippled by too strongly established presumptions – could and should try to avoid the unsatisfactory views of the library and librarianship in information science.[2] However, so far there has not been very much interest in the special issues of library and librarianship within documentation studies or the 'neodocumentation movement' either (see e.g. the programs of the Document Academy meetings in DOCAM 2006).

As a disciplinary field, if compared with information science, documentation studies has the merit of better comprehending the various stages of existence of its objects (cf. e.g. Hjørland 2000[3] and Frohmann 2004,[4] e.g. 6-16). Documentation

---

1 The article – despite its title "*Library and* information science: the science of information seeking" (my italics) – can well be considered as the program declaration of Finnish information studies (as information science is called in Finland).

2 Or *library and information science*, which actually more or less means subsuming the library and librarianship under information and information science concepts, see e.g. Bennet 1988.

3 Hjørland suggests that "the object of study" should be changed "[...] from mental phenomena of ideas, facts and opinion, to social phenomena of communication, documents and memory institutions" (Hjørland 2000, 39), while in other respects still manifesting the userist undercurrent of information science in understanding library and librarianship, culminating the problem (of the discipline, of memory institutions, and presumably of librarianship as well) of investi-

studies, by the very notion of documentation and document, refers to material objects, which are the result of material production that also have economical aspects. They can be produced for the market, owned, sold and bought, etc., and which for these and other reasons also have juridical and political, and – last but not least – semiotic aspects.[5] The library and librarianship are about documents, not just about some abstract ideal information understood as knowledge or content of mind.

On the other hand, a reflective look at the library and librarianship would perhaps require that we adopt a more sophisticated understanding of history, culture and society, and of the human life and existence in them, as well. My point of departure in this respect is that, basically, the library and librarianship have to do with long lines of culture and society, the lines making a connection between past and present in the existence of culture and society, and in the human cultural and social existence. The Library and librarianship, after all, are things that have existed for some thousands of years. Consequently, we could compare them with phenomena like law or education. It would be plausible to think that the library has to do with some rather fundamental functions in the existence of culture and in our cultural existence.

Gadamer (1960) sees the basis of the hermeneutical problem in "man's finite, historical mode of being" (277). Especially important for Gadamer in this regard is the 'back-limit' of this existence. His theme of "rehabilitation of tradition and authority" (277-285) could be expressed in a concise form: We all start when it is our turn, and we always start something that already is there. 'What is there' matters, not only as a resource we can benefit from, but as an existing reality that is the basis of our existence. It has to do with cultural reproduction and the very constitution of our cultural and social existence.

The philosophical implication of this for the library would be that its specific and fundamental cultural and social role and responsibility would be especially related to that which already is present. In no library has any book been written in the future. On the other hand, some libraries have tried to collect all the books published so far. It is the part of the library in the social division of labour to look backwards – or rather that through it, society and culture may look backwards.

---

gating "information seekers' behaviour" (Hjørland 2000, 35-38). For similar positions, cf. also for instance Suominen 2002 and 2004, and Noruzi 2004.

4 Frohmann actually treats issues of scientific documentation, not librarianship.

5 Frohmann (2004, 6-16), however, in the same spirit as Blair (1990, 132-136), seems to totally play out the semiotic aspects, which – in my view – is not a well warranted attempt. I will not develop my counter-argument further in this respect, however, see Suominen 1997, 200-203 for further elaboration on this subject.

Then, perhaps the most important knowledge a librarian needs in his/her professional practice, the core of his/her proper professional expertise, would be knowledge about books and some other forms of documents that actually are existing. A librarian should know the books. Consequently, we could suggest – at the least – that one proper and perhaps the most important scholarly basis of librarianship would be their research.[6]

The perspective of documentation studies that is especially important for librarianship, in my view, would then be the study of existing documents, a study that can ask either

1) What documents are there? or
2) What kinds of documents are there?, and further, as a corollary of this question,
3) Are there some systematic or regular relationships between the kinds of documents?

The simplest form of bibliographic enumeration would be an answer to the first question. Even this "simple enumeration", however, requires some implicit or explicit structural premises. To enumerate, for instance, we must recognize units. To enumerate systematically we must have some structural principles and thus some structural analysis of the object. However, the question 'What kinds of documents are there?' brings the problem to a considerably more demanding level.

In this and the next chapters my aim is to outline a methodology for creating and developing knowledge that would answer question 2 above: What kinds of documents there are? There I especially focus on the knowledge about the *contents* of documents, which perhaps is the most interesting though certainly not the only interesting part of this question. The question of and focus on content makes classification, a traditional library-scientific tradition and practice, a plausible methodic basis. The basic model of the classificatory approach in this paper is in Colon Classification by Ranganathan (CC 1960).[7]

---

6 This suggestion basically is an answer to a question: What things should a librarian have special knowledge of? In this practical respect, it also approaches the question of the curriculum for librarianship, and in this regard, my suggestion comes close to the ideas of Jeng (1993).

7 I use here the 6th edition from 1960, which is more illustrative for my purposes than the more recent edition.

2 Conceptual premises for metadocumentary content reconstruction for bibliographic studies with book-historical emphasis

2.1 The concept of metadocumentary content reconstruction

Classification in the literature of LID-studies, and more specifically, on information retrieval (IR), is typically regarded as one form of documentary language and as one method of content representation, which should serve the purpose of searching. In the present article this is not the exact purpose of classification, but more widely and rather simply to create general knowledge about existing documentary contents. It would represent a form of quite descriptive but systematic empirical research on the documentary contents, or a kind of mapping them. We would classify in order to know, not only in order to mark contents. For this reason, to avoid the limitations of the concept of content representation, in this article I shall use the term *metadocumentary content reconstruction*, instead of the term content representation, as the generic concept under which classification, too, would be subsumed.[8]

The classificatory approach to metadocumentary content reconstruction here would be a methodology for something we could call *bibliographic* (or, using a more general term, *documentographic*) *studies with book* (or *document*) *historical emphasis*, rather than a method for just IR. These bibliographic studies, in turn, within LID-studies, would be especially important for librarianship. From the point of view of librarianship, documentary contents should perhaps be conceived as the cultural and historical environment we are living in, not only, or not so directly, as resources.

2.2 Explication of the idiographic

Furthermore, mapping documentary contents creates knowledge about one level of the historical and cultural environment we are living in, and in that sense it shares its general motivation and interests with other studies on our culture and history. The methodology to be outlined here would find its basic rationale in the

---

8 However, metadocumentary content reconstruction in itself, as a concept not subordinated to IR, even if not identical with content representation, could *also* have a role in IR. Emphasis on some search strategies like browsing, as well as some aspects of relevance actually would imply that a wider familiarity with documentary contents would have significance for IR as well. Saracevic's (1976) "subject literature view of relevance", for instance, suggests that relevance should not be seen as a function between the user and the document alone. The existing literature 'around' the document in question should also be considered.

cultural and historical nature of documentary contents as the object of study. This essence can be grasped, using Rickert's concepts (1910), by the distinction between *nomothetic sciences* aiming at explanations of phenomena in terms of general laws, and *idiographic sciences*, meaning historical sciences, where this general aim basically is not plausible. Metadocumentary content reconstruction would fundamentally belong to the idiographic.

As a consequence of the distinction between nomothetic and idiographic, a distinction can and should also be made on the methodological level, for instance between explanation as related to nomothetic phenomena and *explication* related to idiographic, cultural and historical phenomena (see Suominen 1997, 79-85). The present paper aims to provide quite rudimentary basics of the explication approach to (the structures of) documentary contents, to serve as a starting point for the practical and hermeneutical interests of preserving and expanding "intersubjectivity of possible action-oriented understanding" (Habermas 1965, 310). Explanation by contrast serves the interest of "technical control over objectified processes" (Habermas 1965, 308-309).

In any case, explication also requires generalizations, and in this respect there is a tension between the ideas of idiography and explication. This tension should be seen as a part of the fundamental constitution of the methodology outlined here. We could see it as an inevitable result of the pursuit of intelligibility with material that in itself is historical, cultural, and (it is to be assumed) not produced according to some patterns we have in mind, but rather side-by-side with the emergence and evolvement of those patterns themselves.

2.3 Basis in the theory of faceted classification: the model of Colon Classification

I shall not reproduce the ideas behind CC in detail here, as I assume that they are familiar to members of the LID community. The following aspects, however, are worth noting for my purposes:

1) PMEST categories (Personality, Matter, Energy, Space, Time)
2) First division of main classes (MC) based on disiplines; this level of division is also called Basic Facet
3) Manifestations of PMEST categories defined separately for each of the MCs.

Ranganathan only applies the idea of facet analysis starting from MCs, which in themselves are defined on a different basis, basically by enumerating existing disciplines or fields of knowledge. For instance, the manifestation of PMEST categories in the main class of Education (T), is as follows:

P: Educand;

E: Problem (incl. 3 Teaching Technique, 4 Curriculum, 5: Educational Measurement);
2P: Subject (for 3 Teaching Technique, 4 Curriculum, 5 Educational Measurement in [E])
2P2 Method (CC 1960, 1.113)

and in L, Medicine, as follows:
P Organ
E Problem (incl. 4 Disease)
2P (4) Cause (for 4 Disease) of [E]
2P2(4) Handling (for 4 Disease) of [E] (CC 1960, 1.88).

The methodology I am here suggesting for metadocumentary content reconstruction has basically the same structure as CC; a structure consisting of first recognizing some content areas (MC's in CC) and thereafter constructing structural schemata for them. The recognition of content areas prior to constructing the schemata can here be seen as recognition of the historical and cultural nature of the material described, and this actually, in my view, is also a highly interesting feature in CC, which otherwise so markedly emphasizes structural aspects.

Furthermore, the structural schemata themselves also have the character of historical description in this context, as they are structural schemata or descriptions of something that is in itself historical and cultural. This is an important methodological aspect from the standpoint of my idea of metadocumentary content reconstruction. To a certain degree this also relates the present paper to the ideas of domain analysis (see Hjørland & Albrechtsen 1995). However, while Albrechtsen and Hjørland are talking about domains born in the social division of labor, my starting point is much more modest, merely various content areas that can be recognized in documentation.

2.4 The method of basic facet formulas and 'Great Systematics'

The method of metadocumentary content reconstruction I am outlining here can be summed up by two terms:
1) basic facet formulas for content areas
2) 'Great Systematics'

By basic facet formulas I mean quite simply that some initial assumptions about dimensions content are structured on some content areas. Basically, in this sense the examples of CC given above could be basic facet formulas. They express some typical aspects of documentary contents in a given content area.

On the other hand, by 'Great Systematics' I mean a complex of all possible articulations of all possible categories to be articulated in documentary contents. The notion of 'Great Systematics' clearly is quite an illusory concept. No person could build or have such conceptual complexity in his/her mind. Furthermore, such a complex would not help us configure the documentary contents. It would no more be a map, but rather the reality itself.

However, by the notion of 'Great Systematics' I can express the direction of the classificatory work which could lead towards familiarity with documentary contents - as part of the professional competence of a librarian, for instance. Furthermore, research that takes the first steps in that direction could provide highly useful content for building that kind of professional competence in the students of LID studies.

2.5 Simplifying the contents, and the notion of aboutness

In content representation as well as in content reconstruction, as understood in this article and thus in classification in general, a certain simplificatory relationship to the original documentary contents is essential. In both cases this simplification is motivated by the most fundamental practical purposes. In IR, simplification is necessary so that the expressions of the needs for information can meet with the representations of the contents of documents.

In metadocumentary content representation, simplification is needed to reduce the endless multiplicity of documentary forms and contents to a scale where we can somehow configure it. In the practices of library and librarianship, the results of using the methodology outlined here could perhaps produce knowledge about or familiarity with (the contents) of documents. This also poses demands for the form of the results. They should be in a 'knowable' form, and the problems of keeping them in mind and of using them as tools to configure the enormous multiplicity of documentary contents should also be considered. The progress from basic facet formula towards 'Great Systematics', as presented above, would in itself be a cognitive process as well.

This simplificatory function has been illustrated by the discussion on the notion of "aboutness" within LID. The problem has generally been illustrated by the question: "What is the book about?" The most concrete starting point for understanding the notion of aboutness here is provided by Beghtol (1986a), according to whom aboutness (which illustrates my theme well) is a "*macroproposition*" expressing the overall 'message' of the text, where the text is conceived as a kind of hierarchy of propositions, the 'lower' ones giving details and explaining, and also making the 'upper' ones understandable.

When defining aboutness as macropropositions, Beghtol interestingly contrasts *aboutness analysis* and *text comprehension* with each other. In aboutness analysis, the text is reduced to a macroproposition by "controlled forgetting", while text comprehension consists of "inserting frame-knowledge" to make individual words, sentences and arguments of the text understandable. These opposite moves, the "*bottom-top*" movement of aboutness analysis and the "*top-bottom*" movement of text comprehension are, however, prerequisites for one another: to be able to forget in a controlled manner, one probably has to understand the text, and to be able to insert appropriate frame knowledge, one again has to already know what the text is all about.

Here the meaning of aboutness as an answer to the question 'What is this all about?' becomes manifest. The dialectics of aboutness analysis and text comprehension, with inherent cognitive aspects, also has to do with my requirement above that the resulting description should be 'knowable'.

2.6 The interest of syntactically partly-controlled enumeration

In the methodology to be outlined, there are two major, in certain regards almost conflicting elements:

1) the historicity of documentary contents, which is the object of perhaps the most important professional core expertise of a librarian, and which comes from the concept of culture and human cultural existence on which I base my concept of library, and
2) strongly structural elements of the methodology I outline, which, in turn, comes from the requirement to get a hold on the cultural and historical multiplicity of the (contents of) existing documentation.

Perreault (1969) in his classical article *Transparency and self-definition in classification* outlines a tension of syntax, which adds to transparency in classification on the one hand, and to opaque but inevitable enumeration on the other. The basic messages of Perrault's article for this paper are that

1) Dismantling opaque enumeration into syntactically constructed complexes produces transparence and "self-definition"; it allows us to more concretely see and conceive unique units of content in their relations to both the general category and their 'neighbours' in the articulation of that category.
2) In spite of the benefits of syntacticity, we can not avoid enumeration and opacity, "if we are to get beyond a purely *a priori* classification as a philoso phical exercise", to true bibliographic practice (Perrault 1969, 117).

The second thesis above, the inevitability of enumeration, is essential for my theme, for in it the essentially enumerative nature of bibliography is defined. The interest of *syntactically partly-controlled enumeration* emerges from the fact that, due to the essence of bibliography, the syntactic control always remains incomplete, but on the other hand, even partial syntactic control may create transparency, which helps us to configure the vast multiplicity of documentary contents. Thus, bibliographic scholarship, when using syntactic methods, always and inevitably remains caught in the tension between transparent syntax and opaque enumeration – or logic and history.

I call this *the historicity principle of documentation and bibliography*. In a sense, Ranganathan's 'compromise', starting with disciplines, instead of trying to create a general logic of facets, reflects a kind of (unconscious or even involuntary?) recognition of the historical character of the contents of documentation. The history of disciplines comes first, the logic of facets only thereafter.

3 Outlining the methodology: the basic facet structures for wide content areas

In this chapter I outline a system of categories and other conceptual distinctions by which we could characterize different areas of documentary content on a quite general level. The division of content areas I have in mind is as follows (loosely based on the first division of decimal classifications):

a) philosophical fields, partly including religion (including esp. dogmatics and theology, but excluding, for instance, the administration or history of church and religious movements)
b) social sciences and literature or other documentation on society and social phenomena in general
c) art studies and literature or other documentation on art in general
d) artistic documentation (i.e. documents that are works of art or the essential content of which is a reproduction of a work of art)
e) technology
f) natural sciences and and literature or other documentation on nature in general
g) history

In chapters 3.1-3.2 I present my 'arsenal of concepts' and in chapter 3.3 I briefly demonstrate how it would work in the characterisation the content areas. The choice of categories and distinctions there is partly based on an objective of somehow giving a special characterization for the areas of documentary contents listed above, to be able to 'say something' about each. The description of the contents of more specified areas could require more distinction on the part of the 'arsenal' as well.

3.1 The categories and some other structural distinctions

The system of categories, in terms of which I shall outline the syntactic characterization of documentary contents in some content areas, consists of the following distinctions
1) disciplinary vs. referential
2) process vs. action;
3) process or action vs. actant, where there is still
4) a suggestion for some subcategories of actant

The system of categories is described quite briefly in the following.

3.1.1 Disciplinary vs. referential

The distinction of the categories 'disciplinary' and 'referential' is based on the 'common sense ontology of a document', where a document is considered to be something 'in itself' (-> disciplinary) and further having, perhaps, some referential relationship, a 'telling' relationship to some reality outside it (-> referential, which may also be called the subject). This in a sense already presumes the semiotic character of documents in some sense as well, and I would still add here the distinction of contents or meanings, on the one hand, and the perceivable reality that can have meanings, on the other.

A similar 'common sense ontology' can be found, for instance, as the basic configuration of the "bibliographic universe" in the Functional Requirements for Bibliographic Records (FRBRT) by IFLA (see e.g. FRBR 1998).

What a document and its content in itself is, rather than what it tells us about, can on a concrete level be, for instance, a discipline within which the document has been produced, methodological or methodic points of departure in the document, a style or a work of art, forms like dissertation, research report, encyclopedia, pamphlet, or artistic forms like a novel (with various literary genres as more specific forms), symphony, or *nature morte* in painting, etc. If we wish to define disciplinary, it perhaps is best to do so indirectly by saying that the disciplinary is everything that is not subject in a documentary content, because subject or referential is easier to define through a referential relationship between the document and some other thing that the document tells us about.

By the expression disciplinary I wish to emphasize what a document, as a cultural product, is in itself. It manifests some cultural form, which often has the character of a norm coming from tradition (like a novel, treatise, dissertation, symphony, etc.). What I here call disciplinary has actually been quite a common dimension of differentiating documentary contents in the traditional schemes of classification, for instance, in their discipline-based main divisions. On that level, it is not stated what the documents actually tell, but rather what they in themselves are, i.e., philosophy, theology, sociology, etc. (see e.g. DDC 1989, BC 1952, and also CC 1960).

My claim is that every document must have some disciplinary character; every document must 'obey some discipline', while its referential character is by contrast optional. Some documents refer to something, others do not, but every document must have some form. A novel normally 'tells something' (usually something fictional), but a piece of so-called absolute music does not. Thus, the question of whether or not there is a referential character can be a function of the disciplinary, and furthermore, the disciplinary can determine which kind of referentials there can be. In this sense, the disciplinary is, besides obligatory, a dominant category in regard to referential as well. This could also be seen as exemplified in the basic structure of CC, in the enumeration of disciplines prior to the more structural and logical facet schemes.

However, the distinction disciplinary vs. referential should also be seen in a sense as relative. We may say that every a single and simple piece of knowledge, a fact or factual statement, for instance, has inherently disciplinary elements in it: the language the knowledge is expressed in, the presuppositions the piece of knowledge is based on, etc. This is in accordance with my claim that the disciplinary is a necessarily present element in documentary content, but at the same it makes somewhat difficult to make the distinction between disciplinary and referential clear. One could even claim that the disciplinary elements determie what I here call referential in a more fundamental sense than I claimed above. One could claim that the object we know something about actually is created by our concept, which would be a disciplinary element.

In any case I think, even if relative and problematic, the distinction also has many merits. As based on an (even if 'common sense') ontology of documentation, it has a solid grounding in the points of departure of documentation studies. It talks not only about abstract knowledge, but about the concrete ways content exists in documents. It also often seems to me that arguments based too harshly epistemologically in their generality may only serve to hide practically substantial aspects, which here would mean practically significant differences between different areas of documentary contents.

3.1.2 Action vs. process, their actants, and the subcategories of actant

The next part of my 'arsenal' of structural concepts, the subcategories of the referential, comes more typically from literature on classification and documentary languages. It consists of the 'family' of categories action, process and actant, and the subcategories of actant.

Dahlberg (1977) explicates the PMEST categories of CC as a manifestation of what she calls "the logic of linguistic expression", taking E as the correspondant to the verb and the other categories as the correspondants to the nominal members of a sentence. Taking this as a starting point, we can introduce the notion of "actant" to our vocabulary. Actant is the name which the 'father' of dependency grammar and valency theory, the French linguist Lucien Tesnière, used to denote the nominal members of a sentence (dependent on the valency of the verb, which then is the dominant category in the grammar outlined by Tesnière, see Tesnière 1953). Later in this paper I shall use the notion of actant as the most convenient general concept of some more specified syntactic categories.

The more specified syntactic categories, in turn, can for instance be deduced from the case categories of Fillmorean case grammar. Fillmore's categories (originally put forward in the classic article "Case for case", 1968; later the number of categories grew) are as follows:

Agentiv (A), the case of a typically animate perceiver instigator of the action identified by the verb.
Instrumental (I), the case of the inanimate force or object causally involved in the action or state identified by the verb.
Dative(D), the case of an animate being affected by the state or action identified by the verb.
Factive (F), the case of the object or being resulting from the action or state identified by the verb or which is understood as a part of the meaning of the verb.
Locative (L), the case that identifies the location or spatial orientation of the state or action identified by the verb.
Objective (0), the semantically most neutral case, which defines anything representable by a noun whose role in the action or state identified by the verb is identified by the semantic interpretation of the verb itself (Fillmore 1968, 24-25).[9]

The distinction of process and action belongs to some of the most classical differentiations of categories, being even included in the system of Aristotle, and it may be found in the literature of classification and documentation, as well (see for instance Vickery 1960). In terms of Fillmorean categories, we can define the difference between process and action quite simply by saying that a process never has an agentive while an action always has it.

---

9 On the base of Fillmore's case categories, Hutchins (1975, 65) gives a longer list of categories. Fillmore's case categories are obviously – due to their semantic grounding and fairly clear intuitive content – rather promising regarding the syntactic problems of representation of documentary contents.

By the categories differentiated above, we can, for instance, characterize the difference between social sciences and fields of social knowledge, on the one hand, and natural sciences, on the other. Action would be a category, a type of content typical to the former, and process to the latter. Furthermore, this choice between process and action has implications as regards the subcategories of actant.

3.2 Additional distinctions

Here I shall make some distinctions which can be used as additional features to characterize certain content areas. They are not distinctions of categories in the same sense as the ones presented above, but rather distinctions of rather formal characteristics. These distinctions applied to the concepts under the categories presented above, especially the subcategories of referential.

3.2.1 Unique vs. general

The distinction of *unique vs. general* comes close to the distinction of proper names and general concepts in grammar. We could say that "unique", as I use the term here, is a kind of widened proper name.

Basically, the distinction between unique and general makes it possible to syntactically illustrate the difference between sciences and history, with the social sciences remaining somewhere in between. Science, for instance physics, formulates its themes quite exclusively in terms of general concepts. There are no special physical laws, for instance, for some particular Andrew or for London. In history, on the other hand, (like partially also in geography) there are uniques like the proper names (persons, places, etc.), but also times, for instance, which actually are not quite proper names but nevertheless refer to something unique. Furthermore, there are kinds of uniques in social sciences and fields of social knowledge, as well, for instance. Different countries have different institutional arrangements, and the institutions in them can not be regarded as general concepts in the sense of the concepts of physics.

The distinction between general and unique can be relative, but it has importance if we consider the possibility of using their concepts as tools through which to achieve familiarity with documentary contents. Thus content areas in which general concepts are typical (like physics) also typically aim at building up conceptual systems where concepts are related to each other. By contrast, in content areas where uniques of one kind or another are typical (history fields, partly social sciences and social fields, etc.), the reduction of the multiplicity of concepts to some general concept is much more problematic. If one wishes to have some familiarity with documentary contents of fields like this, one cannot avoid memorizing a lot of separate factual knowledge.

3.2.2 "Natural" vs. "unnatural"

We could make yet another perhaps useful distinction between something we could (and in our everyday communication would) call *"natural"*, and other things that are in the same sense *"unnatural"*. On the level of everyday communication, the meaning of this distinction should be clear. Horse is natural but unicorn is unnatural. This distinction would have significance in expressing the specific nature of some content areas, even if it certainly is somewhat problematic in some respects.

On the other hand, if formulated in a more sophisticated way than above, it could also help us to keep a distance from the so-called realistic philosophy of classification. In my opinion, a classification of documentary contents should not take any stance as regards possible world views. It should not say which of the things dealt with in documents are "real" and which are "unreal". The only reality that such a classification deals with and in this sense recognizes is the cultural and semiotic reality of documents. Taking this into account, we could reformulate the distinction between "natural" and "unnatural" just to a question of whether or not an activity, process or actant belongs to the class of social or natural activities, processes and actants. Be that as it may, I here also include this distinction in the conceptual arsenal I will use in the following chapter to characterize some areas of documentary content.

3.3 The map, or application of the methodology for hypothetical characterization of some macro content areas

The concepts above could now be used to configure the various areas of documentary content, and the result would be a kind of map. Basically, this kind of map would
1) provide a basis for familiarity with documentary contents as the professional expertise of a librarian
2) provide a basis for deepening and developing our knowledge of documentary content to more detailed level.

Here I only briefly illustrate the idea on quite a general level in the form of a list, just outlining rudimentarily what kind of content could be recognized in some broad areas of documentary content as listed at the beginning of chapter 4 (in chapter 3.1.1 I claimed that the disciplinary is always present in documentary content, as 'every document obeys some discipline', and consequently it in principle should be mentioned in each of the descriptions below (which, however, I will not do, to have a more clear focus on the most characteristic features of each area):
a) philosophical fields, partly including religion (esp. dogmatics and theology)
   - necessary disciplinary contents (school of thought, confession)

- possibly any kind of referential (either "natural" or "unnatural", like *substance* as a concept in metaphysics, *angel* as a theological concept, etc.)

b) social sciences and knowledge
- necessary referential social activity or process or their actant
- typical disciplinary schools of thought in social sciences

c) art studies
- necessary referential activities, processes or their actants (e.g. work of art, artist, etc.)
- typical disciplinary schools of thought in cultural or social studies

d) artistic documentation (i.e. documents that are works of art or the essential content of which is a reproduction of a work of art)
- necessary disciplinary artistic forms
- typical disciplinary artistic styles, aesthetic ideas, etc.
- possibly any kind of referential (either "natural" or "unnatural", like various creatures in fairy tales or paintings)

e) technology
- necessary referential natural or social processes and social activities
- typically referential instrumentals as actants of process (cause) or as actants of activity (instrument)

f) natural sciences and knowledge about nature
- necessarily referential natural processes or their actants
- typically referential instrumentals as actants of processes (cause)

g) history
- necessarily referential uniques (a person that actually lived, an artifact that actually existed, an event or time and/or place etc.)

There is not enough space in the present essay to comment widely on these both sketchy and generally formulated descriptions. Just a few remarks might, however, help to read them.

In case (a) my idea is that philosophy is constituted as philosophy on the basis of the way a subject is dealt with, rather than on the basis of the subject itself. As regards familiarization with the contents of documentation in philosophy, as is also perhaps the case with theological and dogmatic contents, it might be most useful to try to get a grasp of the vocabulary consisting of philosophical schools and "-isms" (like marxism etc.), various religious confessions etc.

In cases (b) and (c) I have mentioned the disciplinary school of thought as a typical feature. This in turn is typically a strongly empirical (though here based only on an educated foreknowledge) claim, and it reflects my impression of the factual state in these fields today. There are many disciplinary "-isms" that constitute characteristic features of particular works of social or cultural studies. This claim would be a true Kantian synthetic sentence *a posteriori*. Probably we can also say that even generally in social sciences and in cultural studies, the consideration of alternative isms and schools of thought is a more typical phenomenon than in, say, physics (or in medicine, even though in medicine we actually do have schools, namely the schools of alternative medicine).

The distinction between activity and process, in turn, also helps to characterize the distinction between the contents related to social sciences or social and human issues (c-e), on the one hand, and natural sciences or issues of nature (f), on the other. In natural science and the phenomena of nature there are only processes, but neither activities nor agents (if one does not count, for instance, animals and their behaviour in ethology). In case (e) I have mentioned as necessary both the referential process and activity, and this, in turn, actually comes close to a kind of definition of technology.

Among the additional structural features, presented in chapter 4.2.3, the unique, of course, would be the specific characteristic of history, and what I (with many reservations) called "unnatural" would characterize various forms of fiction, and also philosophical and religious thinking, due to their 'special disciplinary ontologies'.

I hope these few remarks give a hint of how the descriptions of the macrocontent areas should be read. Basically they aim at a kind of map in which we can recognize in one place areas with some typical features, in another place other areas with some other typical features, and perhaps in a third place a mixture, for instance. This is still very much on the level of the basic facet formulas, but could also provide a basis for classificatory work towards the 'Great Systematics'.

On the other hand, once we have the map, i.e. an explication, we also could widen the sphere of phenomena outside the documentary contents, and perhaps proceed to a kind of explanation, though I assume it would be fragmentary by nature. However, perhaps we could make some statements on the relationship between, say, the medieval political, ideological and disciplinary realities, to explain the relatively stable structure of content in the summa-literature, for instance.

4 Concluding remarks

The methodology I have here outlined is strongly empirical, though in this article no other empirical material than my foreknowledge of the nature of some content areas has been used. It is even flatly empirical, although to a certain extent philosophically justified by a conception of culture and human cultural existence that is hermeneutically motivated. To put it very plainly, the somewhat philosophical consideration of the library and librarianship tells us that there are things that a librarian should know, in quite a flatly empirical mode. Some further remarks in this respect are still necessary.

4.1 Uniqueness of the disciplinary and the historicity principle of documentary contents

The distinction between general and unique here also has wider and methodological significance. This distinction comes close to the other distinction between nomothetic and idiographic I used in chapter 2.2 to illustrate the essence of metadocumentary content reconstruction in bibliographic studies with book historical emphasis. I claimed that metadocumentary content reconstruction would naturally be fundamentally idiographic.

Further, we may claim that the disciplinary always is an unique. Disciplines, methodologies, schools of thought, or artistic styles, they all are historical by nature and consequently unique in the sense of the word I have used here. Still taking into account my claim that the disciplinary is an necessary and dominant element in documentary content, we could now rephrase the historicity principle of documentary contents in my rather technical category concepts as follows: *Unique is always present in documentary content as a dominant element.*

The fact that I can use a rather technical conceptual distinction I made to especially characterize the structures of content in history for characterizing the whole of metadocumentary content reconstruction, can be understood in the light of the fact that the former in itself would be a historical discipline. This has also to do with the strongly empirical nature of the methodology I have emphasized.

4.2 Disciplinary as a step towards mature hermeneutics in librarianship and documentation studies

After all this, however, it would be hard to avoid considering the argument that knowledge about documentary contents perhaps also in itself is an issue where hermeneutics might have something to teach us. It probably is a question of sharing meanings, too. This means, of course, that what we know about documentary contents always of course is our interpretation. This, however, should be seen as a methodological reservation, rather than as an ideal.

On a more substantial level, the notion of the disciplinary in my methodology in a sense does involve a kind of hermeneutics. Recognizing the disciplinary in the content of a document actually means that the content of that document is in a sense situated in the context of its author or producer, related to the form in which (s)he has produced it. Further, the idea of the disciplinary as a dominant category leads to an effort to somehow achieve the essential structure of each discipline, which fortifies the hermeneutical character of the disciplinary.

Thus, the methodology outlined consists of
1) the rough history produced by enumeration
2) structural analysis, the aim of which (as I mentioned above) is to make intelligible the multitude produced by enumeration, and
3) some attempts at understanding in a hermeneutical sense.

Furthermore, we can also regard the function of the structural level in yet another perspective, in the sense of Ricoeur, by including structural analysis as a part or intermediate stage of interpretation and appropriation, "hoping "to change hermeneutics from naïve to mature understanding, via the discipline of objectivity" (Ricoeur 1969, 34; or Betti's, 1962, "canon of coherence of meaning", which intends to avoid arbitrariness in interpretation). Then, the structural level would represent objectivity, the object of interpretation, not only our wish to configure the multiplicity.

Thus, a (mature) interpretation would, according to Ricoeur, require structural analysis, which in turn, according to Perreault, requires or cannot avoid enumeration. However much we wish to interpret and understand, we should not try to avoid enumeration, its flat empiria, or the true bibliographic practice, which, after all, is what librarianship fundamentally is about. Yet, this kind of research could also contribute to documentation studies as a whole, perhaps move it towards further maturity by providing it with a basic level of historical knowledge about the phenomena it investigates.

References

BC, 1952. *A bibliographic classification.* Vols. 1-2. 2nd ed. New York: Wilson.

Beghtol, Clare, 1986. Bibliographic classification theory and text linguistics. *Journal of Documentation* 42(2), 84-113.

Bennet, George E., 1988. *Librarians in search of science and identity: the elusive profession.* Metuchen, N.J. and London: Scarecrow press.

Betti, Emilio, 1980 [1962]. Hermeneutics as the general method of the Geisteswissenschaft. Translated by Josef Bleicher. In *Contemporary hermeneutics: Hermeneutics as method, philosophy and critique*, Josef Bleicher. London; Boston and Henley: Routledge and Kegan Paul, 51-94.

Blair, David C., 1990. *Language and representation in information retrieval.* Amsterdam; New York; Oxford; Tokyo: Elsevier Science Publishers.

Buckland, Michael, 1997. What is a 'document'? *Journal of the American Society for Information Science* 48(9), 804-809.

CC, 1960. *Colon classification.* 6th ed. Asia, Bombay.

Dahlberg, Ingetraut, 1978. *Ontical structures and universal classification.* Bangalore: Saranda Ranganathan Endowment for Library Science.

DDC, 1989. *Dewey Decimal Classification and relative index.* Ed 20. Albany; New York: Forest Press.

DOCAM, 2006. *The Document Academy.* Online: http://thedocumentacaemy.hum.uit.no/events/docam/index.html (accessed 14 August 2006).

Fillmore, Charles J., 1972 [1968]. The case for case. In *Universals in linguistic theory*, eds. E. Bach, and R.T. Harms. Repr. London: Holt, Rinehart and Winston, Originally published and cop. 1968. First printed in Great Britain 1970. Reprinted 1972, 1-88.

Frohmann, Bernd, 2004. *Deflating information: From science studies to documentation.* Toronto; Buffalo; London: University of Toronto Press.

FRBR, 1998. *Functional requirements for bibliographic records. Final report. IFLA Study Group for the functional Requirements for Bibligraphic Records. Approved by the Standing Committee of the IFLA Section for Cataloquing.* Frankfurt am Main: Deutsche Bibliothek.

Gadamer, Hans-Georg, 1992 [1960]. *Truth and method.* Translation revised by Joel Weinsheimer and Donlad G. Marshall. New York: Crossroad. The revised English edition based on the revised and expanded 5th German edition, 1986.

Habermas, Jürgen, 1972 [1965]. *Knowledge and human interests.* Translated by Jeremy J. Shapiro. London: Heineman.

Hjørland, Birger, and Hanne Albrechtsen, 1995. Toward a new horizon in information science. *Journal of the American Society for Information Science* 46(6), 400-425.

Hjørland, Birger, 2000. Documents, memory institutions and information science. *Journal of Documentation* 56(1), 27-41.

Ingwersen, Peter, 1992. *Information retrieval interaction.* London: Taylor Graham.

Jeng, Ling H., 1993. From cataloguing to organization of information. *Journal of Education for Library and Information Science* 34(2), 113-126.

Järvelin, Kalervo, and Pertti Vakkari, 1988. Kirjastotiede ja informatiikka – tiedon hankinnan tiede. *Kirjastotiede ja informatiikka* 7(1), 18-32.

Lund, Niels Windfeld, 1999. Omrids af en dokumentationsvidenskap. *Norsk tidsskrift for bibliotekforskning* 12, 24-46.

------. 2004. Documentation in a Complementary Perspective. In *Aware and responsible: Papers of the Nordic-International Colloquium on Social and Cultural Awareness and Responsibility in Library, Information and Documentation Studies (SCARLID)*, ed. W. B. Rayward. Lanham, Md.: Scarecrow Press, 93-102.

Mikhailov, Aleksandr I., and Rudzhero S. Giliarevskii, 1971. *An introductory course on informatics/documentation.* Rev. and enl. edition. The Hague: FID.

Noruzi, Alireza, 2004. Application of Ranganathan's Laws to the Web. *Webology.* 1(2), December 2004. Online: http://www.webology.ir/2004/v1n2/a8.html (accessed 23 September 2006).

Otlet, Paul, 1989 [1934]. *Traité de documentation: le livre sur le livre, théorie et pratique.* Bruxelles: Editions Mundaneum, Palais Mondial.

Perreault, Jean M., 1969. *Towards a theory for UDC.* London: C. Bingley.

Rickert, Heinrich, 1910. *Kulturwissenschaft und Naturwissenschaft.* Zweite, umgearb. und verm. Aufl. Tübingen: J.C.B. Mohr

Ricoeur, Paul, 1969. *Le conflict des interpretations.* Paris: Seuil.

Saracevic, Tefko, 1976. Relevance: A Review of the Literature and a Framework for Thinking on the Notion in Information Science. *Advances in Librarianship* vol. 6, 79-138.

Suominen, Vesa, 1990. *Dokumentaarisen viestinnän semiologiaa.* Tampere: Tampereen yliopisto.

------. 1997. *Filling empty space.* Oulu: University of Oulu.

------. 2002. User interests as the rationale of library operations: a critique. *Scandinavian Public Library Quarterly* 2(2002), 17-19.

------. 2004. Hermeneutics of metadocumentation and librarianship. In *Aware and responsible: Papers of the Nordic-International Colloquium on Social and Cultural Awareness and Responsibility in Library, Information and Documentation Studies (SCARLID)*, ed. W. B. Rayward. Lanham, Md.: Scarecrow Press, 141-167.

Tesnière, Lucien, 1953. *Esquisse d'une syntaxe structural*. Paris: Klincksieck.

Vickery, Brian C., 1960. *Faceted classification: A guide to construction and use of special schemes*. London: Aslib.

Evelyne Broudoux

Construction de l'autorité informationnelle sur le web

1 Utilisation du terme autorité pour la recherche d'informations

Depuis plus d'une dizaine d'années, les outils informatiques ont modifié considérablement les modalités de repérage/indexation des documents. En particulier, les algorithmes utilisés pour la recherche d'informations sur le web (PageRank, Hits, Salsa, etc.) basent leurs calculs statistiques sur les liens hypertextes entre les sites web vus comme des relations entre des entités sociales (qui pointe vers qui?). Ces relations sont caractérisées par analogie: votes (PageRank), indicateurs d'autorité (Hits). Érigé en standard du web, le mode de recherche/indexation PageRank amplifie la diffusion des documents en classant en tête des réponses aux requêtes les documents référencés par les liens les plus nombreux. Pour tenter de limiter les effets de popularité dus aux calculs quantitatifs, *Google* a lancé le TrustRank, dont la particularité est d'introduire un indice de confiance à l'aide, entre autres, d'une opinion humaine sur la source.

Plus récemment, on a vu *Technorati*, un moteur de recherche spécialisé dans les blogs, se servir de la notion d'autorité et la proposer en tant que fonctionnalité additionnelle à la recherche des internautes effectuées dans la blogosphère.[1] Pourtant cet affinage par "autorité" des requêtes de *Technorati* n'est pas pour autant synonyme d'amélioration de la pertinence car les résultats obtenus ne sont pas toujours à la hauteur des attentes. Popularité a été confondue ici avec autorité.

L'utilisation de cette notion d'autorité provient de l'idée que dans le cas de recherche d'informations sur des thèmes larges, un tri adéquat des résultats peut être obtenu par le classement de sites web en deux catégories:[2] les "hubs" et les "authorities" (Kleinberg 1999). Si l'emploi de cette opposition binaire "hub/authority" a entraîné dans un premier temps le développement de nouveaux algorithmes,

---

1 http://fr.techcrunch.com/2006/02/14/technorati-lance-le-filtre-par-autorite/ (consulté 5 décember 2006).

2 Les "hubs" étant les pages ou sites à partir desquels de multiples liens pointent vers des ressources faisant autorité et les "autorités", les pages ou sites les plus pointés par les hubs; leur caractère de hub ou d'autorité se renforçant mutuellement.

cela a aussi favorisé l'émergence de l'examen structurel des réseaux par leur représentation graphique vectorielle. A partir de l'existence d'agrégats de liens, des communautés thématiques ont ainsi pu être extraites (Ghitalla 2005).

Le fait que les procédés de recherche/indexation du web s'effectuent encore sans métadonnées référencées et normalisées – la plupart du temps en dehors de tout "contrôle d'autorité" par les documentalistes et bibliothécaires – freine le développement du web sémantique. Pourtant, une écrasante majorité d'utilisateurs considère que les résultats donnés par les moteurs de recherche sont fiables et questionne peu la pertinence des résultats.

Enfin, du fait de l'absence d'explications claires divulguées au grand public, sur les procédés employés pour générer des résultats, on peut avancer que les moteurs de recherche **font autorité** par opacité ou omission d'informations.

Il apparaît significatif que l'apparition d'indices de "confiance" et d'"autorité" est révélateur d'une volonté de recherche d'amélioration de la pertinence des résultats obtenus sur le web. Mais l'emploi du terme "autorité" sans véritable définition du terme, couplé au fait que les procédés d'indexation/recherche sont trop souvent incompris de l'internaute lambda, incite à préciser les flous de la notion.

2 Approche historique de l'autorité

Pour tenter de saisir le concept d'autorité tel qu'il est vécu par une large partie occidentale de la planète, il est nécessaire de faire un (rapide) détour historique jusqu'à ses racines romaines car notre monde moderne s'est développé dans une "crise de l'autorité" qui trouve son origine dans le fait que l'Autorité a disparu (Arendt 1954). S'enracinant dans la tradition qui donnait sens à toute chose, l'autorité romaine avait pour unique objectif de consolider ses fondations, seule garantie de sa stabilité.

Nous retiendrons de l'analyse historique d'Arendt que:

- l'ordre autoritaire exige l'obéissance sans violence (là où la force est employée, l'autorité a échoué), ceci implique une **soumission volontaire** à l'autorité,
- l'autorité donne des avis qu'elle recommande de suivre et est incompatible avec la persuasion par arguments qui présuppose une relation d'égalité, l'autorité implique un **ordre hiérarchique**,
- sa **transmission** se fait **par cooptation** dans l'objectif de ne pas rompre la tradition avec le passé.

Si nous appliquons cette notion classique de l'autorité aux pratiques de pointage des sites entre eux, on voit surgir quelques contradictions:

- le fait de citer un site en posant un lien n'est pas toujours agréer son contenu,
- le fait pour un site d'être cité ne signifie pas qu'il ait autorisé la citation,
- les liens réciproques (bidirectionnels) ne peuvent induire seuls un ordre hiérarchique.

Si soumission volontaire il y a, c'est au système hypertexte en général qui impose ses "contraintes" de citation.

De multiples contradictions apparaissent donc avec l'emploi de la notion classique d'autorité dans le contexte de la description documentaire du web qui sont seulement en partie résorbées par le concept d'autorité cognitive.

3 Approche cognitive de l'autorité, synonyme d'influence

Dans le domaine de la construction des connaissances où ce qui s'acquiert vient plus du savoir accumulé par les autres que par l'expérience personnelle, l'**autorité cognitive** a été définie comme une relation d'influence de pensée[3] impliquant au minimum deux personnes, l'une accordant à l'autre sa confiance parce qu'elle maîtrise un domaine spécifique de compétences (Wilson 1983). De plus, la notion concerne aussi les livres, les instruments ou les organisations qui sont vus comme autant d'artefacts susceptibles de devenir des autorités cognitives pour une personne ou un groupe à un moment donné. Cette confiance accordée étant susceptible de s'étendre au-delà du domaine concerné, Wilson distingue l'autorité cognitive de l'autorité de l'expertise. Pratiquement synonyme de la notion d'influence choisie, l'autorité cognitive est dépendante de la **crédibilité** et de la **réputation**, deux critères de bases sans lesquels la confiance nécessaire à l'exercice d'une influence ne pourrait s'établir dans le domaine de la construction du savoir.

Cette définition de l'autorité vue en tant qu'**influence choisie** est plus à même de s'accorder avec les pratiques de pointage des sites et des blogs entre eux (blogroll). Cependant, elle est encore limitée car la blogosphère favorise les liens de réciprocité (trackbacks et blogroll). Or, qui dit réciprocité, présuppose l'égalité, ce qui entre en contradiction avec la notion d'autorité.

D'autre part, pour rester dans l'exemple des blogs, la réalité montre qu'ils sont nombreux à être instrumentalisés dans le cadre de campagnes publicitaires, de relations publiques ou de marketing politique, pour créer du trafic et donc de l'audience. Les auteurs eux-mêmes jouent à multiplier les identités sous différents

---

3 "Cognitive authority is influence on one's thoughts that one would consciously recognize as proper" (Wilson 1983, 15).

blogs ce qui contribue à brouiller l'authenticité et les limites des entités sociales. Ceci nous éloigne de l'idée d'**influence juste**. Il apparait donc difficile de modéliser l'autorité cognitive dans l'objectif d'établir un classement qualitatif et rationnel des sites web.

4 Acteurs de l'autorité cognitive et réseaux d'influence

Alors que les mots-clés utilisés dans les balises meta html ne sont plus pris en compte par les robots d'indexation des moteurs de recherche les plus connus, d'autres méta-informations ou métadonnées sont employées par des systèmes qui permettent leur classification et leur moissonnage par les robots de recherche (Dublin Core, Open Archiv Initiative etc.). Leur normalisation et leur interopérabilité croissante en font des vecteurs de transmission de l'information extrêmement fiables, puissants et rapides. Le web sémantique pourrait ainsi progressivement s'imposer comme une solution aux problèmes évoqués plus haut.

Les innovations technologiques se diffusant toujours en subissant des transformations pour élargir leurs cercles d'usagers, ce qui faisait partie du cœur des métiers des professionnels de la documentation, la maîtrise des taxonomies organisant de manière structurée le savoir, est parvenu au "grand public" sous la pratique du "taggage" et cette pratique a pris le nom de folksonomy.

Nous définissons cette folksonomie comme un système flottant de catégorisation conduit par les utilisateurs permettant de naviguer dans un corpus à large spectre composé de ressources hétérogènes instables et non pérennes.

Générée par une nouvelle famille d'outils axée autour du concept d'auto-indexation, cette pratique consiste à catégoriser soi-même des ressources, et ce par l'intermédiaire de services disponibles en ligne (communément rassemblés sous le nom de web 2.0).

Ces pratiques d'appellation qui construisent un vocabulaire commun possèdent deux caractéristiques:

- l'influence du choix des mots-clés de l'utilisateur par suggestion de mots-clés par le système (**collaborative filtering**) ou/et visualisation des mots-clés déjà utilisés par les taggeurs lorsque la ressource est déjà référencée;
- une cristallisation autour de conventions d'appellation par:
  - o regroupement de mots par caractère de séparation (ex: _ ou + ou:) ou absence de caractère de séparation (ex: CamelCase)
  - o émergence de mots-clés et compétition entre termes révélant différents points de vue (ex: public sphere *vs* public space, collabora-

tivejournalism *vs* citizenjournalism, participatorymedia *vs* citizenmedia).

Dans la pratique, trois fonctionnalités caractérisent principalement ces systèmes de partage de ressources dont les pratiques pourraient être rassemblées sous le terme de **collaborative tagging**:

- trois possibilités d'écriture (ouverture obligatoire d'un compte "utilisateur" avec login et mot de passe):
    - dépôt et suppression de ressources (posts) se présentant sous la forme de signets, fichiers images, textes, sons, vidéos, etc.
    - catégorisation (taggage) de ces ressources par indexation à l'aide de mots-clés quelquefois suggérés mais librement désignés,
    - qualification (annotation) ou légende caractérisant la ressource, pouvant servir à la remémoration ou à l'information des lecteurs,
- partage des ressources et des mots-clés avec la "communauté" des inscrits,
- création de réseaux d'utilisateurs en fonction des thématiques choisies, avec repérage des "maillons" ouvrant vers des sous-réseaux.

Il faut ajouter ici que les systèmes constituent un outil de prélecture efficace pour l'activité de découverte sur le web et de partage de signets: les posts étant repérés et indexés par leurs thèmes pour être lus ensuite.

Ces fonctionnalités entraînent des activités de stockage, de partage et de veille d'une part sur des ressources documentaires (collecte des ressources numériques postées sur des mots-clés choisis) mais aussi sur des ressources humaines (création de groupes d'utilisateurs et réception de leurs "posts"). Cette dernière option a été récemment amplifiée sur des outils comme *del.icio.us*, dans l'objectif de créer des réseaux sociaux qui favorisent la **réciprocité**. Ceci nous permet de reconnaître des actions imputables à l'autorité cognitive dans la mesure où des utilisateurs repèrent des informations grâce à d'autres taggeurs auxquels ils accordent une confiance due à leur crédibilité et leur antériorité.

Les principaux bénéficiaires de ces systèmes en termes de **notoriété** sont les bloggeurs et les organisations qui s'auto-publient en ligne car il est possible de s'identifier et d'ajouter l'adresse d'un site web et sur celui-ci de publier les liens menant vers ces systèmes.

Une caractéristique à ne pas oublier est que ces réservoirs de contenus sont alimentés par tous (aussi bien les ressources d'utilisateurs néophytes que celles des professionnels) ce qui provoque un mélange et une hétérogénéité dans les données rassemblées et des effets de **sérendipidité**. Ce qui compense peut-être l'absence de hiérarchie dans les classements thématiques que propose ce genre d'outils.

Une des principales conséquence est que ces systèmes sont bâtisseurs de **réputation** et de **notoriété**. Des informations émergent qui sans cela seraient restés dans l'ombre et n'auraient pas été portées à la connaissance d'un plus large public; des documents sont susceptibles de se former intéressant de multiples sphères collectives. On peut donc dire qu'ils servent à faire émerger des auteurs, des documents et des groupes. Il pourrait s'agir d'**outils sociotechniques d'autorité cognitive** dans la mesure où ils provoquent la construction de réseaux d'influence.

5 Autorité informationnelle

Nous nous proposons ici de définir l'**autorité informationnelle** en nous servant du terme "informer", synonyme de "renseigner sur", c'est-à-dire porter un événement à la connaissance d'une sphère sociale ou d'un individu. Nous présupposons que l'autorité informationnelle est le résultat d'un jeu de forces entre ses composantes. Contrairement à l'autorité cognitive, l'autorité informationnelle, susceptible d'être portée par un individu ou un groupe, un objet ou un outil cognitif ou encore un média, n'a pas pour fonction principale l'influence mais celle d'informer (donner une forme).

Distinguer l'autorité informationnelle de l'autorité cognitive permet de faire coexister les acteurs qui concourent à créer l'autorité informationnelle, rendant possible l'examen du jeu d'équilibres qui les fait tenir ensemble.

Si nous reprenons les définitions de Max Weber qui dans son approche sociologique de l'autorité distinguait l'*autorité traditionnelle* fondée sur la croyance et le respect de l'ordre établi où la légitimité provient du temps, de l'*autorité rationnelle et légale*, impersonnelle, fondée sur le droit, et de l'*autorité charismatique* fondée sur une seule personne, susceptible de conduire à la dictature, nous pouvons les faire correspondre avec d'autres tentatives définitoires:

- l'**autorité traditionnelle** correspond à celle définie par Arendt,
- l'autorité rationnelle et légale peut se nommer **autorité institutionnelle**,
- l'**autorité énonciative** (Leclerc 1996) serait une forme préalable à l'établissement d'une autorité charismatique.

Ceci nous permet de bâtir un premier concept d'**autorité informationnelle** composée de:

- l'**autorité énonciative** où la figure de l'auteur (individuel/collectif) se manifeste parmi d'autres acteurs de la création (compilateur, commentateur, interprète, etc.);
- l'**autorité institutionnelle** ou groupe régulé par des règles hiérarchiques séparant strictement la fonction au sein du groupe et la personne qui l'occupe (éditeur, distributeur, etc.);

- l'**autorité de contenu** du document:
  - genre: littéraire, musical, graphique, éditorial,
  - qualité: précis, utile, volatil/pérenne, micro/macro, panoramique/angle restreint, érudit/vulgarisé,
  - sources: auteur(s), compilation,
  - paratexte: éditeur, autres médiateurs, fabricant;
- l'**autorité du support** de publication:
  - type: imprimé-cd-cassette, etc.,
  - caractère de la publication: périodicité, unique, quotidien, hebdomadaire, à éditions multiples, etc.

Ces formes que peut prendre l'attribution d'autorité sont en réalité interdépendantes. L'institution qui publie un document prend la décision de le faire paraître en fonction de sa connaissance de l'auteur, sa connaissance du sujet traité, son programme de publication, ses possibilités commerciales. La notoriété de l'auteur est susceptible d'augmenter selon les actions publicitaires des groupes ou institutions auxquels il s'est affilié. L'auteur dans ses processus créatifs doit prendre en compte les contraintes du support de diffusion dont l'éditeur a habituellement la responsabilité.

5.1 Acteurs de l'autorité en contexte pré-numérique

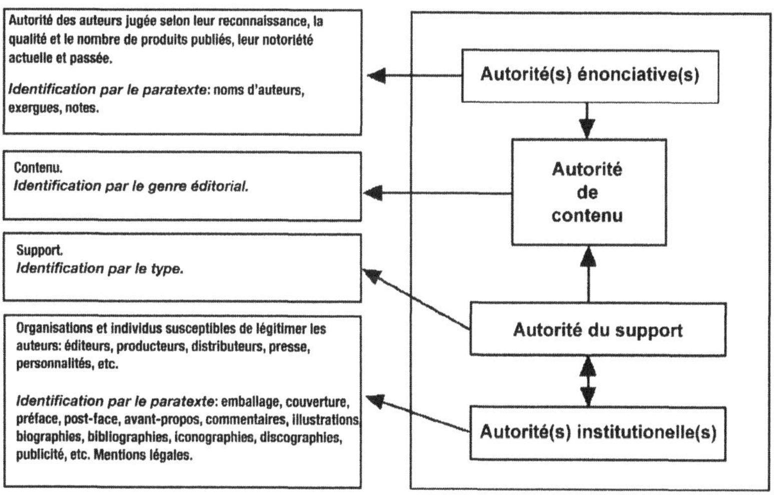

Présence de signes d'autorité autour de la production d'auteurs sur un document édité et porté par un support máteriel.

Dans une situation pré-numérique, le schéma 1 présente les différentes influences que subissent les entités susceptibles d'intervenir dans l'élaboration d'un document édité par une institution et publié sur un support (imprimé, cd, cassette, dvd, etc).

Dans ce schéma traditionnel, un auteur est tenu de s'inscrire dans un genre, totalement dépendant du support géré par l'autorité institutionnelle (en général l'éditeur). Nous voyons que l'autorité institutionnelle est à même d'exercer une autorité de support sur les autorités énonciatives.

5.2 Acteurs de l'autorité en contexte numérique

Nous tentons ici d'évaluer les déplacements de force dans la notion d'autorité informationnelle en publication numérique (web). Dans le contexte du numérique, plusieurs indices indiquent un changement de paradigme:
- l'apparition d'espaces de discussions, publications, référencements, ouverts à tous,
- la baisse du filtrage institutionnel en matière éditoriale, éducative, politique, économique,
- les changements d'échelle (filtrage par les pairs, rédaction collective massivement distribuée, auto-publication, micro-paiements, "longue traine", etc.),
- la réutilisabilité des contenus numériques et l'apparition de licences d'usages (ex: creative commons).

Dans la publication web, de multiples solutions diversifient le champ documentaire:

- l'**autorité énonciative** perdure mais la figure de l'auteur s'élargit (diversification dans les tâches) ou s'estompe jusqu'à disparaître: auteur/ amateur, individuel/collectif;
- l'**autorité de groupe** vient s'ajouter aux autorités institutionnelles: il s'agit d'un **groupe informel** rassemblé par un réseau sociotechnique pouvant se transformer en **groupe institué**;
- l'**autorité de contenu** est dépendante de la stabilité du proto-document ou du document:
    - genre: littéraire, musical, graphique, mixtes, éditoriaux émergents (publication wiki, webradios, blogs, podcasts, videoblogs, etc.),
    - qualité: volatil/pérenne, micro/macro, panoramique/angle restreint, érudit/vulgarisé,
    - sources: auteur(s), programme,
    - architexte, paratexte: nom de domaine, éditeur, autres médiateurs, fabricant.
- l'**autorité du support-logiciel**:

- type: outil logiciel de publication (wiki, blog, cms, ou fabriqué par l'auteur = autopublication), moteur de recherche,
- périodicité: unique (auto-pré-post-publication), quotidien, hebdomadaire, etc.,
- lectorat: participatif, commentateur, auteur, etc.

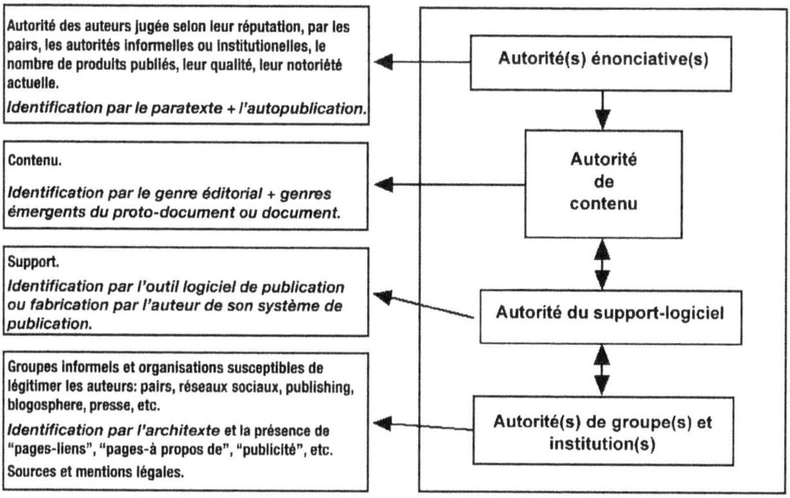

Présence de signes d'autorité autour de la production d'auteurs portée par un support de type outil-logiciel de publication.

Le support numérique connaît deux changements majeurs par sa composition logicielle:
- sa dépendance aux autorités institutionnelles s'affaiblit car il est construit et modelé par les groupes informels de réseau: cas du logiciel libre, du web 2.0, etc;
- il est susceptible d'être directement approprié par les autorités énonciatives: cas de l'auto-édition, auto-publication.

5.3 Relations entre autorités de support-logiciel et énonciatives

La différence entre le schéma 1 et 2 tient aux relations entre autorité du support et autorité énonciative. Dans le cas du support de type outil-logiciel de publication, l'auteur peut choisir de disparaître au profit d'une œuvre collective (publication wiki) mais il peut aussi s'auto-publier, c'est-à-dire fabriquer son propre système de publication: l'auteur est alors éditeur et "publisher", il cumule les fonctions. Dans ce contexte, l'autorité énonciative personnelle s'appuie sur la capacité autoritative à autopublier ses propres œuvres, textes élaborés ou simples commentaires.

Rappelons que l'autoritativité procède d'une conscience d'être conduisant à la modification créatrice de la réalité – ce qui passe par la confection d'un artefact – et à la décision personnelle de rendre public cette construction modifiante (de faire partager à un groupe social cette découverte). Cette capacité du devenir auteur passe par une conscience de soi active, une disposition que l'on a entraînée, une capacité à se distancier qui nous permet d'examiner, tout en étant partie prenante des situations, notre position et celle des autres; posture à partir de laquelle on peut exercer des actions sur soi et son environnement.

L'autopublication est liée à l'autoritativité par sa double signification. Il peut s'agir de la décision de se passer d'intermédiaire pour porter à la connaissance du public ce qui a été réalisé dans une forme publiante existante (comme le genre éditorial préformaté du blog ou du wiki), dans ce cas elle peut être assimilée à de l'auto-diffusion. Mais il peut aussi s'agir d'un travail créatif consistant à fabriquer cette forme publiante (un site web réalisé en flash par exemple), dans ce cas l'autopublication concerne la fabrication de l'objet de communication qui entre comme composante dans l'œuvre réalisée. De nombreux exemples sont disponibles dans le secteur des arts et de la littérature numériques.[4]

Enfin, nous faisons entrer dans la catégorie "support-logiciel", les moteurs de recherche, car ils médiatisent l'information.

5.4 Relations entre autorités énonciatives et institutionnelles, support-logiciel et groupes informels

Les relations entre "autorités énonciatives" et "autorités institutionnelles" apparaissent chamboulées par le renouvellement des espaces de publication. L'auteur se passe quelquefois d'éditeur et se réfère à ses pairs et à l'autorité du groupe informel de réseau dans lequel il s'est inscrit (blogosphère, groupes de discussions, réseau de type web2.0, archives ouvertes, etc.).

Souvent, le support-logiciel de publication est à la base de la création d'un groupe formel ou informel. Un groupe peut cependant décider de le faire évoluer et reprendre sa capacité d'autorité en le transformant (ex: voir les nombreuses versions de Spip[5] modifiés).

---

4 On trouvera sur ce sujet de multiples exemples comme celui d'Albertine Meunier, alias Catherine Ramus: http://www.albertinemeunier.net/ (consulté 5 décember 2006).

5 Spip (Système de publication pour l'internet partagé) est un CMS (Content Management System) francophone qui a rencontré un gros succès dans le domaine de la publication web).

Le cas de Wikipédia illustre parfaitement la reconfiguration s'exerçant entre autorités énonciatives, de groupe et de support-logiciel. Il s'agit d'un cas emblématique de création qualitative de contenus alors que les autorités énonciatives apparaissent être en retrait et les autorités institutionnelles absentes.

Ce qui frappe tout d'abord sur l'encyclopédie Wikipédia, c'est la multiplicité des auteurs anonymes abandonnant leurs prérogatives d'auteurs pour exercer l'activité d'édition de pages.

Ensuite, c'est l'institutionnalisation progressive du groupe informel avec une diversification dans les rôles et les fonctions[6] attachées à la publication (administrateur, administrateur-développeur, développeurs, bureaucrates, stewards, vérificateurs d'adresse IP, etc.) et à l'édition (médiateurs, arbitres). Enfin, l'insertion progressive des lecteurs-auteurs dans le dispositif éditorial avec le volontariat (wikipompier, patrouilleur, etc.) permet d'ouvrir largement le dispositif.

Les diverses difficultés que rencontre Wikipédia à s'imposer en tant qu' "autorité de contenu" auprès des experts et des encyclopédies concurrentes couplée à la médiatisation dont ces difficultés ont fait l'objet incitent à penser que l'installation d'une nouvelle forme d'autorité informationnelle provoque des remous dans un paysage façonné par les habitudes anciennes.

5.5 Vers un changement de régime auctorial?

Ce balayage nous permet de mieux comprendre les changements de régime de l'auctorialité, en phase avec les changements sociotechniques modulant l'autorité. Un virage était déjà bien identifié: de la Rome antique aux siècles des Lumières, étaient considérés comme auteurs les Dieux puis celui qui avait commandé l'ouvrage, celui qui l'avait inspiré, et non celui qui l'avait réalisé (le constructeur, l'écrivain). Jusqu'à la fin du XVIIIe, le "bon" écrivain était celui qui reprenait les textes des anciens en "variant" avec bonheur.

Puis il y a à peine trois cents années, l'auteur "original" émerge et est considéré comme "bon" auteur celui qui produit quelque chose venant de lui-même. L'autorité traditionnelle s'éloigne au profit des autorités institutionnelles (apparition de l'éditeur, droits de l'éditeur et de l'auteur), en même temps qu'apparaissent de nouvelles techniques de reproduction à l'identique (imprimerie à caractères mobiles).

---

6 http://fr.wikipedia.org/wiki/Wikip%C3%A9dia:Statuts_des_utilisateurs (consulté 5 décember 2006).

Vraisemblablement, nous avons entamé un nouveau virage avec le XXe siècle, au vu:

- des figures émergentes d'auteurs:
    - o décentralisé: multi-auteurs sans figure d'auteur collaborant au sein d'un réseau sociotechnique institué et décentralisé (Wikipédia),
    - o collectif: multi-auteurs rassemblés sous une figure d'auteur unique (R.T. Pédauque),
    - o machinique: programmes produisant des œuvres artistiques, documents sans auteurs produits par assemblage informatique (communiqués météo, pages html dynamiques);
- des nouveaux modes de filtrage des textes (filtrage a posteriori dans la publication distribuée),
- de l'installation de nouveaux "intermédiaires" de l'information comme les bloggers dans le champ de l'information professionnelle,
- de l'apparition de groupes sociotechniques informels:
    - o partage de ressources (Del.ico.us, Digg, etc.)
    - o partage et création de contenus (Flickr, YouTube, Ekopedia, etc.)
    - o constitution de communautés (MySpace, TagWorld, LinkedIn, etc.)
    - o auditeurs (Last.fm), lecteurs (BookMooch), etc.
- la décentralisation et la distribution des activités éditoriales.

L'apparition de groupes informels issus de réseaux sociotechniques exerçant de nouvelles formes de filtrages, l'affaiblissement de la reproduction d'exemplaires en série au profit de prototypes, les transferts d'activités entre auteurs, éditeurs, publishers-diffuseurs, tout ceci augure d'évolutions devant modifier à terme le paysage des "industries culturelles" et celui du champ documentaire.

6 Conclusion

Alors que le critère d' "autorité" entre comme argument publicitaire dans la recherche d'informations, il était urgent de faire le tour des approches scientifiques déterminantes pour un concept difficile à délimiter. Si le concept d'autorité cognitive est opérationnel, il ne prend pas en compte les composantes qui exercent leurs jeux de force dans la formation de l'autorité en tant qu'influence. La proposition d'autorité informationnelle vise à préciser le poids des différents acteurs susceptibles de faire autorité dans la production d'informations. Le changement de support dû au passage au numérique remet en question les "autorités" sur lesquelles étaient basées l'attribution de confiance, la vérification et la légitimation de l'information. En particulier, l'arrivée de nouveaux acteurs et la redistribution des rôles dans la fabrique de l'information sur un support dynamique laisse apparaître un nouveau tournant pour l'auteur qui découvre d'autres pratiques.

7 Bibliographie

Arendt, Hannah, 1954. *La crise de la culture.* Folio/Essais (1989).

Burton, Stéphane, 2004. L'émergence dynamique des autorités épistémiques sur le web. Mémoire de DEA de Sciences cognitives. EHESS.

Endrizzi, Laure, 2006. L'édition de référence libre et collaborative: le cas de Wikipedia. Les dossiers de la Veille scientifique et technologique de l'INRP. En ligne: http://www.inrp.fr/vst/Dossiers/Wikipedia/sommaire.htm (consulté 5 décember 2006).

Forsé, Michel, 2002. Les réseaux sociaux chez Simmel: les fondements d'un modèle individualiste et structural. In *La sociologie de Simmel (1908). Eléments actuels de modélisation sociale*, par L. Deroche-Gurcel et P. Watier. Paris: PUF, 63-109.

Ghitalla, Franck, Le Berre, Alain, Matthieu Renault, 2005. Expérimentations autour de radiographies documentaires du web. En ligne: http://wiki.crao.net/index.php/HyperTexte (consulté 5 décember 2006).

Kleinberg, Jon M., 1999. Authoritative sources in a hyperlinked environment. *Journal of the ACM* 46 (5), 604-632.

Leclerc, Gérard, 1996. *Histoire de l'autorité. L'assignation des énoncés culturels et la généalogie de la croyance.* Paris: PUF.

Marlow, Cameron, Naaman, Mor, Boyd, Danah, and Marc Davis, 2006. Position Paper, Tagging, Taxonomy, Flickr, Article, ToRead. En ligne: http://www.rawsugar.com/www2006/29.pdf (consulté 5 décember 2006).

Origgi, Gloria, 2006. Autorité épistémique et Internet scientifique: la diffusion du savoir sur Internet. En ligne: http://jeannicod.ccsd.cnrs.fr/ijn_00000678/en/ (consulté 5 décember 2006).

Pédauque, Roger T., 2006. *Le document à la lumière du numérique.* C&F Editions.

Rieh, Soo Young, 2002. Judgment of information quality and cognitive authority in the web. *Journal of the American Society for Information Science and Technology* 53(2), 145-161.

------. 2005. Cognitive authority. In *Theories of information behavior*, eds. Karen E. Fisher, Sanda Erdelez, and Lynne E.F. McKechnie. Medford, New Jersey: Information Today, Inc. (Published for the American Society for Information Science and Technology), 83-87.

Wilson, Patrick, 1983. *Second-hand knowledge: An inquiry into cognitive authority.* Westport, Connecticut; London: Greenwood Press.

Manuel Zacklad

Réseaux et communautés d'imaginaire documédiatisées

1 Introduction

Dans le renouveau des travaux actuels sur le document (cf. Pédauque 2003) l'accent est souvent mis sur leurs usages professionnels dans le contexte de l'entreprise, de la recherche scientifique, des institutions artistiques ou culturelles, par exemple. Dans ce texte, nous souhaitons mettre plus particulièrement l'accent sur l'importance des documents dans le contexte des usages "grand public", de leurs rôles très divers auprès de populations de tous âges dans le cadre d'activités qui sont souvent qualifiées d'activités de loisir. Nous verrons que, dans ce cadre également, la numérisation transforme profondément les pratiques et que les théorisations actuelles du document et notamment notre approche en termes de processus de documentarisation, permet de les appréhender de manière originale. En particulier, nous défendrons l'idée selon laquelle ces nouveaux usages sont caractéristiques d'une nouvelle forme de socialité que Pédauque (2006) qualifie de "post-moderne" et qui correspond pour nous à l'expression de "modernité sans frontière", pour reprendre le titre de l'ouvrage de l'anthropologue indo-américain Arjun Appadurai "Modernity at Large, Cultural dimension of globalization" (Appardurai 1996).

Parmi les nombreuses idées avancées par l'auteur relatives à l'ère de la mondialisation et de l'inter-culturalité qui l'accompagne, nous retiendrons cellesci:

- Les migrations et l'urbanisation n'ont jamais été aussi importantes et chaque individu, chaque communauté, cherche à reconstruire une forme de localité en maintenant des liens interpersonnels avec des proches grâce aux TIC et des liens culturels avec ses communautés d'origine grâce à la circulation des œuvres culturelles via les média de masse.
- Il y a une subversion créative permanente des contenus culturels par un travail de l'imaginaire qui produit une hybridation et une redéfinition du sens des œuvres et des contours des pratiques culturelles dans toute la planète. Cette vision est à opposer à la vision d'une domination culturelle américaine radicale.
- L'imaginaire (référence à Castoriadis 1975) est plus que jamais le ciment des communautés de migrants et celui-ci échappe de plus en plus au contrôle des états nation.

Dans cet article, nous défendrons deux thèses. Nous considèrerons d'une part que la problématique de la migration, de l'urbanisation et de la nécessité de reconstruire de nouvelles formes de localité concerne aujourd'hui bon nombre des habitants de la planète. Certes, les populations qui réalisent de grandes migrations géographiques sont particulièrement intéressantes et innovantes de par la soudaineté de leurs déplacements et l'importance des efforts de reterritorialisation qu'elles doivent réaliser. Cependant, la prise en compte de leurs spécificités est susceptible d'être généralisée à d'autres types de migrants, dont les mouvements sont moins spectaculaires mais qui sont concernés par des problématiques en partie similaires. Dans les mégapoles, mais aussi dans les régions moins urbaines qui accueillent, par exemple, de nouveaux travailleurs, de nombreux habitants sont à un titre ou à un autre des migrants.

D'autre part, nous pensons qu'il faut prolonger la proposition d'Arjun Appadurai en montrant que les documents tendent à jouer un rôle aussi important que les mass-médias traditionnels (télévision et radio) qui sont d'ailleurs eux-mêmes engagés dans une mutation profonde tendant à favoriser la documentarisation de leurs contenus. Ceci est particulièrement le cas depuis la généralisation des usages grands publics du web qui ont transformé les modalités de diffusion des œuvres culturelles. En particulier, l'usage des documents et particulièrement des documents numériques, permet de passer de la notion d'imaginaire constitué par un "public" à la notion de réseau et de communauté d'imaginaire.

Pour argumenter en faveur de ces thèses, nous rappellerons les définitions du document, de la documentarisation et de la redocumentarisation. Nous préciserons ensuite, dans un assez long détour, le rôle que nous donnons à l'imaginaire dans le cadre de la "théorie transactionnelle de l'action" et de la manière dont celui-ci contribue à la constitution non seulement des individus mais également de différents types de collectifs. Cette partie théorique est néanmoins nécessaire pour appréhender les nouvelles formes de créativité distribuées qui émergent en grande part grâce au web et qui rendent compte des nouvelles pratiques de socialisation médiatisées par des documents. Ces pratiques permettent la constitution de communautés "virtuelles" (Rheingold 2000) interagissant essentiellement à travers l'échange de documents que nous caractérisons ici comme constituant des communautés documédiatisées.

2 Documentarisation et redocumentarisation

Une des caractéristiques de la postmodernité ou de la "modernité sans frontière", est la nécessité pour chacun de redéfinir un environnement matériel inédit qui lui permette d'entretenir le tissu imaginaire nécessaire à la fois à la réception réitérée des productions sémiotiques et à l'exercice de sa propre créativité, condition d'une adaptation réussie à son environnement. Cet environnement matériel est de plus en plus privé, spécifique, mobile. C'est l'environnement du domicile prolongé par les dispositifs matériels permettant la réception en mobilité des œuvres de toutes natures qui permet individuellement et collectivement d'exercer la fonction imaginaire donnant du sens au quotidien et autorisant le maintien des appartenances identitaires.

L'accès généralisé aux œuvres par le biais des réseaux de grande distribution, des ondes ou du web, sur des supports éphémères ou pérennes (documents), est au cœur de la capacité à re-créer du local dont se dotent les individus et les communautés réparties auxquelles ils appartiennent. Pédauque (2006) invoque quatre fonctions associées au document: mémorisation, organisation des idées, créativité et transmission. Toutes ces fonctions sont pour nous étroitement interdépendantes mais la première sur le plan logique est toujours pour nous d'ordre transactionnel. Dans l'approche transactionnelle de l'action (notre cadre théorique, cf. Zacklad 2006a), la documentarisation vise à permettre la ré-exploitation des productions sémiotiques, que celles-ci soient destinées à des tiers lointains, à des intimes, ou à soi-même. Le document possède donc deux composantes indissociables relevant toute deux d'une problématique transactionnelle élargie: celle dans laquelle prédomine l'échange avec un tiers (composante sociale dominante) et celle dans laquelle prédomine l'échange avec soi-même associé au travail de pensée "individuelle" (composante cognitivo-émotionnelle dominante).

La force du document est qu'il permet un travail de redocumentarisation dotant les individus et les collectifs d'une autonomie inédite. Rappelons que, selon notre approche de la documentarisation (Zacklad 2004, 2006b), un document est une production sémiotique transcrite ou enregistrée sur un support pérenne équipé d'attributs permettant sa ré-exploitation. La documentarisation s'exerce selon les deux dimensions de l'articulation documentaire interne et externe. La première transforme matériellement le support pour permettre l'accès aux différentes parties du contenu sémiotique selon un découpage éditorial donné (titre de chapitre, numérotation, table des matières, métadonnées...). La seconde transforme matériellement le support pour permettre son rangement cohérent dans des collections ou des archives (titre, cotes du document, mots-clefs...). Selon cette approche, la catégorie *document* n'inclut pas exclusivement les textes écrits mais également les documents multimédia de toutes natures: œuvre graphique, photographie, cassette audio et vidéo, CD, DVD, jeux vidéo, etc., voire des objets manufacturés à vocation artistique, des objets liturgiques, ou encore des instruments essentiellement dégagés de leur fonction utilitaire pour remplir une fonction principalement sémiotique (cf. Briet 1951).

Que le support utilisé soit éphémère ou pérenne, il s'agit dans les deux cas d'un recours à des médiations substitutives permettant de pallier à la perception directe des productions sémiotiques à partir du corps de l'auteur comme dans le cas du spectacle vivant (cf. Zacklad 2004, 2006b). Mais alors que le recours massif au support des ondes a été une des caractéristiques majeure de la modernité du vingtième siècle (en prolongement de l'imprimé), le "retour" aux documents numérisés, enrichis par tous les possibles du multimédia, nous semble, ainsi qu'à Pédauque (2006), une des caractéristiques de la post-modernité du vingt et unième. Un de ses principaux intérêts est la possibilité offerte aux destinataires des documents de procéder à un travail de redocumentarisation. Selon Pédauque, le préfixe "re-" suggère "à la fois un retour sur une documentarisation ancienne et une révolution documentaire". Cette révolution est associée à divers phénomènes: transformation rapide des relations sociales, évolution des traditions documentaires, intégration des niveaux personnels et collectifs en lien avec les média de masse.

Dans le cadre de cet article, nous nous en tiendrons à la première signification soulignée par Pédauque (2006) en relation avec notre propre définition de la documentarisation. Redocumentariser, c'est documentariser à nouveau un document ou une collection en permettant à un bénéficiaire de réarticuler les contenus sémiotiques selon son interprétation et ses usages à la fois selon la dimension interne (extraction de morceaux musicaux pour les ré-agencer avec d'autres, ou annotations en marge d'un livre suggérant des parcours de lecture différents…) ou externe (organisation d'une collection, d'une archive, d'un catalogue privé croisant les ressources de différents éditeurs selon une nouvelle logique d'association). Dans ce contexte, la numérisation offre des opportunités inédites pour la réappropriation des documents et des dossiers en vue de satisfaire les intérêts de nouveaux bénéficiaires.

Pour analyser plus finement les pratiques de redocumentarisation, il nous semble nécessaire de passer en revue l'ensemble des collections documentaires privées qui structurent l'environnement matériel personnel des acteurs et qui contribuent à la gestion des contours de leur self dans les sociétés ouvertes et changeantes associées aux formes contemporaines de la mondialisation. Pour ce faire, nous proposerons une première ébauche de classification des documents personnels qui s'appuie elle-même sur une analyse des différentes logiques dans lesquelles se déploie l'action, envisagée dans le contexte de la théorie transactionnelle de l'action (Zacklad 2004, 2006b).

3 Logiques d'action dans les transactions

Selon notre approche théorique, la nature transactionnelle de l'action concerne les relations de la personne avec elle-même ou avec d'autres personnes individuelles ou collectives. Les personnes engagées dans la transaction sont en position de réalisateur (ou co-réalisateur) et de bénéficiaire (ou co-bénéficiaire), toutes les configurations de symétrie et d'asymétrie entre ces positions étant possibles. Les transactions se déroulent durant des situations d'activité, toujours médiatisées par des artefacts, soit avec une coprésence du corps des transactants, soit "à distance", par l'intermédiaire d'artefacts circulants d'un corps à l'autre. Certains artefacts sont des productions sémiotiques dont le support, quand il est pérenne, peut être documentarisé.

Les différentes situations transactionnelles (situation d'activité effectives des transactants) sont reliées entre elles par des flux transactionnels qui se diffusent de manière plus ou moins aléatoire ou systématique (Zacklad 2006c). Les transactions sont de nature créative ou routinière. Dans le premier cas elles induisent toujours une transformation ou une production aussi bien des artefacts médiateurs, les œuvres, que des personnes, les sois. On identifie trois dimensions des personnes (sociale, psychique, corporelle) et des œuvres (signifiante, énergétique, matérielle) qui sont générées par les transactions.

Logique d'action au croisement des trois domaines et des deux postures	**Logique affectivo-esthétique** Beau/Bon	**Logique philanthropique-moral** Bien/Juste	**Logique scientifico-pratique** Vrai/Utile
Posture analytique (rationalité en valeur)	Champ de l'esthétique (critères de jugement du beau et du bon)	Champ du politique, du spirituel et du religieux (critères de jugement des engagements philanthropiques)	Champ de la scientificité (critères d'évaluation des actions pratiques)
Posture synthétique (rationalité en finalité)	Affectif-Fictionnel (les goûts et les attraits…)	Moral-Idéologique (les pratiques et les attitudes engagées…)	Pratique-Efficace (savoir faire utiles, méthodes...)

Tableau 1: Six logiques d'action définies par le croisement de trois domaines et de deux postures.

Pour décrire le déroulement des transactions, on identifie quatre étapes: la virtualisation (le bénéficiaire potentiel exprime la vision d'un projet auquel adhère le réalisateur ou réciproquement), l'acquisition de compétence (le réalisateur ou les coréalisateurs acquièrent les compétences nécessaires à la réalisation du projet), la performance (transformation plus ou moins simultanée de l'œuvre et des sois réalisant le contenu du projet), la sanction (rétribution plus ou moins symbolique du réalisateur par le bénéficiaire).[1] Une situation transactionnelle peut donner lieu à la réalisation d'une transaction complète ou d'une étape de la transaction. Les flux transactionnels sont notamment orientés par l'enchainement de ces étapes.

Les transactions relèvent de différentes logiques d'action que l'on peut, par hypothèse, regrouper dans six catégories définies à l'intersection de trois domaines (affectivo-esthétique, philanthropique-moral, scientifico-pratique) et de deux postures (analytique et synthétique). Ce nombre de catégories n'est pas absolu. Une déclinaison selon les sphères culturelles est bien sur tout à fait envisageable (voir le tableau 1).

4 Registres psychiques du soi

Le déroulement des transactions, qui relève généralement d'une logique d'action dominante, met en scène différents registres psychiques qui ont un impact sur l'ensemble des dimensions de la personne et qui peuvent être mobilisés à chaque étape de la transaction. Ces registres sont définis à partir des théories pragmatiques et notamment de celle de G.H. Mead (1934), mais ils peuvent être mis en correspondance avec certaines approches psychanalytiques. Ce sont eux qui permettent de rendre compte de la dynamique créative des personnes individuelles et collectives, dans un compromis entre l'héritage issu des traditions qui les constituent et leur positionnement singulier dans une multiplicité de situations transactionnelles inédites. Les registres psychiques sont ceux du "je-spontané" (le "I" chez Mead, interventions libres de la personne laissant s'exprimer désirs et croyances), du "moi-stéréotypé" (le "Me", expression du contrôle social, des rôles stéréotypés et des traditions) et du "soi-innovant" (le "Self", compromis entre les désirs du je-créatif et les traditions véhiculées par le moi-stéréotypé). Les productions sémiotiques médiatisées par les documents relèvent de manière plus ou moins tranchée de l'un ou l'autre de ces registres.

Ces registres permettent de remplir plusieurs fonctions qui sont nécessaires au processus de création, de transformation des situations, de production des artefacts et des personnes. Le registre du "je-spontané" est associé à la fonction imaginaire. L'imaginaire offre des ressources internes pour l'interprétation créative des situations et l'exploration libre de possibilités de transformation et de production. Le "moi-stéréotypé" est associé à la fonction symbolique-structurante. Cette fonction offre les ressources symboliques et langagières qui sont les matériaux à partir desquels les variations imaginaires sont construites. Mais tout en proposant

---

1 Nous nous inspirons de la sémiotique Greimassienne exploitée dans le domaine de la communication organisationnelle par F. Cooren (2000).

de nombreux cadres structurants elle tend aussi à refouler la créativité libre exprimée par le je-spontané en sanctionnant les inventions du point de vue de la tradition, de la légitimité, de la conformité aux modèles.

Le soi-novateur remplit alors une fonction de production d'un réel-innovant correspondant à l'affirmation du soi par la projection dans des œuvres qui réalisent un compromis entre le foisonnement imaginaire et les contraintes véhiculées par le symbolique-structurant. La notion d'innovation, que nous distinguons de la notion de spontanéité ou de créativité pure, signifie que l'idée ou l'invention a été sanctionnée positivement au cours du processus transactionnel. A l'issue de la transaction une double transformation a été opérée: un artefact répondant aux souhaits des (co-)bénéficiaires a été produit et les selfs ont été transformés par l'échange dans les différentes dimensions sociales, psychiques et corporelles. Ces différents registres psychiques se retrouvent dans les différentes logiques d'action présentées plus haut (tableau 2).

Registres psychiques et logiques d'action dans la Théorie Transactionnelle de l'Action.	**Je-spontané, liberté d'association: imaginaire**	**Moi-stéréotypé, normativité: symbolique-structurant**	**Soi-novateur, solution sanctionnée positivement: réel-innovant**
Logique affectivo-esthétique Beau/Bon	Imaginaire associé au loisir, contes et traditions populaires, jeux, spectacles, convivialité…	Formes symboliques issues de l'histoire de l'art, des goûts, alimentaires, stéréotypes…	Innovations dans le registre affectivo-esthétique.
Logique philanthropique-moral Bien/Juste	Imaginaire religieux, idéologique, politique…	Formes symboliques religieuses, politiques, idéologiques…	Innovations dans le domaine politique, moral, idéologique…
Logique scientifico-pratique Vrai/Utile	Imaginaire pratique, hypothétique, Scientifique…	Formes symbolique dans le domaine pratique, scientifique, méthodologique…	Innovations pratiques, scientifiques, techniques…

Tableau 2. Les registres psychiques croisés avec les logiques d'action

5 Structure psychique: types de connaissances et degrés de conscience

Dans le paragraphe précédent, on a vu que l'imaginaire était principalement associé au registre du "je-spontané". Si l'imaginaire correspond pour nous à une forme de liberté d'association créative il relève également d'un type de connaissance constitué par des représentations élaborées dans le cadre de transactions intra ou inter personnelles. Mais ces représentations libres puisent elles-mêmes dans d'autres formes de "connaissances", tacites ou largement inconscientes, qui sont une des sources des émotions et qui génèrent les associations selon des mécanismes qui ne relèvent pas de structures de raisonnement conscientes à caractère hypothético-déductif ou narratif.

Croisement des registres (je-spontané, moi-stéréotypé, soi-novateur) et des niveaux de connaissance et de conscience	**Je-spontané, liberté d'association: imaginaire**	**Moi-stéréotypé, normativité: symbolique-structurant**	**Soi-novateur, solutions sanctionnées positivement: réel-innovant**
Les **images-modèles**: représentations riches et multimodales qui se développent avec l'expérience dans différentes situations transactionnelles organisées en domaines d'activités cohérents	Images-modèles produites par l'imaginaire	Images-modèles véhiculant le symbolique-structurant	Images-modèles véhiculant le réel-innovant
Les **règles-opératoires**: représentations opératoires guidant l'action étroitement liées aux caractéristiques tangibles des situations (objets et lieux)	Options possibles issues de l'exploration libre d'une situation concrète (objets, lieux...)	Normes associées à une situation concrète	Jugements personnels élaborés dans une situation concrète
Les **automatismes-inconscients** incluant les croyances (source tacites des attitudes), les désirs (source tacite des attirances), les automatismes moteurs: ils agrègent les expériences vécues par la personne depuis sa naissance d'une manière tacite selon des processus de condensation et de déplacement	Pulsions, croyances, séquences gestuelles qui fournissent des ressources vives pour l'exploration et l'imaginaire	Forces du refoulement, structures symboliques inconscientes qui surdéterminent la personne à son insu	Compromis psychique issus d'un travail de sublimation permettant de concilier pulsion et refoulement

Tableau 3: Croisement des types de connaissances et des registres psychiques du soi.

Ceci nous amène à introduire trois niveaux de connaissance qui correspondent également à trois degrés de conscience en nous inspirant à la fois des typologies de la psychologie cognitive et de celles de la psychanalyse (tableau 3):

- le niveau des "images-modèles", qui contient des connaissances déclaratives (au sens de la psychologie cognitive) et des images-mentales relevant de différents registres sensoriels. Les représentations élaborées à ce niveau sont dépendantes des systèmes sémiotiques en permettant l'expression (langues, graphisme...), systèmes dont la mise en œuvre nécessite des supports externes. L'imaginaire, qui implique l'évocation et la construction de représentations, relève pour nous de ce niveau de connaissance dans le registre du je-spontané;
- le niveau des "règles-opératoires", en partie conscientes mais fortement liées aux caractéristiques tangibles des situations (objets et lieux) et n'étant pas nécessairement dotées d'une organisation systématique hors de celle fournie par la situation considérée.;
- et le niveau des "automatismes-inconscients" correspondant à des "connaissances" largement tacites (ou inconscientes) que nous subdivisons en trois sphères, celles du désir (sources tacites de l'attirance pour des artefacts ou des personnes), celles de la croyance (source tacite des attitudes vis-à-vis des artefacts et des personnes) et celle des automatismes moteurs (enchaînement procéduraux de mouvements n'impliquant pas un contrôle délibéré).

6 Structures sociales associées aux flux transactionnels

La diffusion des productions imaginaires fait l'objet de multiples transactions de nature très diverses: transactions des personnes avec elles-mêmes lors d'activités de rêverie, activités ludiques et amicales entre intimes, activités communautaires, réception de productions sémiotiques par le biais des mass-médias, etc. Ces activités sont réalisées dans des situations transactionnelles, dans lesquelles les transactants sont effectivement engagés dans la coproduction de l'œuvre et des selfs. Les transactions se décomposent elles-mêmes en de nombreuses sous-transactions qui tantôt complètent la transaction principale tantôt en relancent de nouvelles en vertu de contrats de réciprocité ou d'une logique conventionnelle de don/contre-don.

Les situations d'activité transactionnelle sont donc reliées entre-elles pour de nombreux motifs. Selon la disponibilité et la localisation des transactants, selon les facilités d'accès à l'œuvre ou aux œuvres intermédiaires, selon la pression des échéances sociales ou des désirs personnels, les situations d'activités transactionnelles interdépendantes s'enchaînent sur selon des rythmes plus ou moins soutenus en constituant ce que nous appelons des flux transactionnel (Zacklad 2006c).

L'analyse de ces flux plus ou moins récurrents et systématiques peut se faire selon deux points de vue. Le premier privilégie la production collective de l'œuvre, son évolution et sa diffusion. Le second privilégie l'analyse des relations entre les personnes, leurs engagements mutuels, leurs relations de dépendance plus ou moins consenties. L'analyse de l'enchaînement des situations transactionnelles au sein d'un flux transactionnel par la mise en évidence de structures récurrentes d'interactions permet de définir plusieurs types de structures sociales. Elles sont, selon-nous, au nombre de sept:

1. Structure sociale intra-personnelle: Transactions de l'individu avec lui-même associées à la réalisation de ses actions quotidiennes et de ses projets de vie.
2. Structure sociale réseau relationnel: Transactions entre personnes sans inscription dans un projet collectif dans le cadre de fréquentations amicales, intimes, de voisinage... Ces transactions peuvent exprimer une solidarité importante et peuvent être poursuivies sur de longues années. S'il n'y a pas de projet collectif, il y a néanmoins un engagement à renforcer chacun dans ses projets personnels.
3. Structure sociale communautaire: Transactions entre personnes réunie par un projet commun qu'ils contribuent à définir en interagissant directement entre elles dans le cadre de relations interpersonnelles (famille, association pérenne de voisinage, association militante ou de loisir de taille restreinte, regroupement de professionnels au sein d'une organisation, etc.). On distingue de nombreux types de communautés selon la force du projet commun et de l'association: d'intérêt, de pratique, épistémique, d'action, etc. L'appartenance à la communauté est plus ou moins volontaire.
4. Structure sociale organisationnelle: Transactions entre personnes associées par un projet impliquant une définition formelle des rôles et des interactions. Les organisations sont extrêmement diverses de par leur taille et leur caractéristique. Elles sont souvent caractérisées par une forte spécialisation et la mise en place de puissants mécanismes de coordination qui permettent des transactions nombreuses sans interactions directes et sans relations interpersonnelles étroites entre l'ensemble des membres. A l'intérieur de l'organisation, il existe des relations hiérarchiques formalisées réglementairement ou juridiquement. L'appartenance à l'organisation est généralement librement consentie.
5. Structure de type "public": Au sein d'un public, les transactions sont très dissymétriques. Le public est constitué par la réception d'artefacts le plus souvent d'œuvres sémiotiques et est d'abord défini par l'intérêt qu'il porte à ces œuvres. La caractéristique du public est qu'il s'agit d'une structure sociale qui ne permet pas d'interactions directes entre ses membres sauf par le biais de mouvements transitoires lors de la présence aux manifestations quand celles-ci ont lieu. Les membres du public interagissent le plus

souvent très indirectement avec le réalisateur de l'œuvre soit par des actes de consommation, soit par des actes d'expression d'opinion plus ou moins formalisés: vote, réponse à enquête, courrier... Le public peut être de taille très variée. Il existe des publics de masse mais également des publics très étroits et spécialisés. Les transactions avec le public sont souvent médiatisées par un ensemble d'intermédiaires (éditeurs, distributeurs, etc.).

6. Structure sociale de type agencement contractuel: L'agencement contractuel coordonne et régule des transactions essentielles qui concernent généralement une vaste population partageant le même territoire. Il est considéré comme relevant de l'ordre des "institutions" au sens économique. Le dispositif de l'agencement contractuel est à la fois diffus et contraignant et relève de l'ordre juridique quelque soit son degré de formalisation. Il est souvent partiellement implicite et s'impose aux habitants du territoire qui n'ont que peu de moyens de le faire évoluer ou alors à un rythme généralement lent. Le dispositif inclut des organisations chargées de le faire fonctionner et de sanctionner les personnes qui contreviennent aux règles. Des agencements contractuels typiques sont constitués par les règles marchandes, les droits citoyens, les éléments de code civil relatifs à la propriété, par exemple. De nombreuses autres structures sociales s'appuient par ailleurs sur les agencements contractuels considérés comme une forme de structure sociale garantissant certaines transactions se déroulant en leur sein (par exemple, au sein des organisations). Symétriquement, l'agencement contractuel serait le plus souvent vide de sens s'il ne s'appuyait pas sur d'autres structures sociales permettant de réguler la vie quotidienne ou les activités économiques (réseau relationnel, communauté, organisation).
7. Structure sociale transitoire: Les structures transitoires correspondent à des transactions éphémères dans le contexte d'un phénomène collectif ou micro-collectif (le plus souvent dans des lieux public où les personnes ne se connaissent pas) associées à des évènements plus ou moins ritualisés (comportement de foule, rituels de salutation entre étrangers, comportements fugace d'entre-aide ou d'évitement...).

Une même transaction relève souvent de différentes structures sociales. Une transaction peut simultanément relever de l'appartenance à un public d'amateurs et permettre de renforcer un réseau relationnel et inversement. Ou encore, un flux transactionnel de type organisationnel peut s'appuyer tout à la fois sur des structures sociales de type communautaires et réseau relationnel. Le document étant selon nous un artefact sémiotique médiatisant une transaction, l'indentification de la structure sociale qui la régule est indispensable pour analyser son statut et les pratiques de documentarisation.

7 Analyse des documents privés sous l'angle des logiques d'action

Nous disposons maintenant d'un cadre théorique qui va nous permettre de caractériser le statut de la documentation et des archives constituées au sein du domicile sous forme papier et dans les différents dispositifs de stockage numérique personnels. Chaque type de document est un médiateur vis-à-vis de transactions dont le lecteur est partie prenante dans le cadre d'une structure sociale donnée et selon une logique d'action particulière dont le déroulement mobilise tel ou tel registre psychique. La première classification a priori que nous présentons est basée sur l'analyse en termes de logiques d'action dont relève les transactions, qui correspond à une mise en évidence des genres documentaires eux-mêmes liés aux genres de discours (cf. par exemple Bakhtine 1977).

Domaine esthétique (posture analytique):
- Documents d'histoire de l'art et encyclopédies artistiques diverses (littératures, arts de vivre, arts plastiques…);
- "Œuvres" au sens traditionnel servant de référence au jugement esthétique dans les domaines littéraires, musicaux, picturaux, filmiques;
- Certain titres de presse relatifs à ce registre.

Domaine affectif-fictionnel (posture synthétique):
- Romans de différents genres (action, sentimental, aventure, fantastique, policier, saga philosophique…);
- Certains titres de presse contenant des œuvres de fiction;
- Documents musicaux de différents genres (notamment enregistrements numériques);
- Film de différents genres (notamment enregistrements numériques):
- Photos, poster de différents genres, photos personnelles…;
- Objets "artistiques divers".

Domaine politico-spirituel (posture analytique):
- Documents doctrinaires de référence engagés politiquement;
- Bibles, divers livres "sacrés" ou de philosophie existentielle;
- Certains titres de presse relatifs à ce registre.

Domaine moral-idéologique (posture synthétique):
- Documents militants;
- Documents liés à la mise en œuvre de pratiques liturgiques…;
- Certains titres de presse relatifs à ce registre.

Domaine scientifique (posture analytique):
- Des documents présentant des résultats de sciences humaines;

- Des documents présentant des résultats de science de la nature plus ou moins vulgarisés;
- Certains titres de presse relatifs à ce registre.

Domaine pratique-efficace (posture synthétique):
- Les documents techniques en relation directe avec la mise en œuvre d'un outil ou d'une pratique opératoire dans un contexte donné (manuel d'utilisation, livre de recette, livre de méthode, etc.);
- Les documents administratifs (preuves des transactions administratives ou commerciales);
- Certains titres de presse relatifs à ce registre.

Ces documents ont deux sources principales: certains sont édités par des organisations externes (administrations, entreprises de bien de consommation divers, éditeurs d'ouvrage culturels...), d'autres sont produits par les personnes elles-mêmes (photos, enregistrements personnels de vidéo, musique jouée par les personnes...), d'autres, enfin, sont hybrides et directement en prise avec le processus de redocumentarisation (sélection ou enregistrement à partir de sources de diffusion publiques ou commerciales, de performances réalisées par d'autres artistes). Par ailleurs, ils sont disponibles sur des supports variés: papier mais également supports d'enregistrement divers (CD, DVD...) et de plus en plus sur les mémoires de masse des ordinateurs à partir desquels ils ont été téléchargés.

Aujourd'hui, ce sont souvent les documents du domaine affectif-fictionnel, que nous appellerons dorénavant, "documents culturels de loisir", qui sont les plus nombreux dans le domicile privé, ceux qui font l'objet des investissements financiers les plus importants et des pratiques d'échanges, notamment pair-à-pair, les plus massives. Ce sont également les productions sémiotiques relevant de ce domaine qui sont évoquées par Appadurai comme jouant un rôle particulier dans les activités imaginaires et qui permettent une forme de relocalisation, notamment dans la sphère privée du domicile. La figure 1 schématise le rôle complémentaire jouée par les documents associés à une posture analytique ou synthétique dans le processus de création de nouvelles productions sémiotiques pouvant elles-mêmes être ultérieurement documentarisées.

Insistons bien sur le fait qu'il n'y a pas une stricte équivalence entre la logique d'action dont relève un document (par exemple, esthétique vs affectif-fictionnel) et son statut dans le processus de création. Pour un scientifique produisant de nouveaux documents, la frontière qui sépare les documents sources d'inspiration et les documents intervenant comme des contraintes (figure 1), peut se situer à l'intérieur de l'ensemble des documents du domaine scientifique en distinguant des articles correspondant à des connaissances stabilisées et des articles porteurs d'hypothèses non totalement corroborées ou issus d'une autre spécialité. Il est également possible que le même document joue tantôt une fonction de source d'inspiration, tantôt une fonction référence normative source de contraintes. Mais le plus souvent, les documents relevant d'une posture analytique, d'une (rationalité en valeur), offrent des critères de jugements pour l'évaluation de productions sémiotiques relevant d'une posture synthétique (rationalité en finalité). Une nouvelle œuvre de fiction sera, par exemple, évaluée en fonction des principaux canons correspondant aux références du genre dont elle est susceptible de relever, à la fois pour contrôler qu'elle n'est pas qu'une simple reproduction à l'identique et pour vérifier qu'elle peut s'interpréter de manière plus ou moins décalée dans des genres existant ou en création.

Dans la partie suivante, nous montrerons comment les pratiques de redocumentarisation contribuent à transformer les activités de réception du "public" en activités communautaires visant délibérément à rassembler des œuvres sémiotiques pour entretenir un imaginaire commun.

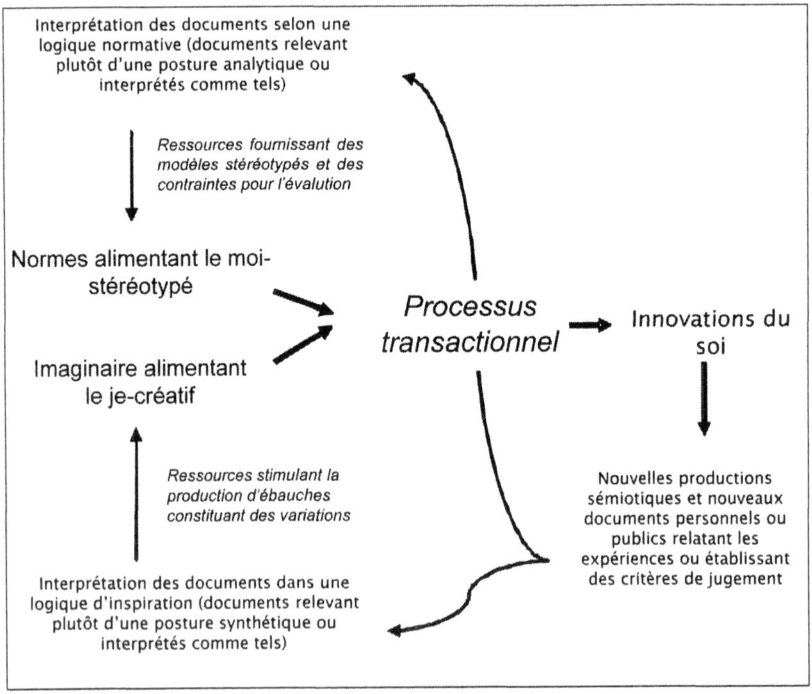

Figure 1. Rôles joués par les documents dans le processus d'adaptation créative.

8 Du public à la communauté d'imaginaire documédiatisée: importance de la redocumentarisation des collections

Si la plupart des structures sociales que nous avons présentées sont en mesure de développer des activités créatives relevant du "je-spontané" et donc de développer une fonction imaginaire plus ou moins explicite, le développement de cette activité imaginaire n'est parfois une finalité que pour la moitié d'entre-elles (intra-personnelle, réseau relationnel, communauté, public). Par exemple, quand les structures sociales intra-personnelles (dialogue intérieur privé) privilégient des logiques d'action affectivo-esthétique sans revendiquer d'activité de production innovante spécifique (soi-novateur), on peut considérer qu'elles visent essentiellement à entretenir une fonction imaginaire propice au déploiement de l'activité du "je-spontané". C'est également le cas des structures sociales communautaires, dont certaines ont comme finalité constitutive des activités de loisir propices au développent d'un imaginaire collectif associé au sport, au tourisme, à la musique, ou encore aux art-graphiques ou culinaires. A ce titre, nous considérons qu'elles constituent des "communautés d'imaginaire", des communautés dont la motivation principale est le développement d'images-modèles communes dans le domaine affectivo-esthétique

Face à la déterritorialisation induite par les différents régimes de modernité sans frontière et au relatif isolement dans lequel se retrouvent les personnes, la société de consommation répond d'abord par la diffusion et la distribution d'œuvres culturelles constituant différents publics. Aux transactions ludiques et festives qui caractérisaient de nombreuses rencontres quotidiennes dans les modes de vie traditionnels, s'est souvent substituée la réception d'artefacts sémiotiques sur un mode asymétrique dont la circulation est de plus en plus mondialisée. C'est dans ce contexte qu'Appadurai décrit la manière dont les diasporas construisent des mondes imaginaires, notamment par le biais d'une consommation culturelle de loisir, qui les constitue en "publics spécialisés". L'entretien d'un monde imaginaire nécessite la constitution d'une collection personnelle, elle-même basée sur les recommandations de différents prescripteurs: éditeurs, distributeurs, critiques de presse et réseau relationnel.

Mais la généralisation des usages grand public du web a transformé la donne. Les collectifs d'amateurs peuvent échanger les œuvres qu'ils apprécient par le réseau, s'engager dans des interactions médiatisées par des forums, des chats, des listes de messagerie, créer des sites web et des blogs. Ils interagissent de manière plus ou moins réelle avec les artistes qu'ils apprécient. Ils constituent ainsi de nouvelles communautés d'imaginaire recourant à la documédiatisation, c'est-à-dire échangeant, organisant, évaluant, des documents culturels de loisir.

La documédiatisation est un néologisme qui exprime en un seul mot le processus de médiatisation documentaire. Une structure sociale, comme une communauté, peut être dite documédiatisée quand l'essentiel des interactions entre ses membres sont réalisées par le biais de transactions documentaires. Dit encore autrement, une communauté documédiatisée, est une "communauté virtuelle", pour reprendre le terme popularisé par Rheingold (2004), qui recourt principalement à l'échange et la coproduction de documents digitaux, le plus souvent des documents pour l'action (Zacklad 2004, 2006a) du type de ceux que nous avons déjà évoqués (messages électroniques, blogues, forums, wiki, fichiers annotés...). En mettant l'accent sur les spécificités de la documédiatisation, on souligne le fait que les processus transactionnels dépendent en partie de l'organisation documentaire sous-jacente, du degré de structuration des documents, de leurs modalités d'indexation, des possibilités d'accès à ceux-ci, des moyens de recherche disponibles, etc.

Certes, tous les groupes de "fan" ne constituent pas des communautés documédiatisées et nombreux sont ceux qui continuent à être des "publics" au sens traditionnel: leurs membres ne participent pas aux forums d'échanges et fréquentent peu les sites web. Mais même parmi ceux-là, certains amateurs échangent des fichiers par des systèmes pair-à-pair et élargissent leurs collections en échappant au strict contrôle des maisons d'édition et des réseaux de distribution. Dans ces systèmes d'échanges, il est de plus en plus possible d'accéder à la collection de titres possédée par les autres internautes et stockée sur leur disque dur, à la recherche de nouvelles associations, voire de rentrer en relation par courriel avec eux.

Notons, d'ailleurs, que si le web permet le développement de communautés d'imaginaire, il facilite également de plus en plus le développement de réseaux relationnels documédiatisés basés sur un imaginaire commun. Ces deux types de structures sociales (communauté et réseau) sont elles-mêmes plus ou moins facilitées par les structures documentaires offertes par les fournisseurs d'accès, les sites portail et les différents sites de réseautage social. Ainsi, là où les sites communautaires dédiés et les forums induisent plutôt de la mise en place de communautés d'imaginaire (qui relèvent de la catégorie plus générale des communautés d'intérêt), les blogs et les sites de réseautage sont plutôt basés sur la métaphore du réseau social. Mais le fait qu'un site de réseautage comme Myspace encourage la mise en visibilité de sa liste d'amis, sans toutefois leur donner la possibilité d'interagir directement entre eux à l'aide d'outils de type forum, permet de créer une visibilité réciproque du réseau et finalement à lui donner potentiellement une forme "d'identité collective" (le groupe des "amis de untel"), ce qui montre que les frontières entre la documédiatisation d'un réseau relationnel basé sur un imaginaire commun et d'une communauté d'imaginaire est ténue.

Le partage de fichiers véhiculant des documents culturels de loisir correspondant à des goûts, des intérêts, des appartenances ethniques... est ainsi au cœur de la constitution des communautés d'imaginaire documédiatisées. Ce phénomène amplifie le rôle qui a toujours été joué par les collections. En effet, celles-ci ont toujours rempli une double fonction: une fonction cognitivo-émotionnelle associée à la définition de corpus rassemblant les œuvres d'un même auteur ou d'auteurs différents pour les inscrire dans des courants esthétiques apparentés et mieux percevoir leurs points communs et leurs différences et une fonction sociale correspondant à la définition des membres possédant, partageant, ou appréciant ces œuvres et se reconnaissant de ce fait comme appartenant à la même communauté d'amateurs.

La numérisation, en autorisant notamment la redocumentarisation des documents multimédia (extraction de morceaux pour les inscrire dans de nouvelles séries), renforce la possibilité offerte à chaque personne de se constituer des collections hybrides de documents culturels, mais plus encore d'interagir avec d'autres pour sélectionner, filtrer, hiérarchiser certaines œuvres culturelles de loisir permettant de s'inscrire dans une diversité de communautés d'imaginaire (comme le font, avec d'autres méthodes et finalités, les communautés scientifiques, par exemple).

Ainsi, la possibilité donnée au citoyen de la modernité sans frontière de se constituer facilement des collections multiples et diverses, peut faire de lui un amateur éclairé réglant en permanence son degré de participation aux communautés d'imaginaire à partir desquelles il se définit. La collection documentaire apparait ainsi comme un instrument qui est tout à la fois au service des communautés dans la définition des représentations de référence de leurs membres et au service des individus pour explorer de manière systématique des imaginaires de référence en s'inscrivant de manière plus ou moins cohérente, persévérante et fidèle dans un certain nombre d'entre elles.

9 Conclusion: quelles conséquences pour la conception des dispositifs de gestion des collections?

Le parallèle de plus en plus apparent entre gestion d'une appartenance collective et gestion de collections documentaires fait également ressortir des parentés frappantes entre les modes de développement des réseaux et communautés d'imaginaire, scientifiques et d'affaire recourant à la documédiatisation pour n'en citer que quelques uns. L'accroissement de la numérisation des documents et la facilité avec laquelle il est aujourd'hui possible de les diffuser et de les échanger augmente considérablement les possibilités de gestion créative des collections à l'aide desquelles les communautés et les individus structurent leurs diverses activités imaginaires, pratiques, scientifique, professionnelles, administratives...

De ce point de vue, les projets de recherche autour des dispositifs de création, de gestion et d'archivage des documents, qu'ils soient de nature technique, organisationnelle ou juridique, doivent être mis en perspective avec ces problématiques de développement psychologique, social, politique, économique des individus et des collectifs. Par exemple, et pour conclure en référence aux débats actuels sur le droit d'auteur, il nous semble nécessaire, en prenant en considération ces différents enjeux, de ne pas privilégier à outrance le pouvoir des "majors" c'est-à-dire d'un secteur particulier de l'économie, tout le monde s'accordant sur la nécessité d'une juste rémunération des auteurs et sur l'utilité du rôle des éditeurs quand ceux-ci n'abusent pas de certaines rentes de situation.

La prolongation des droits d'auteurs sur des durées toujours plus longues, le plus souvent au bénéfice exclusif des éditeurs et des ayant droits et le désir de "verrouillage technique" des possibilités de copie des contenus (Digital Right Management), constituent non seulement un frein aux possibilités d'accès aux œuvres dans les bibliothèques virtuelles publiques, mais également au libre partage des œuvres stockées dans les bibliothèques virtuelles personnelles, une liberté qui a toujours été associée à la propriété de ces biens (prêt de livre, de disque, de cassettes...). Ces restrictions sont également des restrictions au développement des imaginaires individuels et collectifs que l'on ne saurait pourtant accepter de voir outrancièrement et exclusivement soumis aux offres restreintes des campagnes publicitaires du moment.

10 Bibliographie

Appadurai, Arjun, 1996. *Modernity at large: cultural dimensions of globalization.* Minneapolis, Minn.: University of Minnesota Press, Trad. Fçse, Appadurai, A., 2001. *Après le colonialisme - Les conséquences culturelles de la mondialisation.* Paris: Payot.

Bakhtine, Mikhail (Volochinov, Valentin N.), 1977. *Le marxisme et la philosophie du langage: Essai d'application de la méthode sociologique en linguistique*, Paris: Minuit.

Briet, Suzanne, 1951. *Qu'est-ce que la documentation?*. Paris: EDIT.

Castoriadis, Cornelius, 1975. *L'Institution imaginaire de la société.* Paris: Éditions du Seuil.

Cooren, François, 2000. *The organizing property of communication.* Amsterdam/ Philadelphia: John Benjamins Publishing Company.

Mead George Herbert, 1934/1967. *Mind, self and society from the standpoint of a social behaviourist*. Chicago: The University of Chicago Press.

Pédauque, Roger T., 2003. *Document: forme, signe et médium, les re-formulations du numérique*. Working paper. En ligne: http://archivesic.ccsd.cnrs.fr/ (consulté 5 décember 2006).

------. 2006. *Document et modernités*. Working paper. En ligne: http://archivesic.ccsd.cnrs.fr/ (consulté 5 décember 2006).

Rheingold, Howard, 2000. *The Virtual Community: Homesteading on the Electronic Frontier*. Secker & Warburg. London. En ligne: http://www.rheingold.com/vc/book/ (consulté 5 décember 2006).

Zacklad, Manuel, 2004. Processus de documentarisation dans les Documents pour l'Action (DopA): statut des annotations et technologies de la coopération associées. *Le numérique: Impact sur le cycle de vie du document pour une analyse interdisciplinaire*, 13-15 Octobre 2004, Montréal. En ligne: http://archivesic.ccsd.cnrs.fr/ (consulté 5 décember 2006).

------. 2006a. Documentarisation processes in Documents for Action (DofA): the status of annotations and associated cooperation technologies. *Computer Supported Cooperative Work* 15(Numbers 2-3/June), 205-228.

------. 2006b. *Gestion du connaissant et du connu dans la théorie transactionnelle de l'action (TTA)*. Working paper. En ligne: http://archivesic. ccsd.cnrs.fr/ (consulté 5 décember 2006).

------. 2006c. *Une approche communicationnelle et documentaire des TIC dans la coordination et la régulation des flux transactionnels*. Working paper. En ligne: http://archivesic.ccsd.cnrs.fr/ (consulté 5 décember 2006).

Andreas Vårheim

Evolving and Devolving Institutions: A Perspective on Norwegian Public Policy towards the IT industry 1945-2000[1]

1 Introduction

Throughout the IT sector the development, production, organization, and use of digital documents have had a substantial economic impact in advanced political economies worldwide. While constituting part of an advanced economy, the Norwegian IT industry has not been very successful. The end of the 1980s and the beginning of the 1990s proved a disastrous period for the Norwegian IT industry. Among other calamities, the two flagships of the industry, Kongsberg Våpenfabrikk and Norsk Data went bankrupt. Kongsberg Våpenfabrikk, originally a state-owned armament company and manufacturer of the (at least in Norway) famous Krag-Jørgensen rifles, played a central role in the Norwegian high- technology industry after the Second Word War. The market areas it supplied included defence, automobile, energy, data, offshore, aviation and aerospace industries. Norsk Data was primarily a producer of minicomputers (a minicomputer is a midsized computer between a workstation and a mainframe), and also made a wide range of software applications.

In addition, in Norway it proved impossible to develop the GSM–standard for mobile communication industrially and commercially. The Swedes (Ericsson) and the Finns (Nokia) succeeded. However, the standard chosen for the GSM-system ("Groupe Speciale Mobile" or "Global System for Mobile Communications") in 1987 was developed by the Norwegian scientist Torleiv Maseng at Elab-Sintef/University of Trondheim, and financed by "Televerkets forskningsinstitutt", the research department of Norwegian Telecommunications, now Telenor (Sogner 2002, 113; Gran 2004; Thyholdt et al. 2000).

---

1 This paper is a revised version of a paper presented at the 3rd Document Academy Conference at the School of Information Management and Systems, University of California at Berkeley, 7-9 October, 2005. I thank the participants and Peter Arbo for their helpful comments. Olav Wicken is thanked for making figures and tables available.

Contrary to Norsk Data, Kongsberg Våpenfabrikk was restructured. The problem for Kongsberg was not lost markets, but a halt in government funding necessary to service accumulated debts. The Kongsberg conglomerate was split up, and the different activities were continued by new independent companies. The major activity was defence, and continues today in Kongsberg Gruppen or "Kongsberg" only in English. In recent years, Kongsberg has expanded its operations in maritime electronics and systems through organic growth as well as several strategic acquisitions. Civilian activities have been developed especially within areas of technology related to defence activities.

There has been some success in the Norwegian IT industry in the 1990s, but its impact on the economy is small compared to other OECD countries. The high-technology share of manufacturing exports from Norway in the 1990s was less than half of the OECD average and in 1999 only New Zealand, Turkey, Portugal, and the new eastern European members of the OECD exported less high-tech products than Norway, as well as Spain and Italy, which scored marginally lower (OECD 2001, 207). Regarding the average annual growth rate in export value in high technology manufacturing, Norway was only ahead of Japan and Italy in the 1990s (OECD 2001, 209). Considering that the 1990s were not particularly good for the Japanese economy Norwegian achievements are nothing to write home about.

This introduction leads to the question of why Norway has become such an ICT "loser", as a representative of the young and outspoken generation would put it, and this not only compared to neighbouring Finland and Sweden and other small Northern European economies like Ireland, but also when compared to most OECD countries.

The 1980s marked the end of what was considered a bright future for the Norwegian ICT industry. The reasons for the failure of Norwegian ICT industry are of course complex, and constitute a puzzle many scholars have tried answering from different perspectives. However, we know for example that the Finnish industrial/innovation policy and industrial policy institutions have been considered instrumental in creating ICT industry growth in Finland (Castells and Himanen 2002; Moen 2002). The same applies to Ireland (Ó Riain 2004; Vårheim 2005). Regarding industrial policy and innovation policy, there are clear indications that institutions matter - so what about the development in Norwegian institutions and policies in the relevant period? This paper is explorative and will hopefully be one step towards elucidating institutional mechanisms in the formulation of ICT policy.

Firstly, an outline of the development in Norwegian ICT-relevant industrial policy after WWII focusing on the 1980s will be presented. Secondly, I will interpret changes in Norwegian policy towards the ICT industry from a historical institutional perspective on how institutions and policies evolve.

2 The 1950s: cheap energy trumps technology investment

The making of post-WII Norwegian high technology policy and IT policy can be seen as a struggle between the two main paradigms for modernization of the Norwegian economy (Wicken 1992a; Arbo 1996, 178; Ørstavik 1999, 7, 11). One policy paradigm is the macroeconomic paradigm or economy paradigm. In its early formulation based on Keynesianism, economic growth according to this way of thinking is maintained by regulation of demand and credit. The second policy paradigm is the paradigm of science-led economic growth; we shall call it the technology paradigm. The Second World War meant that both policy paradigms were strengthened significantly. The so-called "social economists" of the Oslo school (originally a Keynesian variant) have dominated Norwegian economic policy-making since 1945, regardless of whether Labour or the Conservatives have been in power.

Figur 1

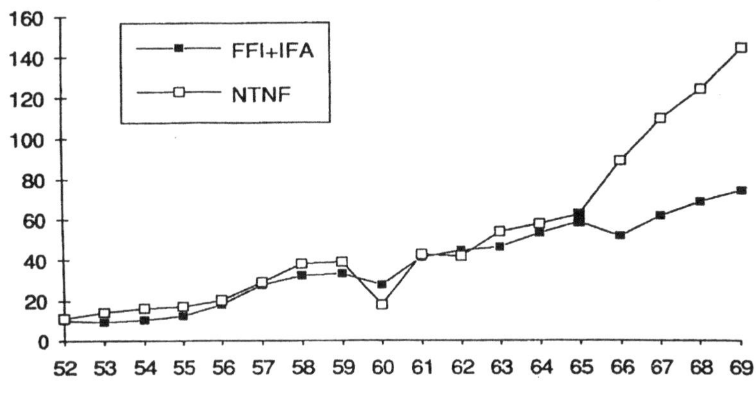

Figure 1. Relationship between military related research spending (FFI+IFA) and civilian technology research (NTNF). Current NOKs (Wicken 1992b, 8).

Even before Norway became one of the founding members of NATO in 1949, "Forsvarets Forskningsinstitutt" – the FFI (the Norwegian Military Research Establishment) had been set up in 1946. This meant the introduction of the ideas of science-led economic growth in Norway. The technology paradigm was significantly strengthened by the advent of NATO, especially in monetary terms by American dollars. Defence funding including American financial support was by far the biggest contributor to the overall Norwegian research effort. Figure 1 shows the development of military research funds and civilian funds in the 1950s and 1960s. From 1966 onwards, civilian research seemingly overtakes military research. One reason for this is that the distinctions between what was military research and what was civilian research became increasingly blurred. A second reason is that formerly military research, e.g. within IT, from the 1960s was conducted in civilian institutions.

Year	Funding from NATO/allies	Total Funding	NATO funding as percentage of total funding
1946/47	0	1 467 000	0
1947/48	0	1 779 000	0
1948/49	0	1 579 000	0
1949/50	0	2 960 000	0
1950/51	0	3 201 000	0
1951/52	0	3 913 000	0
1952/53	0	4 476 000	0
1953/54	1 550 000	4 867 000	31,8 %
1954/55	499 000	5 123 000	9,7 %
1955/56	1 264 000	5 770 000	21,9 %
1956/57	417 000	7 190 000	5,8 %
1957/58	1 257 000	8 468 000	14,8 %
1958/59	7 274 000	12 601 000	57,7 %
1960	8 226 682	17 188 400	47,9 %
1961	5 753 511	17 378 800	33,1 %
1962	3 738 382	23 416 300	16,0 %
1963	12 263 221	19 012 800	64,5 %
1964	6 865 908	22 633 500	30,3 %
1965	2 339 307	25 305 700	9,2 %
1966	6 861327	23 010 900	29,8 %
1967	8 536 758	32 798 000	26,0 %
1968	13 750 187	40 422 800	34,0 %
1969	23 019 776	53 099 200	43,4 %
1970	15 396 526	42 856 300	35,9 %
1971	2 724 347	37 296 000	7,3 %
1972	1 420 482	37 520 000	3,8 %
1973	2 692 517	41 530 295	6,5 %
1974	1 236 500	44 431 000	2,8 %
1975	1 478 000	50 977 000	2,9 %
1946-75	**128 564 431**	**592 270 995**	**21,7 %**

Table 1. Funding from NATO allies to FFI 1946-1975 in current NOKs and relative to total FFI income (adapted from Njølstad and Wicken 1997, 503).

In table 1, we can see one example of American support in the case of FFI. From the table we literally can read off the varying temperatures of the Cold War.

As in the US and the UK, the structure of research funding in Norway meant that most public sector research money was allocated to defence research and nuclear energy research. In the 1950s, nuclear energy and missile development were popular, in the 1960s space technology and information technology were given priority (Wicken 1992b, 4-5).

In spite of the perceived imminent threat from the Soviet Union and the strong military build-up in response, the technology paradigm did not dominate in the 1950s as one would expect. Many economists were sceptical about the benefits of science for economic growth, and the industrial policy focus was on exploiting natural resources, mainly energy in the form of hydroelectric power and energy related industry like aluminium and other metallurgical industry (Ørstavik 1999, 7, 11). Despite its boost by defence spending, the failure of the research effort in generating economic results in the1950s, especially in the nuclear energy sector, gave the economy paradigm the upper hand. In addition, parts of the 1950s, e.g. 1957/58, were years of stagnating economic growth and increasing unemployment.

3 The 1960s: technology policy activism

However, the advent of Sputnik in 1957 and the alleged technology gap meant that the 1960s became a decade dominated by the technology paradigm (Ørstavik 1999, 7). Also, advances in economic theory indicating that technology was an important factor in economic growth contributed in turning the tables (Ørstavik 1999, 7, 11; Arbo 1996, 182). The profits from the huge investments in general manufacture in the 1950s were considered too low.

The 1960s are characterized by many government industrial policy initiatives (Arbo 1996, 183; Sogner 2002, 27). Several industrial development funds were set up, and ensured strong government participation in the formulation of industrial strategies. The IT industry was given high priority within the fund system. This was the result of close cooperation between the head of defence research, Mr Finn Lied, who became Minister of Industry in the early 1970s, and the head of the Central Bank, Mr Erik Brofoss, former Finance Minister and the leading character in the industrial development fund system (Sogner 2002, 28). The importance of closer cooperation between research institutions was emphasised in policy documents, and the need for more knowledge-based industry in the future was acknowledged (Arbo 1996, 184-185). The technology paradigm came victorious out of the 1960s, while the economists revised their theory.

4 1970s: technology activism combined with counter-cyclical economic crisis management

In the 1970s, the government continued and enhanced its industrial policy effort, in particular towards the IT industry (Sogner 2002, 44). The system of funding was strengthened, and the establishment of a holding company for state-owned companies was proposed. This was partly implemented within the IT industry, where it caused a small wave of mergers and acquisitions within the industry, focusing on the big indigenous companies. One electronics firm, Tandberg, became state-owned due to financial difficulties. Overall, the technology paradigm seems to have increased its influence during this decade.

As already hinted at previously, the 1970s were also a period of economic problems. The Norwegian government, newly rich in oil, implemented a counter-cyclical economic policy, granting huge industrial subsidies which resulted in structural problems, high inflation, high interest rates, high wages, and decreased competitiveness compared to other economies. Because of this, the 1970s meant that active state involvement in industry was discredited, and in particular involvement in the IT industry because of the Tandberg affair: Tandberg went bankrupt in spite of state ownership and subsidies.

5 1980s: IT industry breakdown, government inaction and economy paradigm consolidation

The 1980s did not put an end to all the traits of an active IT industry policy, but during this time the development of a few national champions was no longer concentrated upon (Ørstavik 1999, 17; Sogner 2002, 70). The policy was instead redirected towards a few strategic technology areas rather than specific firms, and one area was ICT (Remøe 2004, 21). However, the hallmark of the 1980s is the use of market mechanisms in industrial support rather than direct state intervention (Hauknes and Wicken 2003, 28; Remøe 2004, 23). Government industrial support from now on was expected to be neutral in regard to what kind of industries were supported. The policy ambitions of both paradigms were reduced in the 1980s. However, the economy paradigm came out as the clear winner, although it was a very changed economy paradigm. It had moved from Keynesianism to neoliberalism. Of course, these change processes involved differences of opinion within the economy paradigm.

Until the year 1986, the 1980s proved a fantastic boom period for the Norwegian IT-industry. This meant that industrial policy actually did not seem very important. A crucial factor relating to the IT industry success needs to be mentioned, however: the significance of the petroleum industry and the petroleum revenues for IT industrial development. Oil was and is important in at least four ways. On the positive side, it represents a market that the Norwegian IT industry uses to specialize in oil-relevant technology, and this has been successful. On the more negative side is that this market niche does not constitute a mass market, and limits the growth potential of the IT industry. Another factor is that the oil revenues and resulting public sector expansion made companies like Norsk Data complacent about their market position and technological solutions. When economic crisis and public sector contraction set in in the late 1980s, and the PC became ubiquitous, Norsk Data lost its biggest market. Fourthly, the Norwegian petroleum economy with its huge surpluses has made the government opt for an economic policy that, out of fear of overheating of the economy, means that investments are made abroad, rather than at home. The Norwegian government invests in foreign enterprises and in the multinational IT industry, but not at home. Most people find this policy reasonable in the short term, but in the long term, when the revenues from petroleum are history, this policy might prove unwise.

6 Theory and discussion

The economy paradigm won the battle with the technology paradigm in the 1980s, and it is still winning. Why is this so? The situation is different in, for example, Finland and Ireland. The obvious answer is the oil revenues, but the oil income is no actor in itself. What are the properties of Norwegian institutions that give them such a short-term financial perspective? Compared to Finland and Ireland, it seems that the Norwegian problem is a lack of coordinating capacity in a fragmented system. The prime minister's office is weak. In Finland and in Ireland important policy areas are given a lot more attention from the top (Moen, 2002, Vårheim, 2005).

Public policies are important cases of political institutions (Pierson 2006; Vårheim 2001). Insights about institutional effects can consequently be used in studies of policy effects. Major policy changes and institutional changes occur that are not the results of external shocks to the political economy, and that are not the outcome of punctuated equilibria and critical junctures. Accumulated incremental change can add up to gradual transformational change (Streeck and Thelen 2005; Thelen 2004; Pierson 2004). Social order manifests itself in institutions that in the context of advanced political economies can be defined as systems of social interaction under formalized normative control (Streeck and Thelen 2005, 16).

Institutional development is characterized by ongoing conflict between political coalitions during institutional genesis, and later the point of contention shifts from the form of institutional arrangements to what effects they have, although the form often remains controversial, together with functions and salience (Thelen 2004, 32; Streeck and Thelen 2005, 19). Resilient, previously losing coalitions or paradigms can, over time, develop as important forces of institutional change and ultimately effect institutional transformation, either gradually or as a revolution in the form of breakdown or replacement.

Shifts in the balance of power are the basis of institutional change, regardless of the magnitude of the change. Reproduction and change both form parts of institutional development. Institutional survival is dependent on the ability of actors to construct an institutional development process synchronized with the political and economic environment. Within this parameter of institutional survival, actors pursue their own agendas for institutional development (Streeck and Thelen 2005, 19). The ability of actors to tip the balance of power is heavily dependent on earlier institutional development limiting the menu of choice, as well as their ability to build coalitions around their own interpretation of policies satisfying the necessities of survival (Pierson 2004, 141, 152-153; Thelen 2004, 289).

Gradual and at the same time transformative changes happen in different ways. One comprehensive overview is given by Streeck and Thelen outlining five different models (Streeck and Thelen 2005, 19-30): displacement; layering; drift; conversion; and exhaustion. Here, I will concentrate on displacement, as that seems the most relevant to our case. *Displacement* means that less important institutions gain more relative importance compared to the dominant institutions within an institutional system. The dominant institutions are abandoned by a growing number of actors. Alternative institutional arrangements have already coexisted within the institutional system, or they invade the system of institutions/society from outside, through occupying powers that are subsequently domesticated, or by the importation and integration of foreign practices.

Within Norwegian ICT industrial policy we have seen how the positions of the technology and the economy paradigms have varied over the years, and how losing policies have existed within the institutional system waiting for their comeback. Furthermore, we have seen how the paradigms have managed to adapt to environmental change, and how policy content has changed while losing policy paradigms have not been fully exterminated, but have instead survived and come back with a perceived environmental change.

One example is furnished by the industrial policy development in the 1980s, which can be interpreted as a process of transformative change through displacement. In the 1980s, the economy paradigm grew in importance at the cost of the technology paradigm. The economic crisis of the 1970s was supposed to indicate the failure of an active policy towards technology development and the ICT industry, and the importation of monetarism/economic liberalism (coming from the wallet of Mr Reagan and Mrs Thatcher's handbag) gave the economy paradigm the upper hand. The old, seemingly industry-neutral basis of Keynesianism found a new companion in economic liberalism. Even old-timers like Finn Lied, Jens Christian Hauge and the rest of the Labour establishment abandoned their activist policies. The balance between the two paradigms or coalitions was tipped. Energy resources underpinned "neutrality" in both the 1950s and the 1980s. Huge public investment in electricity development and oil is understood as industry-neutral. It seems that the meaning of neutrality at times can be very elastic indeed!

7 Conclusion

In relation to historical institutional theory, this paper has not disproved the main tenet that institutions or policies can go through transformative change gradually, not only through "big bangs" in times of extreme crisis. Institutions and policies evolve and, as in this case, they also devolve. The active, technological-oriented industrial policy of the 1960s and 1970s disintegrated. This does not necessarily entail the end of an active industrial policy; according to the theory I have laid out here, the active industrial policy can be in hibernation, rather like the brown bear waiting for spring to come, so he can eat wild berries and, perhaps, the occasional economist passing by in the wilderness.

8 References

Arbo, Peter N., 1996. Fra industriorientert til kunnskapsorientert modernisering: Om Nord-Norges plass i kunnskapssamfunnet. In *Det nye Nord-Norge: Avhengighet og modernisering i nord*, ed. E. O. Eriksen. Bergen: Fagbokforlaget, 175-246.

Castells, Manuel, and Pekka Himanen, 2002. *The information society and the welfare state: the Finnish model.* Oxford: Oxford University Press.

Gran, Even, 2004. Inventor of the GSM system. *Gemini. Forskningsnytt fra NTNU og SINTEF,* Trondheim. Online: http://www.ntnu.no/gemini/200501e/gsm.htm (accessed 6 June 2005).

Haukenes, Johan, and Olav Wicken, 2003. Innovation policy in the post-war period. *STEP report 01-2003.* Oslo: STEP – Centre for Innovation Research.

Moen, Ellen, 2002. Globalisering og industripolitiske strategier: en sammenligning av Finland og Norge. *Rapportserien/Makt- og demokratiutredningen 1998-2002, 41*. Oslo: Makt- og demokratiutredningen 1998-2003.

Njølstad, Olav, and Olav Wicken, 1997. *Kunnskap som våpen: Forsvarets forskningsinstitutt 1946-1975*. Oslo: Tano Aschehoug.

Ó Riain, Séan, 2004. *The politics of high-tech growth: developmental network states in the global economy*. New York: Cambridge University Press.

OECD, 2001. *OECD Science, technology and industry scoreboard: towards a knowledge-based economy*. Paris: Organisation for Economic Co-operation and Development.

Pierson, Paul, 2004. *Politics in time: history, institutions, and social analysis*, Princeton, N.J.: Princeton University Press.

------. 2006. Public policies as institutions. In *Rethinking political institutions: the art of the state*, eds. I. Shapiro, D. Galvin, and S. Skowronek. New York: New York University Press.

Remøe, Svend O., 2004. Governance of the Norwegian innovation policy system: contribution to the OECD MONIT project. *Rapport: Norsk institutt for studier av forskning og utdanning/Senter for innovasjonsforskning* 6/2004. Oslo: NIFU STEP.

Sogner, Knut, 2002. *En liten brikke i et stort spill: den norske IT-industrien fra krise til vekst 1975-2000*. Bergen: Fagbokforlaget.

Streeck, Wolfgang, and Kathleen Ann Thelen, 2005. Introduction: Institutional change in advanced political economies. In *Beyond continuity: institutional change in advanced political economies*, eds. W. Streeck, and K. A. Thelen. Oxford: Oxford University Press.

Thelen, Kathleen A., 2004. *How institutions evolve: the political economy of skills in Germany, Britain, the United States, and Japan*. Cambridge: Cambridge University Press.

Thyholdt, Thomas A., Kai Nystuen, and Cato Salter, 2000. *At the frontier of an emerging industry: a description of the development of the cellular mobile telephone company Simonsen Elektro during the period 1970-1991*. Sandvika: Norwegian School of Management (Handelshøyskolen BI).

Vårheim, Andreas, 2001. Paradigmeskiftet i distriktspolitikkens tekster på 1990-tallet: omgivelsesdrevet punktering eller institusjonelt valg? *Norsk Statsvitenska-pelig Tidsskrift* 17, 76-103.

------. 2005. Kapitalismevarianter og politikkendring – betydningen av politiske institusjoner i Irland og Norge 1987-2000. *Tidsskrift for samfunnsforskning* 46, 329-360.

Wicken, Olav, 1992a. *Forskningsdrevet industripolitikk i Norge 1945-1970*. Oslo: Norges teknisk-naturvitenskapelige forskningsråd.

------. 1992b. *Kald krig i norsk forskning*. Oslo: Institutt for forsvarsstudier.

Ørstavik, Finn, 1999. *The historical evolution of innovation and technology policy in Norway*. Oslo: STEP-gruppen.

Ronald E. Day

"A Necessity of Our Time": Suzanne Briet's *What is Documentation?*[1]

1 The "Cultural or Functional Specialization" of Documentation

Suzanne Briet's small book, *Qu'est-ce que la documentation?* (*What Is Documentation?* (Briet 1951; English translation, Briet 2006), is not only of historical interest, but also of theoretical interest. In this article I would like to pull together several theoretical issues from Briet's work, largely concentrating on the notion of "culture", and I will end by discussing the importance of one of Briet's particular understandings of the term "culture" for the future of libraries as a particular type of documentation agency. With this reading I wouldn't claim to exhaust the very admirable complexity and subtlety of Briet's book, but rather I want to simply emphasize a certain reading of her work, focusing upon the meaning of "culture" within it. Such an exploration also involves, however, coming to terms with her understanding of the epistemology of documents, a question which we will first engage.

Michael Buckland's article "What Is a Document?" (Buckland 1997) brought Briet's works to historical and critical consciousness in the library and information science community in its discussion of the first few important pages of Briet's *What Is Documentation?*. In this article, Buckland poses the question of what constitutes a "document". Briet's *What Is Documentation?* first suggests, citing the definition of "document" from the French Union of Documentation Organizations (UFOD), that documents can be defined as "all bases of materially fixed knowledge, and capable of being used for consultation, study, and proof" (Briet 2006, 10). From this beginning, Buckland in his article examines documents from the aspect of their being evidence in any physical form.

In her book, though, Briet immediately "counters" this initial definition of documents as evidence, offering another one that less opposes and more amends the first definition, one which, as she writes, has been suggested by "linguists" and

1 This article is a slight revision of "'A Necessity of Our Time': Documentation as 'Cultural Technique' in Suzanne Briet's *What is Documentation?*" originally published in Briet 2006.

"philosophers": "any concrete or symbolic indexical sign [*indice*], preserved or recorded toward the ends of representing, of reconstituting, or of proving a physical or intellectual phenomenon" (Briet 2006, 10). In the pages immediately following this statement, Briet provides a range of examples demonstrating how and in what social and discursive contexts documents are indexical signs. Documents are shown to be examples – or "evidence" – of things or larger groupings of things: a star is not a document, but a photograph of a star is; a pebble isn't a document, but a pebble in a mineralogical collection is; a wild animal isn't a document, but an animal in a zoo is. A document is evidence insofar as it is an example. Buckland's emphasis, from Briet's initial definition, of documents being any physical form or format remains in this latter definition, but the notion of evidence is developed and begins with intensional, rather than extensional, reference, and it starts with constellations of reference, rather than the self-announcing "fact".

In *What Is Documentation?* Briet then develops the notions of "initial", or primary, and "secondary" documents. Initial documents are the initially cataloged thing. Secondary documents are all that follow from this. Briet's privileged example is that of a newly discovered antelope. It is a primary document insofar as it is cataloged as an antelope. From then on, the animal is taken up in various other discourses and activities and, in the words of the philosopher Raymond Bayer, whom Briet quotes, "immediately becomes weighted down under a 'vestment of documents' [*vêture de documents*]." The documentary "fertility" of the original "fact" is, from its discovery through its continuous unfolding in social and cultural spaces, dependent upon these discourses, their differences, and their powers for its initial and secondary identities. We may call the primary system of discourse that cultural field which first defines the object as some type of object or initial or primary document (zoology is the field in the case of Briet's antelope), and we may call the secondary system of discourse those cultural fields which make use of an initial cataloging or classification. These secondary systems, for Briet, cover a wide variety of scholarly and popular arenas.

For example, as Briet shows, there are the documentary systems of the popular media, of the cinema, of the academic lecture hall, and many others. These "documentary systems" are, at least in some cases, what we would now call in some disciplines "discursive systems". However, the common documentary event of these discourses and their accompanying social networks is that of naming objects according to institutionally or socially normative systems. In cataloging, objects are placed in relation to other objects based on shared and essential properties and, so, the objects are named accordingly. In formal systems, such as library catalogues, indexes, and so on, these names are composed out of formal classes. The relation of the catalogued name to the object is descriptive within classes. In brief, the naming of an object within Briet's notion of *indice* has a double indexical relationship: the name points to the object and the name reflects the networks in which the object first appears as a named thing, that is, as an example of something (for example, as an example of a new type within the class "antelope").

Surely, given the time and place of Briet's writing (Paris, probably slightly before 1951) and given the epistemology of documents presented in Briet's book, we may suggest that structuralism and semiotics were the 'philosophy' and 'linguistics' that Briet writes led her to a definition of documents as *indice*. With this latter definition the earlier definition of documents given in the book is not left behind, but rather, it is developed away from a positivist understanding. For Briet, "facts" are rich in meaning through their appearance in multiple forms and series of documents.

As I have pointed out elsewhere (Day 2001), such an extensive network model of scientific and documentary production as Briet's book suggests would not be conceived again until Actor Network Theory nearly 50 years after the publication of *What is Documentation?* As I noted, the rhetorical similarity between Briet's narrative of the discovery of an antelope and its portrayal in various discursive structures and, much later, Bruno Latour's account of the capture and representation of exotic fauna in one of his texts (Latour 1996) is striking. We may suppose that Briet's development of a type of network analysis based on the indexical nature of signs and collections of signs originated not only from her familiarity with the "philosophy" and "linguistics" of her day, but also from her background in librarianship and documentation, which involved a practical understanding of naming in library and documentary cataloging and classification systems in relation to specific cultures of scientific and professional practices.

In *What Is Documentation?* Briet's theoretical differences with earlier documentation and with librarianship are clearly presented. The most cutting of Briet's observations in *What Is Documentation?* must be in regard to the dream and the attempt of the father of European Documentation, Paul Otlet, to assemble a universal bibliography. Both praising Otlet's leadership in international bibliography and also marking a substantial break between what we might see as Otlet's first generation documentation and Briet's second generation documentation, Briet writes,

> Little by little, the theory of documentation has grown since the great period of the typographical explosion that began in the third quarter of the 19th century, which corresponds to the development of the historical sciences as the progress of technique. OTLET had been its magus, the international leader, with his Institute of Bibliography in Brussels, his universal decimal classification system, his Council of Scientific Unions, and his Mundaneum. Others, less ambitious – or,

> more prudent – plowed the furrows of a culture that failed, in Otlet's circle, to descend from the clouds. *Documentology* lost nothing in alleviating itself of a Universal Bibliographic Catalog [*Répertoire Bibliographique Universel* - RBU], which everyone had considered a dream and which did not offer a comparable attraction to the most localized of union catalogues (Briet 2006, 12).

For Otlet, documentation would be successful in so far as it provided a universal bibliography, centralized in a world library in a world city. From this storehouse of knowledge, users could be served, one day using television screens to deliver the information to the user who could view it from his or her workstation or armchair (Otlet 1935). Briet, however, rejects this model as idealistic. The reason for her rejection is central and is illustrated not only in the first few pages, but throughout, her book. For Briet there is no need for a centralized universal bibliography; a universal bibliography is better served by a network model of multiple documentary organizations or agencies. Through standardized training universal bibliography could be achieved much more efficiently than with a bibliographical center (Briet helped found the National Institute of Documentary Techniques [l'Institut National des Techniques de la Documentation (INTD)], which is still part of the National Conservatory of Arts and Crafts (Conservatoire National des Arts et Métiers – the Parisian technical university). Local agencies of documentation must serve their user population by not only warehousing documents, but by "prospecting" the boundaries of known fields. The documentalist must not only be the "milkmaid" of science, retrieving new documents for the scholar, but as Briet puts it elsewhere, documentalists must be like the "dog on the hunt, in advance of the researcher, guided, guiding" (Briet 1954). This role of not only professional service, but expert prospecting, within and the edges of a given "cultural field" of science is an important attribute that we will soon return to.

Briet's break with Otlet's vision of documentation not only occurs in regard to the centralization of bibliography and the "cultural" expertise of the documentalist, but in regard to the role of the documentalist in relation to the users of documentary services. This is where the user emphasis of the American library tradition, and in particular, the special library tradition, comes into conflict with the European tradition stressing collection building and closed-stacks. Briet, as we may recall, was the founder of the Salle des Catalogues et Bibliographies – the reference room – at the Bibliothèque Nationale. For Briet, the documentalist must locate him or herself conceptually, and even institutionally, beside the researcher. The reasons for this are several. First, there is the need for expertise in the technical or academic field in which the documentalist works. Second, there is the need for the documentalist to find new materials at the cutting edge of research in the field and as the field overlaps with other fields. Third, is the importance that Briet places upon documentation as part of scientific research. Since prospecting for information is part of the documentalist's job, Briet views the documentalist as integral to discovery and communication in science and in scholarship as a whole.

This division between the first (Otlet) and the second (Briet) generation of documentation runs parallel to the difference between librarianship and documentation that Briet marks in *What Is Documentation?* The difference here is that documentation is involved not simply with subject specialization, particularly in regard to the privileged form of the book. I; instead, documentation is a "cultural" specialization from which the material and aesthetic form of the document issues. For Briet, the "human sciences" (and with them, libraries) are largely concerned with the value of accumulated materials. The traditional form of this accumulation is the entity of the book. The sciences, on the other hand, are "revolutionary". For Briet, the sciences function by advancing or overturning past work, and so they neither are limited to nor do they privilege books, and with them, libraries. Whereas "the book" for Otlet was the privileged material object, as well as a trope that stood for all forms of documentation, the practice of documentation, and the whole of human knowledge, for Briet the book is largely a relic of an earlier type of scholarship that lingers in the human sciences, and its form has since become dispersed in other documentary forms more suited to more networked and "revolutionary" types of intellectual production. The documentation agency sees books as but one – a historically specific and important, but increasingly minority – form of documentation.

Since Briet sees prospecting and the documentary diffusion of materials as central to the documentalist's work, the documentalist, claims Briet, both has a central role and a creative role in the development of knowledge across "multi-formed documents". This claim marks a strong difference with the traditional library task of building collections of largely paper-based and paper-bound materials. The gravitational center of libraries traditionally has been towards books and book collections, and the central orientation of librarians, even today, is toward these forms. The gravitational center of documentation centers is the social or professional network that is serviced and the various types of materials of any physical type or form that may be used therein. Whereas the library ethos precludes performing creative, scholarly work for the scholar, Briet argues that documentalists may be involved with reading and abstracting materials for the scholars they serve as well as with the "creative" tasks of juxtaposing and likewise arranging materials to produce new insights. The documentalist is focused upon the "cultural" or "functional" networks (inclusive of discursive networks) and tasks of a specialization. What Briet terms cultural "orientation", or what we may call cultural "attunement", is central for the documentalist profession:

> Thus, we now perceive two tendencies: with librarians, the concern is that of producing card catalogs, and consequently increasingly

> vast, almost universal union catalogs which are able to respond to the question: where can one find a particular work, a rare edition? – without respect to the subject involved. On the other side, with documentalists, there is an effort to prospect and divulge the very diverse means of access to multi-form documents, with the means specific to each discipline. These two tendencies correspond to the specialty of the professions: the former is essentially related to the form of documents, the latter is centered on the cultural or functional specialization. The researchers and scholars find their rewards in these two enterprises of current awareness and orientation (Briet 2006, 29).

2 "A New Cultural Technique"

Given this "cultural or functional specialization" within a practice, Briet's concept of the "cultural necessity" of documentation might, however, also be read as having a grander, more historical, referent than that of specific sets of practices and discourses in science or scholarship: "Culture", with a capital "C", as we might write. There is some evidence of this in her writing. Here, one must closely examine the rhetorical structure of her texts that marks a particular form of historiography, that of progress and development: "efficiency", "dynamism", "inevitability", "necessity", "our time". For example, looking back on *What is Documentation?* Briet writes,

> It is necessary to return to [Robert] Pagès. His message has not had, at the moment or when he made his statements, all the discussion that is merited, because it lacked an audience prepared to receive it. This is why, two years later [in *What Is Documentation?*], we attempted to explain those things, which, in our eyes, were documentation: a technique of intellectual work, a new profession, a need of our time. Pagès' dialectics and axioms are irrefutable. They may be summarized through some phrases pulled from his text and placed end to end: the crisis of definition which we suffer from is only a symptom of an organizational crisis and a division of cultural work; an inevitable industrialization of intellectual work has produced the machinery (organizations and tools) that make the evolution of a new cultural technique necessary, a technique which will soon be socially decisive. Documentation is a segment of culture, but it includes the domain of librarians: the librarian is a particular case of the documentalist – both are distributors of culture. The duties of the librarian, in fact, aren't fulfilled until she learns general documentary technique (Briet 1954, 44).

"Homo documentator", Briet states in the beginning of the second chapter of *What Is Documentation?*, is "born out of new conditions of research and technology [*technique*] ". Here, the French word *technique* could just as well be translated both with the English words, "technology" and "technique". Throughout *Qu'est-ce que la documentation?* there exists for the English reader an ambiguity in the French word *"technique"*. The word can mean the equivalent of either "technique" or "technology". The cultural conditions that Briet sees documentation being born within are those of industrial modernity and its means of production through techniques, tools, and various combinations of these. For Briet, technique and technology – production by means of "the brain" and "the hand" – run parallel to one another and converge in modern production:

> The moment has arrived to prove that the exercise of documentation, with all its possibilities and all of its perfected means effectively constitutes a *new cultural technique*. Documentation is becoming more and more technical, as a specialized skill. M. Le ROLLAND has told us that the hand provides for thought, just as a task which is partly manual serves culture, that is to say, it enriches man. He cites Julian HUXLEY: "The hands receive a precise tactile image from the materials they handle, the eyes receive a precise image from what they see...The most complete definition of objects by conceptual thought has been followed by their most complete mastery by means of tools and machines." The hand has served the mind; the tool has developed the brain. The brain in turn guides the hand. Such is the omnipresence of intelligence. "Documentation is to culture as the machine is to industry" (PAGÈS). (Briet 2006, 17).

The blending of technology and technique and intellectual and mechanical tools in documentation leads Briet to praise the work being done at MIT in cybernetics:

> The progress of cybernetics, especially at the Massachusetts Institute of Technology, links the complicated precision of an already old automatism to the flashy quickness of more effective electro-technical applications. The documentalist will be more and more dependent upon tools whose technicality increases with great rapidity (Briet 2006, 29).

But beyond the technical/technological character of documentation, there are other cultural elements that make it "a necessity for our time". Briet's book clearly spells these out: documentation's "dynamism" and "efficiency" give to it a certain "rhythm". This rhythm is a sympathetic response to the more general information and communication technologies that have affected scholarship and which documentation, too, incorporates:

> Still, the tools of intellectual work have deeply transformed the attitude of the scholar, whatever his specialty may be. The factors of space and time intervene much more than in the past. The hourly calendar, the telephone, the microfilm reader, the typewriter, the Dictaphone, and the teletype give to intellectual work a *different rhythm* (Briet 2006, 14).

This observation may be Briet's most important, at least in terms of cultural theory, and it underpins her book's attempt to argue that documentation is not *just* a "cultural technique" (in terms of its fitting into particular cultural modes of production), but that it is an *exemplary* and *necessary* technique of cultural modernity as a whole. Information and communication technologies may introduce a "new rhythm" to society and culture, but they themselves are a "symptom" of Western social development. Modern technique and technology are historically and socially specific cultural symptoms which documentation appropriates in its functions and professional aspirations. Along with technique and technology, leading to specialization, there is also the modern tendency to spread this technology toward its global expansion. Thus, the double "rhythm" of documentation tends toward both analytical specialization and global expansion. Since Briet's task is not to question, but rather, to adapt to and, indeed, to grasp and control the rhythms of modernity through documentary techniques and technology, she doesn't seem to see the cultural and social perspective and privileging that is involved with this orientation. Her critical acumen, as is so often the case in *What is Documentation?*, is subordinated to her professional practice and advocacy. The "new humanism" she speaks of seems very much that of a culture, namely, what she sometimes identifies as the Western "modern":

> It is not too much to speak of a new *humanism* in this regard. A different breed of researchers "is in the making". It springs from the reconciliation of the machine and the mind. Modern man cannot repudiate any aspect of his heritage. Relying on the rich experiences of the past that have been passed on to him, he resolutely turns toward the world of tomorrow. The constant development of humanity requires that the masses and the individual adapt. Here, technology [*technique*] is the symptom of a social need. "One characteristic of modern documentation is that of the coordination" of diverse "sectors in the same organization".
>
> Thus, documentation appears as the corrective to ever advancing *specialization*. Closed within the more or less spacious limits of his specialty, the researcher needs to be guided through the frontier regions of his particular domain. Orientation along the margins of a

> subject, prospecting some of the sources in an area of research, determining expertise – these are the many requirements involved in the coordination of diverse activities (Briet 2006, 17).

Techniques and technologies are expressions of culture for Briet, and this "heritage" of culture, according to Briet, cannot be refused. In terms of scholarly writing and publishing and in terms of documentary production and use, Briet saw her culture undergoing a radical historical change. The change was from a medieval and early modern manner for the composition and production of knowledge, based on personal understanding, small personal libraries, and, later, books and book distribution, to a modern scientific manner of knowledge production, based on cultural, social, and documentary networks for knowledge production and multiple documentary forms for its embodiment and distribution. The medieval *intellectus* (the universe as contemplated by the intellect, substantiated in, and signified as "the book") is replaced by multiple authorship and the social accumulation of knowledge; the book as the container and the trope for knowledge (Otlet) is replaced by networks of multiple documentary-form objects. Equally, this new emphasis upon networks of knowledge rather than a centralized "book" or site of knowledge means a new importance given to "bibliography" (using the "predocumentalist" term) as not only a documentary event but also a cultural and social event. The essence of networks as cultural grounds lie in the "references" that run through them, as their rhizomic "roots". In the mode of documentation, even libraries are seen to rest on these rhizomic roots of "references":

> During the reorganization of the internal services and stacks of the Bibliothèque National [*sic*], Paris, in 1934, a separate place was found for the Catalogues and Bibliographies Room: – it was installed in the basement. Subterranean, cryptic, with its roots running in every direction through the substructure of knowledge, bibliography can be fairly said to fit into the foundation of library science. Without it there can be no scholarly research, no positive identifications, no enlightened acquisitions, no guides to reading. It is, at the same time, the source and nourishment of the intellectual life of our time. Napoleon once said something like this, "Give me your references and I can do without your report" (Briet 1950, 52).[2]

In Briet's modernity – the modernity of "documentation" – knowledge is explicitly *embedded* and *emergent* in cultural and social production. The documentalist is located in specialized centers, working with, but also in a sense, ahead of, the scientist or scholar. Documentation doesn't serve personal understanding as we sit in our armchairs in each of our own personal studies, but instead, documentation

---

2 I am grateful to Michael Buckland for finding this source and for pointing out his passage.

is part of public spaces of production – that is, it is embedded in social networks and emergent out of cultural forms. Knowledge, for Briet, is primarily social and cultural, and the production of documents is part of the social and cultural production of knowledge. Briet's lengthy description at the beginning of her book of all the networks through which the newly discovered antelope is embodied suggests both the constituting power of social-discursive networks and cultural forms in giving value to an object and the power of the object to shuttle across discursive boundaries and to create relationships – quite literally, worlds – where none existed previously:

> In our age of multiple and accelerated broadcasts, the least event, scientific or political, once it has been brought into public knowledge immediately becomes weighted down under a "vestment of documents" (Raymond Bayer). Let us admire the documentary fertility of a simple originary fact: for example, an antelope of a new kind has been encountered in Africa by an explorer who has succeeded in capturing an individual that is then brought back to Europe for our Botanical Garden [*Jardin des Plantes*]. A press release makes the event known by newspaper, by radio, and by newsreels. The discovery becomes the topic of an announcement at the Academy of Sciences. A professor of the Museum discusses it in his courses. The living animal is placed in a cage and cataloged (zoological garden). Once it is dead, it will be stuffed and preserved (in the Museum). It is loaned to an Exposition. It is played on a soundtrack at the cinema. Its voice is recorded on a disk. The first monograph serves to establish part of a treatise with plates, then a special encyclopedia (zoological), then a general encyclopedia. The works are cataloged in a library, after having been announced at publication (publisher catalogues and Bibliography of France). The documents are recopied (drawings, watercolors, paintings, statues, photos, films, microfilms), then selected, analyzed, described, translated (documentary productions). The documents that relate to this event are the object of a scientific classifying (fauna) and of an ideologic [*ideologique*] classifying (classification). Their ultimate conservation and utilization are determined by some general techniques and by methods that apply to all documents – methods that are studied in national associations and at international Congresses (Briet 2006, 10-11).

Modernity, for Briet, involves the growth of networks of knowledge within the progress of "civilization". Thus, as Briet states in the conclusion to her book, documentation is an essential mechanism of the "growing society" that she sees as a fact around her, one that spreads to the colonies and the "hinterlands". Quoting Paul Perrier, the ideals of Enlightenment Europe, particularly after the Second

World War – "universal suffrage, compulsory schooling, the battle against epidemics, the progress of feminism, social laws, the organization of work, constitutions and political parties", spread through both "imitation" as well as "economic necessity". For Briet, though in a different way than for Otlet, the world grows toward unity, following the global diffusion and establishment of ideals, values, associations, and materials.

For Briet, documentation is part of the spread and diffusion of "science" and Western modernity, in general. For Briet, "science" and "development" are worldwide cultural events that are brought to postcolonial countries, following in the wake of "the United Nations flag". The following needs to be quoted in full, for it is a powerful rhetorical passage that demonstrates the historical, social, and cultural destiny that Briet sees in documentation:

> Since the Second World War, UNESCO has played the chief role in assembling and energizing experts and organizations in the educational and cultural field. Its Division of Libraries, under the direction of Edw. CARTER, has systematically pursued, in relation to other sections of UNESCO, a cultural policy that guarantees that its current results will be passed onto the future. "The living republic of minds" (J. TORRES-BODET) is being created through a subterranean evolution with the United Nations as the temporary perhaps, but useful, frame. Some outposts of scientific cooperation (Manila, Delhi, Cairo, Montevideo) are points of departure for missionaries of a new type, charged with the cultural development of the more or less uncultured masses and with multiplying contacts with scholars. The technical assistants of UNESCO, in fact, have available a sometimes immense "hinterland" to explore and organize. It is through reciprocal actions and reactions that these outposts spread out and are scientifically informed. The battle against illiteracy, the organization of a reading public, of librarianship, and of documentation in all its forms, comes in the wake of this exploration vessel flying the United Nations flag (Briet 2006, 39).

The "cultural technique" of documentation issues both from particular occupational cultures in Western modernity and from Western modernity as a whole. Today, Briet's faith in the inevitable and necessary spread of Western modern science and knowledge may be perplexing. Equally striking, in a different manner though, is the difference between Briet's vision of documentation's globalism and that of Otlet's. Otlet saw all the cultures of the world centrally assembled – bibliographically, diplomatically, educationally – in European institutions and cities. European soil and the European Enlightenment would be the literal and intellectual grounds for world culture. Briet's vision of globalism is, however, that of postwar Western internationalism and "development": the necessary and active diffusion of Western ideals into other cultural, social, and geographical spaces. For Briet, Western scientific and Enlightenment values are the seeds through which the world as a whole grows together.

3 Cultures and the Collapse of "Culture"

One area where differences in culture can be immediately grasped, particularly in a documentary domain, is that of language. For Briet, on the one hand, linguistic multiplicity allows a work to be read in multiple languages. On the other, however, the "Babel" of languages hinders the diffusion of documents and ideas. Whereas internationalists of Otlet's generation took some hope in an artificially created language (Esperanto) in order to mediate global linguistic Babel, Briet's internationalist vision, instead, poses three privileged languages (English, French, and Spanish) as documentary intermediaries to other languages. Here, once again, we can see Briet's documentation in contrast with Otlet's documentation: for Briet, documentation is founded on key institutions and standards as routes for connecting more localized or specialized cultures (in the senses of both organizational and national cultures). European culture provided these standards and its history of colonialism provided their conduits. However, we must remain aware that, by sort of a reverse capture, just as the living being that is then called an "antelope" is appropriated by the West, so even more are the words, concepts, attitudes, and other cultural materials of "the West" appropriated by its "others", not only outside, but also within the geographical boundaries of what we think of as Europe and the Americas. Though Briet's book doesn't explicitly mark this reverse appropriation, its valorization of local cultures as originary sites for documentary meaning and production lead to this concept.

The extension of Western modernity – in a sense, the overextension and "implosion" of the meaning of "culture" in the West – may be seen as the limit to Briet's use of the term "culture" in the grander, historiological, sense of that term, that is, Western "Culture" with a capital "C. " Briet depends upon the notion of Western modernist Culture for not only arguing for the "necessity", but also implying the historical inevitability, of documentation. But what would happen to documentation if the notion of "culture", in the sense of "localized" or specialized cultures, were extended to the point that there was no "Culture", per se, which one could point to as being the former sense's guiding and determining historical spirit? Analogously, one could ask today, which "English" is now spoken worldwide? What is the meaning of "democracy? " Is there *a* culture in Europe or North America today? Can we speak of "the West" in either a determined historical, geographical, or cultural sense, or must we see "the West", and along with it "Culture", as time and space specific social practices and expressive affordances ("western" and "culture", instead of "the West" and "Culture")? Indeed, the practical service of documentation to cultures seems to promote the collapse of the concept of "Culture", as well as the concept of "the West", as concepts upon which one could dream the harmony of a single world or dream of a historical spirit or destiny.

And yet, in Briet's time and work, and as we have suggested, in a different way in Otlet's earlier time and work, the dream of world harmony was the very goal of documentation:

> It has become commonplace, however, to affirm that humanity strives toward unity. The historical sketch that Paul PERRIER has given of this evolution over the centuries is striking. He insists on the ineluctability of the law of unification that he has discovered in his patient, historical work. He explains the success and failure of regressive or progressive human enterprises. He has put into perspective the role of international relations in our time [...] (Briet 2006, 40).

With this collapse of *Culture* by *cultures*, we are left with a question: what is the meaning of documentation without Culture? Where does documentation – specifically, its historical necessity – issue from if not from Culture? One may be reminded here of Walter Benjamin's description of Baudelaire, imaginatively stabbing into the crowd with his pen in order to control the chaos into which the unique individual, as the basis for lyric poetry, had fallen in the modern city and in its commodity culture. If Benjamin was correct, that an older form of expression adjusts to new social rhythms that put inexorable pressures upon it, by attempting to duplicate the opposing social rhythms in its own expressions, so today, in documentation, we now see an expansion of documentary forms far beyond writing, the explosion of scholarly fields into other fields (so much so that the notion of "fields" becomes problematic) and cultural fusions of many types. "Documentation" seems now to be less an expression of Western (modernist) Culture, less to be characterized by the tropes that were supposed to represent that culture (foremost in modernism, efficiency, and dynamism) and now to be more constituted by material necessity. It is material necessity that seems, today, to constitute the call of documentation, not Culture or at least, not any one culture. And where that material necessity leads, and what documentation expresses of it, will very much vary depending upon the people who use "documents". "Culture", in this sense, is not a unifying term (as in Otlet), nor is it a historical *Geist* or *esprit*, and there is no particular "development" which documentation can ride in the wake of and claim as the origin of its own historical necessity. Rather, "cultures" may be seen in the expressions of various documents and documentary practices. This open, "cultural" reading of "culture", as well as documentation, is the one that Briet's book suggests, even as it allies itself with the legacy of a historicist reading of "culture", seemingly for professional reasons.

The culture of documentation, as "a necessity of our time", is that of documentary cultures operating within, and as a product of, various types of other *cultures*, specific cultures that the documentalist must be familiar with and prospect at the edge of. Cultures give us whatever we may call, subsequently, "documents" and from this, documentalists. In this, Briet demonstrates herself an interesting theorist, not only of the library and the documentary professions, but also a cultural theorist at large. Documentation is, for Briet, the way forward for "culture" but it is the way forward that will dissolve "culture" as a unifying term. Information and communication technologies and techniques are privileged in Briet's work as a force that collapses Culture into cultures, allowing the many cultures to disseminate and dissolve the metaphysical entity of "the West". What remains of "modernity" is precisely what Briet most emphasizes: technologies and techniques, now appropriated by those "other" cultures for who "the West" remains somewhat more material than the term "culture" suggests, and more pressing than a narrative of transcendental historical "necessity" allows. Such a vision stood opposed to Otlet's centralizing model, and it still stands opposed to some visions of the global future.

4 "Culture" and the Future of Libraries

Needless to add, "libraries" are often seen as the seat or heart of "culture". Libraries, as we know them today, are very specific to modernism, particularly to nineteenth-century modernism. Briet's vision of documentation as encompassing, but historically advancing beyond libraries and librarianship, points to the dispersal or dissolution of physical libraries, just as it points to the dissolution of Culture. The dispersal of the concept of the modern library and the dissolution of its physical presence is seen in our own time in the shift to digital libraries, which are beginning to follow the decentralized model for collection and service that Briet's understandings of documentation centers and agencies and the roles of the documentalist point to. The term "bibliography" now covers the notion of citation across the entire Internet and across physical forms different from books. "Reference" – in its various meanings – constitutes part of bibliography, but also involves social networks, just as Briet suggested by her grounding of documentation in social networks and cultural forms. Indeed, Briet's understanding of documentation points to the end of libraries as we have known them as cornerstones or "centers" of Culture and toward "libraries" – in whatever institutional or non-institutional form this term may be imagined in the present and future – as techniques and technologies of linkage between documents within "cultures". Briet's book seems to say, "Do you understand? Here is the future: libraries are no longer the center of documentation, but instead, we must now concentrate on techniques and technologies of documentation serving and being used by specific cultures across a broad range of documentary forms, social networks, and cultural means of expression. These will be our new 'libraries'". Briet's "documentation centers" are, after all, founded through cultural productions, not before them. Instead of libraries as the cornerstone of Culture, documentation centers and other agencies embody particular techniques and technologies as services of, and to, cultures. The material form and the privileged trope of "the book" have been surpassed in numbers and kind by the document, of which the book is only one kind among an unclosed set of kinds. There is no end to the physical forms or formats of documents since documents are products of cultures and, thus, there is no end to types of documentary centers and the techniques and technologies that they employ. The term "library" no longer simply refers to a physical space that concentrates on the collection and lending of books, but now the term refers more generally to collections of data or documents of any type, organized to serve cultures of users.

Thus, Briet's *What is Documentation?* remains a "necessity of our time" in that it points to the possibilities and limits of "culture" and with that, the possibilities and limits of any professional practice that seeks to justify itself on "cultural" grounds. On the one hand, the concept and the privileged material form of "the book" marked the height of Culture (as Otlet proclaimed), and particularly, what has been called "the culture of the book". On the other hand, Briet's understanding of documentation marks the importance of particular, more "localized" or specialized cultures in terms of their material needs, their specialized vocabularies, and the techniques and technologies needed to provide documentary services to these groups. It isn't that books will disappear, but rather, that books, and with them, libraries as the temple of books, are becoming specific cultural items, rather than exemplars of Culture. These transformations will take some time, but they are already occurring and are inevitable – not by historical necessity, but by social and technological changes. Different cultural groups use and demand a potentially infinite array of types and forms of what may be called "documents". Thus, the notion of a "library" is expanded to such a degree that its modern cultural-institutional meaning breaks down and its institutional power becomes dispersed and even, at points, disappears. Just as Culture is transformed in cultures, so the Library is dispersed into documentary techniques and technologies, becoming a sort of "library in general". The promise of the Enlightenment is achieved with the end of historical spirits and destinies and the realization and valuing of material necessities on a global scale. In this way, the notion of the Enlightenment empties itself out, as does the notion of the "Library". This is something that still needs to be seen and reckoned with in library education and in library institutions and discourse. Briet wrote of it a half century ago, and these changes have only increased since then.

5 References

Briet, Suzanne, 1950. Bibliography in the Basement. *Special Libraries*, February, 1950.

------. 1951. *Qu'est-ce que la documentation?*. Paris: EDIT.

------. 1954. Bibliothécaires et documentalistes. *Revue de la Documentation* XXI, 43.

------. 2006. *What is Documentation? English Translation of the Classic French Text*. Transl and ed. by Ronald E. Day, Laurent Martinet, and Hermina G. B. Anghelescu. Lanham, Maryland: Scarecrow Press.

Buckland, Michael, 1997. What is a 'document'? *Journal of the American Society for Information Science* 48(9), 804-809.

Day, Ronald E. (2001). *The Modern Invention of Information: Discourse, History, and Power.* Carbondale: Southern Illinois University Press.

Latour, Bruno, 1996. Ces reseaux que la raison ignore: laboratoires, bibliothèques, collections. In Le *Pouvoir des Bibliothèques: la Memoire des Livres en Occident,* eds. Marc Baratin, and Christian Jacob. Paris: Albin Michel, 23-46.

Otlet, Paul, 1935. *Monde: Essai d'Universalisme: Connaissance du Monde, Sentiment du Monde, Action Organisée et Plan du Monde*. Brussels: Editiones Mundaneum.

Michael Buckland

Northern Light: Fresh Insights into Enduring Concerns

In this volume's introductory chapter on the early years of the Documentation Studies ("Dokvit") program at the University of Tromso, Niels Lund, the founding director, addresses the challenge of building a discipline and creating a profession. The Dokvit program has been a new and innovative program, not because the central concerns addressed were new, but because the program has been characterized by fresh insights.

Concerns that really matter to society are likely to be complex and are unlikely to either entirely new or ever finally resolved. Sustained attention to them is needed and, always, fresh insights are needed. Ronald E. Day's chapter describing the powerful insights of Suzanne Briet (1894-1989), who pioneered the first program in Documentation Studies some forty years earlier in Paris, is very fitting. Briet was the founding director of studies of the Institut National des Techniques de la Documentation at the *Conservatoire National des Arts et Métiers* in Paris (Briet 2006).

It is not accidental that new insights arose when a serious real-life problem was addressed. The Norwegian law requiring new publications to be deposited at the National Library had been updated to include more modern forms of publication. This change required the library to deal with new and unfamiliar forms of documents, but the practical difficulties of providing sustainable access to publications in new media forms were not well-understood. Examining the National Library's task of preserving and providing access to publications in new media addresses a large part of the future challenge facing archives, libraries, publishers, museums, and any agency expecting to make use of new media. In this case, a single library's need for help touches the interests of a range of academic fields, most obviously librarianship, but also communications, information science, media studies, and broadly across the humanities. Addressing practical problems, though often inconvenient and sometimes considered undignified, is an excellent path to deeper insights and new ideas. Any practical difficulty may provide stimulating challenges and may generate funding, but individual problems need to be framed in more general terms if what is learned is to be of wider, future use. New forms of documents are being widely adopted across a wide range of organizations even though the consequences of this are not well understood. The impact on industry, government, research, and society are extensive, so the study of documents can only increase.

Three dimensions

The usual approach when developing new programs in this field has been to combine the notoriously ill-defined notion of *information* with an invocation of interdisciplinarity. This process leads to an incoherent collage. The result may contain interesting elements, but the lack of coherence inhibits rational planning and makes the program hard to explain to outsiders. The Tromso Dokvit program, like Briet's, was wiser: the notion of a *document* was taken as the central defining concept and was understood to include any signifying thing. *Documentation* was seen as both the process of *documenting* and also the outcome of that process. So *Documentation Studies* ("Dokvit") includes the systematic examination of all aspects of *document* and *documentation.* This clear and practical formulation has conceptual and practical advantages and may be considered in three dimensions: meaning, technology, and economics.

Meaning
Meaning is at the heart of documentation in three ways: First, creating a document is ordinarily a matter of expressing some meaning; second, reading, viewing, or otherwise perceiving a document is a matter of inferring or constructing meaning; and, third, search and selection require the formulation of queries or other navigational moves which are commonly a matter of finding an effective way to express a meaning.

Meaning is rightly recognized as central to the humanities: Interpretation is the central concern of the arts, architecture, music, dance, literature, theater, and the rest of the humanities. So Documentation Studies should fit well into the humanities, but, so far, it has not. In some countries, the human sciences are broadly understood. In North America the humanities are typically fragmented into narrower foci defined in terms of individual media (e.g. music) and/or geo-linguistic cultural areas (e.g. Italian studies). But in all cases the concern is with the expression and interpretation of meaning. Since Documentation Studies necessarily embraces multiple media and multiple geo-linguistic areas, it has affinities with Media Studies and Cultural Studies, also cross-cutting enterprises, but it differs from both in being primarily a practical and professional field. One result of these three characteristics – multiple media, cross-cultural, and professional application – is that Documentation Studies, although sharing Humanities concerns, does not fit into the orthodox academic organizational structures of the humanities. On the other hand, one of the enigmas in the intellectual history of Library and Information Studies has been a chronic failure to understand the relevance of the humanities in a field concerned with the expression and interpretation of meaning (Buckland 1996).

Technology/technique

All documents have physical manifestations. There are different types of expression ("media types"): Texts, images, numbers, diagrams, drawing, gesture, sculpture, explanatory models, and sounds. And there is a gradually increasing range of physical media (paper, film, analog magnetic tape, digital bits, etc.). Here, again, library schools and information schools have had a rather impoverished record. There used to be an emphasis on the history of the book and of printing, occasional attention to "non-book" (aka "audio-visual") resources, and, now, an understandable and necessary emphasis, now, on digital and electronic technologies. But there has not been a sustained systematic and comparative attention to media types, whether sound, sight, smell, or touch, on the one hand, or physical media – whether clay, paper, electronic, or a human performance – on the other. It is difficult to see how library schools, information schools, or documentation programs can generalize their interests without a comparative attention to technologies and techniques. Barlindhaug's chapter on analog sound and digital technology shows that inferences from textual documents should not be generalized to music and it illustrates the need to examine and compare diverse examples.

Socio-economic aspects

Traditional studies in library schools of the history of the book and of printing (as "historical bibliography" or "analytical bibliography") acquired a narrowly technical focus, had very limited utility outside of rare book collections, and gradually withered. Recognition that book production was socially-situated came later and arose largely outside of library schools, notably through the work of Donald Mackenzie and French historians of the book. Only recently, has a fresh impetus from studies of the social practices of science begun to transform the vast but shallow reaches of "library user studies" into a far richer, more nuanced kind of investigation (e.g. Bishop et al. 2003).

It is a characteristic of modern society that we know less and less by ourselves. We are more and more dependent on data, messages, and records of every kind. Documents play an ever greater role in society: Lawyers and law courts use documents as evidence, as proof; schools use textbooks to teach, simultaneously increasing teachers' effectiveness and reducing their freedom; scientists use documents (articles, offprints) as the archive of achievement and for personal status; media specialists and publicists use documents to persuade; governments use documents to exercise social control; religions use documents for authority and adherence; patriots use documents to commemorate and to reinforce loyalty; artists create documents to inspire and to challenge; commerce is based on documented transactions, with the transition to reliable digital documents being a major challenge. (Choksy's chapter explains how one genre of document, contracts, create, define and maintain society). Documents shape our lives more and more. Modern society is nothing if not document-pervaded.

A useful by-product of defining a field of study is that it can stimulate fresh analyses of related fields. See, for example, Souminen's discussion of library studies and librarianship and Niedenthal's chapter on studies of light.

Specific empirical and methodological traditions

Each academic field adopts, adapts, and develops its methodological practices. The Tromso program in Documentation Studies selected four specific thrusts:

Who? Human agency: Who created this document? Texts, Drucker tells us, are social productions, not the work of individuals. A wide variety of people are involved in differing ways, so this question reaches far beyond traditional questions of authorship and into the rich sociology of co-production. Anderson, O'Connor, and Kearns refer to *The Birds* as "the Hitchcock film", thereby privileging, understandably, the Director, but a major motion picture, like an opera, is a good example of a document that depends for its creation on many different hands. Further, documents commonly have a series of lives, with different players involved in differing ways at successive stages.

What? Materials and technologies: What technologies were used? What resources exploited? The phrase "information technology" is ordinarily and inappropriately restricted to electronic and digital technologies, even though more and more paper is used every year. What were the effects of innovation in the materials and technologies selected? Barlindhaug's examination of the interplay of analog sound and digital tools illustrates how complex the interactions can be.

How? Techniques adopted: What techniques were used? How were the technologies deployed? (The chapters by Back, Billsus, Denoue and Hilbert and by Bootz and Hautbois provide stimulating examples.) Innovation is commonly a case of existing materials and existing technologies being used in new and different ways. It is not enough to make a document available if those who read it do not believe what it says. The chapters by Broudoux and by Francke examine issues of credibility and authority.

Why? What purpose, what outcomes? The central question "What does a document document?" has several aspects: What was the purpose? What is revealed, often unintentionally, about the creators? More generally, how do different forms of documents compare in different situations in their effectiveness for different purposes? Innovative combinations of analytical techniques are in order. Anderson, O'Connor and Kearns provide a striking example of combining radically different qualitative and quantitative analytical methods in their discussion of the dramatic opening sequence of Hitchcock's *The Birds*.

Specific conceptual framework

The distinguishing features of Documentation Studies are, first, the adoption of a document-centric perspective and, second, an inclusive "pan-documentary" field of vision. In practice, as in the first assignments given to the first students in "Dokvit", three complementary lines of inquiry can produce a rich analysis: Document analysis; social interrogation; and comparison of practices across different genres and traditions.

1. *Document analysis*. Taking a single document and examining it closely concerning its origins, purposes, roles, contexts, and fate can, like a good biography, provide a wealth of insights. A passport, a website, an opera, a published short story, or a theatrical performance can each evoke a complex microcosm of life with mental, social, and material culture, if examined closely. A comparative analysis will be implicit if not explicit, and showing how a text may change when transferred from a printed book to a CD should indeed be complemented by an analysis of how the content of CD might be transformed when moved to the format of a printed book. Analysis of medical records has proved a fertile area for document analysis as Olsen and colleagues show.

2. *Human agencies*. As already noted a single document may be the product of the efforts of many different individuals and groups. In a document-permeated society, analysis of who is involved in the many roles played is not only necessary for understanding the document, but also shines a beam of light into the ways that societies function. (Note Zacklad's chapter on the impact of the adoption of digital techniques by the general public.)

3. *Traditions and genres*. Human life and human cultures form their patterns. Ludwig Wittgenstein argued that meaning is constituted through activity, through the use of language ("language games") within specific contexts; that language usage differs in different language zones (different dialects); and that language is disambiguated within contexts and through specialized dialects. Documents, too, are used for expression and the same kind of mechanisms obtain. Genres of document (specific purposive combinations of materials, methods, and intended outcomes) arise among particular groups situated in a specific period and context. A major contribution to Documentation Studies is the insight by Frohmann (2004)

that Wittgenstein's approach to language can fruitfully be applied to document studies. Further, his chapter on "The multiplicity, materiality, and autonomous agency of documentation" shows that this approach can reveal inadequacies in widely held assumptions. Authorship, for example, is not always meaningful in relation to texts.

Documentation studies – A period of constitution

New technologies emerge and techniques evolve, but the core problems addressed in Documentation Studies are neither new nor unique (Buckland 1986). Niels Lund points out in his introductory chapter that the issues examined in "Dokvit" are already being addressed, more or less, in Communication Studies, Cultural Studies, Library and Information Studies, Media Studies, and so forth. But that, in itself, is not an argument against investment in Documentation Studies, any more than it is any argument against the existence of Communication Studies or any of the others. Rather, it is confirmation that there are important and enduring challenges that need more attention and an encouragement to be clearer in analyzing our concerns. (See Ørom's discussion of *document* and of *information*). Documentation Studies, like any other field, can justify itself, or not, by bringing interesting new insights or useful practical solutions. At Tromso, the themes are as follows:

Structural Themes
1. Document forms: Study of the anatomy, physiology, and ecology of documents reveals their characteristics. Frohmann's chapter provides a nice example in the study of early modern inscriptional practices, which call into question present-day orthodoxies concerning information. By studying musical documents, Barlindhaug shows that inferences from textual documents cannot always be generalized across all media.

2. Document biography: Tracing the life-cycle of individual documents shows how they are formed, their relationships with other documents and with people, and the influences they have.

3. Docemes: The role of components of complex documents, which commonly also exist as documents in their own right, yields additional insights. Skare's chapter provides the nice example of the impact of a book's cover on the book. And, as Drucker tells us, "The attempt to define a part of a document raises immediate questions about the 'whole' we assume."

Themes of value and policy
What is a good document? Documents and documentation are purposive. So what can be said about "document goodness." An initial approach is to distinguish between effectiveness (How suitable would a document be for some purpose?) and beneficial (What good does it do?). The former is a technical matter, a question of capability; the latter concerns values and policy, including whose values are to be served, including, as in Varheim's chapter, governmental and industrial policy-making.

Cross-cutting insights. Comparison is needed in order to be able to identify what is, in fact, special to any given case; and comparison is also necessary if generalized insights are to be achieved.

A wider agenda. Documentation Studies overlaps in its interests with other existing fields, as has already been noted. Library and Information Studies has always been concerned with documents, but "Dokvit" is concerned with a wider range of documents, including performances. Media studies is concerned with analysis of the effects of new media, but "dockvit" remembers that all media were once new and includes preparation for a wider range of professional roles.

Process of institutionalization

This volume celebrates the first ten years of the "Dokvit" program at the University of Tromso, but it should be mentioned that in addition to the usual involvement in conferences and projects, the leaders of the Tromso program also organized a Document Summer School at Tromso and, in collaboration with the School of Information at the University of California, Berkeley, a series of annual "DOCAM" conferences organized by the informal Document Academy. Several of the chapters in this book were developed from presentations at Document Academy conferences at Berkeley.

Relevance

Programs generally survive in universities if they are perceived as intellectually interesting and potentially useful in some way. The relevance of Documentation Studies in a document-permeated society cannot be in doubt. This volume brings insights from the world's northernmost university. European artists long ago developed a preference for studios with northern windows. They found their work was better when performed in clear northern light.

References

Bishop, Ann P., Van House, Nancy, and Barbara P. Buttenfield, 2003. *Digital Library Use: Social Practice in Design and Evaluation.* Cambridge, MA: MIT Press.

Briet, Suzanne, 2006. *What is Documentation? English Translation of the Classic French Text.* Transl. and ed. by Ronald E. Day and Laurent Martinet. Lanham, MD: Scarecrow Press.

Buckland, Michael, 1986. Education for librarianship in the next century. *Library Trends* 34, no 4 (Spring 1986), 777-788.

Buckland, Michael, 1996. Documentation, Information Science, and Library Science in the U.S.A. *Information Processing & Management* 32, 63-76. Reprinted in *Historical Studies in Information Science*, eds. Trudi B. Hahn, and Michael Buckland. Medford, NJ: Information Today, 159- 172.

Frohmann, Bernd, 2004. *Deflating Information: From Science Studies to Documentation.* Toronto; Buffalo; London: University of Toronto Press.

Contributors

Richard L. Anderson currently teaches behavior analysis for the Chicago School of Professional Psychology and manages the Information Security and Assurance group at the University of North Texas. He has a Ph.D. in Information Science and an M.S. degree in Behavior Analysis from the University of North Texas. Anderson's research is currently focused on the functional interplay between information and human behavior with a particular emphasis on how these relationships emerge, sustain, and evolve in natural contexts.
<rich.anderson@gmail.com>

Maribeth Back is a senior research scientist at FX Palo Alto Laboratory. Back leads the Usable Smart Environments group, researching the intersections between complex ubiquitous computing systems and the people who use them. Before joining FXPAL, she worked on multimodal interfaces, augmented reality, and ubiquitous computing at the MIT Media Lab and Interval Research, and was a founding member of the multi-disciplinary RED group at Xerox PARC. She earned her doctorate in computation and design at the Harvard Graduate School of Design in 1996. <back@fxpal.com>

Gaute Barlindhaug is a musician and art historian, lecturing at Tromsø University's Department for Documentation Studies. Barlindhaug has a background in working with exhibiting contemporary art as well as organizing art symposiums. His musical career involves solo projects as well as collaborations with some of Norway's most renowned exponents of electronic music. In his academic research he has mainly focused on new technology used in contemporary artistic domains. <Gaute@arcart.no>

Johan Gustav Bellika received a MSc degree in Computer Science from the University of Tromsø, Norway, in 1997 and his PhD degree in medical informatics at the Department of Computer Science, University of Tromsø, in collaboration with the Norwegian Centre for Telemedicine in 2006. He has worked with the Norwegian Centre for Telemedicine for nine years in the area of store-and-forward telemedicine solutions (dermatology, ear-nose-throat, ophthalmology) and trans-institutional access to patient data. His research interests include mobile software agent systems, multi-agent systems, epidemiology, electronic disease surveillance and medical information retrieval. <johan.gustav.bellika@telemed.no>

Daniel Billsus is a senior research scientist at FX Palo Alto Laboratory. His research focuses on intelligent information access, personalization and knowledge management technologies. Dr. Billsus currently leads FXPAL's "Corporate Memory" group – a team of researchers who investigate novel approaches to corporate knowledge management, text mining and collaborative intelligence. Before joining FXPAL, he was Chief Technology Officer at AdaptiveInfo, a personalization software provider he co-founded in 1999. He received a Ph.D. in information and computer science from the University of California, Irvine.
<billsus@fxpal.com>

Evelyne Broudoux is an Assistant Professor of Information and Communication Sciences, teaching in the Velizy Technology Institute, University of Versailles-Saint-Quentin. She received her PhD in ICS with an emphasis on authorship from the University Paris 8, Paragraphe Laboratory. Her research interests include the digital literature field, social networks and information retrieval, the increasing role of online interaction and electronic cooperation in the building of authorship and the legitimization of information. She contributed to the collective work of Pedauque on documentation theory (http://rtp-doc.enssib.fr/).
<ebroudoux@wanadoo.fr>

Michael Buckland is Professor Emeritus in the School of Information and Co-Director of the Electronic Cultural Atlas Initiative at the University of California, Berkeley, and past president of the Amerian Society for Information Science and Technology. His books include Information and Information Systems (Praeger, 1991), Redesigning Library Services (American Library Association, 1992), and Emanuel Goldberg and his Knowledge Machine (Libraries Unlimited, 2006). His current interests include the more effective use of descriptive metadata search and selection and the theory and history of documentation and techniques for the more effective use of descriptive metadata in search and selection.
<buckland@sims.berkeley.edu>

Philippe Bootz is an Assistant Professor in the Hypermedia Department of the University Paris 8. He is also editor of the review of digital poetry alire and director of publication of the review Regards Croisés/Crossed Looks. He is interested in digital poetry theory and the semiotics of new media.
<philippe.bootz@univ-paris8.fr>

Carol E.B. Choksy is an Adjunct Professor in the School of Library and Information Science at Indiana University, Bloomington. Her publications include *Domesticating Information: Managing Documents Inside the Organization* (Scarecrow Press, 2006). She is also a records management consultant and is currently the President-elect of ARMA, International. Her current interests include improving graduate education in records management and creating valid studies of records management within corporations and government. <cchoksy@indiana.edu>

Ron Day is an Associate Professor of Library and Information Science at Indiana University, Bloomington. He is the author of *The Modern Invention of Information: Discourse, History, and Power* (Southern Illinois University Press, 2001), coeditor and cotranslator of Suzanne Briet's *What is Documentation? English Translation of the Classic French Text* (Scarecrow Press, 2006; but also available on the web), and numerous articles. <roday@indiana.edu>

Laurent Denoue is a senior research scientist at FX Palo Alto Laboratory. His areas of interest are user interface and interaction design, document processing and social computing. He received a Ph.D. in computer science from the University of Savoie, France. <denoue@fxpal.com>

Johanna Drucker is the Robertson Professor of Media Studies at the University of Virginia. She was a co-founder of SpecLab, and is currently completing work on a manuscript documenting the projects of that group. Her interests in the role of aesthetics and graphic knowledge production in a digital environment draw on her long experience with the production of books, and her work in the history of writing and typography. Her current project, ABsOnline (www.artistsbooksonline.org), focuses on devolopment of a networked resource for studying artists' books. < jrd8e@virginia.edu>

Gunnar Ellingsen is an Associate Professor in telemedicine and eHealth at the Department of Telemedicine, University of Tromsø. His research interest centres on the design and use of electronic patient records in hospitals and the implementation of telemedicine services. Some of his publications can be found in Journal of CSCW, Methods of Information in Medicine, British Medical Journal, Information and Organization and Journal of IT Standards & Standardization Research. <gunnar.ellingsen@unn.no>

Helena Francke is working on her doctoral thesis on document and information architectures in scholarly e-journals at the Swedish School of Library and Information Science (SSLIS), University College of Borås and Göteborg University, Sweden. She has taught courses in knowledge organization and electronic publishing at SSLIS and is co-editor of the electronic journal *Human IT*. Her research interests concern social influence and historical change in the areas of electronic publishing, scholarly communication, and the organisation and distribution of documents. <helena.francke@hb.se>

Bernd Frohmann is an Associate Professor in the Faculty of Information and Media Studies at the University of Western Ontario in London, Ontario, Canada. His research interests include documentation, the philosophy of information, information ethics, and applications of post-structuralist thought to information studies. In *Deflating Information: From Science Studies to Documentation* (University of Toronto Press, 2004), he applied the social studies of science to investigate the role of documentation in the manufacture of scientific knowledge. <frohmann@uwo.ca>

Gunnar Hartvigsen has been a Professor at the University of Tromsø, in the Department of Computer Science, Medical Informatics and Telemedicine group since 1994. Hartvigsen became Adjunct Professor at the Norwegian Centre of Telemedicine, University Hospital of North Norway in 2000. He has a MSc and a PhD in Computer Science from the University of Tromsø. Hartvigsen has written two books and more than 100 papers on distributed applications, software agents, telemedicine, electronic health records and intelligent homes. <gunnar@cs.uit.no>

Per Hasvold is a University Lecturer at the University of Tromsø (Faculty of Science, Department of Computer Science) and a Research Scientist at the Norwegian Centre for Telemedicine (NST). At NST he has been responsible for establishing the Future Telemedicine Lab and participated in design and development of several systems for telemedicine services. He is currently working on a PhD thesis on participatory design of pervasive computing in healthcare. <per.hasvold@telemed.no>

Xavier Hautbois is an Assistant Professor at the University of Versailles-Saint-Quentin (France). Member of Contemporary Arts Aesthetics Institute (CNRS/ University of Paris 1), his research focuses on the theory of unity in musical works and application of sciences in arts. He has published *L'unité de l'oeuvre musicale: recherche d'une esthétique comparée avec les sciences physiques* (L'Harmattan, 2006) and has contributed to the Second International Conference on Musical Epistemology "Peut-on parler d'art avec les outils de la science?" (IRCAM/L'Harmattan, 2002). <xavier.hautbois@wanadoo.fr>

David M. Hilbert is a senior research scientist at FX Palo Alto Laboratory. His research interests lie in the design and evaluation of novel interactive, collaborative, and ubiquitous computing applications. He received a Ph.D. in Information and Computer Science from the University of California, Irvine. He is a member of IEEE, ACM, and the Phi Beta Kappa Society. < hilbert@fxpal.com>

Alexander Horsch is a senior researcher in medical informatics at the Department of Medical Statistics and Epidemiology of the Munich University of Technology, Germany, and Adjunct Professor at the University of Tromsø, Norway.

His main working areas are medical image processing, computer-aided diagnosis, telemedicine and eHealth. He chairs related working groups of the European Federation for Medical Informatics and the German medical informatics society. <alexander.horsch@tum.de>

Jodi L. Kearns, self-declared wordsmith and grammarian, currently teaches courses in instructional technologies at the University of Akron, Ohio. She holds her Ph.D. from the University of North Texas, a graduate certificate in digital imaging, a Master's degree in library and information sciences, and a couple of Bachelor's degrees from universities in Ontario, Canada, where she spent the first two-thirds of her life. Most of her time is divvied among her three children, and she is a voracious Scrabble competitor. <jkearns@uakron.edu>

Niels Windfeld Lund has a M.A. in History and Ethnology from the University of Aarhus, Denmark, and a D.E.A. in History and Civilisation from L'Ecole des Hautes Études en Sciences Sociales, Paris, France. He became the first full professor in Documentation Studies at the Department of Documentation Studies, University of Tromsø, Norway, in 1996. From 1975 till 1988 Lund was Associate Professor at the Royal School of Library and Information Science in Denmark. Lund has twice been Visiting Professor at the University of California, Berkeley, School of Information Management and Systems, in Spring 2001 and the Academic year 2005-06. In 2001 he founded The Document Academy, an informal international document research network, hosting an annual conference at UC Berkeley on document research (www.thedocumentacademy.hum.uit.no). Currently his main research fields are document theory, experimental document analysis, notably in the domains of telemedicine and the arts, especially the opera considered as a multimedia document. <Niels.Windfeld.Lund@hum.uit.no>

Simon Niedenthal is an Associate Professor of Interaction design at Malmö University (Sweden) in the School of Arts and Communication. His articles on light, perception, virtual space and transdisciplinary discourses have been published in scholarly periodicals including Leonardo, Digital Creativity, Afterimage and the Journal of Architectural Education. He is currently leader of a research project on game aesthetics and emotion, "Shadowplay: Simulated illumination in game worlds", and his paper of the same title was selected "Best Paper" at the 2005 Digital Game Researchers Association (DiGRA) conference. <simon.niedenthal@k3.mah.se>

Brian C. O'Connor shot his first roll of photographs before he wrote his first sentence in elementary school. Currently he is Professor and Associate Director of the Interdisciplinary Information Science Doctoral Program at the University of North Texas. His research deals with production and use of image texts and with information seeking behaviors. He holds his Ph.D. from Berkeley, a Master's degree in film production, and a Bachelor's degree in Greek and Latin literature. He has produced numerous documentary films and builds human powered boats. <boconnor@lis.admin.unt.edu>

Bernt Ivar Olsen received his MSc in Computer Science from University of Tromsø in 2003. He has since 2002 worked within the Medical Informatics and Telemedicine Group at the Department of Computer Science and is currently pursuing a PhD in Computer Science. His current research focus includes Medical Informatics, electronic health record technology to support cooperation healthcare (CSCW) and document-centric system development for this purpose. <bernt@cs.uit.no>

Roswitha Skare is an Associate Professor of Documentation Studies at the University of Tromsø (Norway) in the Department of Culture and Literature. Her research interests include document theory, the relationship between paratext and text, the East German public sphere, German Unification and the Literature of the 1990s. <roswitha.skare@hum.uit.no>

Vesa Suominen is a lecturer in information studies at the University of Oulu. His publications are mostly on theory and philosophy, especially semiotics and hermeneutics of librarianship and documentation, and on documentary languages, especially classification. His current interests are in library philosophy and in applying classificatory methodologies to mapping documentary contents in historical perspective. <vsuomine@sun3.oulu.fi>

Andreas Vårheim is an Associate Professor in the Documentation Studies program at the University of Tromsø, Norway. His publications range from local politics to comparative political economy. His current research interests are in institutional development and policy development, now focusing on public library policy and social trust. Vårheim received his doctorate from the University of Tromsø. Currently (2006-2007), he is a Tocqueville Fellow at the University of Colorado at Boulder. <andreas.varheim@hum.uit.no>

Manuel Zacklad is Professor at the University of Technology of Troyes and head of the multidisciplinary Tech-CICO laboratory (Cooperation Technology for Innovation and Organizational Change). His current research interests include Documents for Action, Socio Semantic Web and Open Information Search, and Knowledge Management and Communities Studies based on Action Transactional Approach (ATA). <manuel.zacklad@utt.fr>

Anders Ørom is a former Associate Professor at the Royal School of Library and Information Science, Aalborg Branch, Denmark. He has taught knowledge organisation in the field of the humanities, general information science, and history of the libraries in the Western World. He has been a co-editor of the journal *Biblioteksarbejde* [Library Work] for two decades. He has published articles and chapters in books on knowledge organisation in the domain of art studies, information theory, library history, and document typology. His current interests include library history as an integrated part of the history of civilizations and cultures, the history of travel books from Latin America, and visual art. <aaseoganders@hotmail.com>

Eirik Årsand received an MSc degree in electronics from the University of Tromsø, Norway, in 1992. He has worked with the Norwegian Centre for Telemedicine for six years in the area of self-help applications for patients with diabetes. His research interests include mobile and wearable eHealth applications, patient-operated sensors, short-range wireless data transfer, and patient-oriented telemedicine applications. <eirik.arsand@telemed.no>

www.ingramcontent.com/pod-product-compliance
Ingram Content Group UK Ltd.
Pitfield, Milton Keynes, MK11 3LW, UK
UKHW020122290926
15471UKWH00003B/218

9 783631 562949